Taken by Force

Also by J. Robert Lilly

CRIMINOLOGICAL THEORY: Context and Consequences
(with Francis T. Cullen and Richard A. Ball)

HOUSE ARREST AND CORRECTIONAL POLICY: Doing Time at Home
(with Richard A. Ball and C. Ronald Huff)

Taken by Force

Rape and American GIs in Europe during World War II

J. Robert Lilly
Northern Kentucky University

First published 2003 as: La *Face Cachee Des GI's: Les Viols Commis par des soldats americains en France, en Angleterre et en Allemagne pendant la Seconde Guerre mondiale*. Preface by Fabrice Virgili. (Paris: Editons Payot & Rivages).

Subsequently published 2004 as *Stupri Di Guerra: Le violenze commesse dai soldati Americani in Gran Bretagna, Francia e Germania 1942–1945*. Preface by Massimo Zamorani. (Milano: Mursia)

This English edition published in 2007 by
PALGRAVE MACMILLAN
Houndmills, Basingstoke, Hampshire RG21 6XS and
175 Fifth Avenue, New York, N.Y. 10010
Companies and representatives throughout the world.

PALGRAVE MACMILLAN is the global academic imprint of the Palgrave Macmillan division of St. Martin's Press, LLC and of Palgrave Macmillan Ltd. Macmillan® is a registered trademark in the United States, United Kingdom and other countries. Palgrave is a registered trademark in the European Union and other countries.

ISBN-13: 978–0–230–50647–3 hardback
ISBN-10: 0–230–50647–X hardback

This book is printed on paper suitable for recycling and made from fully managed and sustained forest sources. Logging, pulping and manufacturing processes are expected to conform to the environmental regulations of the country of origin.

A catalogue record for this book is available from the British Library.

A catalog record for this book is available from the Library of Congress.

10 9 8 7 6 5 4 3 2 1
16 15 14 13 12 11 10 09 08 07

Printed and bound in Great Britain by
Antony Rowe Ltd, Chippenham and Eastbourne

This book is dedicated to

Private First Class Avis Harold Lilly, US Marine Corps, 1945 – "Dad."

Sergeant H. Calbraith Lilly, Cavalry Reconnaissance Troop, 32nd Infantry Division, US Army, 1940–1945 – "Uncle Cal."

Archibald Schurbrooke Lilly, US Navy, 1942–1947 – "Uncle Arch."

A special word of appreciation to

Captain Redman Calloway, 3871st Quartermaster Truck Company, US Army, 1942–1945.

Sergeant Emmett Bailey, Jr., 605th and 3047th Quartermaster Graves Registration, US Army, 1943–1945.

Captain Charles Kirsh, D.C., 829th Aviation Engineer Battalion US Army, 1942–1945.

Captain Theodore Kadin, 8th Air Force, US Army, 1943–1946.

Contents

List of Tables

List of Graphs

Acknowledgments

Strong, timely, and serendipitous support from many kind people allowed me to write this book. Without their time and sacrifices, the work of the last decade would have been impossible to complete. Along the way, I have accumulated many debts. None of them can be paid in full here.

For introducing my work to Francis X. Clines, *New York Times* (February 7, 1993), I am indebted to two "baddies," Ron Wikberg (deceased) and Wilbur Rideau, Angola State Prison, Angola, Louisiana. I am deeply grateful for the undergraduate research assistants – Polly Bunzel, Kelly Moore, Mike Puckett, Charles Klahm, Sara Merkle, Mike Wehrman, and Bobbie Ticknor – who rendered 34 thick volumes of confusing legalese into useful numerical information about patterns of criminal behavior, while keeping their sense of humor.

Mary B. Chapman (formerly Mary B. Dennis), Deputy Clerk of Court, Department of the Army, and Colonel William S. Fulton, Jr., US Army (Ret.), each gave generously of their time and knowledge about military court records. I would have been lost without them. Librarians Phil Yannarella, Steely Library, Northern Kentucky University, and Laverne Mulligan at Chase College of Law (NKU) made several important contributions at just the right moment. Helen Krarup, Librarian, Institute of Criminology, Cambridge (UK) deserves a special note of appreciation for helping a distant stranger track down an obscure reference. Brenda McWilliams, Rhona Mitchell, and Peter Davies never tired, or at least they never complained, of tracking down details circa World War II, United Kingdom. I thank them now, should I have forgotten to do so along the way.

Colleagues and friends Dick Hobbs (London School of Economics), Robin Williams (University of Durham), Rob Hornsby (York University) and Mike Nellis (University of Strathclyde) critically read each chapter. The book is much improved because of their contributions. Comments and questions from Jim Combs, Rex Oachs, and Kevin Eiglebach helped to weld the final draft more readable than would otherwise have happened.

Chase College of Law professors David Elder, David Short, Lowell Schechter Roger Billings, Bill Jones, and Jack Grosse were always more than willing to listen, give advice, provide references, and share lunch. I suspect they are relieved now that the book is completed – I took a lot of their time.

Karen Pape was equally generous and ready to solve computer problems beyond my Luddite technical abilities. Professor Nicole Grant's helpful feminist critique and conclusion that the book was very sympathetic to the rape victims encouraged me to try even harder to insure that their voices be heard. For their sake, and their families and friends, I wish this book had not been possible.

Letters from World War II veterans gave me numerous previously unrecorded recollections of the war's underbelly. The memory of Robert Thomas's contribution of French cuisine, wine, and Cuban cigars during a warm May Saturday night in Paris helped to keep the pages coming on many cold winter days and nights. Conversations in The Netherlands with Jean Perrin and his father-in-law's memories of American soldiers in wartime France provided rich experiential knowledge that supplemented historical resources. Jim Zopp's (FBI Ret.) thorough responses to questions about handling blood, semen, hair, finger prints, and ballistics shed light on murky issues about how the US Army handled evidence circa World War II.

History professors Michael C.C. Adams and Francois Le Roy's encouragement and advice were invaluable and were given in the best tradition of the academy – integrity. Christophe Guias's willingness to let me write "my book," and his soothing words when I was anxious about its translation, speaks well of his editorial and diplomatic skills. None of these comments could be made had it not been for the nugget that Fred M. Kaiser, US Congressional Research Service, sent to me in 1992.

Lastly, for unflinching devotion, love, and friendship, I thank Patty, Catherine, Robert, and Mother.

BOB LILLY
March 2, 2003
Revised on November 1, 2006

Preface to the French Edition

Long considered as an inevitable consequence of war, incidents of rape have acquired a higher profile over the past few years. Much of the responsibility for this is down to the systematic practice of rape in the heart of Europe during the conflicts that have torn the former Yugoslavia apart. Although rape was forbidden by the Geneva Convention in 1949, it was only in 1996 that it was recognized as a war crime and that the first prosecution was made on this count, with the trial of the Serbian, Dusko Tadic, by the International Criminal Tribunal of the former Yugoslavia. This precedent in international law was codified in Article 8 of the Statute of the International Criminal Court that explicitly designates as war crimes rapes committed in the course of international and noninternational conflicts . If these rapes have been committed as part of "a widespread or systematic attack directed against any civilian population," then they are considered to be crimes against humanity.[1]

Thus they could no longer be relegated to the rank of practices considered normal in times of war. In the case of the former Yugoslavia, rape was one of the core practices, along with mass murder, of the process of ethnic cleansing. It was no longer a question of a "side issue" but, indeed, an essential form of the violence of warfare.

There is also a humanitarian aspect to the recognition of rape. The International Committee of the Red Cross, for instance, now publicly condemns armies responsible for sexual violence. It has proposed training for "those bearing arms as part of government forces or armed opposition groups in the rules of international humanitarian law."[2] Furthermore, the duties of its health workers now also include the care of the victims of these specific acts of violence.

These observations in connection with armed conflicts may also be extended to peacetime. Nowadays, sexual violence is repudiated and condemned with far greater clarity than before. It should be remembered that rape has only been recognised as a crime in French criminal law since 1978. The first change took place in the 1970s. In 1975, for the first time, a French lower court declared that it had no jurisdiction in a case of rape, which had initially been described as the minor offence of "assault and battery." In 1978, at the Aix-en-Provence Court of Assizes, the three rapists were found guilty, but, most important, they had now been tried on the charge of rape. On the one hand, thanks to the actions of feminist groups, the Aix trial opened up a real debate around the question of rape; on the other hand, on the legal level, it gave rise to the law of December 23, 1980.

"Any act of sexual penetration, whatever its nature, perpetrated against another person, with violence, force or surprise, constitutes a rape."[3] Rape had thus become a matter for "social debate." Apart from the numerous articles written on the question at this time, it is notable that two books with the same title, *Le Viol* ("Rape"), were published simultaneously in 1976. One was the translation, less than a year after the original English edition, of the book by Susan Brownmiller, which for more than twenty years remained the only reference work on the subject.[4]

Since then, the ongoing action of associations supporting women victims of sexual violence and a slow but steady growth in the government's awareness have consolidated this change of attitude toward rape. As with the Aix trial in the 1970s, a number of other cases contributed to the formation of this new perception of sexual violence. This happened with cases involving pedophilia and several instances of serial killings after rape. Even more recently, there were the "gang rapes," often committed by under-age boys. Then there was the march called "Ni putes ni soumises" ("Neither whores nor submissive") organised in response at the beginning of 2003. However, the changes that have been observed since the 1970s do not mean that problems no longer exist. It remains very difficult to lodge a complaint. Few prosecutions succeed and when they do it is often long after the event. Silence is still often seen as the best option for guarding against social disgrace and the suspicion of having provoked the attack. There is still strong male resistance to the notion that a woman who says no really means no.

Nonetheless, there has been a change of attitude on the part of French society, and this change has also had an impact on historical research over the past twenty years or so.

In 1998, Georges Vigarello published a general history of rape in the modern and contemporary periods. Noting the recent "high-profile visibility" of the crime of rape, his intention was to write a history of attitudes toward sexual violence and the way in which it has been defined. Given the ways in which the shame of the victim and the disgrace of suspicion heaped upon her have changed over time, it was clear that a history of rape was not only possible but also necessary.[5]

It is the same with wartime rapes. In connection with the First World War, Stéphane Audouin-Rouzeau published *L'Enfant de l'ennemi* ("The Child of the Enemy").[6] He wrote that "during the first weeks of the war in 1914 rape of the enemy's women seemed to have been a commonplace phenomenon." Rather than considering this as booty of war on the fringes of the conflict, he placed the fate of the children born from these rapes at the centre of his study. No cloak of silence was drawn over the rapes; rather they were used to publicize the enemy's atrocities. The fate of the "children of the enemy" was one that aroused the concern of judges, journalists, and politicians.

Véronique Nahoum-Grappe has emphasized the extent to which the violence committed in the course of the wars that have torn the former

Yugoslavia apart were initially excluded from analysis, because it was considered to be "an ancient custom of the Balkans."[7] Sometimes, as here, relegated to a custom, mostly considered as an inevitable corollary of warfare, it has taken a long time for war rapes to become the subject of history. They raise questions that coincide with the intersection of several historiographical projects. It is true that their profile has been raised as a result of current events, but the present interest also stems from a new way of studying war. Over the last thirty or so years, historians have turned their attention to new categories. After long being overlooked as a subject of history, since the 1970s women have been the subject matter of a very large number of works. What is conventionally called "women's history" has thus brought out into the open the broader reality of a gendered world. Moreover, war historians have abandoned the triptych of army, politics, and diplomacy in favour of an approach that looks at all aspects of societies at war. Another change concerns those subjects related to violence, sexuality, and the expression of emotions, from which historians have traditionally kept their distance. Whether this was from embarrassment, a sense of propriety, or a fear of overstepping the boundaries of their discipline, all of these together or some other reason, there is no doubt that there has now been a real change and that such matters are perfectly legitimate topics for research.

Finally, the battles being fought around the question of memory have gradually made way for a calmer debate. Whilst the Algerian War is still the main subject of polemical debate and recriminations amongst the French public today, it is becoming easier to question readymade images and to look beyond a number of hitherto sacrosanct clichés.

Any historical account of the Algerian War today will thus logically include the study of the sexual violence that took place at that time. Rapes were carried out as ultimate acts of cruelty and humiliation on men as well as women during torture sessions. Outside the torture chamber, rape was used as a means of asserting the legitimacy of the master's authority and subjugating the opponent absolutely: women through the suffering and violence inflicted upon them; men through their inability to protect them.[8]

How many children were born as a result of the rapes inflicted on Algerian women? Nobody knows for silence and shame have drawn a cloak over this reality. And yet, in 2001, Mohamed Garne, a child born following the rape of his mother by French soldiers, managed to obtain a disability pension from the Regional Pensions Tribunal. Although his application was dismissed at a lower level on the grounds that "the applicant has never been a victim of an act of violence or an attack, directly," he finally managed to win his case because the ill treatment meted out to his mother during her pregnancy was not without consequences for him.

During World War II, the Free French Army, first in Italy and then in Germany, was also not blameless. Thousands of Italian women were raped by French soldiers during the Italian campaign; on this basis, they received an allowance from the Italian government after the war.[9] In respect of Germany, J. Robert Lilly briefly mentions French involvement only in the rapes committed in 1945 during the last months of the war, then during the establishment of the different occupation zones. In Württemberg, it is said that French soldiers committed widespread rape.[10] Thus, 1,198 cases of rape were notified in police reports for the city of Stuttgart alone.[11]

The fact that rape is now considered a fitting subject of history is a phenomenon that is far from being confined to France. Indeed, we are seeing increasing numbers of studies on sexual violence, in connection with World War II. Both the Sack of Nanking in December 1937, in the course of which almost 20,000 rapes were committed by Japanese soldiers, and the forcing into prostitution of hundreds of thousands of Korean women as "comfort women" have figured as the subject of recent research[12] and have given rise to often virulent disputes between Japanese, Chinese, and Koreans.

Knowledge of the rapes committed in 1945 by the Red Army in Germany is becoming more widespread. The figures suggest that several hundred thousand rapes were involved. The extent of this phenomenon indicates the existence of a practice that, although not organised as such, was widely prevalent and moreover to all intents and purposes never punished.[13] It was a true war of vengeance waged by the Soviets against German men and women.

Over the past few years, much research has been published exposing the active participation of the Wehrmacht in the deportations and mass slaughter perpetrated on the Eastern Front. The violence of these atrocities was unimaginable, unlike anything observed on the Western Front. During the campaign in France of May–June 1940, the German Army had a policy of severe punishment for rape. Even so, the fear of punishment did not prevent it from happening. In an order of June 23 1940, General Günther von Kluge, commander of the 4th Army, noted a "frightening increase in cases of rape."[14] Throughout the Occupation, discipline was relaxed, and incidents of rape were regularly reported. From 1944, these increased, along with the numerous massacres that marked the German retreat in France at that time.

On the Eastern Front, it was clear that the violence perpetrated against civilians was never considered as a breakdown of discipline. There was nothing to prevent atrocities from being carried out. Nonetheless, there is still a question mark hanging over the issue of rape. On the one hand, every type of atrocity was possible, because the situation of prisoners and civilians was one of absolute vulnerability to the German soldiers. On the other hand, the Nazis considered the Slavs and the Jews to be inferior peoples, destined for enslavement or extermination. In the thinking of the Nazis, relations with such women were considered defiling and thus prohibited. It would seem that, in some cases, there were incidents of mass rape, and in others, particularly those involving the organization of the mass slaughter of whole Jewish communities, they were unknown.

It is clear from the above, far from exhaustive, list, that the issue concerns most of the countries involved in the conflicts of the twentieth century. However, let us return to the American Army, which is the subject of this book. The archives used by J. Robert Lilly contain documents relating to soldiers present in the European theater of war. As a reminder, we should note that, at the end of the war, there were, in addition to these three million troops, another five hundred thousand in Italy and one and a half million in the Pacific. Japanese women were also victims of rape, as, for instance, was the case during the invasion of the island of Okinawa in April, 1945.[15]

Subsequently, in the course of the sixty-year-long American presence in Japan, there have been regular, sporadic incidents involving sexual relations with the local population. In 2002, there were a large number of protests following a rape committed by an American soldier from the base on Iwo Jima, an island to the south of Japan.

It was during the Vietnam War that the image of the GI underwent a fundamental transformation. If the napalm bombings and the My Lai massacre of March 16, 1968 remain the most striking symbols of the "dirty war," accusations of rape were never far away.[16] Indeed, at My Lai itself, the massacre of the villagers was accompanied by a number of rape scenes, as attested by the commission of enquiry. However, the revelation of the atrocities committed by US soldiers during the Vietnam conflict does not seem to have rebounded on their fathers' generation.

If this book is mainly concerned with the history of Europe, it is also closely tied to the debates preoccupying American society. These obviously include not only the way they conceive their past, present, and future role in the world and the image of their soldiers, but also the issues surrounding relations between whites and blacks in the heartlands of the USA.

The fact that there were more black soldiers prosecuted and severely punished for rape is clearly proven by the records of the military tribunals. This information is corroborated by other evidences, from French sources. The author stresses the extent to which the military justice system was influenced by the racism of the American society and the army in exercising greater severity in respect of black soldiers. One may also add fear on the part of the French and a greater readiness to accuse a black soldier, given the extent to which the alleged crime corresponded to their stereotypical image. J. Robert Lilly perhaps tends to rather overestimate the absence of racism amongst the French population and their familiarity with "colonials" on a regular basis. In a fair number of regions, the sight of black soldiers was quite exceptional, and the image people had of them was not totally devoid of fear of these "savages," even if this fear was not openly expressed.

However, there is no doubt that these questions also relate to a debate taking place in the USA right now. This debate concerning the prison population has also aroused interest in France in connection with issues involving prisoners on death row: the overrepresentation of black people and the shortcomings of a judicial system which has been shown to penalise the poorest sections of the population, including the blacks. Yet the importance of the black/white prism is much greater than that. For the soldiers and officers giving evidence, as well as the prosecutors and judges, the category of "racial grouping" was a way of relating to the world. It was, and still is, even today, an omnipresent classification. Lilly's use of the term "race" thus needs further definition, for the meaning attributed to it on either side of the Atlantic is radically different. In France, since World War II, "race" unquestionably refers to biological difference and Nazi ideology. In the USA, *race* is not just solely a matter of biology. It is also an identity, something one experiences. It is a stamp that figures on almost all official documents, beginning with one's birth certificate. Thus you are *Caucasian*, that is white, or *African American*, that is black. This categorisation takes place today in a context in which positive discrimination coexists with demands around ethnic and cultural issues, as well as a profound social inequality; in 1945, it was more a case of a segregated society, of an all-pervasive racism, and the lynchings which were its most violent, though not exceptional, manifestation.

These remarks relating to concerns that are of primary interest to the American public do not detract in any way from the interest of the documents presented here. There is, however, a need to say a few words about the context, in which the first edition of this book has been published in French. As Lilly points out in his introduction, the book broaches the question of the image of "America's greatest generation," the one made up of men who fought in World War II. Questions may be raised by the fact that this revelation of part of the "dark side of the GIs" comes at a time when the US Army has been engaged in action in Afghanistan and then Iraq since the beginning of the twenty-first century. We should first make it clear that research time is not the same as real time. The choice of subject is, as we have seen, linked to the questions a society is asking itself. The conflicts following the end of the Cold War, in the former Yugoslavia or in the Gulf, have undoubtedly had an influence on the choice of this research topic. On the other hand, for research of this kind, spread over several years, there is no way the author could imagine beforehand how his work would find an echo in reality.

Super-perfect images, hero-worship, the creation of icons, none of these are compatible with the writing of history. Like other soldiers from other armies, US troops raped women during World War II. Whether as allies in the case of British and French women, or enemies when they were German, thousands of women were victims of the sexual violence that is rape. What is demonstrably true from a scientific point of view is difficult to accept from a more political perspective.

September 11, 2001, followed by American military action, make it difficult to publish such a book in the USA, in spite of the existence of a real opposition movement. Thus it seemed preferable to publish an initial version of the work in French translation, before publishing the original in America. The French-reading public will thus be the first to read the results of this research.

The book brings new light to bear on the actual definition of this type of violence. Are these war rapes, meaning acts that directly or indirectly target the enemy? Are they acts of violence resulting from the generalized brutalization of societies at war? Or, again, are they sex crimes similar to those that occur in peacetime, but easier to commit given the prevailing conditions of belligerency?

It is clear that J. Robert Lilly's study covers the intersection of these different forms of violence. The archives on which he has worked allow him to follow the same army – thus, broadly speaking, the same men – through three successive but very different scenarios. In Britain, one can see these men adapting to life in a friendly country, where the length of their posting and the fact that they spoke the same language allowed them to develop certain ties in a situation where combat was still only a future prospect. After June 6, 1944, these soldiers found themselves in France, another country declared an ally and where in any event they were welcomed as liberators but only after bitter fighting. Gestures and sign language made up for their lack of understanding of the language. Finally, from the winter of 1944–1945, these troops ended up in enemy territory, face to face with a population they had learned to hate and with their feelings only intensified by the liberation of the camps for those who had experienced it.

Three elements may be singled out to distinguish rapes committed in Britain from those committed in Germany. There was an increased brutality expressed through a larger number of collective rapes, more systematic beatings, even going so far as murder. There was an increase in the number of convictions; according to one or other set of statistics recorded by the Judge Advocate General, the number of rapes committed in Germany alone constituted two-thirds of the total number of rape cases prosecuted under the jurisdiction of the American Army. The number of convictions increased but, as J. Robert Lilly points out, the sentences were less severe. Unlike in France and even more so in Britain, no soldier was sentenced to death and executed for rape in Germany. The growth in the number of prosecutions, even though only the manifestly more violent rapes were taken into account, did not, however, preclude a greater degree of indulgence on the part of the authorities. This marked a real break compared to France and Britain. This was probably a move away from sexual crimes in times of war, the perpetrators of which were considered as criminals, to war rapes, where the circumstances of the military operations, but, most importantly, the nationality of the victims, made them acceptable. Thus, only the most brutal cases, where the depravity of the culprits could not be ignored, were pursued.

This marks the boundary between two types of rape: rapes of conquest and those which are more of the order of sex crimes in wartime. Herein lies the interest of the research presented here, which is the product of an investigation undertaken by a criminologist over some considerable time. In the USA, in Britain, and even in Northern Europe, criminology has a more important role in the social sciences than it does in France. Thus, many people will find the description of criminality in Britain during the war original. It has much to teach us about a society at war, with not only the well-known explosion of trafficking of all kinds and of prostitution, but also of murders, thefts, burglaries, as well as what may be considered as the characteristic tendency of war to foster crime. More questionable is the author's systematic use of percentages that seem to apply across the board, whereas very often the troops concerned remained limited to a few units, a few dozen at most. Thus, the value of this book's contribution is not so much for its quantitative as for its qualitative analysis. It is for the way in which J. Robert Lilly describes these rapes, or rather allows the reader to access the sources of the military tribunals. These contain all kinds of witness statements, expert evidence, interrogation transcripts, and other official documents. Taken together, they show us what a rape is, in all its horror. These rapes are atrocious and the words used here, crude, precise, violent as they are, express this atrocity. Reading behind the precise language required to establish the facts before the tribunal, one can easily imagine the enormous amount of fear, suffering, and humiliation involved.

There is no voyeurism in the writing of this history. Some will no doubt be shocked, even more will feel deep disgust. However, there can no longer be any question of describing violent phenomena in an elliptical manner without using the words belonging to violence. This history made from blood, sperm, and tears refuses to downplay the reality of the violence. It marks a definitive break with all the romanticized images of soldiers having fun and letting off steam. There is no getting away from what is at issue here. These are crimes. It is war in all its horror.

FABRICE VIRGILI,
Researcher, IHTP/CNRS

(Translated by
MARGARET A. MAJUMDAR)

Preface

Some books have more difficult births than others. The one in your hands had an easy 2003 French birth and an even easier 2004 Italian beginning, but its English arrival was complicated by the confluence of unforeseen events including the United States' invasion of Iraq, post-World War II "greatest generation" myths about US soldiers, and the very topic of the book – rape. The French edition was the result of my affirmative response to French historian Fabrice Virgili's suggestion that the book would be well-served if Paris-based Payot were to publish it. Their previous publications included Virgili's own World War II book, *Shorn Women* (2000), later published in English by Berg. Virgili himself had earlier done a very fine job editing a special issue of the journal *Vingtième Siècle* concerning French women's experience of the twentieth century. The issue included an article by Professor Francois Le Roy and myself about rapes committed by US soldiers in France between June, 1944 and May, 1945. I had confidence in Virgili's professional judgment, the quality of his work, and his faith in Payot's ability to promote my book to both academic and general readers. At the time, I had not attempted to find a publisher of any description, and nor had I ever had a book published in French, but Payot's eventual offer relieved me from the potentially difficult task of finding an appropriate and well-respected home for the book.

By the time Payot and I had agreed on a schedule for the French book's completion and other contractual details, the international political climate between the United States and France was headed for collision over the impending war in Iraq. While the Bush administration favored invasion, the French government opposed it, and sections of both media and public in each country fell to describing the other with clumsy nationalistic jokes and abuse, and chest-beating rhetoric. Cafeterias in the US House of Representatives changed their menus so that "french fries" became "freedom fries" and "french toast," "freedom toast," as a culinary rebuke to France's refusal to support the US position on Iraq; elsewhere wine-drinkers and commercial vintners destroyed their French stock and refused to purchase any more.[17] In some US circles it became popular to show support for the early stages of the Iraq war by deriding the French and anything in their culture. Several US publishers echoed these sentiments when Payot attempted to raise their interest in an English version of my book, *La Face Cachée Des GI's* (*The Hidden Face of the GI's*). One well-established US publisher said, "I wouldn't touch that book with a 10-foot long pole," while another disparaged Payot with "How dare you publish a book like that about American soldiers!"

Today the grip of the collective memory of World War II is somewhat more relaxed – a significant and sad development from just four short years ago. At that time books, movies, and television productions about the United States' heroic involvement in World War II were still finding huge and receptive audiences. The US historian, Steven Ambrose, had died just a few months before the publication of my book. The popular and financial success of his work, most notably the made-for-TV production of *Band of Brothers*, was a measure of the uncritical acceptance of a certain interpretation of the United States' involvement in World War II, particularly in its European Theater of Operations (or ETO, as it was known). In 2003, Tom Brokaw's *The Greatest Generation* was still flying off bookstore shelves, and the glow of Steven Spielberg's 1998 work *Saving Private Ryan* had yet to fade, in sharp contrast to the noticeably weak public response to his and Clint Eastwood's 2006 film *Flags of Our Fathers*. My book, which examined the ugly underbelly of the US army's behavior in Europe, was, in hindsight, perhaps the wrong book at the wrong time for an English-language readership. Since 2003, many thousands of US World War II veterans have died and, arguably, it is now easier – especially in the United States – to find a readership for *Taken by Force*.

Other media responses to the 2003 publication of the French book were positive to neutral on both sides of the Atlantic and, thanks in part to the Internet, unusually large. Just two days before the 60th anniversary D-Day celebrations, Paris-based Associated Press writer Jamey Keaten's article "Historians Looking at U.S. GIs after D-Day," discussed my book and noted that as World War II continued in Europe, some of our GIs were involved in the commission of serious crimes, including black-market trading, armed robbery, looting, murder, and rape. More than four dozen media sources reprinted this story to an audience of approximately one hundred and fifty million people. Other responses were less than positive and one Internet search produced the following rant:

> UPDATE: I just checked, and this Robert Lilly guy isn't an historian at all. He's a fucking sociologist. Real historians check for chucks of sociologists in their stool and in their shoe treads. Sociology is a methodologically unsound, innately political, airy, unfounded, slippery and BS-laden field that, except for luminaries such as the late Robert Merton, deserves to slide into history as a blot on the face of the "social science."

An equally incredulous 2004 email message arrived from Professor Richard Beck, New York Law School, who in response to a *Le Monde* editorial by French television documentary producer Alain Moreau, wrote, "Moreau says the subject of your book is proving that American GI's raped at least 17,000 women in Europe in 1944–45." "This seems wildly improbable." Beck went on: "Of course *Le Monde* is wildly anti-American, as is every other french [*sic*] publication, and this D-Day issue is one of the worst I have ever seen."[18]

Between spring 2005 and spring 2006, public support for the war in Iraq and its two most prominent cheerleaders, President George W. Bush and Prime Minister Tony Blair, continued to wane. At the same time, criticism of the greatest generation motif and its use as a justification for more recent wars showed signs of surfacing in the United Kingdom. Richard Drayton, Cambridge University historian, wrote in *The Guardian*[19] that "Even as we remember the evils of nazism, and the courage of those who defeated it, we should begin to remember the second world war with less self-satisfaction." After all, as *Time Magazine* had reported in September 1945, "Our own army and the British army ... have done their share of looting and raping ... we too are considered an army of rapists." Furthermore, "The destruction of Dresden, filled with women, children and the elderly and the wounded, and with no military significance, is only the best known of the atrocities committed by our bombers against civilian populations." British and the US mythology about World War II, Drayton wrote, ignores our own crimes and legitimizes Anglo-American war-making. Six months after the publication of his article came the release of secret World War II wartime files that indicated that GIs and "good-time" girls had enjoyed London's blackout. Not only had London's Metropolitan Police worried about a flood of prostitutes who would pursue American troops, US military officers had also urged with little effect the police to clamp down on sex trade that targeted responsive GIs.[20]

On April 24, 2006, a *Daily Telegraph* news report titled "Wartime GIs went on rampage of rape and murder" disclosed that "Home Office files kept secret for 60 years show that GIs committed 26 murders, 31 manslaughters, 22 attempted murders and more than 400 sexual offences including 126 rapes."[21] It is against this evolving background of re-evaluating GIs' behavior in the ETO that Palgrave Macmillan were happy to publish *Taken by Force* in an English edition.

* * *

Formally, this book started shortly after the publication of an article in the *New York Times* about the execution of soldiers in the ETO.[22] Its groundwork was begun much earlier, in southern West Virginia. It was there that I first encountered World War II and had my first exposure to capital crimes.

My earliest memory is of standing near a young walnut tree in the back-yard of my parents' first house, a four-room wooden structure on a dusty, dirt road, telling my older brother that the plane overhead was "Daddy in war." It was the year 1945. At that time, my father was in Marine Corps basic training, Camp Lejeune, North Carolina. The last of three sons to enter world war military service, an "old man of twenty-three and father of two boys," when President Roosevelt's invitation to join the Army arrived, he declined in favor of the Marines. "Mom already had one of her boys in the

Army, and it didn't make sense to have another one," Dad explained years later. With his older brother, Cal, in the Army, and the youngest brother, Archie, in the Navy, "the Marines were the only choice I had."

It took five years for the three sons to enter and exit military service. Each came home in due time with individually unique experiences, stories to tell, and wounds to heal. Healing took more time for some than others. To this day the psychological scars remain barely hidden. "It comes back on me if I talk about it," my oldest uncle said shortly after the 50th D-Day celebrations. It prompted me to ask about his 46 days behind Japanese lines, and his highly decorated and heroic Pacific war commander, Captain Herman J.F. Bottcher, whose legs were blown away just before the Japanese surrendered.[23]

In addition to my brother and me, each born during the war, four additional children soon joined my paternal grandmother's round oak dinning room table where, until her death, we had more sumptuous meals than we could count and heard many, many World War II stories that today we fondly remember.

From the early 1940s to the late 1960s, when I left West Virginia and its limited employment opportunities, the World War II stories of my father, uncles, and other kin bound me to that conflict like many millions of others born during the same era. It was inescapable. Beyond the stories were the black-and-white pictures of Dad and his brothers in uniform on the fireplace mantles and clothing dressers. Brownie camera snapshots taken in boot camps here and overseas fueled my imagination of those days that were the defining experiences of so many of our parents' lives. Like so many of that generation, theirs' were not isolated experiences. They were repeated and reinforced almost every time we visited another home in our village, and beyond when we traveled to see distant kin and friends.

Some homes in the surrounding coal towns and rural areas were indelibly marked in our minds as somehow different, and worthy of a greater respect and deference, none more so than grandmother's coal camp home where her three soldier-sons had once lived. Several village families had lost someone during the war, including the family of Dad's best friend, Aviation Machinist Jesse Arthur Crozier, who died on the USS Bountiful during the Philippine invasion, on December 4, 1944. Dad never smiled when we drove or walked past the Crozier property.

Homes with someone in the military had an "A" (Army), "N" (Navy), or "M" (Marines), or all three, displayed in a front window. Beside each letter was a star denoting the number of members of that family who were serving in the military. Bereaved homes displayed a golden star. In some homes, these stars were still in place in the late 1940s when I began walking alone on the dirt and "hard" (paved) roads of Prosperity and Cranberry, West Virginia. Dad removed his Marine "M" from our small living room window late on snowy Christmas eve, 1945. He had spent his enlistment working in the Navy/Marine headquarters, Washington, DC, an unexpected assignment after he had been a courts-martial witness in the case of a brutal Saturday-night assault in a hotel in Goldsboro, North Carolina, the night before he and his buddies were to be shipped to China. Several – eight according to Dad's memory – Marines had mistakenly thought a naked and drunken man found in a hotel room was a "queer" who deserved to be dragged out and thrown down the elevator shaft across the hall, when in fact he was an Army colonel from nearby Seymour Johnson Air Force Base who was celebrating "with a good drunk" the submission of his name to the US Senate for promotion to the rank of brigadier general.

I recall phrases such as "90 day wonder," "shave tail," "D-Day vet," and "eyes and ears of the South Pacific," and names like New Guinea, Australia, and the Philippines were as much a part of our home as those of Arthur Godfrey, Faron Young, Patsy Cline, "Little Jimmy" Dickens, and Hank Williams. Hank died in his Cadillac just a few miles from where we lived.

Old military canteens, aluminum mess kits, marksmen metals, and green webbed belts with sliding brass-buckle catches were used as toys, clothing, and items of boyhood masculinity and identification. Classmates who didn't have World War II artifacts – whether a cloth cap, or an astray made from an 80-caliber shell casing – envied these treasures from Dad and his brothers. Most awesome to me was Dad's handmade knife with the double-honed 12″ curved blade and stiff pig-skin sheath crafted by a local coalmine blacksmith. He "made a knife for all the boys going to war, and mine would have been a good friend in China," Dad said.[24]

My first knowledge of capital punishment also came from home surroundings. My maternal grandfather had told me that he had seen three hangings, and I recall in detail his pained reluctance to discuss them with me. But the current memories of my parents – based on what my maternal grandmother told them – count only one. According to them and historical records, it occurred on October 3, 1890, when my grandfather was a boy of only nine years of age. It was the last public hanging in Raleigh County, West Virginia, and it happened just seven years before the last official hanging in the state.

While the disparity in count between my recollection and that of my parents is significant, it is nonetheless reconcilable when one considers the possibility that grandfather might have been witness to two lynchings. Between the years of 1882–1951, West Virginia had 48 lynchings, some of them not far from where he lived and worked. These are part of the circumstances that permit me to hold true the memory of his claim to having seen three hangings.

I conducted my first undergraduate sociological research project on attitudes towards capital punishment in West Virginia in the 1960s, and in the many years since then, I have often wondered if my grandfather knew those condemned men, or their families, or their victim's families. I have also considered the possibility that, as a white landowner during the age of *de jure* segregation, he might have actively participated in these horrible crimes. Perhaps, too, I have thought that he might have regarded executions as unfair, unjust, or inappropriate.[25] These attitudes would have been consistent with West Virginia's long history of opposing capital punishment.[26] The knowledge that at one time he was a member of the Ku Klux Klan renders these questions even more perplexing than otherwise would be the situation, and it does not change the fact that the answers are lost to history.

Foreword

Rape is so odious an act and for the victim so traumatic and shattering an event that to step forward and volunteer to give evidence is indeed a most difficult thing to do. Exactly how difficult has become clear to me in the course of over a decade of research on the experience and behavior of American troops overseas during the Second World War.

Rape in war and conflict is of all times and all armies. It is, of course, no different for the US military, not even for The Greatest Generation of soldiers who fought The Good War. During a conference in Australia some years ago, distinguished Harvard Professor Charles Maier, in a paper on the Allied bombing of German cities, made the point that given the inevitable moral incongruities of war, perhaps the time had come to stop referring to the Second World War as The Good War. Instead, Maier suggested, we would do better to describe it more accurately as The Good Cause.

That would take nothing away from the sacrifice and valor of America's rapidly fading Greatest Generation. Yet, at the same time, it would disabuse us of the vain thought that any military has ever fought anything like a "clean" war within clearly delineated and rigidly observed moral boundaries. I am convinced that many American veterans of the Second World War would have little difficulty seeing the merit of Maier's argument. As early as the North African campaign in 1942, one of the commanding officers of the 509th Parachute Regiment was urging his men to "forget good sportsmanship on the battlefield," because battle, he insisted, was "not a refereed football game but the dirtiest game yet devised by human minds." Bill Mauldin, the famous war cartoonist who was highly respected by GIs up front, was quick to accept at the Italian front that a war was not fought, as he put it, with his trademark irreverence, "by Marquis of Queensberry rules."

In my research I have found GIs remarkably frank in recounting their war experiences. Perhaps less so in their letters to parents and wives and girlfriends whom they took care to insulate from the worst, although even these letters on occasion contain unsettling observations and confessions. But it is in their diaries and journals as well as in their memoirs, published or not, that American soldiers tend to be far less restrained in characterizing war's dirty underbelly. For some it is a form of much needed therapy and catharsis, for others it is an urgent need to record vital lessons to be passed on to future generations.

And so GIs, through these various sources, talk to us quite openly, for example, of the growing hatred they felt for the enemy as the war dragged on. American soldiers who joined the chase after the fall of Rome confessed to "a bitter hatred of the Jerries" as well as "a burning desire to avenge what they have done to us." An officer of the 35th Infantry Division confided to his journal in January, 1945, that the news of the Waffen SS murders of GIs in the Ardennes had enraged the men. "A hatred," he wrote, "such as I have never seen has sprung up among us against Hitler's armies and all of Germany."

Nor do GIs hesitate to share with painful frankness what it meant to kill a human being. A Ranger in Tunisia who killed his first person in a hand-to-hand fight at Sened Pass could not help vomiting. Afterwards, he felt haunted by a "stained, sodden, guilty" feeling. In December, 1944, a young soldier confessed in a private letter to his father that he had killed his first man face to face. "He was a blonde kid," the tortured boy wrote, "maybe even younger than I – and he probably had a father and mother too." In the postscript he added, "Don't tell Mom about the German kid. I don't want her to ever know."

Still more unsettling it is to have soldiers admit to the numbing dehumanization of war that gradually made killing less painful. After having shot a German soldier in the Hürtgen Forest, a lieutenant was amazed to find that he "could stand there and watch him die and feel absolutely no qualms of any kind." "This seemed particularly strange to me," he continued, "for I was a man who had never gone hunting simply because I had neither the urge nor the heart to kill an animal." A GI who passed Saint-Lô on July 22, 1944, recorded in his journal that the rubble had not yet been cleared and that "the cows, hogs, dogs and Germans lie dead and stinking." The enemy had come to rank low on the ladder of living species. A company commander of the 2nd Infantry Division, inspecting his unit's positions at the Siegfried Line in October, 1944, stared at a dead German whose intestines had been torn out by pigs in a bloody, knotty mess. Next to the remains, one of his veteran soldiers was digging his foxhole with sublime indifference.

Neither did GIs hold back in describing the manifold cruelties of war. A frenzied buddy in Normandy taking the scalp of a dead German, for example, or unscrupulous comrades cutting off the fingers of enemy soldiers to steal their gold wedding rings. Indeed, shocked GIs provide us with quite a bit of information on what could be classified as outright war crimes. In response to the news of the excesses in the Ardennes, men of the 90th Infantry Division at the Saar River took revenge on the Waffen SS in such a systematic manner late in December, 1944, that headquarters had to issue express orders to take these soldiers alive so as to be able to obtain valuable information from them. And GIs admitted that this was a fate that not only befell the hated Waffen SS or despised snipers. A private from the 87th Infantry Division wrote, "Time and again in combat we heard, 'The boys aren't taking any prisoners today,' and that always meant the prisoners were being shot down." Soldiers of the 12th Armored Division had the misfortune of capturing three German soldiers alive at Herrlisheim right before being ordered to move out immediately. Not knowing what to do with the POWs, they killed them on the spot. "Human life," a soldier of the division confessed, "can become a mere matter of logistics."

Yet, what is so noteworthy amid all the frankness about the hatred, the killing, the cruelty, and sheer madness of war is that rape in GI testimonies remains the ultimate taboo. One can hardly expect the rapists themselves to own up to their crimes. But among their comrades too there is a palpable squeamishness and unease about this particularly sensitive subject. On the whole, GIs cannot be said to be reticent in personal documents about sexual experiences and the spectrum of encounters with women. "In a war sex talk gets to be an obsession with men & we're no different than any other GIs," noted a combat engineer who was stationed near Carentan in July, 1944. GIs readily admitted that "fuck" was the most commonly used word in their vocabulary. "This word," observed an officer, "does duty as an adjective, adverb, noun, and in any other form it can possibly be used, however inappropriate or ridiculous in application." Letters expressed the longing, diaries mentioned the wet dreams, and songs advocated masturbation. Prostitution and venereal disease posed tremendous challenges to the US military from Great Britain to Germany, and GI sources show little reluctance in addressing these issues too. In the summer of 1944, a surgeon of the 88th Infantry Division who was in Rome on leave, noticed that the hotel lobbies were jammed with prostitutes. "Everyone has a great time," he jotted in his diary. "There is a rumor that soon a new drug will be on the market that will cure gonorrhea in twenty-four hours."

Again, I have been hard pressed during many years of research to find such openness among GIs where it concerns the issue of rape. Indeed, during the research for my book, *The Crash of Ruin*, I remember coming across no more than two frank soldier references to rape in what must have been tens of thousands of pages of personal testimonies that I examined. Why this reticence? Because rape, of course, does not belong to the realm of consensual pleasure but to that of unmitigated power and control. Because rape is a crime not only of vicious cruelty but also, and above all, a crime of utter subjugation and supreme humiliation. A crime, moreover, committed not against dehumanized and diabolized enemy soldiers but against wholly innocent civilians. It is all this undoubtedly that caused soldiers who witnessed comrades commit rape to feel deeply ashamed. And it is shame more than horror and shock that can cause people to prefer silence.

Shame without a doubt remains the key issue in attempting to understand why the blind spot of rape largely remains even when one looks at the behavior of American troops in the Second World War from the perspective of civilians. Here again my own research in the past years has opened my eyes to the powerful taboo surrounding wartime rape. For my book, *The Unknown Dead*, I examined the fate of the local population during the Battle of the Bulge. It is a story of even more horror and madness as it recounts the experiences not of trained soldiers but of unsuspecting civilians caught between two clashing armies. Research unearthed a catalog of instances of collateral damage, cruelty, and war crimes. I managed to uncover all this by immersing myself in thousands of pages of diaries and journals, interview transcripts and memoirs, municipal archives, and Allied Civil Affairs records. Yet, again, these sources too made me come up largely empty-handed where it concerned rape.

It was certainly not far fetched to expect to find references to rape in the climate of chaos and lawlessness that reigned in the Ardennes in the winter of 1944–1945. Indeed, I was taken by surprise by the vehement complaints of civilians in manifold sources about the behavior of American soldiers when they began to push the Germans out of the bulge. Dirty and disheveled GIs were said to have been "inflamed," to have roughed up civilians, requisitioned their homes in blatant disregard for the extreme cold, and smashed furniture to build fires or simply because they felt like it. Could not rape have been part also of this pattern of aggression and rage? It could not, according to the many published and unpublished sources or the minutely detailed local histories. In all of my research in these sources, I managed to find for my book no more than a single clear reference to rape when villagers of Langlire complained that the liberators had not only thrashed their interiors but had also attempted to violate their women. Events in Langlire cannot but make one wonder how many more women (and their families) in this traditional rural and Catholic area have remained silent out of shame, especially about sex crimes committed by friendly troops. That question becomes even more pertinent when one realizes that in the midst of over-whelming evidence of cruelties and war crimes committed in the area by Waffen SS, Nazi security forces, and Wehrmacht, rape happens to be the one category that barely lights up on the radar even where it concerns the German aggressors, many of whom had been rotated from the notori-ously barbarized eastern front.

That same "code of silence" forms a complicating factor just as much in attempts to gauge the extent and the nature of rape committed by rear area troops. I am currently engaged in research measuring the social and cultural impact of Anglo-American troops on Belgian society during the liberation of 1944–1945. This involves sources on hundreds of thousands of American, British, and Canadian troops. Some did no more than pass through on the way to and from Nazi Germany. Most, however, were stationed in the small country for shorter or longer periods with an eye to logistics and other combat supporting roles. Soldiers from various cultural and social backgrounds in these circumstances had more time on their hands to engage in all kinds of petty mischief and criminal behavior. Almost inevitably therefore, this project is about unearthing evidence on the involvement of Allied soldiers in alcohol abuse, violence, prostitution and venereal disease, and black market activities. What is more, civilians in journals, memoirs, and interviews admit that GIs could be oversexed, at times were outright unrelenting and even given to harassment, and quite often remained nowhere to be seen once pregnancy was involved. But once again, and I hope that at this point I am not boring the reader with the repetitiveness of my argument, civilians seem to draw the line at coming forward with information about rape. More remarkable still, for a variety of possible reasons, even official sources such as Allied Civil Affairs and Belgian state security reports remain almost wholly silent about this particular issue.

I am perfectly happy to accept the risk of sounding repetitive if the end result of my argument is to have demonstrated to the readers of the American Professor Lilly's exceptional book on wartime rape how great its importance is. On the basis of the rich sources of the US Judge Advocate General, *Taken by Force* would have major significance even if all it did was acknowledge the existence and scope of the problem among American troops in the European Theater of Operations. Because that way this study at least does justice to the victims of rape who most often have been forced to suffer in total silence. But *Taken by Force* is more significant still because it provides readers with a detailed and knowledgeable analysis of the phenomenon by a highly respected sociologist and criminologist. An analysis that will teach us much also about the workings of US military justice, the larger issues of race, and the nature of war and, finally, the relative merit of referring to any war as a good war regardless of how worthwhile its cause is.

As the son of Belgians who were liberated by American and British troops in 1944, I can attest to how worthwhile the Allied cause has been in the Second World War. From the very first moments of liberation, Belgians that autumn relished the freedom of expression that the Allies had rescued from the Nazi police state. Professor Lilly is very much aware of the many sensitivities involved in raising the issue of rape where it concerns America's Greatest Generation. To call the publication of his findings a courageous act, however, would be to cause this generation of soldiers the most serious of grievances. For it is for the right to such openness of discussion, even of the most sensitive matters, that these soldiers fought the Second World War. And it is that right, among many others, that will continue to make the Allied cause in the Second World War known as The Good Cause.

DR. PETER SCHRIJVERS
The University of New South Wales,
Sydney, Australia

1
Introduction

At about 7:30 p.m. on the cold, exceptionally dark, drizzling Thursday evening of October 8, 1942, Miss Ellen R. left her home on Rock Lane in the small township of Melling, north of Maghull, Lancashire, England, and walked five minutes to Glover's Shop to buy a loaf of bread. Private Wesley Edmonds, a United States Army soldier in Co. C, 397th Port Battalion, Transportation Corps, was already in the store when Miss R. arrived. He was married and from St. Louis, Missouri, where he had worked at the Morris Hat Co. He and Private First Class John I. Sears, a short, heavyset man, had walked the half mile from their camp to buy cookies (Vanilla Wafers), "Biscuits they call them here,"[1] and soda. When Miss R. left with her purchase, Edmonds quickly followed her outside, introduced himself, and in an attempt to engage her in conversation, shook her hand. Later in court she said she told him she was not interested in talking to him.

Shortly after arriving back home Miss R. decided to go on one of her twice weekly visits to her cousins, the B.s in Lydiate, for 12 lbs of onions. They lived approximately 200 yards in another direction away from her home. For the short trip, according to US military records, she wore a lady's gray-checked tweed coat, a blue felt hat, ladies' brown shoes, a vest, silk stockings, blue knickers, an underskirt, and a pair of pink corsets. She was 34 years old and lived alone with her mother, Mrs. Margaret R., who at this time had two sons "in the Forces overseas."[2] During the last 12 months Miss R. had been employed as a spreader in the munitions works at the Dunlop Rubber Co. in Melling.

As she departed on her bicycle she encountered Edmonds. He again tried to engage her in conversation. In court she testified that he failed once more. Nearly an hour later as she was coming home Edmonds appeared for the third time. His appearance was quite sudden, and Miss R. had to quickly put on her brakes. Edmonds, she said, then grabbed hold of the bicycle saddle, causing her to dismount.

At once Edmonds began "talking love" to Miss R. He wanted her to go around to a nearby haystack. When she refused to do so – she knew about haystacks – he forced her and the bicycle through a gate and inside a field owned by two "Miss Websters." He wired the gate shut and started putting his hands up her clothes. She protested and told Edmonds that she was menstruating. He didn't care what condition she was in; he was going to "fuck her"[3] and she was going to love him.

After placing his coat on the ground, he forced her on to it and then sat on her stomach. Once she almost escaped, but Edmonds caught her and threatened to stab her in the back with a fork if she made any noise or cried out. He hit and bit her on the face and breast. He offered her money if she would comply with his demands. She refused, saying "I'm not that type of girl."[4] She said she was afraid to cry out because "Being a dark man I did not trust him – I did not want to upset him or his temper or anything like that."[5] Despite her efforts to calm him, Edmonds raped her. Afterwards at about 10:30 p.m., he laughed, wiped himself off with her underwear and said, "Now you may go."

Miss R. returned home abnormally late, around 11:40 p.m., in a disheveled condition. Her clothes were dirty, stained, torn, and she had blood on both legs. In court her mother reported that Ellen told her "one of those niggers has had me in Websters' field all this time."[6] They immediately went to their neighbors, the T.s, and called the local police.

Two medical doctors, Robert Reginald Burrows, a police physician, and First Lieutenant Vernon O. Kash, US Army, examined Miss R.[7] Both physicians found her in a distressed condition, numbed and shocked. She had an increased pulse, and she reacted poorly to questions put to her by the doctors. They described her speech as rather slow and halting. Her face, jaws, neck, and ankles had reddened areas, which suggested bruises. The physicians also found an abrasion on her chest and scratches on the posterior surface of both legs and body.

They examined her genitals and found that her hymen ring was torn in three places. They concluded that these lacerations were caused by a brutal entry and that the intercourse was not normal. Nor, they decided, had the intercourse happened with Miss R.'s consent. The damaged hymen had been made when the effort of penetration occurred. It was not the result of an act that had been jointly accomplished.

The next morning at about 4:30 a.m., Edmonds, "a light complected colored man,"[8] was roused out of bed. He was wearing bloodstained woolen underclothing, and he had a fork in one of his pockets, which he acknowledged as his. Miss R. easily identified him as her assailant. Edmonds admitted that he had had intercourse with Miss R.

The US Army conducted Edmonds's two-day trial even though the alleged crime had occurred in England and its victim was a British citizen. It began only 11 days after the assault and ended on October 20, 1942. In it concerted attention was devoted to the details of the rape and Miss R.'s life prior to the assault. According to one of her cousins, she was of a calm, quiet demeanor with an unblemished character and "addicted" to joking on social occasions. On the night of the alleged rape she was in excellent spirits. Her mother testified that her daughter was a Roman Catholic who attended church, twice on Sundays. The court also learned that since leaving school at 14 years, Miss R. had been employed as a domestic dairymaid and at the local Elliptic Home before beginning work at the munitions factory in Melling.

Captain Kenneth R. Wilson, Edmonds's appointed defense counsel, attempted to impugn Miss R.'s rape claim. He asked why she had not screamed, kicked, and scratched Edmonds, or tried to run away during their two-hour encounter. After all, she weighed 10 stone, 10 pounds, approximately 150 lbs, only 18 lbs less than Edmonds's 168 lbs. She was asked again and again to explain what happened. At one point Wilson asked, "Did it occur to you to use your god-given natural defenses?" He also asked about her relationships with men and whether she ever had intercourse before the rape. She repeatedly said no, and when Wilson asked "Did you ever have occasion to observe a male private [sic] before the night in question?" she emphatically answered "No!"[9]

Early on in the trial Wilson asked Miss R. about the size of Edmonds's penis. He wanted to know if she thought her injuries were due to the vigor of his attack or because of the size of Edmonds's penis. She answered that she did not know because "I have not had anything like that before."[10] Wilson wished to demonstrate that the types of cuts in her hymen could have occurred during normal intercourse by the insertion of an abnormally large male organ, one that was "quite a bit bigger than the female."[11]

Before leaving the witness stand, Miss R. was questioned three more times about the details of her rape, once by the court, once by the prosecution, and again by defense counsel Wilson. After the court had asked its questions, the president of the court granted Miss R. permission to make a statement. In it she requested that the court to be lenient with Edmonds. She had previously shared these same thoughts with the Englishman, Dr. Burrows. With this statement Miss R. left the witness stand.

Questions about the size of Edmonds's penis reappeared after four prosecution witnesses were examined regarding more details about the rape. First Lieutenant Augustus A. Marchetti testified about locating Edmonds after the rape in Edmonds's hut. Police Inspector Walter Edward Philpott, Lancashire Constabulary, reported that on the day after the rape he had taken some of Edmonds's clothes and two test tubes of blood to a laboratory in Preston, England.

Police Constable Allan Thompson, N.W. Forensic Science Laboratory, Preston, was vigorously examined about whether he could with confidence tell the court that the clothes he had received from Police Inspector Philpott were indeed those of Edmonds. Police Sergeant Robert McMechan followed P.C. Thompson to the stand, and he testified that at about midnight on the night of October 8, 1942, he visited the home of Miss R. He found her dazed, distressed, and suffering from being exposed to the cold.

The fifth prosecution witness was the Police Surgeon, Robert Reginald Burrows. After presenting his qualifications to the court, he testified about his examination of Miss R.'s hymen. He reasserted that it was torn in three places and that her injuries were not the result of normal intercourse. Upon cross-examination of Burrows, Captain Wilson again addressed the issues of the dimensions of Edmonds's penis. Wilson asked Burrow if Miss R.'s vaginal lacerations could have "depend[ed] on the size of the male?"[12] Burrows answered "yes," only to quickly correct himself by saying that it was not probable that Miss R.'s lacerations resulted from normal intercourse. The court also wanted to know if the wounds could have been self-inflicted. Dr. Burrows answered, "Definitely no!"[13]

Edmonds was to face a life sentence or death if convicted. His testimony and written statement attempted to paint a different picture of himself and of his encounter with Miss R. He portrayed himself as a devoted husband who had just before meeting Miss R. sent his wife some money won in a craps game. He implied, too, that he was a responsible citizen – he said he had voted for presidential candidate Franklin D. Roosevelt in 1931. Regarding what happened at the store where he met Miss R., he stated, "we shook hands – she squeezed my hand" and "so we strolled down the road, talking about different things, about the night, etc."[14] Edmonds insisted that he had asked her for a date and that she didn't refuse. Miss R., he said, agreed to see him at 8:30 p.m. after visiting Lillie. "[Y]ou can see me."[15] "Now, I have to go into the house."

When they were in the Websters' field, Edmonds spread his overcoat on the ground. They sat down and shared "a piece of Chocolate – it was very fine." "[S]he gave me two pieces of Chocolate – I eat [sic] one piece, and save the other for a souvenir."[16] "[W]e sat there and talked about love affairs – we laid down and kissed." "She put her tongue in my mouth – it was very kind of her."[17] He thought "She was very clean" and when Miss R. had "… her dress to her thighs … they looked pretty."[18] When asked if he completed the act, he answered, "No sir."[19]

Miss R.'s plea for the court to deal leniently with Edmonds was heeded – she regretted that the whole thing had happened. He was convicted and on October 14, 1942, was given a life sentence although he could have been executed. Eight of the thirteen members of the military court recommended clemency as did none other than Brigadier General Hedrick, who at the time was in charge of the Branch Office of the Judge Advocate General (JAG) in the European Theater of Operations. His logic was that "after the war and if the conduct of the accused in prison justifies, some clemency may be granted."[20] Hedrick's position, however, was at odds with the opinion of judges under his command. Captain Huber D. Addison, Assistant Judge Advocate, recommended that the sentence was too harsh and should be reduced to confinement for 20 years. Colonel Albert W. Johnson, an Acting Judge Advocate, agreed that 20 years was adequate for Edmonds, but he cautioned that the function of the courts-martial was "to maintain discipline [and] I feel CHL [confined to hard labor for life] should not be reduced at this time."[21]

Addison and Johnson's logic involved cultural, factual, and legal considerations that are important not only to understanding Edmonds's fate but also for comprehending the larger contextual picture of race relations during World War II, its impact on military justice, and much that is examined in this book. First, they reasoned that Edmonds's crime lacked extreme atrociousness in England where the color line was not so noticeable as it was in the *de jure* segregated United States. The life sentence was, they further reasoned, more severe than those imposed by the civil courts in the United States, and a great deal more severe than would have been imposed by the English civil courts for like offenses. They reasoned too that while Miss R. looked like she had been raped, her culpability was in question because she had indeed spent two hours with Edmonds and had actually made a date to see him after she returned from seeing her cousins, the B.s. The last and probably the most important reason that resulted in Edmonds's failure to get a reduced sentenced was Colonel Johnson's argument that unquestionably indicates that the rape of civilian females by US troops was a serious issue in England soon after their arrival:

> *This crime is becoming too prevalent among colored troops.* If this sentence is reduced, the place where such action will receive the widest publication is in accused's organization, and the next widest in other colored organizations located close to his. Such publication will tend greatly to reduce the fear of "death or imprisonment for life," which fear, I believe, is a strong deterrent.[22] [Emphasis added]

At the age of 32, Edmonds became the first ETO soldier in England to receive a dishonorable discharge and life imprisonment for rape. He was soon returned to the United States and was taken to the Federal Penitentiary at Lewisburg, PA.[23]

The impact of the rape on Miss R. did not end with Edmonds's conviction and sentence. Her life did not return to the daily routines she had once known. Edmonds's statement about not "complet[ing] the act" was false. On July 8, 1943, Miss R. gave birth to a baby boy who "was not so dark as it was expected he would be." She submitted a claim to the US government for care and maintenance for a period of 16 years, in addition to a sum for loss of income, pain and suffering, and hospital and doctor bills for herself. As far as we know, she received no compensation, and she never married. She probably raised her son alone.

According to Colonel James E. Morrisette, Judge Advocate General's Office, and Chief of the Military Justice Division, Edmonds had a difficult time adjusting to prison life. In an August 1943 letter to the Adjutant General, Morrisette not only failed to recommend clemency for Edmonds, but he also went to some effort to indicate that a penitentiary report had described him as a "smooth somewhat arrogant type individual with an indifferent attitude toward confinement."[24] It was difficult, according to Morrisette, to predict the type of institutional adjustment that Edmonds might make. In Morrisette's opinion, Edmonds should be required to serve a very substantial portion of his sentence as well as demonstrate "a changed attitude toward society before any clemency is awarded."[25]

Three years later Edmonds's condition had not improved. His mental health had deteriorated to the point that he was transferred from the federal prison in Lewisburg, PA, to Medical Center for Federal Prisoners, Springfield, Missouri.

Segregation, sexual racism, and military justice

On December 19, 1941, 11 months before Miss R.'s rape, Harold Nicolson, (1886–1968), the British diplomat, historian, and an astute observer of public behavior, published a short essay for *The Spectator*. In it he noted how strange it was to be in London the week before because the public seemed unaware of two decisive recent events. The first was that the United States had entered the war after the December 7, 1941, Japanese bombing of the US naval base in Pearl Harbor. The second was that the US Congress had so quickly voted to create an American expeditionary force, which meant that Germany would be beaten. There was good reason for the temporary state of unawareness – the British public had just been stunned by great naval losses.[26] Included among the losses was the German sinking of the British battleship *HMS Barham* in the Mediterranean, the destruction with no survivors of the Australian *HMAS Sydney*, and the extensive damage caused by Italian frogmen to the British battleships *HMS Valiant* and *Queen Elizabeth* in the port of Alexandria, Egypt.

Things had changed in England by the time Edmonds was convicted in October 1942. By then the public was well aware that the US Army had begun its "occupation" of Britain.[27] From January 1942 to December 1945 about three million US service personnel passed through Britain. By May 1942, five months before Miss R.'s assault, more than 1.5 million US military personnel were already in England.[28] Along with its massive buildup of troops, the United States imported three distinct factors that were to have consequences for its soldiers and the women raped in England, France, and Germany. These include *de jure* institutionalized racism, sexual racism, and military justice. We use these factors to analyze the often acknowledged but much neglected topic of rapes committed by US soldiers in the European Theater of Operations, and the military responses to them.

Armed with these tools, the tragic encounter between Miss R. and Edmonds becomes more than the mere question of who, what, when, and where. For him, what was at stake was life itself. Edmonds, in the narrowest of terms, was indeed only a drafted black soldier from the US Army, where rape, though not a capital crime in England, was punishable by either a life or a death sentence. More importantly, he and Miss R. were part of a larger drama and history that had been developing in the United States for hundreds of years. Edmonds was not only a soldier; he was a southern (St. Louis, Missouri) black man whose sexual and verbal congress with a white woman had violated generations of American laws and customs intended to govern race relations. A brief history of segregation and military justice in the United States before World War II will illuminate much of the contents of the forthcoming chapters.

Segregation

At the end of the federal government's reconstruction efforts [1865–1877] to reorganize the states that had seceded from the Union during the Civil War, southern white authorities were determined to end northern and black participation in the region's affairs. The late 1870s to the 1890s witnessed the early development of laws and customs designed by white authorities to give institutionalized advantages to whites and disadvantages to blacks. This era and its laws, often referred to as "Jim Crow," affected every aspect of public and private life. Blacks were barred from basic civil rights including voting, holding public office, and jury service. Beyond these denials of civil rights were laws requiring separation from whites. This applied to transportation facilities; waiting rooms; and public and private facilities open to the public including churches, schools, hospitals, prisons, parks, toilets, drinking fountains, restaurants, stairways, movie theaters, entrances and exits, cemeteries, and even phone booths. As black American historian John Hope Franklin observed, no detail was too small in the frantic effort to seal off social contact between blacks and whites.[29] Blacks and whites were separated into two worlds so tightly proscribed as to render communication almost impossible.[30]

It is debatable whether the segregation statutes were what Derrick Bell called "a massive retaliatory spasm" by a defeated South or an "honest manifestation of the belief" that blacks were such low lifes that whites had to be protected from them.[31] What is generally agreed upon is that *de jure* segregation in the American south alongside *de facto* segregation in the north directly impacted how four post-Civil War generations of blacks and whites experienced public social institutions and aspects of private life before the civil rights movement of the 1960s and 1970s.

There were exceptions to the restrictions of segregation, but they were few, and the US military during both world wars was not included. The military was one of the most rigidly segregated institutions in the United States. In 1940 it had only five black officers – three of them were chaplains – and approximately 4000 black troops on active duty.[32] During World War II, as in World War I, the military required separate training grounds, and eating and sleeping facilities, for each race. Blacks were almost assuredly under the command of white southern officers.[33] Its evaluations and images of black troops during World War II endorsed the idea that they were intellectually and biologically best suited for noncombat units devoted to support services.[34] Exceptions to this interpretation did exist, but they were hard-won and few and far between. A far more likely domestic experience for black soldiers during World War II involved racism and discrimination, some of which was so intense that they created riots and other disturbances in cities (Harlem, Mobile, Los Angeles, and Detroit) and in and around military training camps.

Ample evidence indicates that during World War II black soldiers experienced morale problems. "The sources of low morale among Negro troops were many."[35] Not only was there a disparity between the proclaimed war aims of the nation, but black troops were also constantly reminded by segregation that they were thought of as little more than racially inferior vassals for a white society. Predominant was the concern about their living conditions at military posts and their relations with white troops and commanders. Even when living arrangements and interactions with whites were acceptable, rules and practices applying to black troops often changed. The result was almost certainly heightened uncertainty and intense anxiety. Lee's description of a black soldier's arrival at a new and unfamiliar post is illustrative:

> [T]he first few days could be filled with disturbing questions for the Negro soldier who wished to avoid embarrassment and possibly serious entanglements with local rules and customs. Would he be served if he tried to make a purchase at the main post exchange, or was there a special branch exchange for Negro units? Which theater, which bus stop, which barber shop could he use? Where could he place a long distance call? Which prophylactic station could he use? Was he free to enter the main Red Cross office? The gym? The bowling alley? Would the station cleaning and pressing concessionaire accept his soiled clothes? How would he be received in the nearby camp town?[36]

As the war continued, some of the more obvious hindrances to high morale began to change. Physical conditions in some places did improve for black troops, especially in and around large cities that had favorable attitudes toward blacks in uniforms. But the impact of "More significant blocks to high morale ... occurred on different, less easily apprehended levels."[37] Black troops often had little faith in the importance of the work that was assigned individually and to their units. Neither did they believe much in the "ultimate significance of their roles in the Army's and the country's eyes and motivation for superior efforts and performance fell short in many units."[38]

It was difficult for black troops to have faith in the good intentions of their white commanders, some of who were guilty of imposing segregation and prejudice where none had previously existed in towns near camps. Officers were also often ignorant of the effects of racist language and physical assaults insisting on using "nigger" and striking or beating black soldiers. Still others and sometimes the same officers were unable to gauge the depth of morale problems in their units until serious problems erupted. Requiring black soldiers to pick cotton in Arizona and to clean snow from the streets of Richmond, VA and Seattle, Washington, only heightened "the belief of troops that training for military duties was not to be taken too seriously by

Negro units."[39] According to Lee, the uncertainty of the black troops' status was as damaging to morale as the knowledge of definite restrictions.[40] As the war progressed, morale among black units improved, but it was never as high as that of white units.

Much to its credit, the armed services were the first institutions in the United States to formally endorse integration after President Harry S. Truman issued Executive Order 9981 on July 26, 1948. It declared that there should be equality of treatment and opportunity for all persons in the armed services without regard to race, color, religion, or national origin.[41] The US society at large waited until the civil rights movement of the 1960s and 1970s more fully embraced integration.

Sexual racism was an insidious form of segregation during World War II that had great impact on the military's response to rapes by its troops. By then it had the support of hundreds of years of statutes and customs intended to regulate the sexual relationships between blacks and whites. Miscegenation had been outlawed during America's colonial days, first in 1661 by the Maryland General Assembly and then by Virginia in 1691.[42] Similar statutes developed unevenly across the United States. Missouri, Edmonds's home state, for instance, forbade mixed marriages in 1835.

By the mid-1800s it was clear that anti-miscegenation laws had been less than successful because "an estimated 37 percent of the free Negro population of the United States was part white [with] the figure ... much higher for half of the free Negro population living in the South."[43] By the early 1900s at least 38 states had anti-miscegenation laws of some form.

Whether the root cause of anti-miscegenation laws was the belief that blacks were inferior to whites, and that bars to intermarriage and sexual intercourse were required to maintain the purity of the white race, or whether it was part of a broader pattern of discrimination intended to keep whites in a dominate relationship to blacks, is irrelevant to the present study. What is relevant is that anti-miscegenation is a form of sexual racism that prohibited black men from having sexual intercourse with white women, but it did not attempt to stop the opposite – white men sexually exploiting black females.

This interpretation of proper sexual contact between blacks and whites was still on the law books of many states during World War II, and it continued to exist for more than two decades after the end of the war. Twenty-nine state anti-miscegenation statutes were still standing in 1951 – in 1964, nineteen states continued to have anti-interracial laws. Anti-miscegenation was not ruled unconstitutional until well past the mid-twentieth century in *Loving v. Virginia* in 1967. Paradoxically and ironically, the late-nineteenth century anti-miscegenation laws endorsed the ancient stereotype that blacks, especially males, were more lustful and had greater sexual prowess than white men and women. One late-nineteenth-century illustration of this stereotype was found in physicians' and others' 1880s discussions of the allegedly large size and immunity to erectile dysfunction of the black male penis.[44] After the

American Civil War, great anxiety over whether this was actually correct helped generate unprecedented "fear that black emancipation meant the freedom of macrophallic black men to mate with white women – and, even worse, that white women might actually prefer them."[45] Quite simply, to many white people emancipation had transformed Harriett Beecher Stowe's Uncle Tom of slavery "into a lascivious free 'menace' to all white women."[46] At this time there was little purchase for the tragic complexities of interracial sexual relations that was described later by Richard Wright's *Native Son*.[47]

Sex-based lynching soon became a perverse drama, primarily in the American south, which attempted to control actual and imagined black sexual assaults on white females. On one level of analysis they restored an immediate tear in the fragile local social fabric of segregation.[48] On the other hand, sex-based lynchings and the not infrequent castration of the accused was, according to Calvin C. Hernton, an effort to transfer to whites the "grotesque powers they assigned to the black phallus, which they symbolically extol by the act of destroying it."[49]

The number of lynchings between 1882 and 1951 have been estimated at 4,730, over half of which occurred in nine southern states – Kentucky, Arkansas, Tennessee, North and South Carolina, Mississippi, Alabama, Georgia and Florida. It made little, if any, difference whether the transgressions were real or alleged – the lynchings were nonetheless socially functional. They served four missions: to eradicate specific persons accused of crimes against the white community; as a mechanism of state-sanctioned terror to maintain leverage over the black population; to eliminate or neutralize competition for social, economic, and political rewards; and as a symbolic manifestation of the unity of white supremacy.[50]

It is debatable whether US military justice involving blacks during World War II was more rigorous and brutish than civilian justice. But there is no doubt that its representatives were well aware of the legacy of slavery and that the military practiced segregation. The military court's query about the size of Edmonds's penis in October 1942 was no aberration – in part it reflected the nation's concern with anti-miscegenation laws and customs. It was also a question that likely resonated well with the jury, even though the Englishman, Dr. Burrows, disagreed. The record is silent on what his American counterpart, a 1933 medical school graduate from Kentucky – a state which kept its anti-miscegenation laws until 1978 – thought about the question.[51] The court's query was consistent with the social contexts surrounding black and white sexual relations in the United States during World War II. Rape transcripts from the ETO contain no questions about the penises of white rapists.

The disadvantages that Edmonds and other black troops faced when accused of sexual crimes during World War II were not due to *de jure* segregation alone. They and white soldiers were also members of an American-style citizen soldier *total institution* – the military. It did not permit or practice many of the basic freedoms associated with a democracy. The statutes governing military discipline and justice between 1775 and 1950 were the *Articles of War*. In the eighteenth century they were drawn largely from the Royal Navy and British army, which had adopted them with little modification from the Roman Empire. For the sake of discipline and efficiency the *Articles of War* stripped away most of the individual rights that civilians had before induction. During World War II, soldiers were not permitted to have bail, an indictment by grand jury, impartial judges, or what was known in civilian courts as due process. Neither was it required that accused soldiers be defended by a legally trained attorney. Soldiers indeed had the right to be so defended, but this seldom occurred. Usually, an officer or other military personnel was appointed by the accused's commanding officer to carry out the duties of legal counsel to defend the accused.[52] This created an opportunity for a commander to unduly and capriciously influence those he had convened to conduct a court martial.

How many victims?

The number of unreported crimes has long been a major concern for various academic disciplines and policy makers. Thorsten Sellin and Sir Leon Radzinowicz, two of the most prominent criminologists of the twentieth century, wrote that recorded crime is a mere fraction of the total picture of crimes actually committed. For sexual transgressions the number of unreported offenses is still enormous. Arguably, sexual offenses were even more underreported during the era of World War II than now because of numerous factors, not the least of which was the muted voice of women in general, and of female victims in particular.

Rapes are among the most underreported crimes committed. It is therefore doubtful that the US military's post-war report that nearly a thousand (904)[53] American soldiers were accused of rape, and about half (461) of them convicted, is close to being accurate. If only 5 percent of the rapes are reported as Radzinowicz claimed was the situation more than a decade after the end of World War II, the approximate total number of rape accusations could be 18,080 (20 × 904 = 18,080).[54]

An accurate count of the rape victims is just as elusive. In one of its tabulations the military reported that 710 women were raped. If this is only 5 percent of the total victims, it is possible that there were almost 4,000 (3,880) more assailants than victims (20 × 710 = 14,200). (See Table 1.1.)

Another JAG tabulation, this one for the three leading countries in which the rapes were committed, presents a different picture. This official account indicates that there were a total of 854 rapes in Germany, France, and England. By applying the 5 percent logic, it is possible to estimate that the number of rape victims in these countries was 17,080 (20 × 854 = 17,080). (See Table 1.2.)

A more complete picture of the possible number of rapes per country is important for an understanding of how and why rates of rape changed in

Table 1.1   JAG reported number of victims

German	484 (63.3%) × 20 =	9,680
French	125 (16.4%) × 20 =	2,500
England	101 (13.2%) × 20 =	2,020
Total	710 (100%) × 20 =	14,200

Table 1.2   JAG reported rapes by country

Germany	552 (64%)
France	181 (22%)
England	121 (14%)
Total	854 (100%)

different context of the war. The logic of the 5 percent argument suggests the following:

Estimated rapes per country

Germany	20 × 552 =	11,040
France	20 × 181 =	3,620
England	20 × 121 =	2,420
Total	=	17,080

By country, this logic suggests that the United Kingdom had slightly less than 2,500 rapes, France more than 3,600, and Germany more than 11,000. The total of 17,080 is, of course, an estimate which I think is far closer to being accurate than the JAG's numbers.

*   *   *

This book describes the forcible ordinary rapes (vs. statutory) and the US Army's responses to them between 1942 and 1945. From the first rape in Melling, England, that went to trial to the last one on September 23, 1945, at Regenstaul, Bavaria, Germany, the images of the victims and offenders gradually changed.

The rapes in the United Kingdom occurred within a context of a moral panic largely imported from the United States about sexual relations between black soldiers and white women. The women of these assaults were often described in the records as "innocent victims." Similar language was used to describe French victims, especially if black soldiers had raped them, despite the history and fanciful stereotyped image of French women. In some cases the Germany rape victim's character was maligned with guilt by association with Nazism. Others were "just Germans."

Not surprisingly, the sanctions for rape changed too, with the most severe sentences given to black troops. Black soldiers – but no whites – were executed for rape in England. Soldiers of both races, but mostly blacks, were executed in France. No soldiers were executed just for rape in Germany. Three soldiers were executed for committing murder and rape in Germany – two black soldiers and one native American, a Navajo Indian. None of the three was executed on German soil. Some of the German rapes were explained as "due to the conditions of war" with attendant lighter sentences. By the time of the rapes in Germany, too, black soldiers had been somewhat rehabilitated because of their war contributions – in some quarters they had gained significant respect and admiration.

The picture of US troops presented here is in stark contrast to that chronicled in the United States through official accounts, books, letters, diaries, memoirs, public comments, journalistic reports, and movies. These sources, especially some of the accounts penned by the late American historian Stephen Ambrose, created the myth of US soldiers as the best foreign representatives America had to offer at this crucial period.

The images we have of them in England and France, found in all manner of accounts, portray them as much needed and welcomed friends: generous, benevolent, and selfless. At worst is the impression so aptly captured by the British expression that American boys not only were "over here, over paid and over fed," but also "over sexed."[55] This "All American" image of the US solider in the ETO is unabated. For years the American public has had an insatiable appetite for books, big screen movies, and made-for-TV serials about the "greatest generation any society has ever produced," and its much-heralded contribution to winning World War II and reconstructing the post-war world.[56]

The United States' military participation in World War II, in fact, had a multifaceted, ugly underbelly that remains largely unexamined.[57] This study concerns one aspect of this dark side of that war.[58] In a very real sense, it is about "'a most detestable crime,'"[59] one of the most non-heroic and brutal forms of behavior that occurs during any war. Other dimensions of this side of the American fighting forces that are beyond the scope of this work include thefts, large and small, and brutal assaults on civilians and military personnel alike, including murder. These crimes will be examined at a later time.

It is not my intention to rewrite or alter the record of major – political, ideological, military, or cultural – aspects of World War II. This book was written to illuminate a largely neglected part of American soldiers' misbehavior in the United Kingdom, France, and Germany.

Between January, 1942, and May, 1945, the US Army had prepared and then fought with unparalleled success in three distinctly different and shifting settings. First, it had prepared in England, fought in enemy-occupied France, and entered the enemy's territory beginning with the capture of

Aachen, Germany. The last context occupied the US Army's fighting and command personnel until Germany's surrender on May 7, 1945. For these heroic accomplishments alone it is difficult to write about the rapes committed by US soldiers in the ETO.

The task of examining this subject is made no easier by the fact that the ravages of time are today, in early 2003, rapidly devastating the more than 16 million Americans who served in the armed forces during World War II – now there are less than 5 million veterans.[60] It is not my goal to tarnish their wartime contributions or to besmirch our memory of them. For these reasons alone it is difficult to write about rapes committed by US soldiers. It is so contrary to what we in America think we know about them – it has no glory or romance.

It is all the more difficult to write this story post–September 11, 2001 and the 2003 war with Iraq as the United States struggles to understand why it is so hated in some parts of the world. It almost seems disrespectful, sort of like sticking one's finger in the eye of a dear friend when they are having a bad time. Yet, it needs to be written to help keep the World War II record straight and as a hopeful antidote to the ethnocentric, treacly concoction of the ETO soldiers as "the greatest generation." Perhaps it will encourage some of the rapidly shrinking population of World War II veterans and rape victims to speak candidly about the more sordid aspect of their war experiences. Hopefully, too, it will add some understanding on the neglected topic of wartime rape.

This book offers a systematic examination of the patterns of rapes committed by American soldiers in the United Kingdom, France, and Germany, and the Army's responses to these crimes. In some ways it is a narrow book because it relies principally on the records of the Judge Advocate General Branch of the European Theater. It does not explore whether the British government through its British Foreign Office, or the Free French responded to the sexual violence through normal diplomatic exchanges with the State Department, or the US Army or SHEAF. Neither does it explore race relations in the United States, nor its military during World War II as recorded in the Papers of the NAACP, Papers of Judge William Haste (civilian aide to the Secretary of War Stimson), or the Papers of William O. Davis, the first African American general. To have pursued these avenues would have resulted in a book more concerned with diplomatic history than I wanted to write.

The sources used here contain the verbatim words of the people involved in the rapes. Some of the words were written in longhand, others were typewritten; still others came from the work of the court recorders at the court-martials. Some of the letters are in English, others are in French. We get to hear the voices of the victims as they told their stories in military trials. Their voices come alive, in part, because they are contained in official records. They have the sound of *authenticity*, I think, that is stronger than if we read about them in the newspapers. There the stories would have been competing for space with other news, and they might have been curtailed by the limitations of reporters' time, or the influence of editors and publishers. Here the stories come from the raw records used by the courts, and they have limitations that are discussed in the next chapter.

We, too, get to hear what the victims were doing just before they were assaulted. We learn about their living conditions – almost always it was poor, especially in France and Germany when compared with the United Kingdom. We learn something about what they ate and drank. We get to know where the victims were assaulted, whether it was in houses, apartments, barns, or the cellars of bombed-out buildings. We get to know the crime scenes. We learn about the vulnerability of the rape victims. Were they alone, or living with other victims of the war's ravages and disruptions? Did it make any difference to the assailants if their victims were with their family and friends? When did the rapes occur, day or night?

Their modes of traveling whether by foot, bicycle, train, or hitch-hiking become altogether familiar to us. They help us recreate a bygone and often mythologized era and understand how the victims came into harm's way. The victim's injuries – bruises, wounds, broken bones – from being slapped, punched, cut, beaten, or shot – also become well known to us. The victims and those who attended to them tell us about these things. For children too young or too traumatized to speak, others speak for them.

The primary focus is not on the victims, however. As important as they are, we learn more about the offenders because in the search for guilt or innocence it was the soldiers who were subjected to most of the scrutiny from the military authorities. The military records used here have more information about all the offenders, at least for those soldiers who were tried in England and France. The trial records from Germany, as we shall see, contain significant nuances not found in cases from England and France.

We learn the rapists' ages, and when and where they were inducted into the Army. We learn their rank and what they did for the Army. Sometimes we also learn about their immediate families, including whether they were single, married, separated, or divorced. On occasion we know they are parents. We know what they wore, what weapons they carried and sometimes used on their victims, and the victims' family, children, and friends. We also learn about their drinking habits, and what their buddies and commanders thought of them. They speak about the crimes they were accused of committing. In effect, we learn how the victims' and rapists' daily activities came together almost accidentally.

The prosecutors and defense voices also speak as they argue the facts of the case – at times we hear their barbed asides too. We hear them question victims, offenders, and witnesses. We hear from the army's judges who reviewed the cases before the offender's final fate was decided. Sometimes they revealed their personal opinions about the cases in front of them. We get examples of legal reasoning and how it was used to damn some to death, and to merely slap the wrists of others.

One of the central themes is that not only did the ETO have an as yet unexplored underbelly, but also that its crimes were a complex social matter. The criminal behavior of the soldiers varied depending on when and where the US Army was located. The patterns of raping varied dramatically in France compared to what occurred in England, and later in Germany. The military responses to the soldiers' crimes also fluctuated, not because the soldiers, their crimes, and the military justice system and its personnel had changed. Rather, punishments changed because the ideological parameters within which each country and its citizens (and refugees) were perceived differed. *Time* and *place* mattered.

American soldiers in the United Kingdom had a culture and language that allowed them and their hosts to have more similarities and less day-to-day conflicts than in France and Germany. On the ground, this contributed to a context wherein females in the United Kingdom were comparatively harder to objectify as potential rape targets than in either France or Germany.

The United Kingdom had civilian-based as well as American-sponsored efforts that warned females to be cautious of GIs, especially blacks. The social environment of the United Kingdom, while greatly disrupted and compromised by the war, remained more intact than in either France or Germany.

For this study, these conditions are interpreted to mean that the females in the United Kingdom were in a safer, less rape-prone social world, compared with France or Germany. The United Kingdom, after all, was not invaded or occupied except for two of its Channel Isles, Jersey and Guernsey. Neither was the United Kingdom ever exposed to the consequences of being the vanquished and defeated enemy, and all that that implies for female sexual victimization. The patterns of rape committed by American soldiers reflect and confirm these significant differences.

The extensive details found in the documentation used for this book also make it possible in a limited way to examine the issue of what motivated American soldiers to rape. Was it primarily for the purposes of humiliation and dominance? Or, was the motivation more along the racial and sexual comment as explicitly stated by the crude words of Private James W. Shields, Indiana, a soldier convicted of attempted rape in England, who said, "I want some white pussy."[61]

Whatever might have been the motivations, clearly the victims were overpowered by their assailants and used as sex objects. It also is clear from the records that the *modus operandi* of the assailants varied greatly. Some assailants engaged in "blitz rapes," quickly grabbing their victim, throwing them into bushes, behind vehicles or buildings, raping them and rapidly departing.[62] Other rapists prolonged the ordeal for hours by engaging in conversation and forced sex. Still others spent the night with their victims and had breakfast with them the next morning. Others claimed to be in love and volunteered to marry their brutalized prey.

Some rape convictions followed what the courts-martial and reviewing judges saw as encouraging behavior on the part of the victim. These surviving details, unfortunately, reveal very little, if anything, about the intricacies of sexual objectification associated with gratuitous wartime rape. Very little is revealed about the content or the meaning of sexual objectification by black rapists versus that of white counterparts. Perhaps there was no difference. Neither is anything revealed about the ingredients of the sexual objectification by noncommissioned troops compared to that of officers, or to members of the regular army versus draftees.

Most clearly we learn that the rapes were planned, some rather elaborately, others less so. They resulted from the convergence of three elements common to any other routine activity including crime: a motivated offender, a suitable target, and a differentiation in the absence of capable guardians. Shifts in daily routines that so deeply characterized England, France, and Germany during the war help us to understand why and when the rapes, and other crimes, occurred. Miss R.'s rape is illustrative. She, like so many English females during World War II, found that her pre-war daily routines had been thrown to the wind. Her father and two brothers were gone, leaving her and her mother to cope with the short- and long-term disruptions and tensions of their corner within wartime England. On the night of her rape she found it necessary to leave home for a loaf of bread and a bike ride to obtain onions, activities that normally would have occurred during daylight. Outside her home she encountered Edmonds, who had also ended his day's work for the US Army and was on his own unsupervised for a few hours. Their encounter was uncannily prescient for the patterns of rape that developed in England, France, and Germany.

We begin Chapter 2 with an overview of what is known about wartime rape and a discussion of the sources of the material used here. In Chapter 3 we examine the patterns of rapes in England. We pursue the same questions and answers in Chapter 4 on France, and Chapter 5 on Germany. The last chapter examines how prosecution, defense, and punishments of the rapists shift from one setting to the next.

2
Wartime Rape

Wartime forces drastic changes. It destroys. It disrupts. It hurts, toughens, and gives resolve to people – civilians and soldiers. Expected and unexpected messy changes cause large and small adjustments. In the United States, it created what Perry Duis called a "substitute culture," a temporary replacement for the everyday life of peace. The concept is just as applicable to England, France, and Germany, which saw "temporary replacements for artifacts, institutions and social relationships."[1] Attitudes, fears, confidences, and hopes are altered during wartime, sometimes never to return to pre-war positions. "Things will never be the same" becomes a familiar refrain. New identities are forged for individuals, groups, and nations. Historians, politicians, economists, militarists, and citizens use war as a benchmark to measure the past, interpret the present, and plan for the future. It is simultaneously paradoxical, ironic, and tragic.

The World War II touched nearly all aspects of life in the key theaters of the war – allies and enemies, home fronts and battlefields. This was especially true for the European Theater of Operations (ETO), Italy and Russia, because the war so heavily affected civilians in these places.

The major participants of World War II did not experience the same changes, or make the same adjustments. Far from it – each country had its own unique shocks and adjustments. The blitz (August 1940 to mid-May 1941) was probably England's biggest shock and disruption with a loss of approximately 60,000 lives. In France it was its collapse in May, 1940 and the subsequent occupation of Germany (1940–1944). Defeat was unquestionably Germany's major shock, accompanied by millions of deaths. The greatest immediate impact of the war in the United States was on its domestic employment and economy. With the passage of six decades since the war's end, we seem, at least in the United States, to have forgotten that wartime provides "some of the most intense as well as brutal of human experiences, bringing out the best as well as the worst in people – heroism, comradeship, and self-sacrifice as well as cruelty and viciousness."[2]

Unlike the sanitized post-war view of US soldiers offered by one of the most prolific World War II historians, Stephen E. Ambrose, they were not all glory, high-mindedness and decency.[3] To the contrary, shortly after Hiroshima, *The Atlantic Monthly* published a piece by Edgar L. Jones, a Dartmouth graduate. He had 40 months of war duty, 14 of them as an ambulance driver with the British Eighth Army in North Africa. There he was cited for his rescue of the wounded from an exploding ammunition truck. Later as the *Atlantic* correspondent at Iwo Jima and Okinawa, he wrote,

> What kind of war do civilians suppose we fought, anyway? We shot prisoners in cold blood, wiped out hospitals, strafed lifeboats, killed or mistreated enemy civilians, finished off the enemy wounded, tossed the dying into a hole with the dead, and in the Pacific boiled the flesh off enemy skulls to make table ornaments for sweethearts, or carved their bones into letter openers.[4]

And sometimes they raped.

The crime of rape

Not long ago rape was a taboo subject. At best, it received only glancing notice. Since the publication of Susan Brownmiller's (1975) *Against Our Will* rape has increasingly received attention from scholars, the media, and international policy makers. Earlier it largely had been a subject of legal and religious concerns about the ownership and value of women. Today it is a tragic topic that is often discussed.[5]

Rape in wartime remained almost exclusively an ancillary subject of international law upto and throughout World War II. During the post-World War II Nuremberg trials wartime rape was subsumed but not explicitly identified under "crimes against humanity." Despite solid documentation of German soldiers systematically engaging in rape from *Kristallnacht* (November 1938) until the end of the war (May 1945), no one at the Nuremberg Trials was tried for this offense as a "war crime under customary international law. But it was prosecuted in Tokyo as a war crime."[6] As a result of the Japanese War Crimes Trials, only one general, Yamashita, was executed for a rape-related offense. He was found guilty of *permitting* rape.[7]

Since then wartime rape has increasingly received intensive international scrutiny, most particularly since the early 1990s.[8] In 1946, rape committed during war was recognized as a crime against humanity,[9] a significant development in international law that was reinforced in 1949 when the Fourth Geneva Convention specified (Article 27) that women shall be especially protected against any attack on their honor, in particular against rape, enforced prostitution, or any form of indecent assault.[10] Article 147 of the same Convention designated willfully causing great suffering or serious injury to body or health, torture, and inhuman treatment as war crimes and as breaches of the Convention.[11]

This position was reinforced in the early 1990s when the International Committee of the Red Cross, various states, and the United Nations considered the "weight of the events in Yugoslavia."[12] One significant result was a 1993 UN "statute for the international tribunal to try war crimes committed in the former Yugoslavia."[13] Rape as a war crime was first prosecuted in June 1996, when the United Nations International Criminal Tribunal of the Hague indicted eight Bosnian Serb military and police officers in connection with the rapes of Muslim women during the Bosnian conflict.[14] The indictment marked the first time that *sexual assault*, a much broader concept than wartime rape, was defined as a violation of international humanitarian law, and thus a crime of war. The indictment also indicated that a new era of cooperation had returned to the United Nations and with it an ideology that emphasized the fulfillment of the original UN mandate of peace and security.

The 1993 UN decision did not term the raping of women in wartime a violation of human rights. To do this would have meant that the United Nations condemned the rape of women under *any* circumstances as a violation of human rights. The 1993 decision fell short of this position. It permitted the interpretation that the UN was prohibiting rape only to the extent that it was used for the purpose of illegitimate military ends.[15] The 1993 decision also left the door open to considering other forms of martial sexual assault as war crimes.[16] One possibility includes whether the sexual assaults of men, or by men, can or should be considered war crimes.[17]

In early 2000 this subject received worldwide attention. The *New York Times* reported that male prisoners seized by Russian troops and held in a camp in the northern rebel breakaway capital, Grozny, Chechnya, heard the screams of men who were being raped by their captors. After the rapes, it was reported that their assailants gave the victims new feminine names.[18]

Interpreting rape in war

Some observers hold that rape, whether during wartime or peace, is nothing less "than a conscious process of intimidation by which *all* men keep *all* women in a state of fear"[19] (Emphasis in the original). This broad interpretation is conceptually and methodologically unsound. It says nothing about the role women have played in the distant past and more recently in advocating wartime rape, as demonstrated by Rwanda's Pauline Nyiramasuhuko in the thousands of rapes of female Tutsis in 1994,[20] or the admitted guilt of Bosnian Serb, Biljana Plavsic.[21]

As Lance Morrow has stated, "even sexual assault has its subtleties and protocols."[22] There are rules about rape. "In medieval and early modern Europe, the women of besieged towns taken by storm might be raped, but those in a town that surrendered on terms would not," for example.[23]

Variations in social contexts as explanations for human behavior provide far more useful explanations of wartime rape.[24] This approach is much less simplistic than Brownmiller's (1975) reliance on the over-inclusive *all*. Here it is argued that rape in war results from supportive social structures. These mechanisms range from the highly formal to the informal, and they have been portrayed and analyzed in various formats including paintings, etchings, journals, military reports, historical accounts, and scholarly works.[25]

Rape in wartime, in all of its manifestations, is a gendered subject. Central to the use of context as an explanation are the observations that like all forms of criminal or deviant behavior, rape changes in meaning and measurement, across groups and places and through historical time and in individual lives. Very little has been written about rape victims in "Nicaragua and other parts of Latin America who have expressed *pride* in having been raped in war because their political beliefs taught them that they had given their bodies to the revolution."[26] Civilian rapes prior to the second wave of feminism (1960s–1980s) were usually defined legally as sex offenses. Now they generally are regarded as acts of violence.

An historical portrait of the prevalence of rape in any war lies somewhere among the recorded voices of its victims and their supporters, and the willingness of a victorious military to permit or control it. Within these limitations it is reasonable to conclude that until mechanisms are in place to address each of these factors, the prevalence of wartime rape will be nearly impossible to determine. Perhaps the best documentation of wartime rape occurred in Bosnia and Kosovo during the early 1990s. Not only did thousands of victims bear witness to rape in these wars, but media reports, including television broadcasts, also documented actual rapes.[27]

Some of the first depictions of rape in war appear in paintings, but at times it is very difficult to determine if the rapes portrayed actually occurred. Indeed, several classic paintings of rape in wartime are romanticized allegories laden with numerous symbolic messages and constructed long after the fact. Poussin's *The Rape of the Sabine Women*, for example, was painted in 1635 about an event that allegedly led to the founding of early Rome. Paintings like this provide an example of how rape in wartime has been a reward for unpaid soldiers. Quite clearly these rapes resulted from military organization and culture of the military. Other wartime rapes occurred because of different organizational expectations. To make some sociological sense out of the historical records of wartime the following classifications are helpful. They are not mutually exclusive of each other; – there are bound to be exceptions and disagreements for a subject as vast as wartime rapes. But, they are important for putting the GIs' rapes in the ETO in a comparative perspective.

Mass rape as a cultural and genocidal weapon

The twentieth century witnessed four well-known examples of rape in wartime as a cultural and genocidal weapon. These rapes were well organized, systematic, and public. Perhaps the most well-known example of military rapes during World War II occurred in Nanking.

On December 13, 1937, Nanking, the capital city of Nationalist China, fell to the Japanese after a half-year struggle against Chiang Kai-shek's armies. This occurred eight years before Japanese General Yamashita surrendered to the United States Army in the Philippine Islands and six years into the fourteen years of Japanese domination (1931–1945) in China. By all accounts, including those of surviving Japanese soldiers, the rapes in Nanking were not the result of failed military discipline. They were part of other atrocities, including the mass execution of soldiers and fleeing civilians.[28] As one observer has commented, "What is still stunning is that it was a *public* rampage, evidently designed to terrorize."[29] The raping in Nanking lasted a well-documented seven weeks. At the time the Nazis in Nanking referred to it as the "work of 'bestial machinery.'"[30] Five decades later one observer made the debatable conclusion: "Nothing the Nazis under Hitler would do to disgrace their own victories could rival the atrocities of Japanese soldiers under Gen. Iwane Matsui."[31] This is arguable given the range of atrocities committed by the Germans in occupied Europe.

A more recent example includes the hundreds of thousands of civilian deaths and the massive scale of at least 200,000 rapes by the Pakistani army in 1971 when Bangladesh won its independence. The rapes in Bosnia, far from being a side effect of war, were one of its instruments. According to Amnesty International's report *Bosnia-Herzegovia: Rape and Sexual Abuse by Armed Forces*, "the rape of women has been carried out in an organized or systematic way, with the deliberate detention of women for the purpose of rape and sexual abuses." "[R]apes in Bosnia have almost certainly been committed as a matter of deliberate policy."[32]

The abuse of women as an element of male communication

Another explanation of wartime rape argues that it is aimed at the husbands, fathers, brothers, uncles, and friends of the rape victims. The message is a symbolic expression of the "humiliation of the male opponent" who is told by the rapes that he is unable to protect his women.[33] These rapes serve to wound the masculinity ("honor") and competence of male counterparts. In 1999 the *Cincinnati Enquirer* reported with pictures the story of a Kosovar father who sent his 13-year-old daughter who had been raped by a Serbian soldier to join the Kosovo Liberation Army to kill Serbs. His justification was that she was of no use to him any more.[34] A similar response was often recorded after the battle hardened Russian troops from various backgrounds, including recently released POWs, raped women from East Prussia and Berlin in the spring of 1945. The husbands often held the women responsible for the deed.[35]

At World War II's end and up to the present, these rapes have often been interpreted by Germans of both sexes as one of many examples of German males' failure to protect their female counterparts at the end of World War II.[36] This is an important and perceptive perspective because it helps to expand our understanding of victims. It not only includes the immediate and most obvious brutalization of women and girls, but it also embraces their male relatives and friends as *victims*. It can also accommodate a more circumspect analysis, one that recognizes that the intensity of the violence and brutality of rapes by troops in the same army may change during the course of one campaign, though at the same time generating abuse and humiliation. Beevor makes this astute observation regarding the Red Army, in the spring of 1945.

The Red Army's rapes in East Prussia during January and February 1945 were indiscreet, indiscriminately violent, and revengeful. By the time the Red Army reached Berlin a definite change had developed. "By this stage Soviet soldiers started to treat German women more as sexual spoils of war than as substitutes for the Wehrmacht on to vent their rage."[37] Revenge and lust-based rapes are not likely to have the same meaning for the rapists – a distinction that is probably of little relevance from the victim's point of view. This is not a minor point because at first glance the volume of Russian rapes of German women – often collective assaults sometimes involving 9–12 soldiers[38] – suggests mass rapes of the type reported in Bosnia and Kosovo during the 1990s. Such an interpretation would be an error. The Russian campaign to Berlin did not involve the establishment and maintenance of rape camps. Nor is there evidence indicating that the Red Army raped with the intent of impregnation for the purpose of cultural genocide. This would have required *selecting* rape victims with the promise of fecundity, and *holding* them until they were pregnant. Future research may reveal that this occurred, but for now it seems that the Russian troops raped not only Soviet girls whom they had liberated from German camps, "They raped every German female from eight to 80."[39]

According to some sources, their rapes happened during the relatively short period of time, between late April and mid-May, 1945, though other accounts of these rapes indicate they occurred "at least until the beginning of 1947."[40] In a review of Anthony Beevor's *The Fall of Berlin 1945*, the rapes are said to have continued for three years or more after the Russians had arrived.[41]

Rape as a part of military culture

Unlike other total institutions including mental institutions and monasteries, the military has an unusual configuration of norms regarding masculinity, sexuality, and women. Some observers have found that the confluence of these factors is part of the shared norms that comprises the bonding that occurs in the military. Moreover, it has been asserted that bonding based on these items is conducive to rape by military personnel. By using two sources of secondary data, a law professor Madeline Morris examined this hypothesis and reported that the US military has a "rape differential." It consists of *lower* rates of rapes by military personnel during peacetime than what exists for civilians in the same period. Morris reports that between 1987 and 1992, the Air Force rape rate was only 5 percent of the civilian rate. For the same time span, the Army's rape rate was almost 50 percent of the rate of rape committed by civilians.[42]

Morris's second data source came from the ETO. She concludes, in part, that during "breakout periods" in France when US troops were pursuing the enemy rape increased dramatically. Under conditions of actual combat, the "rape differential" increased, based on what was actually recorded and investigated by US military authorities.

These observations, unfortunately, explain very little about the military culture or military organization during World War II that might contribute to any understanding of rape patterns across the ETO. Morris does not attend to the question of whether the rapes were mostly committed by freebooters, or by "bonded" gang rapists similar to the pattern of Russian rapes reported in Germany, spring 1945. Nor does Morris mention that rapes during "breakout periods" may have involved a "rape differential" composed of more (or less) rear echelon troops than of frontline combatants. Neither does Morris discuss how segregation, sexual racism, or military justice might have influenced the picture of rape she found reported in the records. She failed to report, even though the ETO records she used contained the information – whether accurate or not – that while most of the soldiers accused of sexual offenses were white (57%), most of the convicted men were black (66%). The US Army records report that blacks committed more than 75 percent of the rapes in France alone.[43] As we know, black soldiers in France were not major contributors to fighting in the breakouts – they were behind the front lines. It is quite possible that the complaints against the black soldiers were the ones the army *selected* to record, thus inadvertently creating an incomplete and inaccurate account. This point will be explored further in a later chapter on patterns of punishment.

This is not to deny Morris's argument that the US military between the 1970s and today has a rape-prone culture, or even that it had one during World War II. Rather, it must be remembered that the cultural tapestry of the military during World War II was dominated by racism, not sexism. This does not mean, of course, that sexist language and behavior were absent in domestic training camps or those developed abroad. What it does mean, is that it was highly improbable that during World War II white drill instructors would try to instill bonding and all that that implies by devaluing white women in front of black or white soldiers.

A closely related issue is whether there might have been a "reception differential" among soldiers to any, or all, of the elements of a rape-prone culture. Were white soldiers more receptive than black troopers? Were relatively younger or older soldiers more receptive? Did soldiers who entered the military early in the war rape more often than those who came in later?

Rapes, revenge, and elevated masculinity

Fictional and nonfictional literature contains a plethora of materials that explain male behavior as efforts to elevate masculinity and to confirm loyal group membership. Sports and war literature are especially rich with this theme. Part of the African-American military history, for example, as well as part of the European Jewish military record in World War I and World War II, involves joining the military in hope of proving one's individual masculinity and hopefully, collective worth and patriotism.[44]

The transformative power of the uniform is relevant to this point. Prior to World War II, the Schutzstaffel (SS) was formed as an independent organization within the Nazi Party. Initially it served primarily as Hitler's bodyguards, orderlies for mass meetings, and party propagandists. Later, under Himmler, it spawned more ambitious interests and activities that came to represent "the arrogance of Nazi ideology and the criminal nature of Hitler's regime."[45] Upon reflection, first as a member of one of Hitler's youth organizations, and later as a member of the SS, Peter Neumann noted, "It is unbelievable how the black uniform changes one's personality, hardening the expression of one's face and defining one's features."[46]

The symbolic meaning of the uniform and the earned adornments worn on it are germane to this point. The uniform represents among many things, an approved membership or citizenship in an official, primarily masculine organization. Earned medals and ribbons provide additional identification and confirmation of an elevated masculinity. They speak loudly to the range of behavior that the wearer of the uniform can be expected to exhibit. More importantly to the wearers of military uniforms is the knowledge that the range of acceptable behavior is determined more by peer pressure than by formal rules.[47] Uniformed soldiers may indeed tolerate a wide range of questionable, even illegal and inhuman behavior including rape, from fellow troopers. Much depends on where the deviant behavior occurs.

Marine E.B. "Sledgehammer" Sledge's devastatingly powerful World War II memoir illuminates this observation with poignancy. He writes that at the Pacific battles of Peleliu and Okinawa not all uniformed soldiers were permitted to hunt for souvenirs. Frontline troops had greater freedom than "fresh-looking souvenir hunters wearing green cloth fatigue caps instead of helmets and carrying no weapons."[48] Anyone not in a rifle company were called REMF's, "rear-echelon mother-fuckers."[49]

Black soldiers returning from both world wars soon found, by some accounts, that wearing a uniform in the American south generated hostility and denial that they had been accepted by the military. Sergeant Isaac Woodard's experience is illustrative. He had served 3 years, including 15 months in the South Pacific before being discharged. He was still in his uniform when he boarded a bus for the trip from Fort Gordon, Georgia, to his home in North Carolina.[50] At a stop in South Carolina the bus driver became irritated at Woodard because of the time he took to use the "colored only" toilet. At the next town the driver demanded that the local sheriff arrest Woodard on the charge of drunkenness even though Woodard did not drink.

During the arrest Woodard was beaten with a blackjack by the sheriff and someone "either the sheriff or a policeman, thrust the end of a nightstick into his eyes."[51] He was denied medical care and was locked into a cell overnight. When he was eventually examined at an Army hospital, doctors found that he was permanently blind. "The uniform meant nothing to white authorities determined to demonstrate their superiority over the black man."[52]

Adorning one's uniform with unearned medals can be fatally self-destructive. In 1996, Admiral Jeremy M. Boorda, 56, the Chief of Naval Operations found himself in a difficult situation. He was then the "first sailor to climb from the lowest ranks of enlisted man to four-star admiral,"[53] but embarrassing questions were raised about two Vietnam War combat decorations he wore. They were reportedly called into question by *Newsweek*, ABC News, and the National Security News Service.[54] Just about the same time *Newsweek* correspondent was arriving at the Pentagon for an interview about the medals, Boorda left his office and went home where he "grabbed a .38-caliber handgun, walked outside, rested the gun barrel against his chest and pulled the trigger."[55] In a one-page, typed suicide note he said wearing the medals was "'an honest mistake.'"[56] In the days following his death several Navy officers and legal experts reviewed Boorda's life in the military, and the medals he wore. Most agreed that he was not authorized to wear them because he was not in a war zone during the war. "The shame and dishonor were too much for him,"[57] especially during a time when the Navy had been tarnished by a number of scandals.

As an expression of striving for elevated masculinity, rapes in wartime have explanatory value, especially for new recruits whose squad members may take rape as a sign of masculinity and solidarity. In 1993, *Time* reporter Lance Morrow discussed rape as part of his coverage of the Bosnia War. He noted that while professional soldiers receive intensive indoctrination on decent behavior and what offenses, including rape, would result in courts-martial, this logic got turned on its head. The "elite" units of Serbian irregulars, such as the White Eagles, "evidently made rape a gesture of group solidarity. A man who refuses to join the others in rape [was] regarded as a traitor to the unit."[58] The theme of solidarity is also found in interviews with surviving Japanese soldiers from World War II who learned to rape and kill in Nanking.[59]

Rapes are part of the "rules" of war – pay and pillage

It is often asserted that rape always occurs in wartime. Soldiers throughout the ages, according to Bryant and others, have engaged in various forms of pillage, including rape. For unpaid soldiers the promise of booty – including sexual booty – was often their sole reward. This does not mean that pillage and rape were "unregulated" and without rules. "To allow uncontrolled pillage was, in effect, to lose control of the army."[60]

Historical records, for example, indicate that Moses instructed the Israelites not to cut down certain of the enemy's fruit trees. The Athenian general Xenophon ordered his retreating soldiers through Asia Minor to behave with moderation. Roman troops on occasion were punished for violating orders not to sack cities. In early Muslim holy wars (*jihad*), armies were restrained from "unnecessary harm to fruit trees, bee hives, wells, camels ... [and] noncombatants."[61] Widespread rape whether during or after battle(s) is therefore not without rules and social purposes. Quite simply, military (and civilian) rapes do not occur in social vacuum's absent rules about what they mean to the respective worlds of the victims and assailants.

Sexual comfort rape

During World War II, the Japanese high command decided to create an underground supply of women for the sexual pleasure of its soldiers. The plan was straightforward. The Japanese military hoped by using women – lured, purchased, or kidnapped from Korea, China, Taiwan, the Philippines and Indonesia – they could reduce the incidence of random rape of local women.[62] They also hoped to contain sexually transmitted diseases through the use of condoms and to reward "soldiers for fighting on the battlefronts for long stretches of time."[63] At the risk of sounding fetish about the number of victims, it has been estimated that between 80,000 and 200,000 women were forced to serve as "comfort women." The idea of establishing brothels for soldiers was not unique to the Japanese use of "comfort women." General Patton made a similar suggestion during World War II when he installed a "medical team in the six largest brothels of Palermo."[64] The record is silent, as far as I know, on who Patton wanted to use – enemy women or women from someplace else.

Strategic rape

These rapes are deliberate and intended to provoke or intimidate individuals or relatively small groups. A most notable recent example of this form of rape involved General Augusto Pinochet, President of Chile (1973–1990). While on a visit to England in 1998 he was placed under house arrest after Spain requested his extradition for being an accomplice to the disappearance and murder of Spanish citizens during his dictatorial reign.[65] Pursued in part because of the 1988 UN Convention against Torture, Pinochet was alleged to have used rape as a form of torture, a matter of state policy directed against his political opponents. During his dictatorship, approximately 4,000 people were tortured and between 1,200 and 3,100 victims disappeared.[66] Suspected of human rights abuses by a panel of the UN Human Rights Commission because he unexpectedly canceled a 1975 visit to Chile, and long shunned by the international community, lawyers for Spain unsuccessfully sought

Pinochet's extradition for 34 instances of murder and torture committed since 1988. It was alleged, for example, that he used specially trained dogs to rape women.[67]

During East Timor's long struggle for independence, strategic rape was reportedly used against young Catholic women. Graphic photographs of sexual abuses of East Timor women became available on the Internet in early 1999.

Rape as an "imperial right"

This form of rape is a type of sexual assault that occurs in social structures and communities that are not engaged in declared war. Succinctly described by the French phrase *droit du seigneur*, it refers to an alleged custom of medieval times by which the feudal lord might have sexual intercourse with the bride of a vassal on the wedding night, before she cohabited with her husband. The existence in law of *droit du seigneur* is a matter of dispute.[68]

Rape as gratuitous/random behavior

This form of wartime rape differs from the others. It does not have any formal organizational support, and it is prohibited by civil and military law, both of which provide for harsh punishments. Nevertheless, it does happen. It is one of the several forms of sexual misbehavior that was documented in the US military during the twentieth century. Other forms of sexual misconduct during World War II included homosexual encounters, bestiality, and statutory rape. There are no data that documents US soldiers engaging in any form of rape except gratuitous self-serving assaults. These are the type of rapes that the military has acknowledged and for which soldiers were punished.

It is possible, indeed highly probable, that US soldiers have raped for revenge, bonding, and/or enhanced masculinity. However, the limited forms of data available from the US military about rape do not lend themselves to exploring these possibilities. At best the data might at times contain information about the context or setting of specific rape(s) that would permit such a conclusion. The interest here is not the individual level of analysis. The focus is explicitly on *patterns* of rape over time. The US military has a long history of prohibiting and punishing soldiers who have violated this proscription. It is therefore reasonable to conclude that it has not employed or developed rape as a cultural or genocidal weapon, an element of male communication, pay, privilege, pillage, or sexual comfort.

Between 1916 and 1919, the death penalty was adjudged 145 times for capital offenders.[69] Of these, 35 were executed, 11 of whom were put to death for rape, and 3 for rape and murder. The first US soldier reportedly to have been executed abroad for this kind of case was an infantryman, Private Frank Cadue. He was hanged in France on November 4, 1917, for the murder and rape of a seven-year old French girl.[70] Of the 11 soldiers executed in France between 1917 and 1919 for murder, murder/rape and murder/attempted rape, 8 (73%) were black.

Few armies readily admit that their troops would rape. During World War II, however, US Army General Patton expressed this perspective. He said,

> I then told them that, in spite of my most diligent efforts, there would unquestionably be some raping, and that I should like to have the details as early as possible so that the offenders could be properly hanged.[71]

It is not clear what motivated Patton to make this statement other than that rape was a violation of the 92nd Article of War. Maybe he saw rape only as a threat to discipline that he wanted to discourage. On another occasion he is alleged to have said, "If a soldier won't fuck, he won't fight."[72] The record is silent on what if anything Patton thought about US soldiers raping friendly British and French women compared to enemy's women.

Joseph Stalin, by comparison, found little reason to be concerned with Soviet units raping in northeastern Yugoslavia. During the fall, 1944, Stalin's Red Army engaged "in such action."[73] Remonstrations against this behavior infuriated one of the Soviet generals to the point that he bitterly protested that such outcries were "insults" directed at the glorious Red Army. When the protests reached Stalin, he is reported to have stated about a male Yugoslavian partisan's concerns: "Can't he understand it if a soldier who has crossed thousands of kilometers through blood and fire and death has fun with a woman or takes some trifle?" Later, when Soviet troops' behavior caused more complaints during the East Prussian campaign, it is reported that Stalin's lack of sensitivity allowed him to say, "We lecture our soldiers too much ... let them have some initiative."[74]

James Wakefield Burke's *The Big Rape* (1952), a documentary novel provides a graphic and sensitive account of the Russian soldiers "initiatives" in and around Berlin, Spring, 1945, 50 years before Beevor's work.

Since Patton's observation, several people have acknowledged that US soldiers raped in the ETO. Relying on some of the same information used for this book, Peter Schrijvers wrote,

> Rape became a large problem in the ETO only with the invasion of the Continent. A first big wave occurred while the Americans broke out of Normandy and rushed through France in August and September 1944. The second wave was registered in March and April 1945, when American troops were swiftly conquering large parts of Germany.[75]

As interesting as this information is about "waves" of gratuitous rapes, it offers no other information other than to suggest that the rapists were infantrymen. Nor does it mention that US soldiers raped in both allied territories, England and France, as well as in Germany.

A similar conclusion can be made about what may be the only war narrative from US soldiers in World War II to mention an American soldier engaged in attempted rape.[76] It comes from the ETO and is found in the excellent autobiographical account of *The Men of Company K*. The incident occurred in February 1944, when Company K, 33rd Infantry, 84th Division, was in the battle for the small German town Hardt, located almost due east between the Roer and Rhine rivers. Company K's Sergeant George Pope, a Regular Army man, reported,

> When I was making my rounds that night I found our dead-end guy trying to rape this German broad. The mother and father were right there in the goddamn house. I was ready to shoot him there on the spot.[77]

Here we get a hint about what kinds of social factors that might have been involved in the rapes committed by American soldiers in Germany. First, the incident occurred at night, suggesting a possible pattern of when the rapes happened. Second, the attempted rapist is referred to as "our dead-end guy," which could mean a host of different things. Perhaps he was a slacker, or a goof-off or maybe an enlistee who was disdained by the regular army troops because they were in the army only for the duration of the war. Whatever it meant to Sergeant Pope, it suggests that rapists and attempted rapists might not be regular army, or at least less than good soldiers. Pope's comments also indicate that the threat of violence accompanied the attempted rape. This, too, suggests what might be a wise line of investigation into the ETO rapes. Did various forms of threats and violence accompany the rapes? And, were the rapes committed in front of the victims' family and friends? Were the victims predominately young? Finally, did the rapes involve only one soldier, or were the rapes "social events" in which more than one soldier participated?

* * *

The defeat and occupation of Japan at the end of World War II has generated significant recent discussions of rape by US soldiers. According to Yuki Tanaka, widespread rapes by American personnel occurred during a period of ten days between August 30 and September 10, 1945. He states that there were over 1,300 cases of rape of Japanese women by US soldiers in Kanagawa prefecture. "If these figures are extrapolated to cover the whole of Japan – and if it is assumed that many rapes went unreported – then it is clear that the scale of rape by US forces was comparable to that by any other force during the war."[78]

The number of rapes also interested post-World War II Japanese scholar, John Dower. He cites Japanese sources calculating that the number of assaults on Japanese women amounted to "around 40 *daily* while the R.A.A.

[the Recreation and Amusement Association, a Japanese-organized prostitution service for occupation troops] was in operation."[79] After the R.A.A. ended the assaults allegedly rose to 330 per day, a development, if correct, that was consistent with the Japanese wartime propaganda that portrayed "Americans ... as demonic figures ... possessed [with] oversized sexual organs that could injure them."[80]

The accuracy of the number of rapes is questionable based on the fact that neither Tanka or Dower offered details on how the counts were recorded. Less in question is that some occupying soldiers likely did rape Japanese women before, during, and after the RAA. was established. The RAA was, after all, created to accommodate the sexual appetites of the occupying troops, but there is no evidence on the effectiveness of the Japanese organization.

Recently several voices have claimed that US soldiers committed rapes during the Korean War; however, verifiable resources on this issue are difficult to locate. When Brownmiller came to this subject in her landmark treatment of rape, she relied on an interview. From this she stated that between May 31, 1951, and May 30, 1953, there were 23 courts-martial convictions for rape and 9 for attempted rape.[81]

Discussions and documentation of rape by US soldiers in the Vietnam war are, by comparison, easier to obtain than those of 1975; then Brownmiller found it difficult to get access to courts-martial statistics for all branches of the service.[82] In 2000, however, Marine Lieutenant Colonel Gary D Solis's (Ret.) discussion of the sentences of Marines for crimes committed in South Vietnam relied upon a 1976 publication of the *Marine Corps Gazette*. He reported that between 1965 and 1973, the military had 42 courts-martial convictions for rape. A majority of 25 convictions came from the Army. One conviction came from the Navy and 16 from the Marine Corps.[83] The fact that the military in Vietnam committed specific crimes and atrocities is well documented. The My Lai incident involving Lieutenant Calley's platoon and its murder of innocent women, children and the aged, is no doubt the most infamous offense from this war.

The Gulf War provided a new twist to sexual assaults by US servicemen – this time the victims were the Army's female soldiers. The precise number of victims and rapists is difficult to precisely identify. One media report said at least "two dozen US Army women were raped or sexually assaulted while serving in the Persian Gulf – and not by the enemy."[84] According to the US Army Criminal Investigation Command, two female privates reported that they had been raped or assaulted by superiors. One victim said a male sergeant grabbed her privates as she was walking to her vehicle and then dragged her "at knife point into the desert and rape[d] her."[85] In the same publication, a 24-year-old private said she was assaulted in a male captain's tent. She was "French-kissed" and fondled above and below her waist.[86] Another victim, a 29-year-old Army reservist who served in the Gulf War told the US Senate Veterans Affairs Committee that she "was forcibly sodomized by her sergeant while on duty in a bunker near the Iran border."[87] In one of the few instances where the voice of the victim is heard, she reportedly stated, "I was very proud to serve my country, but not to be a sex slave to someone who had a problem with power."[88] I have found no records indicating that women native to the region of this war were raped by Americans. (If this is indeed correct it is very likely the only time American servicemen on foreign soil during a war did *not* rape native women.) Nor is it reported if all of the Gulf War rapes were committed singularly, or by several soldiers.

On January 16, 2000, a *New York Times* article reported that an American soldier, Staff Sergeant Frank J. Ronghi, was charged with sexually assaulting and killing an 11-year-old Kosovo Albanian girl named Mertia Shabiu. The soldier, 35 and divorced, was a weapons squad leader from Company A, Third Battalion, 504th Parachute Infantry from Fort Bragg, NC.[89] The crime was also reported on Serbian state-run television with the comment that it "'exposed an unprecedented disgrace.'"[90] This incident was but one of the many complaints made against US troops in Ronghi's unit in the interval between their arrival as peacekeepers in the small town of 5,000 in June 1999, and the date of the girl's murder in January 2000.

Ronghi had sexually assaulted and killed the girl in a yellow apartment building, in what was described as a "soulless town of ugly government buildings and small shops."[91] After she was dead, he solicited a private to help dispose of the body. After the body had been wrapped in plastic they loaded it into an armored vehicle and drove it "up to woods outside of Vitina, where it was dumped."[92] According to the private, Ronghi told him "'It's easy to get away with this in a third world country,'" because "'he had done it in the desert.'"[93]

Nine months after the crime Ronghi was tried before a jury of six Army officers, and found guilty of murder. He was sentenced to life without parole. At one point he insisted he was innocent and being framed, but later he pled guilty. "[T]he evidence that he had carefully planned the killing proved ... compelling."[94] According to one witness, Ronghi had told some soldiers that he "had a plan to 'grab a little girl and rape her, but would have to kill her to get away with it and would blame the Serbs.'"[95]

Earlier, in August 1992, the US Senate Veterans Affairs Committee held hearings to try to determine the extent of sexual harassment and assault problems in the US military. According to the data received by the Committee, as many as "60,000 of the nation's 1.2 million female veterans may have been raped or sexually assaulted while on duty."[96] By 1996, sexual harassment was reported to remain a big problem, "but not quite as big as it used to be."[97] On the basis of the largest survey of its kind, 55 percent of the women in the military reported that they had been assaulted either by rape, groping, assault and pressure for sexual favors, but this number was nine points lower than that was reported in a 1988 survey. Between the two surveys, the military had made efforts to "raise the consciousness and reduce rape, raunchiness and sexual rowdiness in its ranks."[98] The military's largest and most serious sex scandal, however, began to unfold just a few months later in November.

This time various reported assaults and rapes were committed by drill instructors – the victims were their *trainees*. While not the only place this occurred, the focus of most of the media attention was on the United States at the Aberdeen Proving Ground, on the shores of the Chesapeake Bay,[MD].[99] Staff Sergeant Delmar G. Simpson, one of the 12 men who were charged with sexual offenses,[100] received 58 charges of various forms of sexual assault involving 21 women. Among other offences, he was charged with 19 rapes, forced oral sodomy, battery, and threatening to hurt or kill women who complained. He was charged with raping some of the women more than once. In the trial, he was described as an "evil predator who abused the power of his rank ... [on] ... the most vulnerable women under his command."[101] In high school and prior to the charges, Simpson, a black, had an exemplary record. He once captained his basketball and football teams, and had been awarded the Army's Good Conduct Medal.[102] His lawyer claimed the case was the result of racial bias – most of the accusers were white. Simpson received a 25-year sentence.[103]

As the final touches were being made for publication of this book, the US's military policies on sex abuse came under intense scrutiny again. Several – at least 20 – US Air Force Academy cadets reported that they had been raped or sexually harassed by fellow classmates, and subsequently treated badly by the Academy's administration when they complained. Their accusations raised serious questions about the military's current policies about handling complaints about sexual harassment within its ranks. Not all of the victims were, however, female cadets. "One case detailed by local newspapers involves a 22-year-old male cadet at the academy, Robert Burdge, accused of molesting a girl of 13 who attended Falcon Sports Camp on the academy campus for two weeks in June 2001."[104]

Despite the fact that the Academy has admitted females for several years, at this late date it continues to publicly display a slogan that reads: " 'Bring Me Men ...' Sam Walter Foss July 4 1894."[105]

Beyond what has been learned about wartime rape (and the peacetime rapes at Aberdeen), several questions remain unanswered. *Which* soldiers in war rape? At the juncture of some eighty years after the end of World War I and some sixty years after the end of World War II, there is no evidence that US troops engaged in any form of rape other than gratuitous ones, but *which* US soldiers actually raped? Was it the soldiers from the infantry? Or, was most of the raping done by behind-the-front-line support personnel? Does the pattern in World War I of executed rapists being black carry forward into World War II's ETO? Were the rapists in the ETO primarily black? Were the rapists volunteers and draftees, or were they mostly career-oriented regular army personnel? Or were they, as suggested by popular historian Stephen E. Ambrose, replacements "who had arrived too late to see any action."[106] Were the rapes well-planned or random incidents?

Who were the victims, and how did they come to find themselves in harm's way? Were they predominately young women, as suggested by Sergeant Pope's account of attempted rape in Germany? Were they assaulted by lone soldiers, or were they raped by more than one soldier? Did the age of the victims help determine who was assaulted? Were the rapists under the influence of alcohol? Did the soldiers threaten or otherwise abuse their victims with knives or guns? Did they assault others, perhaps members of the victim's family? Once apprehended, what evidence was used against them? And when convicted, how were they punished? Were they executed as Ambrose claims?[107] Answers to these questions are found in the materials used for this study.

The data come from the official records that were generated by general courts-martial trials for rapes committed by US soldiers in the ETO. Initially the records were compiled as a result of directions given by President Franklin D. Roosevelt to establish the Branch Office of the Judge Advocate General (JAG) for the United States Army in the British Isles. This office was first established on May 22, 1942. Later, on November 9,1942, it became the Branch Office of the Judge Advocate General for the ETO.[108]

The records exist in three different but closely related forms. First, the rapists' trial transcripts contain the most detailed accounts – they are held in the National Archives. Second, are the published opinions of the Judge Advocate General's Board of Review. These judgements were required before a sentence could be executed. These opinions are contained in thirty-four bound volumes titled, *Holdings and Opinions Branch Office of the Judge Advocate General, European Theater of Operations*. Last, at the end of the war the Branch Office of the Judge Advocate General issued a two-volume history of its work. It summarized the formation and activities of the ETO Branch Office of the Judge Advocate General. Much of this report is statistical.

It must be appreciated that lesser military courts and other military options could handle serious offences including rape. Acting Judge Advocate Colonel Albert W. Jackson's comment on reviewing the *first* general courts-martial sentence for rape in the ETO admits this point. In reference to the fact that offender Private Edmonds was black, Jackson said, *"This crime is becoming too prevalent among colored troops* (Emphasis added)."[109] Rapes handled by lesser courts do not appear in the JAG Branch Office records. Neither do the cases investigated by agencies other than the US Army's Criminal Investigation Division. The Branch Office's surviving statistical picture of the crimes, trials, and sentences in the ETO are based only on the cases it received from the time it opened on July 18, 1942 through February 1946.

By way of an introductory summary, during the time the ETO Branch Office was open, 19,401 general courts-martial records were received involving charges against 22,214 individuals who were tried. Of those tried, 2,123 (9.5%) were acquitted. In addition, 307 had their convictions overturned by the Reviewing Authority. An additional 2,797 individuals received sentences that for various reasons were *less* than what the Reviewing Authority would have approved for a general courts-martial. For instance, 977 officers received sentences that did not involve actual dismissal. In total, 16,987 (76.5%) received approved sentences, which included death, dismissal or dishonorable discharge.[110] Those tried included officers (7.8%), civilians, merchant seamen, general prisoners, and prisoners of war.[111]

Of the 1,737 officers charged with major crimes, 8 were colonels, 48, lieutenant colonels, 96, majors, 320, captains, 621, first lieutenants, 563, second lieutenants, 15, chief warrant officers, 47, warrant officers, and 19 flight officers. Only 30 black officers were tried before general courts-martial. This number included 1 captain, 8 first lieutenants, 14 second lieutenants, and 7 warrant officers, junior grade.[112] When reading these statistics it is prudent to keep in mind that approximately 10 percent of the troops in the ETO were black.

The crimes that lead to general courts-martial include nine broad categories of offenses. From the most to the least numerous for both white *and* black troops, they are as follows:

1. absences (31.2%);
2. disobeying constituted authority (20.3%);
3. violence (13.8%);
4. abuse of military property (10.8%);
5. dishonesty (9.1%);
6. miscellaneous (4.5%);
7. sentinel (3.6%);
8. drunk (3.4%);
9. and sex offenses (3.2%).[113]

A much different pattern of offenses appears when each category is examined by race. Absences, which contained the largest number of recorded offenders (11,252, i.e. 31.2%), had a racial distribution of 85.8 percent whites and 14.2 percent blacks. Sex offenses with the least number of recorded offenders (1,176), contained 57.7 percent white and 42.3 percent black soldiers. Neither absences nor sex offenses reflected white and black soldiers along 90 percent and 10 percent distribution. For each category of crime, white soldiers are underrepresented except for being drunk. For this offense, white soldiers were slightly overrepresented at 91.1 percent Black soldiers were almost without exception overrepresented, sometimes dramatically. According to the HBO/JAG, the top offense for black soldiers involved sex. Sex offenses ranked at the bottom of the recorded offenses for white soldiers.[114]

At first glance, it is reasonable to expect these records to be exceptionally thorough accounts of the number of rapes that occurred in the United Kingdom, France, and Germany because the US military is a well-developed bureaucratic structure with a legendary penchant for details. It is unsound, however, to uncritically accept the military's account of the soldiers' crimes, trials, and punishments as representing the full picture, especially on the question of the volume of crimes they committed. One of the primary reasons for this interpretation is the fact that the American military forces began to arrive in the British Isles in January 1942, approximately five months before the first JAG Branch Office was established, and two more months before the Branch Office was working at full capacity. During this interval more than a million and a half US soldiers had arrived in the United Kingdom, but the records of their serious crimes for this period do not appear in the JAG records. Without doubt, rapes and other major crimes occurred during this period, but they never made it into the JAG Branch Office records.

Another reason why the surviving records must be considered less than complete is because they are statistical in nature. Statistical records, official or otherwise, are the result of human efforts that nearly always contain omissions and errors. This point cannot be overstated. Official records, regardless of the agency collecting them, are flawed for one reason or other as often are records collected by individuals for personal objectives;[115] using them requires caution.

Some clarity about the problems with official records (statistics, official reports) can be quickly gained from the realization that they are made primarily for the purposes of the agencies collecting the information. Official records, not surprisingly, are collected with the expectation that they will serve administrative, in-house objectives. They are not often collected to serve the interests and objectives of other, possibly hostile, audiences, notably social scientists and investigative journalists.[116] Agencies' data may also be compromised because those collecting it may perceive or interpret it as a threat to the best interests of the agency. This means that records kept by official agencies are by the way they are collected likely to be incomplete when used for purposes different from the reasons they were created. Like all knowledge, official statistics must be analyzed as a socially constructed product, and not as a mirror reflecting absolute truth.[117]

This raises two hoary questions. Are the military records of the crimes of the ETO soldiers' accurate reports of what occurred? Or, are the records of these events (as well as other offenses and punishments experienced by US soldiers in the ETO) *merely* a function or result of the military organization producing the reports? To state the concern in a slightly different way, are the reports of military justice portraits of the real events, or simply reflections of the biases in how the military *saw* the crimes and *organized* its official accounts of them?[118] A related question is whether the official records of the capital crimes and punishments for ETO soldiers are accounts of all of the rapes that occurred? Or, do they suffer from what criminologists have identified as dark holes or hidden incidence of crime. There are well-founded reasons for this concern.

First, it is generally recognized that statistical data on the true crime rate cannot be compiled for the simple reason that it is impossible to determine the amount of crime in any given locality at any particular time. Not all crime is reported, and not all crime that is reported is recorded and investigated, so it does not appear in any official report. The underreporting of rape is an especially good example of this problem. Today, some three decades after the various forms of the feminist movement have successfully altered some of the major legal obstacles to reporting rape, some people claim that this crime is still underreported by 95 percent. Except, perhaps, for the rapes committed in England, we can expect the conditions of war – fear, language barriers, uninterested military personnel, objections from family and friends – to have rendered the reporting of rapes by US GIs to a very low level.[119]

The most important point to remember is that rape is underreported for a number of sound reasons that have been acknowledged by scholars for years. In peacetime these have included the age, marital status, and race of the victims and the faith that reporting rape to the criminal justice system will produce positive results. These and other factors associated with war reduced the likelihood of reporting rapes in the countries studied here.

Reporting rape, it must be noted, does not automatically translate it into being recorded and acted upon by authorities. This, too, is made problematic by several factors in wartime military (and civilian) settings. Formal disincentives would include topics deemed more important in the long or short run for military objectives than rape. These could include requisite paperwork, and limited staff and resources. Informal pressures to ignore rape complaints could include personal prejudices and callousness, a desire to prevent embarrassing fellow soldiers and officers from the same unit as the accused, and the possibility that being associated with a formal rape complaint against a fellow solider could taint careers.

The problem of acquiring and interpreting statistical information about crime accurately, of course, still exists. Professor Marc Riedel has recently documented that the ratio of arrests to citizen reports is abysmal. In the 1960s, annual arrest clearances for homicide were over 90 percent. By 2001, they had dropped to 69 percent. In short, no one is arrested for about one-third of the homicides in the United States. Law enforcement in general does not make this fact freely available.

Indexes, second, do not maintain a constant ratio with the true crime rate, because this information is unknowable. Indexes of crime therefore cannot be considered true samples of the whole because the whole cannot be specified. Third, conditions affecting the collection and publication of crime statistics vary from year to year within and across jurisdictions, thus making it extremely difficult to hazard comparisons. Variations in social contexts including how people within one setting actually go about their work, in other words, are so great as to require considerable caution when comparing crimes and the responses to them over time.[120]

This point is extremely important for the present study. On the one hand, the United Kingdom contained allies with shared traditions including law and language. France, on the other hand, was the fighting front where customs and language were more of a barrier. As the ETO developed the US military moved from one shifting context to another shifting context. One of the most obvious questions is whether crimes committed in different contexts received the same responses from the military. If they did not, it must be recognized that the military responses to rapes (as well as other capital and noncapital crimes) were inconsistent. If the military changed its responses to rape as the fighting forces moved from the "occupation" of friendly Britain into enemy-held France, and later when it was in the enemy's home country, it implies rather strongly that its record is only partially accurate. This study is limited almost exclusively to the historical record *constructed by the military nearly sixty years ago*. Unless information from the local police, victims, and witnesses is included in the official records, it generally will not otherwise be discussed.

In sum, the approach taken here is that the official military records of the rapes and punishments in the ETO are not complete. It is not possible to know about the existence of all criminal acts, especially those crimes committed after the invasion of Northern France. In a post-war report titled *Military Justice Administration in Theater of Operations*, Hyer et al. concluded that the handling of cases involving civilian victims was generally satisfactory. However, "because of the rapid movement of the ground forces and overburdened communications," it was often impossible to obtain important records about accused soldiers' prior convictions.[121] In addition, the military police under the provost marshals did not have enough personnel to cope with the "two great waves" of rapes as they occurred in France and Germany.[122] Nor were the inexperienced investigators able to "recognize evidence and valuable clues when they were observed."[123] In some instances of rape "[T]hey did not reach the [crime] scene promptly," and their methods were slow and inadequate for the rapidly moving troops.[124]

The position offered here is that a great range of responses to capital crimes was used by the military. They were influenced by the nature of the offense, the social characteristics of the offenders and victims, the person(s) who received the complaint, and by the immediate social circumstances of the war. It is likely that the records contain information only about the most egregious and brutal gratuitous rapes that came to the attention of authorities willing to respond to them. Clearly the "Inability sufficiently to identify the attackers, especially during the disordered break-through periods was, of course, a principal reason for the failure to try many of the alleged offenders."[125]

Why the rapes occurred cannot be definitively tied to a single explanation. It would be pointless to seek such an answer, a task no less difficult than attempting to explain why French women had love affairs with German soldiers and officers.[126] To attempt to do so requires data I do not have. Insight into what influenced the patterns of rapes is another matter. Multiple short- and long-term themes keep surfacing. One short-term factor was the lack of sexual outlets for masses of young, virile men away from home. Unlike the French and German militaries, the US military made no formal provisions for the availability of women as sexual companions for its soldiers in the United Kingdom, France, or Germany. Ironically, as the journalist and novelist John Steinbeck observed: "When Army supply ordered X millions of rubber contraceptive and disease-preventing its, it had to be explained [to the prudish US public] that they were used to keep moisture out of machine-gun barrels – and perhaps they did."[127]

Exceptions did exist. For a while field commanders in North Africa "… allowed selected brothels with European women to stay open for the GIs."[128] Later, in Palermo, Italy, General George Patton installed medical teams in six large brothels in an effort to fight the spread of VD among GIs. Toward this effort, according to Schrijver, the US's Fifth Army headquarters "kept one large brothel outside the city open and placed all others off-limits to GIs."[129]

Coupled to the lack of army-sponsored brothels is the fact that the army was segregated, and one could argue that even if the English and French were relatively less prejudiced against blacks than in the US, this would not translate into equal opportunity for sexual parity for the two groups of soldiers. Sexual deprivation for black soldiers was relatively high compared to that of white soldiers. This may have contributed to differences in rape patterns for black versus white soldiers.

Perhaps more importantly, the *meaning* of sexual contact with white women for black soldiers was potentially radically different compared to the same experiences for white soldiers. Less than 25 years after the end of World War II, Eldridge Clever wrote insightfully on this subject.

> but I know that the white man made the black woman the symbol of slavery and the white woman the symbol of freedom. Every time I embrace a black woman I'm embracing slavery, and when I put my arms around a white woman, well, I'm hugging freedom. The white man forbade me to have the white woman on pain of death. Literally, if I touched a white woman it would cost me my life. Men die for freedom, but black men die for white women, who are the symbol of freedom … I will not be free until the day I can have a white woman in my bed and a white man minds his own business.[130]

For Cleaver, rape was a revengeful and insurrectionary act.[131] This sentiment may have contributed to the patterns of rapes committed by black soldiers.

Generally, it seems certain that US soldiers in the ETO and Mediterranean Theater of Operations (MTO) were sexually active. The number of sexual intercourses per soldier, according to one report, remained relatively low, with no more than twice a month – "with only 10 percent of all these men having intercourse at least once a week."[132] Of particular relevance here is a finding by the Research Branch, Information and Education Division of the United States Army. In the summer of 1945 it conducted with meticulous care a survey for the Preventive Medicine Branch of the Medical Section at theater headquarters. Among other things it learned that in the MTO Black soldiers reported a higher frequency of intercourse than white soldiers. "[T]he average frequency of intercourse reported by Negroes ... was 2 to 3 times a month, as compared with 1 to 2 times a month reported by whites."[133] Whether the same frequency of intercourse existed for blacks compared to whites in England, France, or Germany is at present unknown.

Of all possible motivations for rape, alcohol was considered to be the most important contributing factor to violent crimes by soldiers in the ETO. It was a "particularly frequent aspect of crimes of violence and involving the sex motive," though it was difficult to isolate it from other factors.[134] The following chapters discuss this point in some detail.

The brutalization of soldiers caused by their exposure to the intimate details of death and injury is now well documented. This may very well have contributed to patterns of rape in France and Germany. For the most part, however, the post-war military reports on the major cause of crimes in general, and rapes in particular did not give much attention to this point. The "induced urge to hate the enemy," which had been part of combat training, has not yet been considered a major contributor toward crime. Hyer et al., concluded, nevertheless, that the attitude of "unintelligent American soldiers toward foreign civilians, particularly enemy civilians, often contributed to offenses."[135] He offered no comments on how "unintelligent" was determined.

There is some question as to whether this point applies equally to black and white soldiers. There is also the question of whether black troops in the service units who raped experienced the same sorts of brutalization faced by white infantrymen in the frontlines. The trial transcripts for some of the rape cases in Germany reveal that the level of punishment approved for rapists was influenced by considering the impact of "the conditions of war."

We begin with the patterns of rape in the United Kingdom.[136]

3
England: White Women

Six decades have passed since the end of World War II, enough time for individual memories to become clouded, and for the details of minor and major circumstances of events to be distorted. In my effort to keep the record of the context as well as the rapes committed by US soldiers defensively accurate, the following overview of wartime England is intended to be more cursive than exhaustive. Calder's *The Myth of the Blitz* (1991) provides an excellent and detailed defrocking of how the story of this period of the war was told then, and recalled later.[1] It is an excellent example of why caution is needed when the "echoes of war" are heard in popular culture.[2]

Arguably, the most enduring collective memories of England during World War II are replete with positive images of what Prime Minister Winston Churchill called "our finest hour" [1940]. Many examples come to mind, none more vivid than John Tophams's 1940 black-and-white photo of London's St. Paul's Cathedral standing intact after the German raid on December 29, 1940.[3] Other cities, Plymouth and especially Coventry with its destroyed cathedral and loss of 70,000 homes (November14–15, 1940), are also indelibly engrained as symbols of England standing alone against the German night Blitz, 1940–1941. All the more remarkable is that while the night Blitz's destruction and death did not snap civilian morale, Britain was simultaneously fighting on two additional fronts – the daytime battle for Britain and its sea battle for its trade. "For a whole year the United Kingdom stood alone amid disaster and depredation, offering resistance to tyranny – an example admired and respected across the world."[4] No single individual's personage represented democracy's opposition to Germany better than the hat, cane, bulk, cigar, and victory sign of Britain's prime minister, Winston Churchill.

His morale-boosting efforts, it is often recalled, were remarkably successful. In his first speech to the House of Commons as prime minister, he was cheered when he told them, "I have nothing to offer but blood, toil, tears and sweat."[5] Later, he frequently took unannounced walks without guards in London and other cities' bombed streets and said encouragingly, "We can

41

take it."[6] The public agreed, often calling out, "Hello Winnie," "You will never let us down," and "That's a man."[7] In the words of Edward R. Murrow, the 32-year-old American radioman for CBS whose broadcasts from London told America about the Blitz, on September 10, 1940, "but not once have I heard man, woman, or child suggest that Britain should throw in her hand."[8] Life was thin – rationing placed tremendous demands on the civilian population – yet, the public did not panic. To the contrary, they bonded together on many different "home fronts" and fought what politicians called "the people's war."[9] According to Calder "the people of Britain [became] ... protagonists in their own history in a fashion never known before."[10] Without the benefit of hindsight, there were contemporary observers of the Blitz who thought there was no other way to defend the island. In response, a number of voluntary associations including "the Home Guard, the Observer Corps, all the A.R.P. and fire-fighting services" came into existence. These and other organizations were of "a new type, what might be called the organized militant citizen."[11] They, too, represent positive images of Britain during World War II.

Well-fed American troops sent over to lend a helping hand in sharply tailored uniforms, chatting up young women, tossing gum and chocolates to children, and with money to burn, conjure up other positive wartime images that survive from England. It was then and is now often agreed that America's "invasion" and "occupation" of Britain 1942–1945, was an all around good experience with "rich relations."[12] In 1946, A.P. Herbert, a Member of Parliament from 1935 to 1950 and author of more than fifty books including his 1919 classic treatment of stress of battle during World War I, *The Secret Battle*,[13] wrote the following in fond homage to the American soldiers:

> Good-by, GI
> Good-By, GI – Good-by, big-hearted Joe.
> We're glad you came. We hope you're sad to go.
> Say what you can for this old-fashioned isle;
> And when you can't – well, say it with a smile.
> Good-by, GI – and, now you know the way,
> Come back and see us in a brighter day,
> When England's free, and Scotch is cheap but strong,
> And you can bring your pretty wives along.
> Good-by, GI, don't leave us quite alone.
> Somewhere in England we must write a stone,
> "Here Britain was invaded by the Yanks,"
> And under that a big and brilliant "Thanks."[14]

These images and sentiments of Britain and its American visitors remain strong in Britain nearly six decades after the fact, yet they are incomplete and misleading. Britain and the American troops had several other less obvious wartime social worlds, which contained mutual skepticism and incomprehension about themselves and each other. Each carried with them many homegrown experiences that influenced their thoughts and deeds. These social worlds began to co-mingle when the racially segregated American troops began arriving in Britain in January 1942. Often these worlds were far from united or harmonious – they generated numerous cultural clashes.

The English setting

The appearance of normal life that was given by the music, warm tea, and scones that sometimes greeted American soldiers belied several serious social conflicts. They developed and intensified throughout the war, though the contours of these worlds themselves were not clearly evident or well understood by many observers until after the end of the war. George Orwell, however, had an exceptionally keen eye for these matters and wrote about them a number of times during the war. In early January, 1943, he wrote that there had been a growth of animosity against Americans as it was increasingly clear in some circles that America was "potentially imperialist and politically a long way behind Britain."[15] Later in 1943, he wrote, "There is also widespread anti-American feeling among the working class, thanks to the presence of American soldiers, and, I believe, very bitter anti-British feeling among the soldiers themselves."[16] Not all of the anti-American feeling was class-based. Some of it stemmed from differences in the behavior of black and white American soldiers. In December, 1943, Orwell wrote that the general "consensus of opinion seems to be that the only American soldiers with decent manners are the Negroes."[17]

Perhaps Orwell was correct – his well-known sentiments about America ranged from anti- to ambivalent[18] – but there is considerable evidence from other sources that alongside its aid for the war, America imported its moral panic about black soldiers having sexual relations with white women. English historian David Reynolds succinctly described this problem when he wrote, "As far as officialdom was concerned, sexual relations were most worrying when the males were not only American but also black."[19] He is of the opinion, and it is hard to disagree, that racial friction over British women was the most frequent cause of altercations among GIs, but as he notes, it was part of larger policy issues. While Britain did not have a "colour bar," it nonetheless had its own style of racism, and it had to decide whether to impose one to accommodate its powerful ally.[20]

This issue was no small matter. Much of its details were considered so sensitive that they were kept secret from the public until a 1971 ruling by parliament.[21] It had powerful supporters on both sides of the issue in Britain and the United States.[22] Some members of the House of Commons objected to the introduction and presence of discrimination against Negro troops by the American forces. On the other hand, a vicar's wife provided a six-point code of behavior for British women which included among other proscriptions, instructions for white women to have no relations with "coloured troops" and "On no account must coloured troops be invited into the homes of white women."[23] England's foreign secretary, Anthony Eden, wanted the US to reduce the flow of blacks into his country because, he said, their health might suffer from the rigors of an English winter. Others, including secretary of state for war, Sir James Grigg, suggested Britain follow the segregation policies of the US, but to allow British officers to interpret the facts of racial situations so as to educate the public. Still others, such as Viscount Cranborne, secretary of state for the colonies, objected to this idea because he "deplored the idea of seeking to guide British citizens into the ways of the Americans."[24]

Officially, the United States and its military were segregated, but there was not a united front on racial matters. Within the military, General Dwight D. Eisenhower, the supreme Allied commander first in the Mediterranean Theater of Operations (MTO) and later throughout the ETO, wanted to maintain a "separate but equal" policy in Britain, which he described as "a very thickly populated country that is devoid of racial consciousness."[25] To this end he ordered his commanders to avoid discrimination due to race and to minimize causes of friction. His position was not, as Reynolds shows, without "constant political scrutiny from back home, from white liberals and black pressure groups."[26] Eleanor Roosevelt, the wife of the President of the United States, was a strong and persistent advocate of equal treatment for blacks. Her voice, though not often heeded on this matter, was nonetheless a potent symbol of the absence of political and social unity on race issues in the United States.

The National Association for the Advancement of Colored People (NAACP), the most influential pressure group that supported blacks troops at home and abroad, was unyielding in its efforts. On more than one occasion it sent visitors to England to assess the situations facing black troops. Equally persistent and vocal were the scores of black newspapers that reported on the experiences of black soldiers in England, and in other places throughout the war where they encountered Jim Crow in the military.

The real issue in England was not Eisenhower's position on racial matters, but how his orders on the subject were to be implemented by those under his command. To this end it is reasonable to conclude that very few, if any, significant changes developed, at least as far as punishment for soldiers was concerned. In 1944 the leadership of the NAACP noted that black troops in England believed that they were punished more quickly and severely than white soldiers.[27]

Offering generalizations about social disorder and changing patterns of crime during wartime is, according to Mannheim, an extremely hazardous enterprise.[28] There are several reasons for this problem, including, most distinctly, the difficulty of getting data, especially in occupied countries. Other hindrances include the fact that large numbers of men were away in the forces, which no doubt skewed some patterns of crime downward. Behavior that was prohibited only during the war, such as theft of food rations, disappeared after the war, thus making long-term analysis impossible. A few generalizations are nevertheless useful, however risky they might be.

During the interim before the summer 1944 invasion of Normandy, approximately 1.5 million American troops lived for various periods of time in Britain. By this time, especially in southern England where the American soldiers were concentrated, social life, according to many accounts, had a great deal of social disorder – the pre-war routines of daily life had been radically changed. In late 1939 alone, between the end of June and early September, between 3,500,000 and 3,750,000 people were evacuated from areas thought to be vulnerable to enemy attack.[29] Family life, especially in the south of England in 1939, was also disrupted most painfully by the evacuation of 800,000 children without their mothers, and additional 524,000 children with their mothers.[30] The nation's educational system suffered, too. With so many children evacuated, teachers and schools experienced "weeks of chaos."[31] School buildings, in some instances, had been taken over for war purposes and statistics indicate that by January 1940, only a quarter of "the school-children in the evacuated areas had ... resumed full-time education."[32] Another quarter of the school-aged children were receiving some form of education while "430,000 children ... were still getting no teaching at all."[33]

The nation's employment resources meanwhile were dwindled by demand for men in the armed forces and by mid-1941, "All people, of both sexes, from girls of eighteen to old men and women of sixty, [were] obliged to undertake some form of 'national service.'"[34] This meant that for the first time in "any civilized nation," women were to be conscripted.[35] For many, this development became emblematic of the stress and strain that Britain faced during World War II. But, it was by far not the only serious social problem. Crime, by comparison, was a far greater problem, a development often discussed by a wide range of post-war commentators.

"Mad" Frankie Fraser, one of London's most well-known and violent gangsters, spoke glowingly in 1995 about crime during the war years because it was paradise for thieves. Everyone, according to Fraser, was "at it" and had money, but not needed goods because of shortages and rationing. It was a time of paradise for thieves, he said, that was made all the better by blackouts and air raids. These not only provided cover for crime, but they were also part of an atmosphere within which people were mindful that they were all 'in it together' and that tomorrow they could be blown to bits. One result was that on occasion passersby, whether air-raid wardens, firefighters, police or curiosity-seekers would kindly offer the thieves assistance, thinking that they needed a helping hand to get valuable goods loaded into their vehicles to be moved out of harm's way. This bountiful time nearly came to an end with V-E Day (May 8, 1945), but, in fact, it continued until the early 1950s when scarcity of needed goods abated. In Fraser's words: "It was wonderful. I'll never forgive Hitler for surrendering, they were great days."[36]

Other English criminals with biographies similar to Fraser's comprise a genre of villains who have attested to the crimogenic impact of World War II. The infamous Kray twins, their associates T. Lambrianou, C. Richardson, and B. Webb, and later Freddie Foreman, who became known as the Managing Director of British Crime, have claimed they were products of the war years. Lambriano, born in 1942, said it best when he described the bombings, taking refuge in tube stations, homes destroyed and the general atmosphere of fear. "All of these things, in their own way, alerted me at a very early age to violence of a certain kind which probably hardened me up to a lot of what happened afterwards."[37]

A more precise summary of crime in England and Wales, yet questionable in terms of statistical accuracy, is found in Mannheim's work. He reported a gradual rise of indictable offences known to the police from 303,771 in 1939 to 415,010 in 1944. By 1947 the number was 498,576. The proportion per 100,000 population of age 17 and older found guilty of indictable offenses fell from 162.5 in 1938 to 150 in 1940. This number increased, however, to 201 in 1941. By 1945 the number was 223.[38]

In 1969, Angus Calder briefly discussed crime in Soho during the war where "Bohemian writers, and artists rubbed shoulders with a still more vigorous criminal community, enriched by deserters who had managed to evade capture."[39] Juvenile delinquency convictions, he reported, increased by more than one-third in England and Wales between 1939 and 1941. Malicious damaging and petty theft rose by "seventy and two hundred per cent respectively."[40]

Written 13 years later, Edward Smithies's classic (1982) *Crime in Wartime: A Social History of Crime in World War II*, is much more detailed and informative. It deserves attention not only for what was included as much as for what was omitted. By using government reports and other sources it provides an excellent portrait of a wide range of criminal behavior during the war.[41] In 1939, 47,223 people were found guilty of crime. By 1945, 72,758 individuals were found guilty – an increase of 54 percent. Expressed in terms of ratios per 100,000 people, 149 were found guilty in 1939 compared to 223 in 1945. Within these broad contours of change in crimes known to the police and persons found guilty, were more detailed changes in crimes.

Theft at work, whether in shipyards by dockers, goods depots, large companies, shop floors, work canteens, grocery stores, and various points of distribution, was thought to be rampant during the war, though precise numbers were impossible to determine.[42] Employer's attitudes toward pilfers did change during the war. Before the war, they were more tolerant as long as theft remained on a small scale. But, as the scale of theft grew alongside an ever-expanding black market for scarce rationed goods (food, gas), employers found that they had to be more accountable to government agencies for their shortages. Under these conditions, theft at work became less tolerated.

Changes in patterns of professional theft were also influenced by the war, especially in terms of a dramatic shift in scale.[43] In the Victorian era, luxury homes and tradesmen who supplied them were targeted and attacked by stealth, craft, and technique. During the war, they were replaced by what Smithie calls a new "technology." The new targets of professional thieves were businesses – the factory, the warehouse, and the distributive network – their objective was to supply the black market.[44] In 1944, the year of the invasion of France, 53 thefts in London were reported with the value of the goods taken put at 1,000 pounds, compared with 41 in 1938. Of these 41, 80 percent (33) involved jewelry, furs, and paintings. These types of thefts dropped to 42 percent by 1944.[45] The scene of the thefts had also changed. In 1938, nearly half of the big thefts in London occurred in private homes – by 1944, it was less than 25 percent.

Increasingly, shops became targets. The Metropolitan Police District, London, had 5,542 reported shop break-ins during 1938. By 1945, the number had increased 58 percent to 13,276 at a time when the population of London was approximately 2 million *less*. This trend was also found in other cities. Between 1939 and 1946, Manchester experienced nearly a 300 percent increase in shop break-ins. The importance of and the contribution made by the government-imposed blackouts on nearly all manner of crime, especially thieving, cannot be overstated. Efforts to control criminal and deviant behavior were diminished under the cover of darkness.

The number of prosecutions involving betting and gaming also soared upward during the war years. The number of persons prosecuted in magistrate's courts for betting and gaming offenses per year between 1935 and 1939 was 14,578, or an average of 2,430 per year. During the next six years, 1940–45, the total number of prosecutions in magistrates courts increased by more than 112 percent, to a total of 33, 271, or, to an average of 5,545 prosecutions per year.[46] These increases were due in part, according to Smithie, to the police orchestrating "the rate of prosecutions," however, the total number of prosecutions in 1945 was 7,595, or nearly half of the total number of prosecutions for 1935–1939. There are reasons to think that the increase in prosecutions was not merely the result of more vigilant policing, however. As Smithie notes, "there [was] evidence to suggest that the police were failing to come to grips with the core of professional crime in both betting and gaming."[47] Non-professional gamblers were at times drawn to games of chance during the war years because of changes in the nature of the prizes. In July, 1943, the police raided an amusement fair in Wembley and found that instead of gift prizes, it was offering *cash* prizes.[48] The magistrate in this case commented that while a powerful magnet for public participation, money should "not be gambled but put into National Savings, a common theme in betting and gaming prosecutions."[49] This admonition may have contained an element of class bias aimed at the working class and the newly rich, instead of the upper class and established rich.[50] During the war the latter often gambled in England at private parties equipped with accouterments resembling a miniature casino, "who in normal and happier times would have gone abroad ... to enjoy ... gambling at the casinos in the south of France."[51]

The war – with its large movement of populations, disruptions of family life and at times large numbers of domestic and foreign troops in transition – also had a tremendous impact on sexual attitudes.[52] While certainly not the only cause of increased sexual liberties, "the arrival of Canadian and, later US armies coincided with and contributed to a radical alternation in sexual attitudes."[53] Some of the new sexual attitudes were captured in a popular wartime joke, which asked: "Heard about the new utility knickers? One Yank and they're off."[54] One of the better-documented examples involves prostitution. In London alone, the number of prostitutes more than doubled in the fifteen years between 1931 and 1946.[55] The anxieties and uncertainties of the times contributed greatly to an "urgent determination to eat, drink and be merry; for though one might not actually die tomorrow, it seemed unlikely there would be much scope for merriment."[56] Known in central London as "Piccadilly Warriors," prostitutes made easy money and, under cover of blackouts, they drew more and more women into the streets, some with connections to criminal interests.[57] By the last two years of the war there was a boom in this trade, which by this time had witnessed a seller's market with a change in price from 3 pounds for "a short time" (10–15 min) in 1943, to 5 pounds in 1945.[58] Unfortunately, Smithie does not discuss what impact the war might have had on rape, a term that does not appear in his index. It is into the above crimeogenic social world that American troops made their own contributions to the minor and serious crimes of World War II.

The exact impact of American troops on the various crime rates in England during the war, cannot, of course, be determined accurately for two important reasons. First, with the Visiting Forces Act of August 9, 1942, the British "gave the United States authorities exclusive criminal jurisdiction over members of their armed forces."[59] Not at all unlike the demands made by the United States in 2002 to exempt Americans from the jurisdiction of the new International Criminal Court, the American authorities did not want US soldiers to be tried by a foreign court. US soldiers were almost always tried in military courts. Consequently, it was the military that had the responsibility and opportunity to record the crimes its members committed, if reported. The press was allowed into these trials only if the crime(s) involved a capital offense against an English citizen.

A rare example of an American soldier tried in an English capital trial involved Private Karl G. Hulten. For the sake of impressing his 18-year-old girl friend, Elizabeth Jones, Hulten, 22, shot to death World War I veteran and London cabby, George Heath.[60] He was tried, convicted, and hanged under the authority of English law. Otherwise, for the most part, the American soldiers were tried within the confines of a court martial without the presence of the press.

The press also engaged in self-censorship, in part because it was thought undiplomatic to criticize in public such an important ally as the United States. Orwell observed in early 1944, "Discussion of inter-allied relations is still avoided in the press and utterly taboo on the air."[61] But these were not the only reasons the press contributed to underreporting the crimes of American soldiers. It was recognized that there was, according to several observers including Orwell, much jealously between white and black American troops. But, again according to Orwell, the press shut down on this subject so that "when a rape or something like that happens, one can only discover by private inquiry whether the American involved is white or coloured."[62] But there is little doubt that American soldiers made significant contributions to the crimes and social disruptions during wartime England. Fortunately, it is possible to examine the major contours of the rapes committed by American GIs by using military trial records.

American rapes in England: findings

The *History Branch Office of the Judge Advocate General with the United States Forces European Theater* summarized the rapes committed by American troops in the European Theater of Operations (ETO). Its chapter 1, "Statistical Survey – General Courts Martial in the European Theater of Operations," contains several charts about the offenses committed in the ETO. The charts with the information about the three leading countries in which the rapes were committed states that 121 ordinary (vs. statutory) rapes occurred in England. Forty-one (33 %) of the soldiers convicted of these offenses were black. The record states that 101 of the victims were "English girls."[63] The reason for the difference of 20 between these numbers is not explained. One can reasonably speculate that some, if not all, of the 20 victims were American military personnel and war refugees who were not counted as English victims.[64] The statutory rape victims are more accurately identified as "girls." Here the *HBO/JAG* 's Chart 17 reveals that 258 of these cases were tried in the ETO, "All except for ten of the statutory rape cases occurred in the United Kingdom."[65]

The *HBO/JAG* records, however informative, do not identify the names of the rapists and their victims, or the date and place of the assaults, information essential for this study. To find it I relied upon ETO's 34 volumes of Judge Advocate General's summary and opinions. Each volume was searched for ordinary rape cases. Most of the information summarized here is based on this source.

According to these records, between October 8, 1942 and December 3, 1944, the US Army tried 27 cases of ordinary rape, not 101 as one would expect from the *HBO/JAG* report.[66] These cases were from England and Wales; they involved 27 victims. The number of soldiers at the scene of the rapes totaled 38. Of this number 25 were black. Far less than expected on the basis of numerical proportions of white versus black soldiers in the United Kingdom, only 11 of the soldiers were white. The race of 2 rapists is unknown. Of the 38 soldiers at the crime scene, the US Army tried 36 soldiers, 23 of whom were black, 11 white, and 2 whose race is unknown. The prosecution used some of the soldiers who were not tried as witnesses against the accused. One of the most significant findings is patterns of rapes committed.[67]

Patterns of rapes

Date rape:

A date rape required that the male and female participants had agreed to meet for a social engagement. None of the ordinary rapes in England, Wales, or Ireland met this stipulation. Acquaintance rapes came close to being date rapes.

Acquaintance rape:

This type of rape involved individuals who had a relationship that was less intimate than a friendship or a dating relationship. It included some knowledge of each other sufficient to render that they were not partial strangers or total strangers. They had seen each other, perhaps exchanged names but their contact had been very limited, indeed fleeting. Three of the 27 ordinary rapes involved acquaintances.

Annie P., a 20-year-old factory worker met Private Kenneth M. Waite, white, Replacement Company "B" Separate, at the bar of a pub in Aintree, Lancashire, on Thursday, July 23, 1943.[68] It was the first day that Waite's organization had moved in. When the pub closed, Miss P. and a girl friend, Grace D., left with Waite and another soldier. "On the way home Annie and [Waite] stopped in a doorway for about an hour, "necking, kissing and talking."[69] He asked her if "she would," but she declined, saying she wasn't that kind of girl. Waite apologized, saying he knew where to find that "kind of girl," but "he didn't want them."[70] They made a date for the following Sunday, July 25, 1943, but it was not kept.

On the following Monday, August 2, 1943, Miss P. and Gracie returned to the same pub, where they drank 4 or 5 half-pints of mild beer and "draught" Bass.[71] Near closing time, Miss P. "accosted" Waite outside the pub and gave him a cigarette. Later at about 10:30 p.m., she walked down Ormskirk Road with Waite toward his barracks – Grace was walking ahead with another American soldier who got the two of them a lift in a jeep. As Miss P. and Waite continued to walk they approached an American storage camp that was on a cul-de-sac. Here, Waite grabbed Miss P. and said "I have got to have you."[72]

She and Waite struggled and he ripped and tore her underwear, hit her in the face every time she screamed for help, called her a "darn fool," and held his hand over her mouth. After struggling for "a good bit he got his private inside me," and "it hurt me."[73] He soon told her to take off her blouse, which she explained was actually a dress. To comply with his demand, she stood up and said, "I want to go to the lavatory," and promised to come back. To secure his trust, she "gave him my handbag and ... walked away from him and then ... ran down the lane into the main road."[74] She made it to a camp where she encountered an "RAF chap" who was on guard duty. He, in turn, took Miss P. to Corporal Holland, who then took her to a police station. Between 3:20 a.m. and 7:45 a.m., a civilian physician, Dr. Ronald Sinclair, Antree, Liverpool, and US Army medical officer, Lit. Victor Lampka, concluded that she had been raped.[75]

Waite was convicted and sentenced to 20 years of hard labor. His life sentence had been reduced in no small measure because over a period of weeks Miss P. had been encouraging Waite. It helped, no doubt, as with the first ordinary rape trial of Private Edmonds, that the victim had indicated in a letter that she had been very troubled by the life sentence. All members of the courts-martial agreed to the reduced sentence.

Partial stranger rapes:

These rapes involve even less prior contact and shared knowledge between the victim and rapist(s) than acquaintance rapes. Here the victim had at least been seen by the assailant(s) prior to the offense, the time elapsing before the rape may have been as little as a few minutes to a few days. Seven of the ordinary rapes involved this type of assault.

Ivy Doreen C., 17 years old, single, lived at Burton-on-Trent. At about 10:15 p.m. on Saturday, October 3, 1943, she, Miss Dorothy F., 16 years old, John V. Blackshaw, 19 years old, and a British soldier named George A. Price, were sitting on a bench in Memorial Park. A black soldier walked up and down "before them three or four times, bent over and peered into their faces."[76] Price commented that the soldier, Private Thomas (NMI) Bell, Company C, 390th Engineer Regiment, appeared lost.[77] At one point Bell put his hand on Price's arm and asked him why he thought he was lost. Shortly after this exchange, Ivy and Blackshaw got up from the bench and walked away, but returned when they noticed that Miss F. and Price were still talking to Bell. Blackshaw then reminded Miss F. that her father was waiting for her, and the two couples went to the corner of the park. Bell and another black soldier followed them.[78]

The two couples separated. Ivy and Blackshaw walked down a path toward Lichfield Street. They were followed by Bell, the larger of the two soldiers. At the corner of Lichfield Street, Bell seized Ivy's arm and after a few words were exchanged, Bell said, "Don't you scream or else I will kill you."[79] She noticed something in his left hand, which seemed to her like a knife. Unsuccessfully, she tried to grab the arm of another soldier who was passing by, but failed to get his assistance. Next, she tried to run by slipping her coat off and leaving it in the hands of Bell, but he caught hold of the collar of her dress, saying: "Come with me or I will kill you."[80] Blackshaw, hearing her protests that she did not want to go with Bell, attempted to pull her way. He, too, had observed that Bell had a "'slasher, cut-throat' type of razor where the blade folds back into the handle."[81] With the blade folded back across the fingers of one hand, Bell held Ivy with the other.

Two other soldiers came by and spoke to Bell – he told one of them to "take care" of Blackshaw. They grasped Blackshaw by the arms, made him walk a short distance and told him, "if a white man took a white woman from a colored soldier, the colored soldier would kill the white man."[82] They offered him a cigarette, and when he turned around, Bell and Ivy had disappeared. Blackshaw tried to get away, but the two soldiers held on to him. When they finally released him, he went to his home to get his "mate" who lived next door. Together they then went to Ivy's home and then to the police.[83]

Meanwhile, Ivy was taken by Bell down Abbey Street to the rear gates of an inn. Here, he asked, "Will you give me sugar?"[84] She indicated she did not know what he meant, to which Bell replied: "Don't try and be funny. Remember, I still have the knife in your back." When two more soldiers passed by, Bell put his hand over her mouth to keep her quiet and soon took her down behind some houses on Fleet Street.[85] Here, at number 4 Fleet Street, they encountered Miss Margaret H. in the yard of her home. According to the record, Ivy asked Miss H. to "save her," but Bell refused to heed Miss H.'s request to free Ivy. Miss H. testified that they all stood in the yard for about ten minutes until she "got tired of it," got her key and went inside.[86] In a few moments she checked on the couple and later stated they were "walking up the alleyway apparently arm in arm."[87]

They proceeded, Bell holding her all of the time, into Green Street near some flood gates and a wall. Near the wall, Ivy slipped, falling flat on her stomach. For a few minutes she was unable to get up, during which time Bell threatened again to kill her. He helped her up and put her on the wall – it was not as tall as she. On the other side, Bell knocked her down on to the grass and told her to undress. She refused, and Bell continued to struggle to remove her knickers. Frustrated, Bell told Ivy to "shut up," [and] put his hand over her mouth, and raped her.

Afterwards, Bell and Ivy both dressed. He put her back across the wall, and told her not to mention the incident to anyone. She arrived at home about

11:15 p.m., and called for her father, James W.C. She was nervous and hysterical. Her right stocking was ripped, a hand was cut, and she told her father that a black soldier had got hold of her and dragged her along Fleet Street. Around midnight, October 3, 1943, Division Police Surgeon, Dr. Francis L. Picket, 181 Hornblow Street, Burton-on-Trent, examined Ivy. He found her hymen had been torn "within an hour or so."[88]

Five days later on October 8, 1943, after Ivy had attended two identification parades and had not picked out anyone, she attended a parade of eight colored soldiers. This time without hesitation she picked out Bell. One month later he was found guilty of rape and sentenced to be "hanged from the neck until dead."[89] This sentenced was reduced to life imprisonment. He was still incarcerated in 1950.

Nine months later, a similar partial stranger rape occurred. This time it involved an older woman. Mrs. Beatrice Maud R., a World War I widow, lived in Gunnislake, Cornwall. She had a full life. In addition to being active in the British Legion, she was "chairman"[90] of the British Legion Hall, and she kept house for her invalid brother. At 10:40 p.m. on July 26, 1944, she left the hall to walk home. Soon Private Madison Thomas, 23 years old, a black man from Louisiana, and a member of the 964th Quartermaster Service Company, was walking alongside Mrs. R. He asked if she had far to go, and she replied "No," and suggested to him that he had better hurry to catch his ride back to his camp. She did not care for his company.[91] Thinking that he would go away, she stopped to chat with Miss Jean Elizabeth B., who was sitting just outside her home. Thomas went on down the road, and Mrs. R. thought he was gone. However, he decided not to go back to his camp. Instead, he reappeared and starting talking to Miss B. At this point, Mrs. R. walked on alone, until she came to the loneliest part of a hill. Here, to her surprise, Thomas reappeared, and he again asked if she had far to go. Mrs. R. again said "no," and to her horror, Thomas seized her and, despite her struggle, picked her up and in the form of a "blitz rape," put her across a hedge.[92] She unsuccessfully pleaded with him, telling him that she was old enough to be his mother. Thomas replied, "that didn't make any difference." He wrenched her gold wristwatch from her arm and told her she could have it back when she gave him what he wanted. Mrs. R. said: "That will never be boy [sic]." Despite her resistance, Thomas knocked her to the ground, ripped off her underwear, held a very sharp doubled-edged five-inch knife with pearl handles to her throat and raped her. After the rape, Thomas showed Mrs. R. a .30-caliber carbine bullet and said, You see this bullet, if you make any attempt to run, you'll get it."[93]

In the early morning of the next day (4:20 a.m.), Police Constable James H. Elliott, Cornwall, Constabulary, along with Miss B. went to the Whitchurch Down Camp. Thomas was put into a parade of his entire company and Miss B. positively identified him as the soldier who had talked to her the previous night. Less than a month after the assault, Thomas was tried on August 21, 1945, and by unanimous vote of the court he was found guilty.

On October 12, 1944 he was hanged in Shepton Mallet Prison, in southern England, at 1:00 a.m. by two civilian executioners, Thomas W. Pierrepoint, and his nephew, Albert Pierrepoint. Thomas's last words to Captain Andrew J. Zarek, Chaplain, were: "look after my pictures in my cell and send them home for me. I would like you to write home and tell my mother about it and send my pictures home."[94]

Stranger rapes

This type of rape has a beginning and an end during which the rapist(s) and victim(s) have never met or seen each other before. They have had no prior contact. They are total strangers. Most of the rapes prosecuted by the military involved females who were raped by a soldier they did not know. Altogether, more than half of the rapes tried in England involved this type of assault. A more complete picture of the social distance between the victims and their assailants emerges by combining the partial stranger rapes with the stranger rapes. Almost all of the rapes committed by US soldiers in England involved these two types of sexual assaults.

A year earlier and just two days shy of the same day as Mrs. R.'s [partial stranger] assault on July 26, 1944, at about 10:00 p.m., Mrs. Dora Amy B. got off a bus on its way to Hollington Corner. She had just returned from Newbury, and she had about a mile to walk home. As she crossed over the crossroads on the Andover Road, she saw "two colored boys to the left ... with two girls."[95] Private William Cooper, Jr., 21 years old, Detachment "A," Company "D," 383rd Engineer Battalion, was there walking the other way. As Mrs. B. continued to walk up a fairly steep hill toward home, she soon heard footsteps and thought it was probably the "two colored men with these girls."[96]

Private Cooper had caught up with her, and he was breathing hard because he had just run up the hill. He said "goodnight" to Mrs. B., who remained silent. He said "goodnight" twice again, and thinking he would go away if she spoke, said something to him. Cooper,[97] frustrated, asked, "Why don't you speak to me – all the girls around here do." She replied, "I'm not in the habit of speaking to strangers." At this point, Cooper grabbed her wrists. She started to scream, but he stuffed a handkerchief into her mouth. Cooper dragged her to some bushes, threw her to the ground, and managed to remove her shoes and stockings. As he sat on her stomach, he said, "if you don't let me get what I want I'll strangle you."[98] Mrs. B. stayed conscious until Cooper pulled out a condom, and then she fainted. When she came around, the handkerchief was out of her mouth and in court she testified that at this point she was too weak to "cry for help," but she did hear Cooper say "Why didn't you tell me you were unwell?"[99]

Mrs. B. asked if Cooper would let her go. He said: "I'll go out into the road to see if there is anybody coming."[100] While he was gone, she tried to crawl back through the hedge to get to a path to a nearby lodge, but it was too overgrown. She couldn't get through it, and stood waiting for Cooper to return. He told her no one was coming, caught her hand and pulled her toward the road. She asked about her stockings and shoes, and Cooper went back through the hedge and retrieved them, including the bags she had been carrying before the attack. Before letting her depart, Cooper asked Mrs. B. if she "would see him next week at the dance."[101] She responded, "No, I don't go to dances." Cooper then reasoned, "If you keep quiet about this I'll give you a pound-note."[102] He put the note into her hand, but she let it fall to the ground. "I didn't want his money."[103]

In his one-day trial Cooper was found guilty. The Board of Review found that the trial had numerous errors and irregularities, none of which it reasoned, however, had affected "the substantial rights of accused."[104] Cooper contented that two companions were framing him, and he further asserted that the intercourse was consensual. Mrs. B., Cooper testified, had agreed to sexual intercourse for the price of one pound, but he had only a few shillings. She had also agreed, according to Cooper, to meet him a few days later.

The record does not indicate if the Board of Review gave any explicit credence to Cooper's contentions. He could have been executed or sentenced to life imprisonment. Instead, he received a ten-year confinement at hard labor.

Two months after D-Day (June 6, 1944), on August 6, 1944, 112-pound Mrs. Agnes C., a frail 75-year-old woman, was living alone in a small cottage at Sandy Lane, Rugeley, Staffordshire.[105] While in her second floor bedroom, at about 3:15 a.m., she heard someone on the stairs, and then a man appeared in the doorway. She said, "'Oh Dear Master, whatever do you want? If it is money you want, I haven't got it.'"[106] Private Aniceto Martinez, Headquarters Detachment, Prisoner of War Enclosure No. 2, a 22-year-old Hispanic from New Mexico, replied, "'I don't want money. You know what I want. It be a woman I want.'"[107] He placed his hat on her bed, moved her to one side, lifted her nightdress, took out his "'privates,'" and put it in her "'private part.'"[108] She resisted to the best of her ability and Martinez struck her, giving her a black eye and bruises. He soon left.

That night, at about 12:00 a.m., a bed check at Martinez's organization found that he was the only member of his outfit absent. He admitted he had gone into the house and had had "connections with a woman."[109] In his defense, Martinez said he believed he was in a house of ill repute – he did not recall hitting a woman. Six months later, at a trial in Lichfield, Martinez was found guilty of rape on February 21, 1945.[110] General Eisenhower approved his death sentence and on June 15, 1945, Martinez was hanged at 10:29 p.m.

in Shepton Mallet Prison by civilian executioners, Thomas W. and Albert Pierrpoint.

Other sexual assaults

Vaginal intercourse was the primary form of sexual assault committed by the US soldiers during their ordinary rapes. Carnal knowledge of their victims per os (mouth) and anum, however, did occur. These acts were considered "against the order of nature," according to the US Army's 93rd Article of War.

Attempted ordinary rapes:

Between April 5, 1943 and September 6,1944, 27 cases of attempted ordinary rape, which was the same number of ordinary rapes that went to trial with convictions, were prosecuted in England and Wales. Eighteen of the victims were single – the others were married, one with children. The oldest married victim was 52 years old. Fourteen of the assailants were black.

As expected, most of the ordinary attempted rapes happened before the June 6, 1944, invasion of France, after which the presence of American forces in the United Kingdom began to radically decrease. During this time, 19 of these assaults occurred. After D-Day, the number of attempted ordinary rapes decreased to 8.

Statutory rapes:

Though the definition of rape used by the US Army made no reference to the victims' age, in 11 cases the age of the females was emphasized. In these incidents the charge against the soldiers contained language which often stated the victim "who was then under the age of 16 years, and above the age of 13 years."[111] Or, the charge might simply read "a female under the age of sixteen years of age."[112] One victim was seven and a half years old.

Murder/rapes:

Four murder/rape crimes occurred in England and Ireland between September 28, 1943 and April 12,1945. The first of these incidents involved two female victims, one of who was murdered, the other raped by the same soldier.[113] The second murder/rape with two victims occurred on April 12, 1945.[114] The victims were a murdered man, Mr. John Charles P., and his wife, Mrs. Amy Eliza P., 67 years of age, who was raped. They lived in a trailer home or "caravan" at Boundary Lane, St. Leonards, Ringwood, Hampshire.

The first murder/rape with only one victim was Betty Dorian Pearl G., "a female child below the age of sixteen years."[115] She was murdered and raped at Ashford, Kent, on August 22, 1944, by two soldiers. A little more than a month later on September 25, 1944, Patricia "Patsy" W., seven and a half years old, was strangled and raped by a white, 22-years-old, from Ohio named Private William Harrison, Jr. The child was murdered and sexually assaulted at Killycolpy, Stewartstown, County Tyrone, Northern Ireland.[116] He was found guilty and was executed.

Military rape victim:

Second Lieutenant Irene O., 26, a member of the Army Nurse Corps, stationed at the 65th General Hospital, England, was raped on March 5, 1944.[117] She and five other nurses had traveled by "ambulance to attend a dance at the officer's club at Great Ashfield." After drinking a couple of rum and coca-cola, dinner and dancing, the rapist, Second Lieutenant Arthur C. Blevins, Jr., white, 550th Bombardment Squadron, 385th Bombardment Group (H), whom she had met for the first time at the dance, asked her to go outdoors for "some air."[118] They returned to the dance after five or ten minutes – Blevins had gotten bit on the lip after placing his hands on O.'s hips.

Inside, they talked at the bar for about fifteen minutes, and with drinks in their hands, returned outdoors at about 10:30 p.m. They walked over some uneven ground in a field, and about five hundred yards from the surrounding buildings they sat down under a tree. Blevins finished O.'s drink for her, made sexual advances toward her and was rewarded with another bite on his lips. She said, "Please leave me alone," but Blevins persisted. At one point during a lull in their struggle, O. started saying the Act of Contrition, a Catholic prayer. "While she was praying he seized her around the waist from behind," pushed her to the ground, struck her with his fist, stifled her screams by putting his thumb over her nose and the palm of his hand over her mouth, and raped her.[119] He was sentenced to ten years of hard labor.

One of the most unique features of the data used here is that it identifies the soldiers by name, rank, and unit. This information has been used to determine what type of soldier raped.

Who raped?

Wartime rape literature often offers no clear distinctions about which or what kind of soldiers commit rape. One of the best discussions of World War II rapes by Russian soldiers in Germany is found in Ryan's classic 1966 study about the battle for Berlin in April 1945.[120] Though he devotes pages to detailing the fears and realities of what German females suffered at the hands of "lusting Red soldiers,"[121] he makes no distinctions about which or what kind of Russian soldiers raped German women at war's end. The question remains unanswered as to whether the rapists are career soldiers, draftees, fighting men, administrators and soldiers of all ranks and responsibilities. The same can be said about Chang's 1997 *The Rape of Nanking*.[122] In these two instances, unfortunately, this oversight has contributed to the unexamined impression that World War II rapists in Germany and China were fighting infantry, regardless of rank or responsibility. Writing later about the

American soldiers in Europe during World War II, Schrijvers devotes part of a chapter to their "longing for women."[123] He, too, gives the same impression, saying that rapes happened when fighting troops were moving rapidly in France and Germany. Though he does mention that soldiers were "dutifully lined ... up for identification whenever rapes were reported in a town,"[124] he does not mention the responsibilities of the units that were involved. Neither does he say anything about crimes committed by regular (career) troops compared to the crimes committed by draftees/enlistees in for the duration of the war.

Failure to discuss these crucial distinctions and the implications for explaining the crimes committed during the ETO was typical. After the end of the ETO, military summaries of the crimes committed by US soldiers was discussed in the *Report of the General Board, United States Forces, European Theater*, Study Number 84.[125] It was prepared under the direction of Colonel Julien C. Hyer, Chief, Judge Advocate Section whose mission was to prepare a report and make recommendations. Part One – "Offenders and Offenses," – contains no mention of these important distinctions. Instead, it classifies the offenders according to whether they were mentally diseased, mentally deficient, pre-induction criminals, psychopaths and psychoneurotics, chronic alcoholics, sex criminals, and what was termed combat aversion types. The same oversight is present in Morris's elaborate, yet seriously flawed, effort to explain rapes committed by US soldiers in the ETO.

Service units:

The data used here contain very specific descriptive information about the rapists. Surprisingly, most of the soldiers tried for rape in England and Wales were *not* infantrymen.[126] Overwhelmingly, these rapes were committed by *service* troops whose responsibilities were to supply goods – food, water, gasoline, ammunition, spare parts, and other vital supplies- and services to the front line. Because the US Army was segregated during the war, its service personnel were almost entirely comprised of black American draftees. While black soldiers comprised approximately 10 percent of the US Army in the ETO, at least 64 percent of the rapists in England and Wales came from black units – all of whom were certainly under the command of white officers.

The third rape that was tried by general courts-martial in England forecast much that was to follow.[127] On June 4, 1943, Beatrice Annie K., 23 years old and single, walked approximately half a mile from her home at Council House, Whitchurch, to a public dance held between 7:30 p.m. and 11:00 p.m., at the Church Hall in Whitchurch, near Kingsclere, Hampshire. The dance included male and female British civilians, and "colored soldiers of the United States Army."[128] At the dance, a Mrs. H. introduced her to two colored soldiers, "Chico" and "Rock." Her companion, Miss Annie P., and she danced "several times with 'Rock.'"[129]

While the dance was in progress, she and "Rock" went to the Bell, a nearby public house. There she had three glasses of non-alcoholic cider. By 9:25 p.m., she and "Rock" returned to the dance, and she had a few more dances with "Rock," as well as one with another colored soldier, "Vernon." At the end of the dance she, Miss Annie P., and Mrs. H. left the hall together. Outside they met "Chico," "Rock," and an unnamed black soldier. "Rock" asked if he could walk her home, and Miss K. declined and started walking in that direction up Newbury Street and past the White Hart public house.

After passing another public house, Bricklayer's Arms, she heard someone approaching her from the rear – it was a "colored boy," who asked if he could escort her home.[130] She declined, and he continued to follow her until he caught her by the shoulder and asked if he could get under her umbrella. He soon forced her across the road, pulled her up a lane to a gate, knocked her backward to the ground and commenced removing her clothes.

Private Isiah Porter, 434th Engineer Company, (Dump Truck), pulled her knickers down and placed his hands on her privates. She screamed but no one came to her assistance. They struggled for what the record says was a "long time,"[131] she hitting him with her umbrella, while he knocked her about in the nettles and tried to keep his hand over her mouth. Once she freed herself and made it to the gate, but Porter grabbed her again and said, "I'm not going to let you go until I had [sic] F-U-C-K."[132] After throwing her onto her back, she rolled down a bank onto the gravel by the side of the road, where he held her prostrate and repeatedly struck her head on the ground. She lost consciousness and she had no recollections until Porter pulled her to her feet and handed her her handbag and umbrella. She was cold and shivering and in the darkness Porter struck a match to help find his cap. Miss K. found her shoes, and Porter asked her where he could find a phone because he had to find a way back to Kingsclere. She arrived at home about 2:30 a.m on June 5, 1943. Miss K. immediately went to her mother and told her "A black man knocked me down."[133]

The next morning, Mrs. K., Beatrice's mother, reported the incident. During the course of the next two days her daughter was examined by Dr. James Ewing, Whitchurch and Jack Rubin, a surgeon at the Royal Hampshire County Hospital. The evidence was unequivocal – her hymen had been torn.

At the trial, June 30, 1943, Porter, 31, admitted that he had sexual intercourse with a girl whom he "thinks" was Miss K. He verified that the place and time where he had intercourse were exactly the same as the description given by the victim.[134] He was found guilty, and lacking a unanimous jury decision, was sentenced to life imprisonment at hard labor and sent to Federal Reformatory, Chillicothe, Ohio. The US Army's Board of Review examined the trial record and reduced Porter's sentence to 10 years. They commented that his "crime was one of barbaric violence and ... an exhibition of animalism in its most repugnant form."[135] While the Board of

Review opinion is silent on this point, it must be remembered that the Army was segregated and that for a white woman to freely socialize with black soldiers was prohibited by law and custom in the United States. Her admittance to having danced and socialized with black soldiers may have saved Porter's life.

Officers

First Lieutenant Hugh I. Malley was one of the soldiers tried for rape in England, Wales, and Ireland who were not in service units. He was a combat pilot in the 330th Bombardment Squadron, 93rd Bombardment Group. Malley was well thought of; his "air executive," Lieutenant Colonel Howard P. Barnard, Jr., Headquarters 93rd Bombardment Group, said he was one of the most outstanding combat crew members in the group. He said further that Malley performed his duties in an excellent manner and "proved himself under fire and combat."[136] One of Malley's crew members, First Lieutenant Maurice T. Lawhorne, who had been in Malley's crew for ten months testified, "We have gone out together and everybody thinks he is a swell guy. I think so myself. I don't know of a guy any sweller than he is."[137]

On the date of his offense, July 25, 1944, Lieutenant Malley had been the lead pilot on his 33rd and last combat mission. It was also the group's 200th mission and a dance had been organized to commemorate the occasion. Prior to this time Malley had a good reputation for being honest and truthful. Before the rape he had conducted himself as a gentleman.[138]

Miss Hilda Kathleen M., 19, Norwich, Norfolk County, went to the special dance at the request of her friend, Miss B., who herself had been asked by a "boy" if she would "bring some friends out."[139] Miss M. and Miss B.s along with several other girls met at the Bell Hotel and were taken to the dance in three or four buses. The actual dance was held in the Mess building – Malley's living quarters was in a large room at the end of the Dispensary, not far from the Officer's Club.

During one of their several dances together Miss M. requested a Coco Cola. None were available, and Malley instead brought her a "straight" whiskey. She didn't like it and Malley offered to get some lemon powder from his quarters for her drink. Miss M. accompanied him to his quarters. He put the lemon powder in her drink and placed it on a dresser. Malley put his arms around M., who said, "I can't be bothered. I came here to dance. I want to get back to the dance."[140] They returned to the hall, and she danced with no one else. He got her another drink, this time with lemon juice in it. She did not like the drink and poured it into a friend's glass and then pretended to drink what was left in her glass.

As the dance came to its end at about 11:30 p.m., Lieutenant Malley suggested they go to the officer's club where her coat was and because she "had to leave from there."[141] When they reached a turning point, he suddenly seized her and dragged her toward his quarters. She protested, tried to pull away, but Malley held her wrists and pulled her toward his barracks. At one point, he got behind her and managed to get her into the nearby room of a Captain Johnson. This frightened Miss M. and, as she struggled to free herself, Malley started to beat her. She bled from her nose and mouth, and it caused great difficulty with her breathing – she almost fainted. At one point she asked for water and when Malley got up to get it, Miss M. attempted to run away. Malley caught her, hit her on the chin with his fist and threw her on the bed.[142] While on top of her and holding her arms across her chest with one hand, Malley managed to remove her knickers and forcibly engaged in sexual intercourse. At one point during the rape, someone came into the room and Malley shouted, "Get out." He continued raping her for about five minutes more until three "boys" standing in the doorway again interrupted him. Miss M. took advantage of this development and seeing her knickers on the floor, grabbed them and ran out, ducking under Malley's arm as he tried to constrain her. One of the boys helped her get her coat and transportation home. She arrived there at about 1:45 a.m.[143]

Mrs. Mary M., her mother, testified that when Miss M. arrived home, her hair was "matted to her face with sweat and blood," and that she was "crazy with fright."[144] Miss M. told her mother that she "had been attacked by a man."[145] She had difficulty walking, her upper lip was cut, her teeth were bleeding, and two front teeth were loose. She was bruised on the back of her legs and arms. Her knickers were on wrong side out – later they were admitted as evidence at the three-day trial, September 1, 8, and October 14, 1944.

Lieutenant Malley testified that Miss M. was willing, very passionate and that she had removed her underwear herself and that she asked him to "Put something on." After saying that it was not necessary, he "crawled in" between her legs and attempted to have intercourse.[146] In court he stated, "I suppose I did a fraction or so. I didn't put it all the way in."[147]

After a difficult two-day trial – Porter's trial lasted one day – all of the members of the jury found him guilty of rape, but they were less than enthusiastic about sentencing Malley to life sentence or death. Unlike Porter, who was a black and from a menial Dump Truck unit, Lieutenant Malley was a white officer with a distinguished record as a pilot. At one point during the pre-trial investigation, Malley actually said he didn't want to make a statement but did so after being informed that it "would look awfully funny for you as an officer if you don't."[148] Later he asked for the statement to be returned because he said several things in it were not right. According to the records, Malley was nervous.

The jury clearly did not like its task. Before the trial ended its court president allegedly told Malley's defense counsel on the second day of the trial, September 8, 1944, that he "would never have voted for conviction if I knew it carried a mandatory sentence of life imprisonment. *I would have found someway out of it.*"[149] Three-fourths of the jury favored dismissal from service, forfeit of all pay and allowances, and confinement to hard labor for

12 years. The reviewing authority, however, returned the trial record to the court because its proposed punishment was "less than the mandatory sentence required by Article of War 92"[150] – life imprisonment. The court reconvened, and again with three-fourths vote, sentenced Malley to hard labor for life. This sentence was approved, but it was reduced to 25 years, 15 years longer than the same punishment given to Porter.

Two factors explain what appears at first glance to be a classic case of reverse discrimination wherein a white officer is given a heavier sentence than a black soldier with lower rank. First, Porter's behavior was not unexpected or shocking, though nonetheless offensive, abusive, and exploitative. He was, after all, an excellent representative of the imported collective image of rapists in segregated America. Porter was a young, black male in the social company of a young, white female. The fact that he admitted to having intercourse, but was unable to positively identify Miss K. as the victim, was consistent with the stereotype of black males with uncontrollable sexual urges. Second, Miss K.'s *voluntary* socializing with black males helped to ameliorate Porter's guilt. Her behavior, however unintentional, contributed to Porter's relatively light sentence.

Unlike Porter's victim, Miss M. was not guilty by association. In the collective white eyes of the US Army, she had not compromised her reputation by socializing with black males. She had, in fact, been brutally victimized by one of the US military's glamorous white fly-boys who had taken the good fight to the enemy.[151] Malley's rape, however, was not his only major offense. Even though he was not charged with either conduct unbecoming an officer and gentlemen, or general articles,[152] both of which were punished with dismissal from the service, his behavior had soiled and maligned the legitimacy and prestige of his fellow officers. This point had been addressed in England two years before Malley's case in the trial and dismissal of Captain John F. Kenney.[153]

According to Kenney's testimony on the night of July 28, 1942, he went to Glouchester on a motorbike to find a W.A.A.F. with whom he had a date. He could not find her, so he tried to get a date with the first girl's chum. This effort failed too. He next made a date with the telephone operator, a "high school girl of tender years,"[154] Kathleen W. She had been trying to put his calls through. In his trial he said that they had agreed to meet in an alley at 8:30 p.m. during her break. She did not show up and after social drinking with new friends he returned to the alley at 11:00 p.m. to meet Miss W.

Kenney testified that she accepted his offer of a ride for the journey to her house. They stopped a few blocks from her home, and Kenney told her that he did not appreciate having to wait so long to see her. Miss W. attempted to get away, but he grabbed her. Her screams aroused curiosity from nearby women, and a Mr. Egan fought with Kenney to free Miss W. She got away, and Kenney continued to beat Egan to the point that he had to be helped to a house across the street from where Kenney had detained Miss W. After the fight, Kennedy shouted that the English were yellow swine, pig-headed, smug, and curs. He added insult to injury by boasting that he was of German ancestry, and proud of it.

At the end of the two-day trial, the jury found that Kenney had wrongly accosted Miss W. on a public street and had against her will forced her into a vacant area. They also found him guilty of assaulting Mr. Egan, and they recommended that Kenney to be dismissed from the service. The Board of Review agreed with the facts and the sentence. Kenney's behavior was of such a serious nature "as to pass beyond the domain of propriety or good manners. It involve[d] the relationship of American military personnel towards the civilians of an ally in whose country a substantial American military force is stationed."[155]

The Board of Review, however, argued that the sentence be suspended. It reasoned that the US government had made a considerable investment in Kenney because the training he had received. It argued that the "Government should have the opportunity of availing itself of the services ... the accused is capable of rendering."[156]

Brigadier General, L.H. Hedrick, Judge Advocate General, ETO, disagreed. Kenney was a married man who had been in England only two weeks before the incident. He found Kenney's testimony to be less than frank, his memory hampered by liquor, his language and behavior so unacceptable as to force a group of British citizens to free Miss W. Hedrick also emphasized that Kenney's misconduct was not strictly speaking "within the family" of military personnel where often reformation could be accomplished by punishment less severe than dismissal from service. Kenney's behavior was a public embarrassment. It was conduct unbecoming an officer and gentleman. Hedrick recommended that if the commanding general wanted to suspend the sentence he should "be not kept within the British Isles."[157] By early October 1942, Kenney's sentence was confirmed, and he was dismissed.

Kenney's case was the first of its kind in the ETO. It set a precedent that Hedrick was certain would "serve notice on the officers of this command as to what they may expect should their conduct materially fall below the standards desired and demanded of officers of the Army of the United States."[158] Hedrick's ruling also carried, in his words, a message to the British public and British. They were to be assured that the US Army's standards of conduct would be enforced and that measures would be taken to see that violators were punished. A reasonable conclusion is that Malley's sentence had more to do with his rank as an officer than for the rape of Miss M. Hedrick's decision, as will be demonstrated, did not affect the differences in punishments given to black compared to white rapists.

Buddy rapes[159]

One of the most interesting and challenging findings to explain involved learning that some of the rapes were "social events" that involved more than one soldier. The exact meaning of this configuration is unclear. Perhaps it was strategy to assure a successful assault, to ward off interference and competition, or in the case of black soldiers, a means of protection from whites.

Of the 27 rapes, 8 had more than one assailant, 7 of these incidents had 2 rapists; 1 had 3, for a total of 17 "buddy assaults." The first double assault took place at 12:30 a.m., December 4, 1943, and the victim was raped outdoors.[160] The last "buddy rape" occurred within a few hours of the same time, one year later.

On December 3, 1944, Mrs. Joyce M. B., Bonfire Close, Chard, Somerset, married and in her ninth month of pregnancy, left her home about 8 p.m. to go to a cinema.[161] Before getting to the cinema, she became aware that she was being followed. She turned around and found her path blocked by two colored soldiers. They were Corporal Robert L. Pearson and Private Cubia Jones, both of Company A, 1698th Engineer Combat Battalion. They said "Hello," and Mrs. B. replied, "Hello, I don't know you and you don't know me."[162] She tried to get past them, but they grasped her wrists while she protested by saying she was married and pregnant. They ignored her pleas and in the struggle that followed all three fell to the ground. In what might be cautiously interpreted as evidence that one or both of the soldiers had raped before, one of them said to the other, "Keep it up. She will be alright in a minute."[163]

One of them kept his hand over her mouth, and they both dragged Mrs. B. along the road to a gate leading into Bonfire Orchard. She recalled that one of them said, "Lift up," and the next thing she remembered was being on the ground. She begged the soldier to leave her alone, saying again and again, "Don't do it, Don't do it."[164] Pearson and Jones ignored her pleas, and in an attempt to console her they told her that they loved her. Before she was raped she was dragged farther into the field. It was near a hedgerow where she was raped, first by the shorter soldier while the taller one held her on her back. They switched places and after the second attack was completed, the taller soldier started to hand a knife to his companion. Mrs. B. still struggling despite having endured two sexual assaults grabbed the knife and briefly had it in her possession.

Mrs. B. was warned by Pearson and Jones to stay put until they were out of sight. "Don't say anything about this to anyone or we will ... kill you," was the last thing she recalled that they said to her.[165]

The first person she saw as she neared her home was a friend and neighbor, Mr. Frederick B. She told him what had happened, and he reported the crime to Police Sergeant Arthur E. Dought of the Somerset Constabulary at Chard. By 9 p.m., Dought and Dr. Albert E. Glanville of Jocelyn House, Chad, arrived at Mrs. B.'s home. Thirteen days later, Dr. Glanville testified that when he examined Mrs. B., he found her suffering from shock, crying, pale, very distressed, her lip bruised and her nose swollen.

By 12:30 p.m., December 4, 1944, James E. O'Connor, 32nd Military Police Criminal Investigation Section, had advised both soldiers of their rights. Two weeks later, Pearson, 21 years old, and Jones, 24 years old, were both found guilty of raping Mrs. B. Both soldiers were hanged at Shepton Mallet Prison on March 17, 1945.

Modus operandi: targets and time

According to Felson, violent offenders generally need to *conceal* their activities. This requires *selecting* a target that has *value* to the criminal(s), *enjoying* the crime, and taking evasive steps afterwards, including *disposing* of the evidence, perhaps even the victim. No matter how bizarre, rapists have very practical modus operandi. The following contain most if not all of these elements.[166]

Ellen R.'s nighttime rape in October 1942 was the first of 22 assaults that occurred on the ground, outdoors.[167] Mary C., 26, a housemaid living at Stork House, Lambourn, met Private Henry (NMI) Lakas, 9th Airdrome Squadron, VIII Air Support Command, on a public street at about 10:00 p.m., Friday, the 4th of July, 1943.[168] They went into a field and Lakas tried "to get an intercourse' with her," but she told him that she was not that kind of girl."[169] From 11:15 p.m. to 11:30 p.m., Miss C. wanted to go home. Lakas objected and pulled her down a bank, and when she screamed he took out a knife, held it to her face, and raped her. He was convicted and given a life sentence of hard labor.

On Friday, the 3rd of December of the same year as Miss C.'s assault, Miss Lily Rebecca G., the 17 year old who worked as a machinist in a tailoring factory, left her home at 7:40 p.m. and joined Mrs. Mary M. to attend a dance at the Wickstead Park Pavilion.[170] After learning that the local dance was canceled, they took a coach into Kettering to see if a dance was being held there. On their way, they met two white soldiers they did not know before. Together the four of them went to the New Inn for a drink. They left about 9:00 p.m. and went to a public house for a drink and stayed there until approximately 10:45 p.m. Because no bus home was available at this hour, Miss G. and Mrs. M. started walking homeward.[171]

Near midnight, they had walked near to the Finedon Station turn, approximately one and a half miles from their homes. At this point, "two colored Americans, one being tall, the other short and wearing a "peak cap," were approaching them. As soon as the soldiers got close to them, they "'made a grab'" for them, and both ran.[172] Miss G. tripped in the brush, but Mrs. M. escaped. For about 15 minutes she stayed in the vicinity, only a few yards from where Miss G. was struggling with both soldiers. Mrs. M. heard Miss G. shouting "Let me go," and "Please, don't."[173]

In court, Miss G. testified that the smaller soldier kept hitting her in the face, and threatened to kill her, while the taller soldier held her down. Before both of them raped her, "[o]ne soldier had laid his coat on the ground so that Miss G. would not soil her coat."[174] Other rapists were not as "considerate" as Ramsey and Edwards. Both were found guilty, and they were confined to at hard labor for life.

Miss Mable Clarice M., 31, a school teacher, left the home of her sister, Mrs. Edith Enid E., on Sunday, July 2, 1944, to visit friends five miles away in the town of Tetbury, Gloucestershire. Mrs. E. expected her sister back about 11:00 p.m.[175] By midnight she had not arrived. Mrs. E. called Miss M.'s friends and learned that she had departed an hour earlier. Suspecting that something was wrong, Mrs. E. and the friends started looking for Miss M.

At a "camp of colored American soldiers ... located approximately three miles from Tetbury," Mrs. E. stopped to inquire whether they had seen her sister.[176] The soldiers she spoke to said they had not seen her sister, but they did inform Mrs. E. that "there had been 'some trouble along the road.'"[177] At this point, Mrs. E. called the police and continued on toward Tetbury in search of her sister. She found her walking toward her at a crossroad about a quarter mile past the camp. Miss M.'s clothes were dirty, one shoe was missing and she was crying. Later, at home, after having previously sent Miss M. there while she continued investigating what had happened to her sister, Mrs. E. noticed that Miss M. was in worse condition than she had originally thought. Her lips were swollen, eyes bleeding, and she was badly cut and bruised about the face. Her legs were scratched, her hair was thick with mud, and some of her clothing, including her knickers, were missing.[178]

At the crime scene, a local police sergeant found Miss M.'s bicycle in a ditch. Near to it the grass had been flattened, and "the earth had recently been disturbed for a space of six by two feet."[179] Later in the same day, the sergeant returned to where the bicycle had been located. Nearby, in a clover field, he found another area of flattened grass, and the earth showed signs "indicating a struggle not long before."[180] Close by he found a knife, a galosh with a sandal in it, a bicycle seat cover, two diapers and a badly torn pair of knickers.

On Tuesday, July 4, 1944, James R. Thompson, Criminal Investigation Division agent, obtained signed and sworn statements from Privates Alfonso Josie Lewis and Freddie Moses Sexton, two of the 4197th Quartermaster Service Company. They admitted that on the evening of July 2, 1944, both had been drinking beer and whiskey in various places in Tetbury. On their way back to camp, they ran into Miss M. Lewis and claimed that it was Sexton who stopped her and tried to drag her into a field. Together, they lifted her over a gate. Sexton raped her first, but Lewis, apparently too drunk, had difficulty because "it always kept coming out."[181] He had penetration, nonetheless, and after Sexon raped Miss M. the second time, Lewis tried again with the same result he had before.

Both soldiers were judged guilty. Each received a life sentence of hard labor that they began serving at the United States Penitentiary, Lewisburg, Pennsylvania.

The indoor rape of Mrs. Amelia May M., a 95-lb. mother of two small boys, Corby, was not a chance encounter. On Saturday, December 17, 1944, she and her husband first saw her assailant, Private Donald Hicks, 612th Bombardment Squadron (H), 401st Bombardment Group (H).[182] All three were in White Horse pub – the couple did not speak to Hicks. On Monday, December 25, Christmas Day, they were again in the pub and Hicks joined them at their table. He was polite, and whenever Mr. M. went to the lavatory, so did Hicks. He was later invited to their home for Christmas dinner, and he stayed until 2:30 a.m. on the 26th. When asked if he could return again later on the night of the 26th, Mr. M. explained that he would not be home because he worked "on night shift"[183] They agreed to meet the next day at noon in the pub, but Hicks did not show up.

Instead, at about 10:30 p.m. on the 26th Hicks knocked on the door of the Murray home. Mrs. M. asked who was there, and Hicks replied, "Me."[184] She opened the door, invited him in, and he accepted her offer of tea. As she "switched on the electric kettle" in the kitchen, Hicks opened a parcel he had brought with him. It contained cakes made by his wife, he said. When the tea was served, Hicks suggested that Mrs. M. sit beside him on the settee to better see pictures he had of his wife and some "film stars."[185] She agreed, but when he put his arm around her, she objected and said, "Stop it." He persisted, putting his hand on her breast, and soon he had her right hand twisted behind her back. She hit him with her free hand and told him she would never have invited him to the house if she thought he was that sort of person.[186]

For a moment she partially freed herself from Hicks, even though he still held her hand behind her back. "Near a chair in the corner of the room he put his leg underneath hers and both fell to the floor."[187] She did not see him open his trousers because her face was turned away and she was crying, but she felt him inside her. To keep her quiet during the rape, he kept his hand over her mouth. When it was over she said, "Let me go to my child," who had been crying.[188] Instead of going to the child, she ran out through the kitchen to the Green's house, a neighbor. The assault of Mrs. M. was one of only two rapes that occurred within the victim's home.

Hicks, 23 years old, from New York City, was tried on February 4–5, 1944, at the Corby Hotel, Northamptonshire. By three-fourths vote of the court, he was found guilty and sentenced to confinement at hard labor for life. He was taken to the United States Penitentiary, Lewisburg, Pennsylvania.

Temporal dimension

Twenty-one of the rapes occurred at night, usually between 8:30 p.m. and 3:30 a.m. – 19 of these 21 rapes took place between 10:00 p.m. and 3:30 a.m. One of three exceptions of rape during these hours happened on the afternoon about 5:00 p.m. on May 14, 1944. Sylvia Joan N., a housemaid from Middle Wyke, St. Marybourne, Hampshire, was delivering a pail of milk to the home of Bertram John G., Faulkner's Down, Hampshire. She had got the milk from a farmer named Crane.[189] As she rode her bicycle down Faulkner's Lane, a colored soldier, Private First Class Conway Green, 24. Company A, 354th Engineer General Service Regiment, emerged and said, "Good-afternoon." Miss N. made a similar reply and kept on going. Green responded with "Just a minute," and followed her until he was able to take hold of the bicycle and stop Miss N.[190] She protested his behavior, and as she screamed, Green produced a knife and pressed it against her throat. Forced from her bicycle, she placed the milk pail on the ground. Green tried to pull her behind a straw rick. She reluctantly and with resistance complied out of fear he would kill her. Still resisting his behavior, Miss N. continued to scream until Green said, "Either you come or I will kill you."[191] Green then produced a gun and told her, "If you make another sound you know what you will get."[192]

After pushing Miss N. to the ground, Green pulled up her dress, cut the elastic of her knickers, torn them from her body, and raped her. The assault happened near the road, and no one passed by. Green soon departed and Miss N. "mounted her bicycle, picked up the pail of milk and rode to the G.'s house where she reported the incident to her friend Elfrida."[193] She was sobbing, unable to speak and seemed on the verge of collapse. Finally, she told Mr. G. that a "black man ... attacked me ... he's done me, he's done me."[194]

The next morning, Green's absence from his company for the previous night was included in a report to his commanding officer, Captain Bruce R. Merrill. Green, was arrested the same day at 10:00 p.m., and on May 20, 1944, Miss N. identified Green even though he was not wearing the mustache he had during the attack.[195] Green was tried at Tidworth, Wiltshire, on June 27, 1944. With the aid of several witnesses and convincing physical evidence he was found guilty and sentenced to hard labor for life.[196]

Alcohol, weapons, and more violence

Alcohol was involved in more than half of the rapes either on the part of the assailant or victim, or both. Sometimes, the Board of Reviews did not mention alcohol, even though the trial record indicated it had been consumed prior to the incident, especially when the rape happened after a social gathering such as a dance. It was not uncommon for the rape to follow drinking in a pub.

On Thursday, March 30, 1944, Miss Elsie O., 22 years old, a member of the Women's Land Army, lived at a hostel at Michaelston-Y-Vew near Cardiff, Wales. That evening, she met Private Leonard K. Steele, white, 22 years old, Company A, 771st Tank Destroyer Battalion, at a dance held in St. Mary's Hall, Castleton, Wales. Also at the dance was Marjorie E. F., Women's Land Army. She lived at a hostel at Wilta Court, Rummey, near Cardiff.[197] Before Steele and F. departed after the dance they made a date to meet later, but she did not keep it.

Three days later, April 3, 1944, Elsie and F. were together at the Cefn-Mably public house in or near Michaelston-Y-Vew, about one-half mile from where Elsie lived. She arrived about 8:00 p.m., and soon she was talking with Steele and drinking beer he had bought for both her and F.[198] Before leaving the public house at about 9:30 p.m., Elsie had consumed three or four half pints – the record does not mention the amount of beer Steele had consumed. Once outside, Elsie voluntarily kissed Steele as they walked in the direction of the Land Army hostel. Near a stile, he wanted to go one way and she another. As she resisted, Steele lifted her up (she weighed 115 pounds) and over the gate. While still on her feet, Steele dragged her backwards toward another gate, which he pulled her through.[199] Elsie continued to struggle and screamed, but no one came to her assistance as Steele hit her with his fists and threw her to the ground. After raping her and while she was still on the ground, Steele ran down the road.[200] He was convicted and sentenced to 30 years of hard labor.

Fists were not the only weapons US soldiers used to subdue their rape victims in England. Knives were far more prevalent – they were used in eleven (41 percent) rapes. A stick, glass bottle, and a knife and gun, were also used.

Twelve of the rapes involved violence other than the sexual assault. Some victims lost teeth, others had handkerchiefs stuffed in their mouths, one had her head repeatedly hit on the ground, and still another's companion was severely beaten. In one incident, the rape was part of a number of violent acts involving more people than the rape victim. On the same day that Green[201] (see the section on Temporal Dimensions) assaulted Miss N., he also attacked Mary H., a schoolgirl from The Forge, Vernham Dean, Hampshire. She was riding a bicycle about 500 yards from Vernham, when, according to Mrs. Vera M., a housewife from Rowebank, Vernham, who was riding her bicycle behind her, a colored solider stepped from the hedge onto the road behind Miss H., "raised his arm and fired a shot."[202] Green then ran to Miss H. and hit her on the head as she lay on the ground. Prior to shooting her, Green and Miss H. had talked for about 15–20 minutes. He had stopped her to ask the way to St. Marybourne, and as she remounted her bicycle, Green grabbed her by the neck and said, "No, go up this way."[203] She struggled, got free of his grasp, and because Green blocked her way, turned her bicycle to go in the opposite direction toward Fernham. She got only a few yards before Green shot her in the leg. As she lay on the ground, he hit her with the gun. He carried Miss H. behind ricks of hay, and returned to the road to see if anyone was following. During his brief absence she tried to leave, but he called to her and said, "I'll shoot you again."[204] He returned to her, placed her on his shoulder and carried her further into a field, pulled out a knife and said he was going to, "Cut the bullet out of your leg."[205] She protested, saying, "I'll shall go to the hospital to have that out.'" Green then wanted her to go farther into the field, but she refused and told Green, "I shall not go any farther." At this point she was standing and Green ordered her to "Lay down then." She again refused to obey, and Green pushed her to the ground, got on top of her, pulled down her knickers "but did not take them off."[206] Miss H. said she could feel his erection when he was on top of her, but instead of raping her at that moment, he picked her up for a third time. He was just about to carry her farther afield, when she said she saw men coming toward them. "There are some men coming," she said.[207] Green placed her on the ground and ran into the hedges, saying, "If any one catches me you tell them I was drunk."[208]

Green was tried at Tidworth, Wiltshire, England and found guilty of absence without leave, attempted rape and rape. He was confined for life at hard labor.

Victims' social characteristics

Nearly half of the *Board of Review* records did not contain information on the age of the ordinary rape victims. In the 14 cases where age was recorded, the range was between 16 and 75 years of age. The number of teenage victims, 5, was exactly the same as the number of victims in their 20s. Three of the victims were in their 30s. Only one was 75 years old.

More than half (16 in total) of the victims were single. Eight were married, three of whom had children. Two victims, one married and the other single, were pregnant at the time of their assault. One victim was a widow. In two cases, the martial status of the victim was not mentioned.

Less than half (12 in total) of the *Board of Review* summaries contained information about whether the victims were employed outside their homes at the time of their assault. Those victims who had jobs included housemaids, factory workers, members of the Woman's Land Army, a 17-year-old machinist at a tailoring factory, and a 31-year-old, single, school teacher.

Consequences for the victims

Unlike the ground-breaking research on the consequences of wartime rape conducted by Braithwaite[209] and Hagan,[210] it is nearly impossible to address this topic for the victims of US soldiers during World War II. The reasons are simple and direct. First, the information on this aspect of the assaults is very thin because the US military made no effort to follow up on the consequences of these crimes. None of the victims were formally compensated though some of them received letters of apology. In one of the murder/rapes, soldiers in the criminal's unit made a monetary donation to the family.[211] Second, the victimization and feminist movements as we now know them had yet to develop. Rape shield laws, for instance, were unknown during the war. Consequently, wartime rape was not the political and human rights issue that it is today. Nevertheless, a few details are worth examining. They emphasize the human pain caused by what were mostly fleeting and drunken encounters with US soldiers. The lack of more information serves to re-enforce this point.

The number of unwanted pregnancies that resulted from the rapes by US soldiers was not well documented in England compared to Germany. There are two exceptions in England which suggest what might have been a much larger problem.

The rape of Miss R. by Edmonds on October 8, 1942 produced a male child "who was born on July 8, 1943, and at birth was not so dark as it was expected he might be."[212] Exactly one week after the birth, on July 15, 1943, Lieutenant Colonel John W. Rees, Senior Claims Officer, wrote a letter to the Branch Office of the Judge Advocate General. He stated that his office had received a claim from Miss R. that "is most likely to involve a large sum in view of the fact that the care and maintenance of the child over a period of sixteen years is likely to be one item in addition to loss of income, pain and suffering and hospital bills for Miss R."[213] Rees also requested information as to whether "General Prisoner Edmonds is still in the theater in the event it should develop that a blood test is desired if the paternity of the child cannot satisfactorily be determined by other methods."[214] There is no evidence that indicates that Miss R. received financial aid. By the time her request was made, however, Edmonds had been incarcerated at the United States Penitentiary, Lewisburg, PA since December 1942.

A child was also born after the statutory rape of Queenie Margaret F. She was 13 years old when at about 9:00 p.m., June 17, 1944, two black soldiers at Earley, Berkshire, raped her. On the next day she identified one of the rapists. He was a 23-year-old soldier from Georgia, named Private First Class Fred L. Lofton, 4148th Quartermaster Service Company.[215] Queenie and Lofton had seen each other before the rape. She had been "around the camp several times during the previous week and he had given her a cigarette once when she asked for one."[216] The records state, "By stipulation it was shown [that] a medical examination of Queenie on June 19, 1944 disclosed lacerations of the hymen together with oedema of the hymen and adjacent vaginal walls."[217]

Queenie gave birth to a baby with curly hair and according to her, was "sort of light coffee color."[218] Whether the child was indeed of mixed blood was a matter of dispute. The attending physician was "unable to state definitely that the child had colored blood."[219] Lofton, who had an excellent military record, denied the rape. There is no record indicating that Queenie requested financial support.

The records reveal scant testimony about what was an enormous consequence for all of the victims – emotional trauma. Miss K.'s mother, Mrs. K., stated in court that after the June 5,1943 rape of her 23-year-old daughter, she became "very highly strung," and that "'I has [sic] to have someone sleep with her.'" Mrs. Kebby also stated that her daughter "Keeps calling out at night."[220]

After being raped on a clear night, October 5, 1943, by two soldiers Miss G., and her companion that got away, Mrs. M., were so distressed as to be unable to recognize either assailant.[221] Corporal Joan E. Trigg, Auxiliary Territorial Service, testified that just after Mrs. Kathleen Elsie T., a married woman with a five-year old son, from Birch Grove, Barry, Glamorgan, South Wales, was raped, she was "genuinely distressed," "very nervous and practically in a state of collapse," and kept repeating "what will happen to me, don't leave me."[222] Miss Hilda Kathleen M. at first refused to testify in the three-day rape trial that convicted Malley, stating, "The thing is to hard to think about."[223] While unwilling to see the two convicted assailants who had raped her hanged, Miss Mable Clarice M. described the impact of the assault with "they have broken me."[224]

Conclusions

During World War II, England and Wales, especially the former, were far from being places of only strong resoluteness and determination. They were also scenes of radical social disruption, none more evident than with the rapid growth in crime. The exact contribution made to the social disruptions by the arrival and stay of American military personnel is elusive in its exactness, but not totally immeasurable. Some of their victims made complaints about the soldiers' behavior. In the trial records that survive these statements serve as an official voice that speaks with considerable authority on the who, what, when and where.

American soldiers planned and committed ordinary, statutory murder/rapes throughout the entirety of their stay in England, Wales, and Ireland. Most of the rapes that resulted in trials were committed by soldiers from black service units. They raped mostly at night, outdoors. Their victims were mostly teenagers and women in their twenties.

The victims often endured more than simple sexual assault. Often they were physically abused with fists, knives, and sticks. At least one intended rape victim was shot, though not sexually assaulted. The long-term impact of the assaults is unknown, perhaps at this time even unknowable. There is little reason to assume the consequences were soon, if ever in the victims' lifetimes, forgotten.

The patterns of rapes discussed in this chapter include only the first phase of American soldiers' involvement in the ETO. The second stage began on June 6, 1944, with the invasion of France. It lasted until the Allied troops entered Germany and began the fight to Berlin. The rapes in France were, if not almost beyond imagination, certainly beyond what the US Army expected of its troops.

4
France: Liberation, Occupation, and Criminality

The executions of Privates Cooper and Wilson

The morning of January 9, 1945 was cool and crisp with slight flurries of snow. The floor of the L-shaped stone quarry on Route de Chonville, about half a mile southwest of Lerouville, Meuse, France, was covered with a two-inch blanket of snow. In happier times the quarry had provided some of the stones used for the construction of the Empire State Building, New York City. On this day it was the setting for what was to be the first of two doubly ironic and macabre scenes. It again lent support to an American interest. Instead of helping to build, it aided in destruction – the death of an American at the hands of Americans who had come to France to liberate it. The US Army's scaffold was in a portion of the quarry that was parallel to the road. In front of it was an 80-foot high wall. Behind the scaffold the ground had been terraced at three levels to a final elevation of 40 feet. Each level featured tracks, stone blocks, and tools related to quarry work.

Before the condemned, Private John David Cooper, black, 23, from Dover, Georgia, arrived under heavy guard, 70 people – 59 US military personnel and 11 French citizens including rape victims – had assembled. The official and invited witnesses, and the invited spectators, had an unobstructed view of the entire proceedings. The official witnesses stood in a single rank at about 20 paces from the north side of the scaffold. The military and French spectators were 20 paces from the south side of the scaffold. Together they watched as a covered personnel carrier – a 1.5 ton, 6 × 6 vehicle – delivered Cooper to the place of his death. The youngest witness invited to the execution was Mlle. Mireille W., 14, one of the victims of Cooper's nighttime assaults.

Unbound, Cooper was lead in a procession from the personnel carrier to the gallows by Lieutenant Colonel Henry L. Peck, Commander Military Police. Several officials, including a chaplain, Captain Marvin E. Kausler, and three medical officers accompanied him. At the bottom of the scaffold Cooper's hands were tied together behind him before he was assisted up the steps. At the top, Cooper was placed on the trap by guards. Peck stood on the right in front of Cooper. Chaplain Kausler stood to the right of Peck. Peck read the entirety (4 pages) of General Court Martial Order No. 2, followed by, "Private John D. Cooper, do you have a statement to make before the order directing your execution is carried out?" Cooper answered, "No sir, I don't, sir." Chaplain Kausler asked, "Private John D. Cooper, do you have anything to say to me as the Chaplain?" He replied, "I don't have a thing to say, sir."[1]

A hood was put over Cooper's head, the noose was adjusted while Kausler intoned a prayer. Peck signaled the executioner and the trap door opened clearly and hung suspended in the lower screened recess of the scaffold. Cooper's body dropped and remained motionless with no sounds, swaying, or muscular movement.

The witnesses and spectators stood silent and motionless. There were no visible or audible signs of emotional reaction. At 11:14 a.m., Peck signaled for the medical officers to enter the lower screened understructure of the scaffold. All three of the medical officers examined Cooper and at 11:17 a.m. the senior medical officer, Lieutenant Colonel John K. Martin, announced, "Sir, I announce this man is officially dead."[2] Cooper's Battle Casualty Report was sent to his mother. It said he died of "Judicial Asphyxiation."

This scene was played out again on the morning of February 2, 1945. Cooper's partner in the rapes of three French females was Private J.P. Wilson. He was hanged in the same stone quarry before 72 witnesses and spectators. Most of them had been present for Cooper's death. Wilson's execution had been delayed because he had escaped from the stockade after his conviction and returned to the scene of some of his crimes before being captured. But, this time the trap door did not function properly. The executioner quickly descended the stairs, "readjusted the weights and the trap door was released at 1101 hours."[3] A few minutes later, the senior medical officer, Major Andrew J. McAdams, announced Wilson's death. His Battle Casualty Report was sent to his wife in Mississippi. They had a child of sixteen months.

* * *

The Liberation of Europe, starting with D-Day (the landing of Allied troops in Normandy on June 6, 1944), evokes images of glory perpetuated by movies such as *Saving Private Ryan*. The US GIs who landed in Normandy have come to epitomize everything that was good and great about wartime America: courage, selflessness, loyalty, love for country, and democracy. The French, in turn, have been expected ever since to express eternal and unconditional gratitude to the United States without whose assistance – as the cliché says – they would be speaking German today. D-Day was indeed a pivotal event in the history of World War II, and the men and women engaged in its realization and success deserve recognition and have earned the heartfelt respect of the French people.

Yet, it is also important to set the historical record straight, and not only as a mere scholarly exercise.[4] While the public readily imagines the US soldiers in Vietnam engaging in a broad range of criminal activities, it does not usually think of the World War II GIs as looters, robbers, murderers, or rapists. Soon after D-Day, French civilians began to lodge complaints with American military authorities and the French police for criminal incidents perpetrated by US troops. Those incidents involved traffic accidents, looting (souvenir hunting), disorderly conduct, fights, racketeering, organized prostitution, murder, and rapes.[5] Memories of these incidents linger in France – most notably in Normandy where Americans maintained a large and lasting presence – although underneath recollections of happier moments that have become part of the mystique of Franco–US relations and World War II. With the passage of time it is now relatively easy to examine some of the previously unexplored aspects of Liberation's underbelly.

We begin with the context of France leading up to D-Day. It is instructive for understanding the crimogenic setting that US soldiers encountered and for shedding light on the rapes they committed. Many French women, especially the peasants that the American soldiers encountered across Normandy, were often, indeed if not inevitably, vulnerable and unprotected as a result of the disruptions caused by the war with Germany and the following occupation.

The French setting

According to Mannheim, in some countries during World War I and World War II, the social responses to war can be divided into stages, each with its own peculiar criminological characteristics.[6] The initial stage, he noted, produced a general enthusiasm of patriotic sentiments with a consequent decline of crime by civilians. After a few months, by comparison, the positive sentiments declined as a result of dramatic changes in environmental factors. These include, but were not limited to, the dislocation of the economy, loss of jobs without adequate substitutions, disruptions to family life, and a redistribution of the criminal population. As Hurwitz noted, "It is true that the effects of war are an object-lesson in the capacity of environmental factors to induce criminality in law-abiding populations."[7] During this time civilian crime increased. Crime among females and juveniles, according to Mannheim, often increased because, in part, women had lost jobs, their hasty marriages to acquire family allowances dissolved, unhappiness developed, and adultery increased. Evacuations, shortages of consumer goods, rationing and stealing also contribute to the mental and financial strains of living under conditions of war. After the end of a war, "What emerges as one of its most striking features is the primitivity of robbery, murder, and rape."[8]

The war in France was far from being over when the Liberation began. The country had already experienced greater and more horrific disruptions and severe strains on its social fabric than had its cross-channel ally, the United Kingdom. Long gone was the idea that France could win the war it declared on Germany, September 3, 1939. Its mid-1940 defeat by Germany and Marshall Philippe Petain's call for the French to lay down their arms had sealed its fate until near the war's end in 1945. During the interim years of occupation, the French adapted what Swiss historian Philippe Burrin described in 1993 as a multitude of ways to live under the extraordinary predicament of life under Nazi domination.[9]

It is not my intention to add to the rich discussions of the "strange defeat,"[10] or the occupation. Others have done this with great insight and scholarship.[11] Rather, it is my goal to first describe a little of the domestic life and the economic circumstances in France during the occupation. This will provide some understanding of the humiliating and dreadful conditions under which the French experienced the physical and moral suffering that the war brought to them.[12] As Berrin comments, "The war left behind it death, ruins, and physical suffering. The occupation, in contrast, inflicted wounds not so much physical as moral and political – wounds that have still not fully healed."[13]

Oradour-Sur Glane, for example, still serves as what Charles de Gaulle called "the symbol of the country's suffering." In 1998 the *New York Times* reviewed Oradour's World War II tragedy under the headline, "Wartime Nightmare Is Still Alive in French Town."[14] On a bright June 10, 1944, nearly 60 years ago, the SS town of Oradour-Sur Glane became part of a terror campaign "to cow the French Resistance."[15] The SS machine-gunned the men, herded the women and children into a barn and set it on fire, and then burned Oradour. Altogether, 642 people were massacred. It was never known why the village was selected. Today, fragments of destroyed buildings have been preserved that still contain as a reminder of the ordeal, old cars, metal sewing machines, pots and pans and bicycles twisted by intense heat.[16] Only six men survived, one of who was "buried under a pile of bodies in a barn."[17]

Shirer puts the number of French hostages killed by the Germans during the war at more than 29,000. This number does not include the 40,000 who died in French prisons.[18]

The major goal here is to describe and analyze one dimension of the suffering the French experienced, not because of the presence of the Nazis, but from the presence of American soldiers. Unlike the rapes they committed in the United Kingdom where military and civilian efforts to prevent sexual assaults had been relatively successful, the rapes in France were under the brutal and chaotic conditions of frontline combat and its aftermath. It must be stated here that while the US military made efforts to generate and maintain restraint and control of its forces from sexual assaults (and other crimes), it was less than successful. Nor, it must be noted, were there any civilian-based or government-based efforts similar to those exerted in the United Kingdom, to forewarn the French population of pending sexual assaults from American troops.

One notable consequence was that the volume and the viciousness of the rapes were dramatically greater than were committed in the United Kingdom. The French female population was, quite clearly less protected from predatory US soldiers than in the United Kingdom. There they had the benefit of sharing more cultural affinities, including language and history, than were possible in France.

Collectively, the lives of the female population in the northern zone of the occupation had already been greatly compromised for four years before the Americans arrived. Changes in working conditions and family circumstances contributed greatly to making French females more vulnerable both in and out of their homes than had occurred in the United Kingdom.

The US military commanders, too, had objectives and concerns in France that were different from the ones that had occupied them in the United Kingdom. In France the issues for the military were directly related to fighting and winning, while in the United Kingdom they had been concerned with preparation. Quite literally, in the United Kingdom, commanders had more control and could more accurately predict the behavior of their charges than was possible under the conditions of war in France and Germany.

Life in France before Liberation[19]

The disruptions to France's domestic life quickened soon after the German forces crossed the river Meuse. In the general mobilization that followed, the French authorities sent approximately two million factory workers to the front. While this was an effort intended to prevent peasants from bearing the brunt of the war, it contributed greatly to an almost immediate production slump.

The German invasion caused a mass population exodus. It was, according to Kedward, the biggest migration of people in Europe since the Dark Ages. Between eight and ten million people fled their homes under the hot "sun of May and June [1940]."[20] It was a nightmare; hundreds of children were separated from their parents, and the low-level strafing by the German Luftwaffe killed hundreds.

According to Kedward, it is difficult to generalize about the impact of the war effort economy under the German occupation. For some of the French it was a matter of undermining the German's economic demands with strikes, slow-downs, and sabotage. Still others worked resentfully for the Germans. Yet, as Kedward makes clear, production was negatively effected by acute shortages of materials and labor. The latter was influenced greatly by the fact that at one point before French POWs were returned, the Germans had 1.6 million Frenchmen in prisoner-of-war camps.[21] Another 600,000 men were sent to work in Germany after the February 16, 1943 pronouncement of Compulsory Labor Service. An even larger number of men were forced to work in "French mines and industries deemed essential to the Germans, such as bauxite and aluminium, or engaged in construction works."[22]

The Germans also requisitioned, sometimes in staggeringly large percentages, portions of French's agricultural and industrial output. Kedward reports that by 1943, Germany was taking 40 percent of France's industrial production, "including 80 percent of its vehicle production."[23]

On top of these economic losses, the French government had to pay at least 55 percent of its revenue to meet the costs of the German occupation. Per day this amounted to 20,000,000 francs, which was then devalued with a 20 percent exchange rate. In terms of the current value of (December 11, 2002) Euro-dollars, the daily loss to the French governmental revenue exceeds $20 million, plus the 20 percent devaluation. Put simply, the cost of the Occupation for the French was enormous.

It is with little surprise that in the face of a shrunken labor pool, requisitions, and the daily costs of occupation, production suffered. Coal production was only 65 percent of the pre-war output. Industrial production achieved only 38 percent of its 1938 level, while agricultural production dropped by 30 percent. These developments did not reduce the average cost of living. It went up 270 percent.[24]

In the south it was impossible because of the climate to grow extra vegetables – there the deprivation was both rural and urban. Arguably, extra vegetable production was more available in the north because of its climate, but growing crops and maintaining farming property there had the "added scourge of Allied bombings."[25]

As the occupation wore on, food deprivation grew, and the rationing system added its own form of misery by being unpredictable as to what and how much of any category of foodstuff was available month-to-month. At first, the list of rationed goods began with staples including bread and sugar. But it "quickly extended to meat, milk, butter, cheese, eggs, fats, oil, coffee and fish – the last made scarce, even in coastal areas, by the petrol shortages which hampered fishing boats."[26]

Changes in the "make do" circumstances of food for adults in Paris is illustrative. At the beginning of the Occupation, adults in Paris were "making do" with 350 grams of bread per day, 350 grams of meat a week, 500 grams of sugar, 300 grams of coffee, and 140 grams of cheese a month. The daily allowance for bread in 1943 had dropped to 180 grams. The allowance for meat was 90 grams. "The monthly sugar ration stood at only 390 [grams]."[27]

Ousby claims that on the whole, people fared better in rural areas than in France's great cities. Farmers and people in the countryside were more likely than city people to trade with their neighbors, forage for food or fuel than city people were.[28] To the extent that these advantages were real, it may explain or at least make some sense of the fact that by 1942 the mortality rate in Paris was "40 per cent higher than it had been in years 1932–8; death from tuberculosis among the elderly and young doubled."[29] Adolescent females growing up in the poorer sections of Paris between 1935 and 1944 were 11 centimeters shorter, boys were 7 centimeters shorter than their predecessors, and adults lost 4–8 kilos.

Skin color became like winter's pallor with an unnatural paleness and ashenness. The skin cracked, the whites of eyes turned dull, and joints stiffened and became painful. Boils were caused by vitamin deficiencies. They appeared first on the hands and feet and later spreading over the rest of the body. Minor sicknesses persisted longer than would have happened with well-nourished population.[30]

The lack of goods and services generally deteriorated over the course of the war, but transportation was a problem from the beginning, especially in Paris. Driving a car there was restricted from the beginning of the Occupation.[31] Prior to this time, Paris had about 350,000 parking spaces for its driving public, compared to the meager 7,000 permits for private car driving issued by the Franco-German Service Public set up by the police during the winter of 1940. Those permitted to drive were "restricted to people in certain occupations, such as doctors, mid-wives, firemen and nightworkers, though others who cultivated friendly relations with the Germans ... were quick to use their influence."[32] Sunday traffic on Paris's streets, however, "was exclusively German."[33]

The German requisition of car fuel not only contributed to a quieter Paris, it also boosted the city's Metro. Its ticket sales "rose dramatically in spite of the interruptions which more and more often plagued services."[34] Unsurprisingly, both bicycle thefts and sales increased under the Occupation. According to Ousby, by the end of the Occupation, Paris alone had 2 million bicycles, more than three-fourths of them newly acquired.[35]

Mannheims's observations about the effects of war on crime, while harder to confirm in France than in the United Kingdom because of numerous disruptions that affected accurate record keeping were, nonetheless, confirmed by postwar observations. Records indicate that criminality increased in 1941, one year after the occupation began, and it did not decline to pre-war levels until after Liberation. Unfortunately, there is little information about felonies including murder, manslaughter, and rape during the Occupation. Cavarlay, Hure, and Pottier's 1993 summary of crime statistics for 1934–1954 contained nothing about these offenses.[36] Information about lesser crimes, especially those crimes that would be expected to occur during wartime, is available.

Berrrin's discussion of profiteering as a form of Occupation accommodation in a chapter cleverly titled, "Rogues and menials," is insightful. It is also remindful of Hobbs's classic, prize-winning study of entrepreneurship, the working class, and detectives in the east end of London, where "ducking and diving" and "wheeling and dealing" are still part of everyday life.[37]

Behind, Burrin observes, the big business bosses whom the Germans treated "with a certain consideration were mixed ranks of respected wholesalers, arrant rogues, and drudges seeking a leg-up or better pay."[38] For some it was simply a matter of being in the right place at the right time. The man in charge of the professional group that handled the importation and exportation of fruits and vegetables earned "remuneration amounting to 4 million francs," and "a monopoly over the export of fruit and vegetables to Alsace-Lorraine."[39]

Nothing was left untouched. Alcohol, clothing, works of art, Jewish property, banking, and metal are but a few examples. The impact on the population living under the Occupation was wide and deep. In the words of Occupation survivor, Janet Teissier du Cros,

> We were all of us driven to some form of dishonest practice. It was no small hardship having to throw our moral scruples to the winds and settle down to a dishonest way of life, in full view of the children and in contradiction to all we were striving to teach them.[40]

Unlike the United Kingdom which experienced German occupation only in two of its Channel Islands, France's peculiar relationship with the Nazis generated formidable active and passive resistance to their occupation. This was no small matter within France. At times, especially near D-Day and afterwards until the war ended, the resistance in all its forms, including the unique *Maquis*, generated considerable anxiety and mistrust, which added immeasurably to the country's internal strains and disruptions.

Sebastian Faulks's novelistic treatment of Scottish, middle-class, French-speaking, Charlotte Gray's effort to retrieve her lost English lover who had been shot down over France, provides a brilliant and harrowing account of the resistance's responses to the German jackboot.[41] It is also convincingly portrays that participation in the resistance included the energies of unknown French citizens, refugees, and sympathetic foreigners. Pearl Witherington's real-life contributions to the resistance are illustrative. Born in 1914 to an "ancient Northumbrian [England] fighting family,"[42] she lived in Paris in 1940 and fled to England, but parachuted back into France in 1943. By June, 1944, she had a price of a million francs on her head and was running "a private army some 3,000 strong, specializing in cutting railway lines."[43] She was never caught.

Perhaps the opinions of the English working class toward the French were patronizing and superior. After all, the French had been traditional enemies of the United Kingdom, who during World War II "couldn't sort those bloody Krauts on their own."[44] To some English citizens, the French were pretentious, beret-clad, bicycle-riding onion sellers.

As early as July 1, 1944, it was clear that the French resistance to the initial stages of the Liberation "was of substantial value."[45] During this time and later, its members were helping the Allies by serving as guides, collecting and give intelligence information, and "guarding vital installations."[46] It also provided far from the front, a demoralizing factor to the Germans with harassing tactics that "diverted ... troops from the battlefield and shook [German troops] confidence."[47] According to Roberts, arguably the most effective unarmed resistance actions in France were of railway workers.[48]

It is into this context of pain and disruption that the Allies launched their attack on June 6, 1944. In retrospect, it is clear that as the fight for France developed over the months to come, it too, had different contextual features of its own that influenced the patterns of rape committed by American soldiers. We begin with the major findings.

American rapes in France: findings

There are four possible answers to the question of how many women were raped in France by American soldiers. Based on an examination of the 34 volumes of *BOR/JAG* opinions, between June 14, 1944 and June 19, 1945, the US Army tried and convicted soldiers in 68 cases of ordinary rape[49] in France. These convictions involved 75 victims – three of whom were refugees.[50] This number might be accurate, though it is doubtful that it is because of previously discussed problems with statistical data (see Chapter 2). If the 75 victims represent only 5 percent of the rape incidents, the number of rape victims in France might have been around 1,500 (75 × 20 = 1,500).

The number of victims found in the *BOR/JAG* volumes is, it must be again noted, not the same number reported by the *HOB/JAG*. In tabular form, the latter states that France had 125 rape victims that were "French girls."[51] If Radzinowicz's observations – that only 5 percent of the rapes are reported[52] – can be generalized to France, it is reasonable to conclude that 2,500 (125 × 20 = 2,500) French females were raped by US soldiers.

On the same page of the *HOB/JAG* report, however, another table indicates that 181 women were raped in France. It most likely contains French civilians and refugees who were raped. If this number represents 5 percent of the total number of rape victims, it is possible that as many as 3,620 (181 × 20 = 3,620) females were raped in France by American soldiers. The analysis here of the rapes in France is based on the 68 cases found in the 34 volumes of the *BOR/JAG*.

The total number of soldiers that the *BOR/JAG* records place at the scene of the crimes was 139 – 117 (84%) of who were black and 22 (16%) whites. Black soldiers were greatly overrepresented based on their membership in the Army, and whites were underrepresented. Of the 139 soldiers at the scene of the crime, the US Army tried 116 soldiers: 94 (81%) were black and 22 (19%) white. All of the 116 soldiers were convicted. Presumably, the 100 percent conviction rate resulted from careful selecting or screening of the cases and convincing evidence. This does not explain the disproportionate number of black soldiers who were tried. The prosecution used some of the soldiers who were not tried as witnesses against the accused. One of the most significant findings are the patterns of the rapes.

Patterns of gratuitous rapes

Date rape

A date rape requires that the male and female have agreed to meet for a social engagement. None of the reported rapes in France met this stipulation, although one date rape occurred in England. No date rapes occurred in France because there were few opportunities for this form of social relationship to develop, unlike the time taken in England for preparing for D-Day which provided ample time for dating and marriage.[53]

Acquaintance rape

This type of rape involves people who have a relationship that is less intimate than a friendship. None of the rapes in France fit this type of relationship. However, in England where the US troops were stationed between January 1942 and until the end of the war, acquaintance rapes happened eight times.

Partial stranger rape

Partial stranger rape means that the rapist has seen the victim(s) prior to the offense. The time elapsing before the rape may be as little as a few minutes to a few days. Forty percent of the offenses in France were classified as partial stranger rapes. In England 26 percent of the rapes involved partial strangers.

Stranger rape

This type of rape has a beginning and end during which the rapists and victims have previously never met or seen each other. With this assault, once contact has been made the victim(s) and assailant(s) are not separated until the end of the encounter. The duration of this assault may be as brief as a few minutes, or as long as several hours, perhaps as long as a day. Fifty-six percent of the rapes in France were stranger rapes. In England, 53 percent of the rapes involved total strangers.

Unknown

Here the record is insufficient on the nature of relationship between the offender(s) and victim(s) to allow classification. The relationship between the offender(s) and victim(s) could not be determined in 4 percent of the rapes in France.

By combining the numbers for partial and stranger rapes, a more complete picture emerges about the social distance between the victims and their assailants. In France, 96 percent of the offenses fell within these two classifications. This figure represents a 30 percent *increase* in partial and stranger rapes. In England, 66 percent of the rapes come within these two classifications. Again, a major finding was which of the American soldiers raped.

Who raped?

The analysis of the rapes in the United Kingdom where there were no front lines found that the offenders prosecuted were primarily blacks from service units. By comparison, it was expected that the data from France would indicate that the rapists would be fighting men on the front line. Such a finding would be consistent with the previously published literature on wartime rape. Surprisingly, the data from France did not confirm the expectation. Most of the soldiers tried for rape in France were *not fighting men*.

Service units

These rapes were committed primarily by black *service* troops, soldiers whose responsibilities under white officers were to supply goods and services to the front line. The first rape that led to a trial in France forecast much that followed. During the early evening (4:30 p.m.) on June 14, 1944, only eight days after D-Day and just 4 miles southeast of Ste. Mere Eglise and in the landing zones made famous by the American 82nd and 101st Airborne Divisions, Aniela S., a Polish refugee (with no undergarments) was raped in a field approximately 300 yards from her home.[54] She and her sister, Zofia S., both of who lived in Vierville Sur Mer, were pulling a wagon toward a field where they had cows to milk. On the road they met four "colored soldiers with rifles" who pushed the wagon through the gateway into the field.

One of the four asked for milk. Aniela started to milk a cow while Zofia went to an adjoining field to round up more cows. As she entered the second field, one of the four soldiers pointed his rife at her head and knocked her down with his fist. According to military records, she and the soldier then fought on the ground for about ten minutes. In court she testified that "He tried to take me by force but I didn't want to give in."

While milking the cow, Aniela looked up and noticed that all but one of the soldiers has gone to the second field. As she walked in the same direction she saw a soldier on top of her sister. She yelled to her sister, who replied, "They put a gun to my head." Realizing their grave danger, Aniela tried to run but dropped to her knees after shots were fired. She was immediately seized by one of the soldiers, who was himself pushed aside by 20-year-old, Private Clarence Whitfield (240th Port Company, 494th Port Battalion, Transportation Corps). At this point Zofia's assailant gave up. He and the other two soldiers left the field, and Zofia ran for help.

After Whitfield, a North Carolina inductee, raped Aniela he "indicated by motions that he wanted her to perform an unnatural sexual act." She refused and soon heard her husband's voice calling her name. Fearing that the black soldier would shoot her husband, Aniela seized the rifle. As she and Whitfield fought over the rifle, the husband entered the field at a run, along with three US Army officers, Captain Roland J.Tauscher, First Lieutenant James P.Webster and Second Lieutenant Walter S. Siciah, from the 3704th

Quartermaster Truck Company. Siciah seized the rifle and Aniela's husband struck Whitfield, who asked, "Why did you do that? I didn't do anything." He was taken away from the crime scene, but not before Tauscher noticed that Whitefield's fly was unbuttoned. The record indicates that witnesses testified that Whitfield had been drinking wine.

At the brief June 20, 1944 trial, Aniela was asked if she attempted to prevent Whitfield from inserting his penis. She replied, "I was very concerned with my life. There wasn't much I could do." Whitfield kept his rifle beside him throughout the rape; he reached for it each time Aniela tried to rise.

Whitfield was tried and hanged on August 14, 1944 "at a point near Canisy, France," by Mr. Thomas William Pierrpoint, a civilian executioner from England. At the top of the gallows, Colonel William H.S. Wright, Cavalry, Provost Marshall, First United States Army, asked Whitfield if he had anything to say. Whitfield replied, "No, sir." Captain Albert N. White, Chaplain Corp, then asked Whitfield if he had anything to say. He said, "Yes. What will you tell my mother?" White replied that she would be told that you died in France. Whitfield, just moments from his death, persisted. He asked, "But, I mean, will she get my insurance?" White said, "I will let the Colonel answer that." Wright stated, "Yes; she will get your insurance. Is there anything else you want to ask or request?" Whitfield replied, "No, sir."[55]

After Pierrpoint placed a hood over Whitfield's head, Wright said, "The Chaplain will lead us in prayer." Chaplain White responded with,

> Our Father in Heaven, we invoke Thy blessings upon this young man. And we pray that from this event those who have thoughts of this kind in their hearts may be cautioned therefrom. Bless this young man's mother back home, and bless him. We ask all these blessings in Thy name in Thy cause Amen.[56]

* * *

Only 3 of the rapists tried in France were in non-service units; two of these criminals were Privates Melvine Welch and John H. Dollar, both of Battery D, 537th anti-Aircraft Artillery Automatic Weapons Battalion. They were white. On August 24, 1944, almost one month since the American "break through" against German forces, they took turns raping Madame Georgette A. in her bedroom.[57] According to the persecution's evidence, between 9 p.m. and 10 p.m., the two soldiers had ridden horses to the home of a Madame Germaine D. and demanded drinks. Both were drunk, especially Dollar, who played with one of Madame D.'s children. Despite their friendly gestures, they frightened Madame D., her husband, and children, as well as a female refugee who was living in the same home. The refugee left the house when one of them indicated he wanted to sleep with her. In about an hour three more American soldiers came to the home, and they took Welch and Dollar away.

Madame A. and her husband, E.A., 45 and 49 years of age respectively, lived some 300 yards from the D. home. About 10:30 p.m. of the same day, Welch and Dollar rapped on the door. They were given food and had emptied a bottle of cider. When Madame A. was retrieving another bottle of cider from the cellar, she saw one of the soldiers guarding her husband with a German Luger, or revolver. One of the soldiers locked the kitchen door and Welch asked Madame A. to go into the bedroom with him. She refused, and at gunpoint he forced her into there. Once in the bedroom, he said he "wanted to do mother and father with" her, while beating her about the face and legs with his arms. Her husband heard her screaming for help for about an hour as he was forced to remain in the kitchen with Dollar who had a knife on the table.

After Welch had finished with Madame A., he returned to the kitchen and at the point of a pistol took E.A. to the cellar for more cider. Meanwhile, Dollar forced himself upon Madame A. for about 15 minutes but he was too drunk to complete his assault. When Welch returned from the cellar he again threw Madame A. on the bed, stripped off his clothes and most of hers, and raped her again. He stayed on her about an hour while her husband was guarded by Dollar, who fired twice threw the window. According to the records, this time her husband heard no struggle or fight, only his wife's crying.

Buddy rapes

The data contained details about the number of soldiers involved in the rapes. Out of a total of 68 rape incidents that led to trials, 42 involved more than one soldier either as rapist(s), or as non-raping participants. These 42 incidents had 88 rapists. Thirty-five of these 42 cases involved 73 black rapists. In addition to the multiple rapists, there were soldiers who did not rape (at least not in the rape incident with which they were identified). At times, these soldiers held others at bay, acted as look out, or held the victim down. A total of 111 participants were involved in the 42 multiple rapes.

Gang rapes did occur, however, the *HBO/JAG* makes no mention of these types of assaults happening in France. On the same day as Whitfield's trial and its unanimous vote of guilty, a few short miles away from Vierville Sur Mer, a similar pattern of rape was repeated in Neubille-au-Plaion, Village Le Port, Manche. There on "about 20 June 1944" three black soldiers from Company B, 29th Signal Construction Company, at approximately 11 a.m., arrived at the home of Madame B., 26. Living with her at this time was Mons. Alphonse L. and wife, Madame L., Mons. Auguste M. and his wife, Madame Jeanne M., 28, and the small children of the M.s.[58] After the soldiers asked for cider, Madame B. filled their canteens, and the soldiers departed. A few minutes later, they returned with five more colored soldiers. All were served cider as they stood and sat about the yard.

Pleasantries were exchanged – Madame B. cut roses and gave them to the first three soldiers who had asked for cider. They, in turn, showed her photographs. Some of the soldiers were already asking about women, some were making signs and gestures indicating their desire for sexual intercourse. They also used a French-English phrase book to express "I want to pass the night."[59] The demeanor of the men frightened Madame B., and she departed to get the help of a neighbor, Mons. D. He soon appeared at the B. home, while Madame B. remained at the D. home. The soldiers departed, but after a short interval they returned to B.'s home between noon and 12:30 p.m. By this time Madames B., M., and L., and the M. daughter were in the B. home.

Two of the soldiers compelled Mesdames L. and M. and the little M. girl to leave the house and enter the courtyard. Mons. L. was also forced into the courtyard. Madame B., who had remained in the house managed to escape into the courtyard, but one of the soldiers pointed his carbine at her and forced her back into the house. Once in the house, two different solders raped her. After her second rape, one of the soldiers menaced Madame M. with his rifle and marched her into the bedroom. There the same two soldiers who had raped Madame B., raped her, too.

Stunned and shocked by what was happening to them and while still being assaulted, Madame B. asked Madame M., "What are they going to do to us?" Madame M. replied, "I don't know." Madame B. exclaimed, "Be quiet, they might kill us." Their ordeal was not over despite each having endured being raped twice by two different soldiers. While two soldiers were raping Madame M., a third and unidentified colored soldier who was not part of the original trio who had asked for cider, entered the room and raped Madame B.[60]

The third soldier of the original trio meanwhile kept the rest of the B. household under guard in the courtyard with a machine pistol across his knee and a carbine aimed directly at the group. Four or five more colored soldiers arrived before the rapes ended.

One of the most brutal gang rapes in France involved a 56-year-old victim in the vicinity of Plougar, Finistere, August 24, 1944. She was attacked by at least 9 black soldiers, 7 of who were tried and found guilty. All of the accused were from the 447th Quartermaster Troop Transport Company. On the day of the crime, Madame F., a resident of Bourg de Plougar, and three friends and neighbors, Messieurs Marcel M., Antione P. and Pierre C., rode bicycles to the soldiers' camp with the intention of trading wine for gasoline. They entered the camp and commenced negotiations, but their efforts failed. After being in the camp for about one and one-half hours they were informed they had to leave. They were escorted to the camp gate by a soldier, and accompanied by "about twelve or fifteen colored soldiers of whom three were armed."[61]

When they reached the road, Antione and Marcel pushed their bicycles ahead of Madame F. who followed on foot with Pierre. As they walked toward Bourg de Plougar a black soldier suddenly seized Madame F.'s bicycle. Pierre returned to lend assistance and in the melee that followed, other black soldiers joined in. Madame F.'s and Pierre's bikes were thrown to the ground, and they were pulled to one side of the road by a hedgerow. Ordered to keep their hands in the air, one of the soldiers aimed his gun at the woman.

She screamed and ran toward Marcel, but she was prevented from reaching him. In desperation, she attempted to run to Antione and Pierre, but she was intercepted by some of the soldiers. Marcel escaped on his bicycle for assistance. Meanwhile, Madame F. ran along an intersecting road to a meadow where a soldier grasped her by the throat, threw her to the ground, tore off her pinafore and knickers, and raped her.

Another soldier held his hand over her mouth to assist the first rapist. Then, another soldier raped her. Following this assault, two additional soldiers took her by the arms and led her about three meters distance. She was again thrown to the ground where a hand kept her from screaming. Her third, fourth, and fifth assaults were committed in consecutive order while other soldiers fought among themselves to see who would be next. Eight of the assailants were sentenced to confinement at hard labor for life.

"Buddy rapes" became so prevalent that the Judge Advocate General's (JAG) Board of Review found it worthy of comment following an assault that occurred three months after Liberation, on September 6, 1944, near Dimancheville, Lioret, in central France. It involved two black soldiers who raped 34-year-old Yvonne B. in her home at night while her husband and baby were put under threat of their weapons. The court said,

> The evidence presents an all too familiar pattern of joint nocturnal invasion of the privacy of a French home and intimidation of the occupants culminating in joint rape of the woman of the house. [T]he intercourse ... was obviously effected by terrorization at the point of a gun force through mutual aiding and abetting.[62]

Initially, the offenders were sentenced to be hanged by the neck until dead, later their sentence was reduced to life imprisonment.

Images of the rapists

The language found in the trials[63] and *BOR/JAG* records is very instructive regarding what the military thought about rapists among its troops in France. It is quite clear that rapists were often considered despicable deviants, sexually depraved, bestial, and inclined toward "crimes against nature," deceptive, crude, and an assortment of other descriptions. In some cases, a combination of these images is found in a single rape incident.

On Saturday, January 6, 1945, 34-year-old Sergeant Obbie L. Myles, 663rd Ordnance Ammunition Company, along with two companions, all black, raped Mademoiselle Arlette M., a 16-year-old virgin.[64] She was walking on a public highway from Coucy to Pinon, Aisne, when the three soldiers drove past her in a weapons carrier. After seeing her, they stopped and turned around. Two of the soldiers grabbed her and forced her into the back seat of the vehicle. She was stripped of her clothes and repeatedly raped. The court let stand the victim's testimony that the offense "exhibits the bestial crime of rape in its most detestable and brutal form."[65] One soldier was sentenced to a life sentence at hard labor.

Technician 5th Grade Kenneth W. Nelson, 14th Ordnance MM Company, entered the army in November 1941. Between early 1942 when he arrived in Ireland and his arrest for having carnal knowledge per os with Miss Ann H., Saint Laurent, he had served in England, the African campaigns, through Salerno to Venafro, to Anzio and from there to France. Without any prior convictions, and with a "Good Conduct Ribbon" and six battle stars, he nevertheless was found guilty of rape and sodomy. The latter was described as "against the order of nature," and blamed in part on foreign influences "among soldiers who had served in Africa and Italy."[66]

There are no US military records indicating that US troops forcibly detained their rape victims in poor living conditions or deprived them of food. Neither were they forced to cook or do household chores, kept available for constant use, sold or given to other soldiers for sexual purposes. The rapes were, nevertheless, "organized" sociologically because the criminal behavior – though illegal and undesirable – followed patterns that reflected the social context within which the crimes were committed. The American soldiers' rapes in France were committed within the context of war where the norms of social life were severely strained if not temporarily destroyed. Sometimes the rapes contained extreme brutalization of the victim(s) and as well as an extraordinarily depraved insensitivity on the part of the rapist(s).

Explanations

The courts-martial trials were concerned with proving that a specific crime had occurred, instead of pursuing its cause(s). Sometimes the records contained language that reflected the trial courts assumptions about why the crimes occurred. Offender(s) were described as "fiends" and "bestial," terms which implied that the prosecutors thought of the crimes as resulting from inadequate control of *individual's* motives and/or urges. These descriptive terms contained racial overtones – white soldiers who raped were seldom, if ever, described as "bestial." This case involving Teton and Farrell is a useful example.

Captain Frederick J. Bertolet's, Assistant Staff Judge Advocate, review of the facts required him to discuss whether clemency should be granted to either Teton or Farrell. He concluded,

> There is no recommendation for clemency in this case and none is recommended. A careful search of the record indicates no facts in extenuation, and the age of the victim, the violence employed, and the lawlessness implicit in raping a woman on the ground by her very doorsteps are circumstances that aggravate this crime. The record shows that the old woman cried out for very nearly an hour while the two soldiers *dishonored* her."[67] (Emphasis added)

Surprisingly, Bertolet did not use stronger and more condemning terms. The term "dishonor" is far less harsh, judgmental, and disapproving than "bestial" or similar terms used to describe black rapists. Both Farrell and his victim were white. He was nearly 38 and she, Madame Lucie H., 57.

Differences in the descriptions of the offenders by the military, regardless of how they reflect racist stereotypes, cannot hide the soldiers' onerous objectification of their French rape victims. This illustrates how easy rapes can happen once the victims and the offenders, especially if black, have been reduced to less than full human beings with integrity and autonomy.

Private Anderson, for example, referred to one of his two victims on June 20, 1944 as "meat." He said, "I didn't get any of this meat."[68] Pennyfeather, a black, convicted felon, overcame any language barrier about his midnight intentions by going from apartment to apartment in Cherbourg, August 1944, armed with a knife and with his penis hanging out of his trousers. He referred to his victim as "pussy." More specifically, as the MPs pulled him off of Mme. Julia H., he exclaimed, "I'm getting myself some pussy."[69] He was hanged.

Other soldiers called their victims "dates," although they had never seen their victims prior to assaulting them. Private Henry D. Rorie and George W. Ferguson, black, 582nd Ordnance Ammunition Company, made several self-delusional references to their "buddy rape" of Denise Q. They described the assault in terms of time and as a pleasant social event: "I had my date with her."[70] During the initial stages of McGann's armed August 5, 1944, assault upon Madame Yvonne V., he asked her and a woman who was living with her "for a piece of ass?"[71] McGann, who acknowledged that he had "tended toward the criminal," was convicted and hanged before 38 official, witnesses, and spectators.

In response to investigating an alleged rape of a Cherbourg prostitute, a white military witness arrogantly and condescendingly referred to the victim as one who "sold the favors of her body for trifles."[72] It is unclear whether the same characterization would have been made if the alleged rapists were white, or if the economic deprivation of the victim was understood.

The approach used here emphasizes sociological reasoning. It focuses more on *patterns* of group behavior over time and space, than on causality. This perspective reminds us that the data contain only the most egregious and brutal rapes committed by US soldiers. The data are therefore exceptional in the sense that the more routine and less brutal rapes are not in the records to be studied. If these data were available they might reveal different patterns of rape and suggest sociological explanations not considered here.

First and based on the official records, we know that the rapists were almost exclusively low-ranking black soldiers from service units in a segregated army whose home country had a long history of brutality, prudishness, and intolerance regarding sexual liaisons between black men and white women. One salient implication is that black soldiers had little if any opportunity at home to acquire social skills that would have facilitated the establishment of consensual sexual relationships with white women, especially those who spoke French. Yet, with a wink-and-a-nod, the US army encouraged sexual liaisons by providing condoms for protection from venereal disease, but provided no organized sexual outlets for its soldiers. Unfortunately, the black soldiers found themselves in a foreign country with a mythical history of few sexual inhibitions and a reputation especially among its women ala World War I, of accepting blacks openly.[73] Some black soldiers were "ready" but ill prepared to establish consensual sexual behavior when they got to "liberal" France.

Second, and closer to the ground and the everyday conditions of the war, was the fact that unlike in England, it was practically impossible in France to establish anything but fleeting contacts with females. In contrast to their experience in England, the black service soldiers were less strictly supervised than most of them had been during the build-up before D-Day. There sexual relationships with females while discouraged were nevertheless possible. Combined with the above factors and the horrific experiences of brutalization of war that accompanied being in enemy territory, plus the abundance of strong drink, each contributed greatly to making the sparse population of French females highly vulnerable to sexual attacks.

The language of individual records of the rapists indicated that they were motivated by sexual desires stemming from sexual deprivation. Case after case contains information about what the soldier(s) said during the assault including "fuck," "fucking," "ziz zag," "I want some pussy," and other references to sexual intercourse predominant. Comments suggesting a desire to assault a victim *without* sexual content are absent. Sexual contact was very important to the offenders.

Indecent exposure was also used to express the desire to have sexual contact. During a May 14, 2005 interview that I conducted in cooperation with Program 33 (a Paris – based television company) for the production of its documentary *The Hidden Face of the Liberators*, a World War II male resident and former quarry worker of Lerouville, France, recalled this behavior. According to his recollection, as a boy it was not uncommon to see soldiers expose themselves during their lunches, breaks from labor, and when they were being transported by trucks. Some soldiers, he said, exposed themselves while resting on the running boards of parked Army trucks. It was not unusual, according to him to have to step over or walk around soldiers exposing themselves while sitting on the ground or sidewalks, leaning against buildings. When asked why the United States exposed themselves he speculated that it might have been the result of language barriers and the frustration of soldiers who had limited sexual outlets with females.

I do not interpret this information to mean that domination and submission were not on the minds of the rapists. On the basis of the contents of the records, however, these were not the primary causal factors. While the offenders might have been motivated by the thought that the rape was fantasy come true for the victim, the records are silent on this point. Neither are there indications that revenge and/or anger were causal factors in France or England.

Why so many black rapists?

Why does the official picture of rape in France contain so many black soldiers and so relatively few white ones? One possible answer is that black soldiers actually did commit more rapes than white soldiers. It is reasonable to argue that the black soldiers who were motivated to rape had more opportunities to do so behind the lines than did white soldiers who were fighting in the front. It is also reasonable to argue that women were more available to black soldiers when they returned to their homes after hostilities had ceased, and the front had moved on. The records are replete with examples of this happening. It is also consistent with Felson's arguments that violent criminals *select* their vulnerable targets.[74] The devastation left behind rendered women (and men) more vulnerable than before to attacks by predatory Allied soldiers.

However appealing these arguments and observations may be, they are less than fully compelling. We do not want to overlook the fact that America and its military authorities had a very well-developed image of their rapists at the beginning of the European campaign of World War II. Most of the image was homegrown – it had flourished largely because of the pre- and post-Civil War fears and anxieties white southerners and their counterparts in the northern states had about the sexual desires and behavior of black males. By the time the US Army arrived in France in June 1944, it knew what kind of men it would be looking for when rape accusations were proffered.

Part of the image of blacks soldiers as rapists had come from France during World War I. During this conflict US soldiers had been segregated and the French had been instructed about American *mores* concerning black men. Themes of unbridled sexuality and lust for white women gave "the impression that every black man was a potential rapist."[75] While relatively few black soldiers were actually convicted of rape in France, they, nonetheless, often had opportunities to meet white women who did not treat them as servants.[76] Unfortunately for the soldiers and their victims, the image the soldiers had of French women in Brittany and Normandy in general, did not match. Both regions were primarily rural, predominately Catholic and conservative.

Some southern politicians regarded black soldiers returned to home as rape suspects who had to be taught a lesson. Senator Vardaman from Mississippi, went so far as to publish a letter in his *Vardaman's Weekly* stating,

> Every community in Mississippi ought to organize and the organization should be led by the bravest and best white men in the community. And they should pick out these suspicious characters – those military, French-women-ruined negro soldiers and let them understand that they are under surveillance and that when crimes similar to this [an alleged rape] are committed, take care of the individual who commits the crime.[77]

A few black soldiers were lynched in the south while still in their World War II uniform.

The notion that French women during World War I (aka The Great War) were relatively generous with their sexual favors was not restricted to white southern politicians well known for their racial bigotry. Historian K. Craig Gibson's account of sex and soldiering by the British Expeditionary Forces (BEF) in France and Flanders along the Western Front, 1914–1919, is illuminating. Based on military records, novels, diaries and letters, he found that during World War I the opportunity for sex "was not confined to the cities and large towns where the brothels and hordes of amateur prostitutes made it easy to find."[78] Rural village women on occasion, were responsive to the sexual needs of the soldiers. Quoting P.G. Heath's recollection, "in the French villages the local farm girls always seemed willing to do their best to solve the men's problems."[79] More specifically, Gibson uses soldier's personal accounts of *how* their sexual needs were addressed. One solution, which may have been repeated several times, involved giving a soldier food – in one instance a bowl of warm milk and a large piece of bread prepared by the madame – followed by her approving a mademoiselle's kind invitation (replete with a contraceptive) to join her upstairs.

The seductive and easy image of French women and the lure of Paris were indeed powerful. General Bradley's post-World War II comments are illustrative. He wrote that Major Robert L. Cohen "had anticipated the fever that seized the US Army as it neared Paris ... raised on fanciful tales of their fathers in the AET, Paris beckoned with a greater allure than any other objective in Europe."[80]

The image of less racial prejudice and discrimination in France, coupled with the real or imagined sexual freedom of French women encouraged some black soldiers during World War II to think that all they had to do to win sexual relations with French women was to knock on their door. An incident reflecting this attitude was given to me by Captain Martine S. Nadler, 4257th Quartermaster Battalion.[81] It involved an American black he had defended. Drunk on calvados, he followed a young French woman home and pounded on her door. Alarmed, she locked the door and hid. Unsuccessful in getting her to open the door and grant him sexual favors, he entered her family's rabbit hutch, cut open a rabbit and assaulted it. The US Army paid for the rabbit.[82]

World War I provided many white and black Americans with their first opportunity to become acquainted with French citizens and culture. Because the US military was segregated, its soldiers impressions and memories of the French differ somewhat. Some white soldiers, on the one hand, carried their racial prejudices to France, and were not favorably impressed with the positive reception given to blacks. Black soldiers, generally, were not treated with bigotry. "All accounts agree that both French officials and ordinary citizens welcome their black American guests cordially."[83] In contrast, the French "simply could not understand why Americans would treat their fellow countrymen so poorly."[84]

This does not mean that race relations in France during World War I were without difficulties and conflicts. As Tyler Stovall has written, "World War I would give a powerful boost to the myth of French racial egalitarianism, especially among African Americans, [and] it would produce conflicts contradicting that myth."[85] Racial conflicts during World War I were part of an escalating clash between French capital and labor, exacerbated in large measure by the importation of laborers from Spain, Algeria, Indochina, China, Morocco, Tunisia, and Malagasy.[86]

After World War I a generation of black and white Americans were deeply influenced by the memories of how blacks had been treated by the French.[87] By World War II, those memories were nearly polar opposites. Blacks, generally, thought favorably about the French, while whites did not.

Intermixed among the race-based ideas of the French, Americans of the World War II era thought themselves rather superior and they were arrogant toward the French, especially its men. After all, it was often said, had we not already gone over there once to help them fight the Germans? The quick submission to the Germans in 1940 added more fuel to the notion that the French men were effeminate and unable to protect themselves.[88] With the confluence of these attitudes, plus the differences in the language and culture – including what Kennett refers to as "little shocks GIs had upon observing French manners[89] – it is reasonable to expect some indifference to be expressed by some American soldiers and officers toward the numerous problems the French experienced during World War I and World War II. A late 1945 poll indicated American occupation soldiers preferred Germans by a wide margin, compared to the French.[90]

The American soldiers' attitudes toward the French did not improve immediately after the war. Whether it was because of poor military leadership and training coupled with indifference, or something more basic, possibly the economic plight and attendant woes present in post-war France, it is clear that by November 1945, the relations between American soldiers and civilians were, in the words of a *Time* report, "strained to the utmost."[91] Military records and news accounts from that era report scenes of drunkenness, holdups, rowdiness, swaggering, and the embodiment of "irresistible conquerors to boot."[92] By this time it was reported, the French were often heard saying of Americans, "They have merely taken the place of the Germans," and "I wish they would go home."[93]

Modus operandi: time and place

The rapes in France may have occurred literally around the clock. The official records indicate that most of the recorded rapes occurred between 6:00 p.m. and 6:00 a.m. (See Graph 4.1). It was during this time that Privates Welch and Dollar's crime happened, as did (61%) of the recorded rapes. Twenty-five percent of the recorded rapes occurred between 6:00 a.m. and 5:59 p.m.

Madame Madeliene Q., and her husband were living with her sister on the latter's farm near the hamlet of Prise Guinment.[94] A little before 5 p.m. on August 23, 1944, Private Tommie Davison, 427th Quartermaster Troop Transport Company, armed and with three companions, came to the farmyard and asked Madame Q. for cognac which she did not have. In an arrogant, cross, and nasty mood, the 30-year-old, black Mississippian then asked for a chicken. One was found but he rejected it, insisting instead on

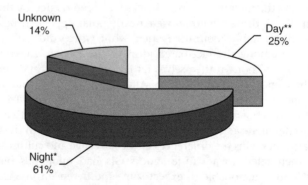

Graph 4.1 Time of rapes – France
*Night: 6:00 p.m.–5:59 a.m; **Day: 6:00 a.m.–5:59 p.m.

a pullet. When two of the women present finally got the chicken he wanted, Davison was given a rope for the purpose of tying its legs. About this time, Heni D., who with his wife and two children along with several other people who were living on the farm, was warned of danger by one of Davison's companions. For sometime Davison had been talking about "fucking" and "zig-zag," accompanying his remarks with suggestive gestures. He also asked D. for a mademoiselle and displayed 500 francs in American invasion currency. Freightened, Heni D. told the women to run away and hide. Davison left temporarily, during which time Madame Q., her husband, and Heni D. and his children locked themselves in the house, and went upstairs.

Davison circled the house, knocked on the backdoor and finally broke open the front entrance. Heni D. tried to run for help as Davison mounted the stairs, but he pushed Heni D. aside, threatened him with a pistol, and kicked a small boy. Madame Q. ran for help and near an apple-crushing mill found another black soldier who told her to hide. Davison pursued her, and pushed this soldier aside and while still holding on to the rope and chicken with one hand, grabbed Madame Q. by the shoulder with the other. Forced to go down a path some 60 meters to a meadow, Davison forced her to the ground and raped her while stifling her cries with one hand over her mouth.

The factors contributing to the rapes coalesced to make the time between late afternoon and early morning the time most conducive for the soldiers to rape. Rapes in the morning accounted for 11 percent of these offenses. Private Frank Williams, 587th Ordnance Ammunition Company, 100th Ordnance Battalion, assaulted Madeline L., 15 years old, on June 29, 1944, at Neuilly La Foret. Helmeted and armed, Williams, from Oklahoma, arrived at about 9:30 a.m. at the house where Madeline L. lived with her foster mother, Odette L., and Odette's 9-year-old little brother. Speaking no French, Williams gestured for cider, and Madeline poured him a glass, which he did not drink. He put his gun down near a clock, and after looking at a picture on the chimney, Williams grasped Madeline by the waist, put her on a bed, and "lifted my skirt … .Then he hurt me."[95]

Williams was convicted and sentenced to life at hard labor.

No place was safe. Women were raped in or near their homes, fields, along roads and waysides, and in military vehicles. At least one woman was raped in a barn, another in a pigsty. On November 23, 1944, Mademoiselle Genevieve C., 27, was employed as a maid at the home of M. and Madame P., in the village of Bain de Bretagne.[96] At approximately 6:15 pm, she was walking toward the P. home when she noticed a "closed" jeep coming near her. Private Luther W. Carter, 667th Quartermaster Truck Company, stopped his vehicle and got out to talk. When she indicated she did not understand him, Carter knocked her to the ground with one slap to the face.

Despite her screams and struggles, Carter picked up Mlle. C., placed her in the jeep, and drove toward Noe Blanche. He eventually stopped along the road and after some preliminary advances, placed her in the back of the jeep and "tried to do what he wanted to." Upon hearing the voice of Emile D., a neighbor who had heard Mlle. C's screams, Carter was distracted, and Mlle. C. escaped through the jeep's rear window. Carter chased and frightened Emile D. away by firing his rifle.

Mlle. C. was again dragged back to the jeep, and Carter drove away in the direction of Saint Sulfice. As the jeep passed through the village of Bain de Bretagne, the local gendarmes who had heard the rifle fire, tried in vain to stop Carter who was singing loudly to drown out Mlle. C.'s screams. A bit further on, Carter turned into a lane, stopped the jeep, and began to remove Mlle. C.'s clothing. In her efforts to resist, she bit Carter's finger. By this time she had little strength left and Carter succeeded in having inter-course with her.

After the rape, he helped her to find and put on her clothing he had pre-viously removed. He gave her a 500 franc note, which she said she kept because she feared that if she did not accept it he might again attack her. Carter then drove her near the P. home where he had first picked her up, and permitted her to depart. He was sentenced to life imprisonment.

Alcohol, violence, and weapons

Alcohol and violence were often involved in the United Kingdom and French rapes. There was a significant difference, however. In England the alcohol was usually beer – fists, knives, and clubs often inflicted the violence after visits to pubs. In France there were no pubs, but there was calvados, brandy, and wine. These were new to the soldiers, especially calvados, and each one was much more potent than the beer available in the United Kingdom. Matters were more volatile in France because the US soldiers were usually, if not always, armed and carrying live ammunition. At least 36 per-cent of the rapists-soldiers were under the influence of alcohol at the time of their crimes. (See Graph 4.2 and Graph 4.3.)

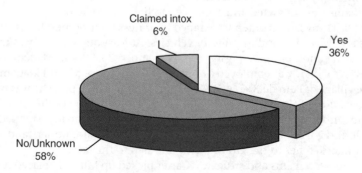

Graph 4.2   Alcohol and rape – France

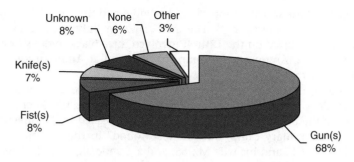

Graph 4.3 Weapons and rape – France

Unlike the rapes in England, the majority of the rapes in France involved guns more than any other weapon. The American rapists in France were armed during their assaults. (See Graph 4.3.)

Guns were reported to be the weapon most often associated with the rapes in France. Sixty-eight percent of the cases contained information about the presence of guns. Knives were reported to be used in 7 percent of the assaults; fists in 8 percent of the rapes. In only 6 percent of the cases were no weapons reported.

Rapes before and after the breakout

During the initial stage – what Blumenson calls "in the wake of the invasion"[97] – the Army reports contained information on only four rapes. The first occurred on June 14, 1944 followed by others on the 20th, 23rd, and 29th. These rapes were prescient to the patterns of rapes that the US Army was to record for its time in France. More often than not, the rapes occurred *behind* the front lines, sometimes during a lull in the fighting. The first rape that led to a trial is illustrative. A black soldier committed it.

He had three companions, one of whom attempted rape. The convicted rapist was in a service unit. The crime occurred in the Omaha Beach region on June 14, 1944, 8 days after the D-Day invasion and approximately 10 miles from the nearest Allied front line. By this time the Allied forces had made considerable progress inland, though not as much as had been hoped for when Operation Overlord had begun. Caen, for example, was targeted to be captured from the Germans on D-Day, but it was not under Allied control until July 9, 1944, according to Eisenhower[98].

The additional rapes on June 20, 23, and 29, 1944, essentially matched the characteristics of the first. All of the offenders were black, and their crimes occurred behind the front line. Two of the four rapes that occurred in June 1944, varied from the first – they included multiple assailants.

The end of June saw the capture of Cherbourg and the end of "first phase of continental operations."[99] The first rape in July that appears in the *BOR/JAG* occurred on the 12th. It involved three black soldiers from the 597th Ordnance Ammunition Company stationed at Ammunition Depot 801 "near Cherbourg, France."[100]

At about 11:30 p.m. three soldiers knocked down the door of a family dwelling. They pretended to be "American Police" looking for "Boche." After the man in the house refused them cognac, they headed in the direction of an American military camp, but "turned around" in the direction of the home of Ernest L. and his wife M., 65, and a granddaughter, 15. They had retired for the night when the soldiers arrived.

The record states that the soldiers used the ruse of looking for "Boche." Once Ernest L. realized the soldiers were black, he did not wish to open the door. The soldiers persisted by putting their guns "between the door so that it broke down, and all three entered the bedroom."[101] Within twenty minutes they in turn raped Ernest's wife and the granddaughter.

Late at night, eight days later, the raping trio returned to the house where they had been refused cognac. They again used the ruse of being American police looking for Germans. This time the man of the house recognized their voices and refused to open the door. They nevertheless entered the house through a window that contained no glass. Disappointed with what they found in the house, they soon departed, but returned in about 15 minutes.

On this visit, the largest of the black soldiers, Downes, climbed upon a bureau and lighted a match. This permitted him to see a cowed and frightened Madame L., a widow. She and her two sons, ages 6 and eight, lived with her 74-year-old father. "He seized her and dragged her out to the floor" and raped her.[102] During the commotion, the closet fell over and the mirror was broken. This gave Madame L.'s aged father the opportunity to flee with what one account says was his youngest grandson. Another, but related, report states that he got away with both children.

The soldiers were convicted; two received life sentences. One, Downes, 29, who had served for sometime in prison before joining the military, was hanged in an open field about 300 yards south of Etienville, Manche. One of the 22 witnesses present was one of his rape victims.

After the June 26 capture of Cherbourg, the Allied forces were bogged down because of several factors including inclement weather and the nearly impregnable hedgerows of the Bocage region. On July 25, this situation changed with what is now described as the Breakout and Exploitation period.[103] The pattern of rapes found in the records for June and July continued as the Allied forces advanced – rapes behind the front lines.

According to a *HBO/JAG* graph of the number of soldiers *accused* of rape spiked close to 175 in June, 1944. (See Graph 4.4). The date(s) on which the rapes happened, as found in the *BOR/JAG* records, indicated a similar picture,

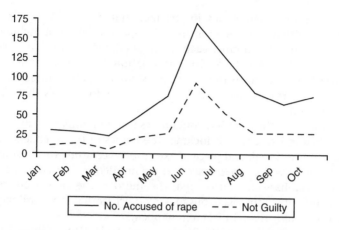

Graph 4.4 No. accused of rape and no. not guilty

Source: HBO/JAG, chapter 1, chart 14.

although at first glance it appears to offer a contradiction. From these records it is learned that only 7 soldiers were convicted of rapes (on 4 victims) *committed* in June.

Similarly, only 4 soldiers were convicted of rapes committed in July, while the *HBO/JAG* report indicates a decline in the number of rape accusations for this month. The number declined to 124 soldiers. The picture for August is the same. While the number of accusations decreased, the number of convictions increased – one hundred soldiers were accused of rape, fifty-one of them were convicted.

The differences between the number of accusations and convictions are expected. Perhaps some of the accusations were false while others were – according to *HOB/JAG* – too difficult to investigate because of the conditions of war. Some of the accusers had established intimate and rewarding relations with German soldiers, and were possibly out for revenge and charged Allied soldiers unfairly – the McGann case contains elements that support this possibility.[104] Sometimes the accused and witnesses were difficult if not impossible to locate.

Another complication in sorting out the differences between accusations and convictions is the fact that the *HOB/JAG* account contained graphed information on the number of soldiers *not guilty*. For instance, the difference between those accused (approximately 50) in June 1944, and those not guilty is approximately 25. A definitive account of the gap of the 25 soldiers found guilty is higher by 18, compared to the 7 convictions supported by the *BOR/JAG's* official records. It is, perhaps, impossible to explain these differences empirically. Perhaps the differences can be explained by convictions being reversed upon review.

A possible explanation lies in the fact that the *HBO/JAG*'s graphs of crimes committed over the months of its operation did not include information on murder *and* rape. Each of these crimes was treated separately. But, the *HBO/JAG* did have this information in a chart under "Death Sentences." According to this chart, 18 soldiers in the United Kingdom, France, and Germany, received death sentences for crimes that included murder and rape.

Appendix 83 in the *HBO/JAG* contains a separate summary of murder/rape that resulted in execution. It includes the names of the offenders, victims, date of crime and trial, and place of execution. According to this source, six soldiers – none white – were executed for murder/rape in France. Perhaps, when the graphs were constructed, the murder/rape cases were counted as rapes, instead of murders – thus making it *appear* that more ordinary rapes occurred *singularly* than, in fact, did happen.

After the initial success of the Breakout and the battle for Falise – "unquestionably one of the greatest 'killing grounds' of any of the war areas" – General George Patton, Third Army, was directed to capture the Brittany Peninsula.[105] To do this he sent Major General Troy H. Middleton westward to capture much-needed ports. By August 14, he had captured St. Malo, "a small port on the north coast of the Brittany Peninsula."[106] By mid-September, 1944, Brest was under the control of Middleton.[107] The fuller force of the Allies had meanwhile turned eastward toward Paris, and beyond to the Rhine River and Germany. The capitol city was liberated in late August and by the 30th, the Provisional Government of General Charles de Gaulle had been established and had begun work.

Rapes were reported and prosecuted in the westward turn into the Brittany Peninsula and in the eastward move toward the Rhineland. The gang rape of Madame L. on August 24 in Plougar, Finistere, is illustrative of rapes in the west. On the next day, a black soldier from 3912th Quartermaster Truck Company, raped Miss Jeannie L., 19. The crime occurred near Paris, at 65 Route de Guerville, Mantes-la-Ville, Seine et Oise. At about 7 p.m. Miss L. arrived at her home and saw the soldier and a companion, standing at one of the doors to the house.

After exchanging greetings, she started to make a fire when she noticed that the "big one" was in the corridor on the inside of the house. The two soldiers asked about a girl who lived upstairs. At this point, Miss L. told them to leave because her mother and father would soon be home and that they should go away. Their response was to ask her if she wanted to spend the night with them.

They ignored her comments, and Washington – the smaller soldier – exposed himself, but the "big one" pushed him away and told him to close the door and the window.[108] Miss L. fought with the "big one," and after he had finished raping her, Washington raped her, too. Then, the "big one" got on top of her a second time.

About this time Miss L.'s little brother arrived. She got up, put on her pants, and combed her hair "because she did not want to make a scandal."[109] The assailants indicated they would bring her chocolates and sweets, and that they were still interested in staying the night with her. According to the *BOR/JAG* records, Miss L. tried to leave after she had got dressed, but the "big one" grabbed her again. It is not clear whether she was raped again. Her parents arrived at about 7:30 p.m., and the soldiers ran away.

Miss L. could not talk very clearly at this point, but she did manage to say "two soldiers," and she pointed to the bed. Her mother understood what had happened. In about five minutes, the "big one" returned and took his helmet from the bed. He also retrieved his rifle, which was leaning against a table.[110] Her father asked the soldier, in French, what had happened. The soldier replied "No compree."

Private Levisy, another companion of the "big one," reportedly had intercourse in the same house earlier in the morning with a girl who lived upstairs. This led Washington to think the home was a house of prostitution. According to Levisy, when the two soldiers arrived later around 7 p.m., Miss L. had already agreed to "ziz, zig" for chocolate, cigarettes, and "D" rations.

Washington's trial was convened at Paris, January 20, 1945. He was found guilty by three-fourths of the members of the court and confined at hard labor for life.

In 1961 Blumenson likened the Allied armies at the end of August to "knights of old who set out in quest of the Holy Grail but were not adverse to slaying dragons and rescuing damsels in distress along the way."[111] This description has considerable merit. "Everywhere the Allies looked in early September, 1944, they saw success."[112] Portions of the pursuit towards the Germans' West Wall were "spectacularly fast and fluid."[113] Northern France, most of Belgium and Luxembourg, and parts of the Netherlands were soon under Allied control.

Their pursuit of the Germans was nonetheless impressive despite the fact that the Allies did not cross the Rhine until March 1945. In the previous few months after overcoming problems with the delivery of much-needed supplies, the Battle of the Bulge, and the loss of thousands of lives, the Allies were successful.

Another rape pattern began to emerge before the last offensive and the Allied drive to Berlin. It is not as well documented as the rapes by blacks behind the lines, but it is suggestive of what might be contained in the bulk of the rapes that are not in the records. One example involved two fighting men whose crimes happened on September 24, almost exactly the day that General Middleton got control of Brest. The place was Au Fayel, Brittany, not far from Rennes.[114] The offenders were members of the Troop C, 17th Cavalry, Reconnaissance Squadron.

Corporal Wilford Teton, 23, inducted in Portland, Oregon, Private Arthur ("Artie" to his mother and friends) J. Farrell, 37, from Newark, New Jersey, set out to find some eggs and cognac. They had been fighting for 47 days and had been out of combat only three days.

Teton, a Shoshone Indian, who the trial record describes as having "typical Indian features, black hair, large brown eyes, and a stolid expression,"[115] bronze in color, had no prior military service and was from a broken-home. He had been raised on a farm with four brothers, all of whom were in the war – two brothers were in the Pacific and two in France. He had gone through the Indian schools, completed a year at Salem Indian School in Chena, Oregon, – junior college – before taking a three-month welding course. He was working as a welder for the Kaiser Company when he was drafted. His outfit landed in France on July 15 and he became part of the breakthrough out of "the Normandy peninsula."[116] He said he never had had a drink before seeing combat.

Farrell, also from a broken-home, had known alcohol for some years. He had had a difficult life and had attended high school until the second year. Since then had worked at several jobs, including being a "runner" for the National City Bank of New York, a records clerk for the Standard Oil Company, a railroad clerk, tractor driver on the American Export Docks, and many other odd jobs. While working for the Standard Oil Company he was charged with manslaughter after backing over a woman with a truck.

He and his first wife divorced after she took up with a bricklayer across the street from where they lived. In 1932 he remarried, this time to a woman one year older than he. Their married life had been "punctuated by numerous quarrels ... because he would 'drink up his pay' and because he wanted a family but his wife did not."[117] It was after an argument with her that he had asked that his draft number be advanced so that he would be called into the army. He met Teton soon after joining the army – both were riflemen, though not in the same platoon. They had not been out together until the evening of September 24, 1944. At the time of his arrest, Farrell was described as a typical heavy drinker with a large bulbous nose and florid complexion. He wore army issue spectacles and his two lower front teeth were missing. Since age 16, he said, he had smoked a pack of cigarettes a day.[118] He had prior military experience between April 1, 1925 and March 31, 1928. During this time his character had been judged excellent.

In their search for eggs and cognac, Teton and Farrell visited at least three different homes between 7 p.m. and 9 p.m. In one home they frightened an extended French family because Teton took out his pistol in an effort to determine if an older woman who was in bed had been shot by the Germans. At another house they banged on the shutters to see if anyone was awake. They departed and soon returned. Meanwhile the 57-year-old female farm laborer who lived in the house alone, got up and started walking toward the village. She said she felt she would be safer there after she had heard her neighbors shouting out in alarm.

Farrell caught up with her on the road, pushed her down, and raped her. She testified that he stayed on her for about an hour. During the rape, Teton kept his pistol on Mme. Lucie H., occasionally kicked her, and he "forced her to take his private parts in her hand."[119] Informed by her neighbors who had earlier in the evening had a visit by Teton and Farrell, First Lieutenant Maurice C. Reeves, 1391st Engineer Forestry Battalion, along with an interpreter and another soldier, drove onto the crime scene. Teton and Farrell ran away, but Farrell was soon apprehended in the possession of a German Mauser pistol. Teton made it back to camp and was arrested the next day.

They were tried together. Teton was found guilty and sentenced to hard labor for life. Farrell was sentenced to be hanged. Before his execution, however, Teton tried to recant his testimony and admitted that it was he who was the rapist, not Farrell. After the military authorities interviewed Teton and Farrell, and others, it was determined that Teton was trying to save Farrell's life, and that he, Teton, feared he would be forced to watch Farrell be hanged.

Teton was immediately confined to prison and served time in three US prisons: Lewisburg, Pennsylvania; Leavenworth, Kansas; and McNeil Island, Washington. He was granted clemency sometime after March 1955. Farrell was pronounced dead at about 12:30 p.m., on January 19, 1945, before 35 people. The day before he wrote to his mother saying that he was innocent. His seven-page letter began,

> Dear Mother:
> Mom, I want you to pay strict attention to this letter, as it will be the last one you will receive from me.

Victims: fact and image

"If they [women] were between 14 and 40, they got raped by American troops," according to the recollections of a former World War II Military Police corporal.[120] The ages of the victims in France were, in fact, more varied, ranging from 10 to 74 years. The victims included children, the elderly, married, single, virgins, mothers and pregnant women. Many of them endured more than the rape. Some victims were severely beaten, shot and crippled, and then raped. One horrific rape with these characteristics occurred between 8:00 or 9:00 p.m., August 8, 1944, and at approximately 2:00 a.m. on August 9, 1944.

Marie G., a 33-year-old unmarried female, lived alone with her 66-year-old father at Le Pas En Ferre.[121] Their two-floor home, a combination of house and barn built with stone, had a kitchen with a stairway that led through the stable and connected the two floors. The second floor had a hallway, attic, and two rooms, one was used for sleeping, the other one was used as a "bee supply room." It was "full of equipment."

Between 8 and 9 p.m., August 8, 1944, near Le Pas En Ferre, two black American soldiers, Private Joseph Watson, a large man, and Technician Fifth Grade Willie Wimberly, Jr., 257 Signal Construction Company, came to the farm house and asked for cider. They were told to return the next day, but they persisted and were given about a liter of the drink. They soon departed and Mons. G. barricaded the door and went upstairs to his bedroom. Marie stayed downstairs where she usually slept. About five minutes later the soldiers made their second visit of the night. They shook the door, broke a windowpane, and forced the door. The barricade gave in.

Frightened, Marie G.called for her father, who immediately came downstairs and reproached the smaller soldier because of the broken window. Wimberly violently struck Mons. G. on the back of the head with his gun, causing blood to flow down his neck. Watson pushed Marie into a chair and then quickly departed. At this time both Marie and her father went to the upstairs bedroom and barred its door with a double lock.

Around midnight both soldiers visited the home for the third time, mounted the stairway and fired a machine gun through the door. Both Marie and her father were wounded, she in the left leg and he in the right foot. They tried to hold the door shut, but the soldiers fired more bullets, demolished the door, and entered the bedroom. Shocked, wounded, and bewildered, Marie's father said, "A pity, a pit, what do you want with this?" He offered them wine and whiskey, but they were not appeased.

Marie told her father to go for help, and he escaped through the door. After his departure, the soldiers then placed Marie, who had yet to undress, on the bed. While one of them held her uninjured leg aside, each in turn "violated" her. Afterwards, Wimberly left, and Watson fell asleep on the bed. Eventually, Marie slipped away and by daybreak was a 1,000 meters away at the house of a neighbor, Alexandre H. Because of her injury it had taken her an hour to drag herself on her elbows to safety.[122] Watson and Wimberly were hanged at the Seine Disciplinary Center on November 9, 1944.

Consequences for the victims

The official records for rapes in France (and Germany) do not contain any information similar to Ellen R.'s request (see chapter one) for financial support for the child fathered by Pvt. Wesley Edmonds.[123] Interviews conducted during May 2005 for *The Hidden Face of the Liberators* do provide evidence about some of the consequences of three rape incidents. Though far too few to allow generalization they are nonetheless helpful for understanding how victims absorbed their sexual assaults both in terms of immediate impact and long-term effect.

Mlle. Mireille W., 14, and Mme. Lucienne B. were assaulted by Wilson and Cooper[124] respectively on September 21, 1944, while the male members of their home were locked in the cellar with a low ceiling and walls that archeologists have dated as "older than Christ."[125] When asked if she recalled the incident, Mireille's recollection was both vivid and faded. "I can't say very clearly that I remember the soldiers. I can't remember seeing them arrive, but they kept us locked together. And they pinned us on the bed like this"[demonstrating with her hands how she and Luciene B. were forced to submit to Wilson and Cooper]. "And they come on us."

She said she could not remember which of the soldiers raped her, but she was certain that "oh, yes, it hurt me too much. I suffered too much from what happened." And "I had no help from anybody, not even the priest." Compared to other victims, however, she did have considerable aid, protection, and comfort from her immediate and extended rural farm family. According to her small, weathered, and bird-like 87-year-old aunt Denise W., who lives near the farm and is the sister to Mireille's father, Paul W., she had near-constant companionship, was never allowed to be alone and she did not suffer from humiliating gossip in part because her assault was never denied by her family. No attempt was made to keep it a secret, not even from her children years later.

Her recollection of the executions indicated that she is a kind and thoughtful person. "They done wrong, but hanging a man is dreadful all the same. That's how I see it. I don't think my father felt as I felt. I think he was glad." Her aunt Denise W., agreed, saying "Paul had no 'armor' [gun] but he would have killed them if he had it." The impact of the rapes on him was tremendous because as he sometimes said, "I couldn't help her." According to Denise, his sister, he died an early death because he felt so helpless when the assaults occurred.

When asked if the rape still bothered her or if it had ruined her life she answered while sweeping a hand over her head, saying, "No. It's all over my head now, gone." Married at 19, she had 7 children and at the time of the interview 19 grandchildren.

Cooper and Wilson's sexual assaults were not limited to Mlle. Mireille and Mme. Luciene B. Three nights before these crimes – sober – they had raped sisters, Mlles.'s Christiane and Germaine P. Sixty years later they were still hurting and bitter. They were also upset that my research had identified them as rape victims. They thought they had forever put their assaults behind them, "having never spoken to anyone about it to any once – not even each other – since it happened."[126] Asked if they would agree to be interviewed for Program 33's documentary, they firmly declined and said that they hated Americans and did not want to be contacted again.

In retrospect, the rape of Mlle. Marie R.O.'s, 19, by Privates Robert L. Skinner[127] and Waiters Yancy, black, 1511th Engineer Water Supply Company, August 1, 1944, at Hameau-Pigeon, France, appears to have been the beginning – or the continuation – of a life filled with tragedy. Her assault occurred while she was employed in the demanding job of a house maid on a farm. She was not alone. She and Madame Xaiver H., her employer, were outdoors finishing chores when the two soldiers approached them and asked for cider. Marie was instructed to fetch some, and the soldiers were given five to six glasses from a porcelain pitcher. They drank quickly and left, only to return in about eight minutes asking for more. This time Skinner and Waiters followed her to the cider shed and just as she got to its door, Waiters aimed his carbine at Mme. H.

Pregnant and wearing wooden shoes she begun to run at which time she heard Marie screaming for help. After a neighbor woman refused to open her door to give her refuge, Waiters caught up with Mme. H. and whacked her on the head with the butt of his carbine and helmet. With Mme. H. immobilized, Waiters rejoined Skinner who already had knocked Marie onto the shed's floor. Together they dragged Marie through a gate into the nearby orchard, "took off her drawers," and raped her for seven to ten minutes. Each soldier stood at the gate and kept watch while the other raped. At one point Waiters had fired a shot into a neighbor's door just as Madame entered their home for safety, and he shot to death a young male farmhand, Auguste L., who had come running from the fields when he and Mr. H. heard Marie's screams for help.[128] Waiters also shot Mr. H. twice in the back before joining Skinner.

Marie fought back as best she could and inflicted two or more bites on Waiters that were later helpful in identifying him as one of her assailants. Her injuries where much more serious – she had lacerations on her forehead, shoulder, bruises, and a depression in her skull that is easily visible in the trial transcript photos.

She was hospitalized for at least 5 weeks, but she eventually recovered enough to return to work and along with her mother and the parents of Auguste L., to attend the February 10, 1945 field executions of Skinner and Waiters. Marie later married but had a hard time of; her husband was a heavy drinker and he beat her. One of her children – perhaps her only one, a girl – was killed in a car accident at 18. Marie died shortly after her daughter was buried.

Punishments

One should be wary of embracing too uncritically the idea that punishment was the means to the simple end of crime control during war for the sake of military discipline. A more complex approach examines the punishments for rape as an exhibition, as well as an influence, of the webs of social relationships and cultural meanings within and beyond the ETO. It is therefore with due caution that I report almost exclusively on the technical aspects of the wartime rape punishments. More will be said about this in Chapter Six.

Of the 116 soldiers (94 black; 22 white) who were tried for rape in France, more than half, 67 (56%) received life sentences. Within this group, 52 (78%)

were black and 13 (19%) were white. The race of two (3%) who received life sentences is unknown. Only one soldier, a black, had his life sentence reduced by the JAG Board of Review.

In France, 34 soldiers were executed for crimes against French citizens or refugees.[129] Of this number, 21 were executed for rape. Of those executed for rape, almost all – 18 – were black, 3 were white. The disproportionate number of blacks executed in France is far in excess of their presence in the Army where they represented only 10 percent of the troops.

Not all of the US soldiers sentenced to death in France for rape were in fact executed. Forty-nine soldiers were sentenced to death but more than half, 26, had their fate changed by the JAG Board of Review and were given life sentences. Twenty-one of these soldiers were black. Only one black soldier, Pfc. George J. Skipper, 24, small and with a scar on his left cheek, who was convicted of raping Mlle. Marie R., also 24, on September 3, 1944 near Mazencourt-Frences, Somme, had a death sentence changed first to life, then to twenty years.

Conclusions

Caution is prudent here – the explanations and examples of rape in wartime are not mutually exclusive. Historical portraits of the prevalence of wartime rapes lies somewhere between the recorded voices of its victims and their supporters, and the willingness of a victorious military to permit and control it. Within these limitations, it is reasonable to conclude that until mechanisms are in place to address each of these factors, the prevalence of wartime rape will be nearly impossible to determine.

The iconography of France's liberation dwells on images of enthusiastic crowds of civilians embracing their American liberators whom they showered with flowers, spontaneous and inflamed kisses, and alcohol. It is well recorded that GIs welcomed the outpouring of popular gratitude and generously distributed chocolate bars and cigarettes to people who had been deprived of such treats for years. These images are accurate, but they tell only part of the story of Liberation.

This work reports other facts and images of France's World War II experiences. It is part of the contemporary efforts to understand and to prevent wartime rapes, as well as to provide a wide range of assistance to its victims. It is also part of French historians' efforts to better understand how its women experienced World War II.[130] The military records of the reported gratuitous rapes committed by US soldiers in the ETO provide excellent data on this neglected aspect of the liberation.

The harshness of the military sentences was consistent with the two cultural traits in the United States: the then popular and legal perspective that viewed women as either Madonnas or less, and the severity of military justice.[131] Often the French women fought with their rapists and thus confirmed

American notion then of how innocent and virtuous females were expected to react to sexual predators. There is no doubt that while the punishments were legal and consistent with military juridical logic, they addressed other cultural consumers. Some of the executions were used for public relations. They were preceded by letters of apology to the victims and were attended at times not only by US military personnel but also by French police, the rape victim(s), and her family and friends. Fifteen of the 21 soldiers were executed in public.

The rapes in Germany occurred in a significantly different context than the ones in the United Kingdom and France. One result is that the "last offensive" provides additional insights into the patterns of rape, rape victims, their attackers and the punishments they received.

5
Germany – Operation Plunder

Three-year-old Ingrid C. was asleep at home in Auerbach, Germany, with her mother nearby, when at about midnight on August 21, 1945, someone knocked on the door for a long time. No one got up to see who was making the noise. Later an intruder broke into the home.[1] Her mother, Frau C., testified that she heard footsteps and the muffled cry of her daughter. For some reason, she did not rise to investigate, perhaps because she thought the knocking and noise was made by the American soldier Private Gilbert F. Newburn, white, 46th Quartermaster Graves Registration Company. He was in the habit of visiting Frau H., who also lived in the house.

Next morning, at about 5:00 a.m., he was found lying beside Ingrid. Her head was close to Newburn's, and she was at the opposite end of the crib from where she had been placed when her mother put her to bed. None of her outer clothes had been removed, but she was naked from the waist down.

There was blood on her body, but no open wound. Blue marks were found on her back. She was sleeping as if exhausted. Newburn was fully clothed, except for his trousers. They were on the floor and they had blood on the front.

A German and an American physician examined the child. They found her genital organs extremely swollen, her vagina was slightly injured and it contained a discharge. Clotted blood, an incontinence of feces and urine were found. Two tears extended from the labia toward the anus. The doctors concluded that penetration of the vagina had occurred, possibly "caused by a rigid penis."[2]

Newburn left the house on the morning he was found in the child's crib and returned near 9:00 a.m. when he repaired the broken windowpane, and departed. At about 5:00 p.m., he again returned to the house and inquired as to why the matter had been reported to an officer. Newburn said he had no idea what had happened because the night before he had been very drunk and could not remember. After being told that the child would need extensive medical treatment, he volunteered to give her poor family money.

He made two extra-judicial comments, one on the 26th and the other on the 30th of August. In each statement Newburn denied knowing anything about the incident. In the second statement, he admitted that he had an appointment with Frau H., which she did not keep. After she did not appear at their appointed place, Newburn said he did go to her house and bang on the door and entered by breaking a window.

Newburn also admitted that he entered the crib thinking that the mother and baby slept together. Then, "thinking the baby was the mother, I inserted my penis into her vagina."[3]

Newburn denied that he was ever in the child's room before. He further denied that he ever saw blood on his trousers before he gave them to Frau H. for laundering. Soldiers in his company testified that he had drunk a large quantity of schnapps on the evening in question. There was no doubt he was drunk.

Consent was not an issue at his trial because of the child's age. It was noted that at common law all sexual intercourse with a girl of tender age was criminal as she was conclusively presumed not to have consented.[4] Newburn's defense boiled down to extreme intoxication. It was contradicted by his pretrial statements that gave evidence to his detailed recollection of his actions on the night of the rape. The court concluded, therefore, that it was unnecessary to consider whether intoxication in any degree short of psychosis ever constitutes a defense for rape. Newburn, 26, was tried in Heidelberg, Germany on October 16–17, 1945, found guilty, and sentenced to confinement at hard labor for life.

* * *

No country in the twentieth century epitomized the image of evil more distinctly in American minds than Nazi Germany – it continues to fascinate and to horrify.[5] It is rather ironic to realize that absent this legacy, the notion of America's World War II soldiers as the embodiment of good – courageous, selfless, and loyal supporters of democracy – would have much less purchase. The fact of the matter is that the American presence in the European Theater of Operations (ETO) had a very distinct and ugly underbelly. As with the previous chapters, I hope that this one helps to redress the balance between the popular image of American soldiers on the way to V-E Day, and the entirety of their conduct. The vulnerability of German women was at its highest during the Allies' presence in Germany. At this time most of Germany's men were away at war, and in some places the country had experienced horrific physical destruction.

The first German rape complaint that resulted in a general courts-martial trial happened just about a month after Eisenhower's armies went on the offensive in the last stages of the Battle of the Bulge, January 1945. The day before the February 7, 1945 crime, Eisenhower had given the orders to mount what was called Operation Grenade. It was designed to strike the German army along the Roer River, just east of the Belgium border and in the German towns of Linnch and Dueren.[6] Some months before, in September and October 1944, nearby Aachen, Germany, had been the "scene of the first major battle fought by Eisenhower's forces on German soil which began the battle of Germany."[7]

The rapist, Private First Class Wardell W. Wilson, was from the black 777th Field Artillery Battalion, XVI Corps, under Major General John B. Anderson. He had left his assigned station at an observation post in Driesch, Germany, at about 5:00 p.m. and traveled to the nearby town of Haaren. There, during a time of approximately three hours, Wilson twice raped Frau Sibilla J., once vaginally, the other time by oral sex. He also had a violent confrontation with Mrs. Helene von D.F.[8] He was found guilty by three-fourths of the members of the court – a unanimous decision would have meant death. Wilson was sentenced to life in prison at hard labor.

Wilson's assaults were just the beginning of numerous forms of sexual abuses that German females experienced at the hands of victorious Allied soldiers, especially the Soviets.[9] Records indicate that no Allied army failed to rape, including the British, French, and Americans. This is the first systematic treatment of the subject outside of a discussion of legal issues that were summarized by the Judge Advocate General (JAG).[10]

The German setting

When the Allied forces landed on the Normandy beaches on June 6, 1944, the nearly six years of war that Germany had initiated in 1939 were close to ending. It took only 11 more months of fighting before the Nazis surrendered at General Eisenhower's headquarters, a red brick boy's school at Reims, on May 7, 1945.[11] By this time Hitler's dream of creating a thousand-year Third Reich (empire) was in shambles. Germany "was prostrate, almost every square inch of territory under the control of victors."[12] Gone were the times of high spirits that followed such feats as "The dazzling victory over France in 1940 [that] had profound effects on Germany."[13] Much had changed between the time of the July 20, 1944 attempt on Hitler's life and Germany's surrender. "Endurance changed to apathy, personal survival became more important than the national interest."[14]

One goal here is to avoid any attempt to explain or to add anything new to the major military and political dimensions of the ETO. Others have done this with better insight and scholarly erudition than I bring to these topics.[15] Here a modicum of military and political history is necessary to illuminate the domestic life and other circumstances that German citizens and its millions of impressed workers endured during six years of war. Most important, I concentrate on the last year of the war as the Allies were closing in on Berlin.

Another goal – as with the discussions of the United Kingdom and France – is to describe and analyze the suffering that German women experienced at the hands of American soldiers. The number of rapes in Germany was much higher than in the United Kingdom where the US military had moderate success in preventing sexual assaults. Living conditions in most of Germany rendered women more vulnerable to rape than in France. German women had few sources of meaningful protection. Not only were housing conditions, especially in larger cities, extremely difficult and compromised, the German women were the *enemy's women*. In the highly ideological context of victors and vanquished, they were the most vulnerable women to the American soldiers.

In addition to their physical, mental, and emotional distress, German women were rendered more vulnerable by the attitudes of some of the American military officers than their sisters were in the United Kingdom and France. MacDonald's astute 1973 observation about plunder and looting is just as pertinent for rape. "How much of this went on depended in large measure at first on the attitude of company, battalion, and regimental commanders."[16] Much closer to the ground Captain Ted Kadin, a Jew and civilian lawyer before joining the US Army, developed a poignant and powerful defense strategy that tapped into anti-German sentiments. At a general court martial, he represented three black soldiers accused of murdering a German man. They had beaten him to death with a table leg after he had tried to remove one or two German women from the building where they were living with the soldiers. In their defense, Kadin devalued the German victim as "just another German." He also said to the court, "Six weeks ago we were praising these soldiers for *killing* Germans. It makes no sense to convict them of *murdering* a German now."[17] The soldiers were found guilty, but not executed.

Since late February 1933, everyday life in Germany was shaped, according to Forster, "by a perpetual state of emergency and by a dictatorial regime that (after September 1, 1939) murdered millions of its racial and ideological enemies."[18] This description should not be taken as evidence that life in Germany was particularly bad or intolerably compromised for all of its citizens. Reminiscences by steelworkers in the Ruhr region recalled Hitler's political party not for its terror and mass murder, "but by reduction of unemployment, economic boom, tranquility and order."[19]

German industry, it must be remembered, was centered around and subordinate to requirements of the Nazis since 1933.[20] "Yet there was no total economic mobilization to counter the probability of attrition in a long war."[21] Until mid-1944, "by and large, business as usual prevailed." At this time the Nazis introduced a series of measures that addressed food shortages, froze prices and wages, and regulated working conditions.[22] Living conditions in German cities generally did not deteriorate significantly until the massive Allied bombing campaigns of 1942–1943.[23]

Before these ameliorative measures were established, the Nazis had followed Hitler's plan of cutting up the European cake, as he called it, by domination, administration, and exploitation.[24] It amounted to nothing less than what in 1960, William L. Shirer termed "The Nazi Plunder of Europe." In his words, "The total amount of loot [taken] will never be known; it has proven beyond man's capacity to accurately compute." To this day efforts continue to address the hoary question of whom or which institutions were accountable for and actually owns pieces of property, art works, and bank accounts the Nazis stole.[25]

Massive amounts of goods were taken from conquered countries. From Russia in 1943, Germany took "deliveries" of "9 million tons of cereals, 2 million tons of fodder, 3 million tons of potatoes, 662,000 tons of meat … 9 million cattle, 12 million pigs, 13 million sheep, to mention a few items."[26] Poland fared no better – hundreds of thousand of Polish farms were grabbed without compensation and given to German settlers. It lost more than 709,000 estates and more than 20 million acres to the Nazis.[27] It is little wonder food rationing in Germany was relatively stable until early to mid-1945.

The first years of war hardly impacted its standard of living. This was accomplished through a number of avenues, including an accumulation of raw materials, adequate food supplies and the fact that some goods could be imported from Russia (until June 1941).[28] Food rationing was first reduced in the spring of 1942. In 1939 and 1940, for example, there was no weekly bread ration for an adult in Germany. In mid-1940, the weekly (adult) bread rationing was 2,400 grams. Between this date and October 1944, bread rationing varied; sometimes it was higher and during other times it was lower. By April 1945, the weekly bread allotment for an adult was 900 grams.

A similar pattern of decline existed for meat. An adult was given 550 grams of meat weekly in September 1939. By April 1945, it was down to 137 grams weekly.[29]

The rationing of fats also declined precipitously. Beginning in September 1939, adults were given 310 grams of fat weekly. By April 1945, the allotment of grams of fat was 74.

As early as May 1943 "there were no more onions," according to the recollections of Edith Hahn Beer.[30] In wrenching detail she recalled her young life – first as law student forced out of Vienna into a labor camp, then as refugee living underground scavenging for food, and later as a Nazi officer's wife who gave birth to their child.

By the outbreak of the war in 1939, unemployment in Germany was virtually nonexistent. Its workforce at this time exceeded 39 million, 14.6 million of whom were women, and approximately three hundred thousand foreign workers.[31] Five years later, the workforce had 28.6 million Germans and 7.1 million foreign workers. "Nearly all of them had been rounded up by force, deported to Germany in boxcars, usually without food or water or any sanitary facilities."[32] In the latter number were 5.3 million forced laborers and 1.8 million prisoners of war.[33] These numbers do not include all of the concentration camp labor. German aircraft production saw a tenfold increase in labor from this source of exploitation in one year – 1944.[34]

By June 1944, the trades had experienced a shortage of apprentices that was so severe that it was used as a justification for kidnapping children abroad between the ages 10 and 14, and shipping them to Germany. This operation – code name "Hay Action – was "not only aimed at preventing a direct reinforcement of the enemy's strength but also as a reduction of his biological potentialities."[35]

The early war did not bring fresh recruitments of women into the factories, as had occurred in the United Kingdom. On ideological grounds, the Nazis resisted the "armed forces' demand for compulsory work service for women and they paid married soldiers generous allowances"[36] so their wives could stay home. In May 1941, for example, there were 400,000 fewer German women in the workforce than in May 1939.[37] As early as 1942, Hitler had ordered Fritz Sauckel, who carried the title of Plenipotentiary General for the Allocation of Labor and who was described by portly Hermann Goring as a pig-eyed little man, to get a half million Slavic women "in order to relieve the German housewife."[38] Women imported for housework were to have no free time. They were prohibited from entering restaurants, movies, theaters, and other similar places, including churches.

It would be an error, according to Wilke, to assume that the enhanced status of German women under the Nazis resulted in households retaining their dominant role in rearing and training children. In its place, schools became "the dominant instrument for the dissemination of racial propaganda [and they] helped to win young minds for the system and made them receptive to militaristic ideas and practices."[39] As the Nazis moved toward war, demands on women changed. They were "expected increasingly to combine the roles of mother, housewife, Party member and industrial worker."[40] In the latter role, they were increasingly subject to the same military discipline as the prisoner-of-war slaves with whom they worked alongside. By May 1944, things had changed dramatically for working women. By then, women comprised more than 50 percent of the native German workforce in what had been the pre-war German territory.

Women, according to Shirer, were almost as necessary as men in the Nazi slave labor program.[41] More than half of the three million Russians forced into German servitude were women who ended up doing heavy farm work or labor in factories. The working conditions for male and female slave workers were atrociously bad. Beatings, disease, and exposure to the cold were commonplace.

According to Shirer, it was such conditions as these that prompted the "senior doctor" of the Krupp gun manufacturing empire to complain to its directors. In an affidavit at his Nuremberg trail, Dr. Wilhelm Jaeger described finding Krupp's female slaves suffering from open, festering wounds, and other diseases. They had no shoes, their sole clothing was nothing but a sack with a hole cut in it for their arms and head, and their hair was shorn. Their food was meager and of poor quality – their barracks were flea invested.[42]

Jaeger's affidavit also contained information about how 600 Jewish women already living in the horrid conditions of the Buchenwald concentration camp in southwestern Germany, were being transported to work for Krupp. Their living accommodations were a bombed-out work camp from which "the previous inmates, Italian POWs had been removed."[43] French prisoners of war in one of Krupps work camps in Nogerratstrasse, Essen, were kept in dog kennels, urinals, and in old baking houses. "There was no water in the camp."[44]

Quite paradoxically the Nazi regime presented itself as the defenders and upholders of conventional law and order, but reality was something else. While it arrested and prosecuted prostitutes, for example, it set up brothels "for German soldiers, foreign workers and in concentration camps."[45]

Before 1939 Germany had already become a centralized state ruled by one party – there were no checks and balances to Hitler's dictatorship.[46] As National Socialism expanded its control over its citizens, "The judiciary, like the police was part of the public security organization, an instrument of Hitler's will to discipline and purge society."[47] Draconian verdicts were commonplace and often motivated by political considerations, but not all judges condemned women and men to the gallows. "Although the statistics of the criminal courts are incomplete, almost 15,000 death sentences were passed between 1933 and 1944, of which over three-quarters were carried out."[48] In late December 1944, nearly 198,000 men and women were in prison.[49]

The military had its own legal system for dealing with crimes against military and civil codes. At one point, it had more than thousand military courts and more than three thousand military lawyers. Its judges' primary purpose was maintaining military discipline.[50] As the war progressed, discipline increasingly became a matter of some urgency. Deserters were a special problem. While it is unclear whether all of the Wehrnacht executions were for this offense, its statistics "reveal that 9,732 persons were executed up to the end of 1944."[51]

Near the end of the war the military established mobile courts, presumably to handle increasing disciplinary problems. The entire courts-martial apparatus worked until May 1945. It may have been responsible for "A total figure of at least 21,000 executions."[52]

The Nazis also had a severe and deadly set of rules and directives for handling recalcitrant male slave workers. One directive, reported by Shirer, prohibited Polish nationals from any longer having the right to *complain* about their working conditions. Nor could they go to church, theaters, or other cultural entertainment. Males were prohibited from having sexual intercourse with Polish females – sexual intercourse with German females was punishable by death. Heinrich Himmler, the SS head, declared in late February 1942 that for severe violations against discipline, such as refusing to work or loafing, offenders would be given "special treatment" – hanging.[53]

By late November 1944, civilian crimes were reported to have increased dramatically. In Berlin, where 60 percent of its 2,000,000 population lived with no windows, "[a]bout thirty murders [were] committed during each air-raid alert, mostly in connection with robbers."[54] The primary crime motive was usually ration cards.

The numbers here are staggering and can only be treated fleetingly in this space. The total number of deaths is unknowable and yet a matter of dispute. Soviet prisoners of war provide an illustrative example. There is no doubt that the SS killed Soviet prisoners of war (POW). As Forster notes, "Apologists estimate several tens of thousands, other assessments begin at 140,000 and go up to 600,000." More Soviet POWs died under other German armed forces than under the SS. "These numbers range from 1.68 million to 2.53 million and up to 3.3 million, out of a total of 5.7 million prisoners taken between 1941 and 1945."[55] These numbers beg for comparison to the number of Jewish deaths caused by the Nazi's Final Solution. In Forster's estimation, "In its magnitude this crime is comparable to the mass murder of the Jews."[56]

Britain's Royal Air Force (RAF) began its bombing of German ports and industrial targets in 1940. Until the Allies joined them they had conducted the entire burden of air warfare against Germany for three years.[57] During this time, the RAF had caused considerable destruction and disruption in Germany, notably in March 1942 at Lubeck, Essen, Cologne – the latter was hit with 1,000 bombers. But the RAF had not been able to inflict massive damage and demoralization to the point of defeating the Germans. Their efforts became more effective with American-made planes, and after the US Eighth Air Force joined the air attacks in August 1942.

The Eighth Airforce was created in the spring of 1942 as part of a massive and detailed Allied-backed effort to develop a concerted program that would be superior to the air power of Germany's *Luftwaffe*. By January 1943, "it was ready for its first attack on Germany proper."[58] Its readiness coincided with the beginning of the year that saw the turning of the tables against Germany.[59]

At the risk of being too succinct, 1943 was a bad year for the German war effort. First, they and their Italian allies were defeated in North Africa in May, which was soon followed by an Allied invasion in Sicily, Italy, on July 10. By July 13, 1943, it was in the Allies hands. Shortly thereafter between July 24 and August 3 Hamburg, Germany, was hit with a series of the most effective to-date air attacks of the European campaign. These assaults caused about fifty thousand deaths and created between 400,000 and 800,000 homeless.

By November 1944, living conditions and morale were so low in Berlin that on average 50 people committed suicide per day, according to "private advices."[60]

Meanwhile, Mussolini, the leader of the Italian Fascists, had resigned and was arrested, at first protected by the Germans and finally shot by partisans, mutilated, and hanged by his heels in Milan in late April, 1945.

Germany's fortunes were no better in Russia. In early July, they launched their last great offensive against the Soviets – by July 22, they had lost half of their tanks and suffered a decisive defeat, and the Russian offensive against Germany was spread across the entire front as the Russians headed for Berlin.[61] The German sea war fared no better, possibly even worse than its land war. By the early 1943, the "Allies had gained the upper hand over the U-boats, thanks to ... using long range aircraft and carriers and, above all, ... radar which spotted ... submarines before the latter could sight them."[62]

It was into these maelstroms that American soldiers entered the last offensive. Most of them had by now become seasoned soldiers. That they had "come fully of age had been amply demonstrated in the Ardennes."[63] By the end of March 1943, some of the American columns passing through German villages were shouting "*schlafen mit?*" (Sleep with me).[64] According to official figures, by this date no less than 82 American soldiers had already committed rape in Germany.

American rapes in Germany: findings

Based on the examination of the 34 volumes of *BOR/JAG* opinions, between January 7, 1945 and September 23, 1945 – date of the last rape it reviewed – the US Army tried and convicted 284 soldiers in 187 cases of rape in Germany.[65] (See Table 5.1.)

These convictions involved 344 soldiers present at the scene of the crime; half (50%) were white. Black soldiers accounted for 158 of the soldiers at the crime scene, or 46 percent. Yet, a slightly higher percentage of black soldiers were convicted (49%) than were present at the crime scene.

If the three Native Americans are counted as whites, the number of whites convicted would be 140, or 49 percent – the same percentage as black convictions. Conversely, if the Native Americans are classified as blacks (they were not), the number of blacks convicted would be 141, or 50 percent.

Perhaps the most significant finding is that the percentage of white soldiers who were convicted is greater in Germany than in either the United Kingdom or France. However, black soldiers were again overrepresented as convicted rapists, while white soldiers were underrepresented. This information is presented in Table 5.1.

A total of 243 females were victims. This figure is based on cases found in *BOR/JAG*. If these numbers represent only 5 percent of the rape victims, the number of women sexually assaulted might have been (20 × 243) 4,860.

Table 5.1   Convictions by race in the United Kingdom, France, and Germany

	United Kingdom	France	Germany
Black	23 (64%)	95 (82%)	138 (49%)
White	11 (31%)	21 (18%)	137 (48%)
Unknown	2 (5%)		6 (2%)
N. Americans			3 (1%)
Total	36 (100%)	116 (100%)	284 (100%)

The numbers from the *HOB/JAG* presented a different picture. Its tabular reports indicate that Germany had 484 "girls" raped by American troops. If this number is correct, and if Radzinowicz's 5 percent rule is applied to Germany, the total number of rapes approximates 9,680 (484 × 20= 9,680). The following discussion is based on the 187 rape cases found in the *BOR/JAG* reports.

It is quite clear – regardless of the source – that the rapes and complaints about them were not distributed evenly over the months the US Army was fighting in Germany. According to the *HBO/JAG*'s account, the number of accusations about sexual assaults began in January 1945 and grew slowly until February. The complaints grew precipitously until April – at this point the complaints peaked, presumably, as did the actual rapes.(See Graph 5.1.)

According to this source, the complaints in April 1945 were approximately two hundred and sixty. The distance between the peak of the bold line and

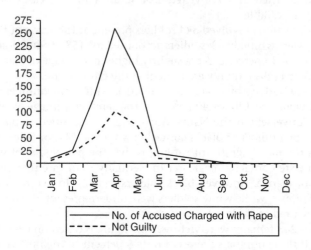

Graph 5.1   No. accused with rape

Adapted from HBO/JAG, chapter 1, chart 16.

peak of the broken line suggests that approximately one hundred and fifty soldiers were convicted. This number, if correct, represents only 10 more convictions that were found in the *BOR/JAG* – it contains 140 convictions for April 1945.

Patterns of gratuitous rapes

The data reported here is incomplete because some of the records were too sparse or vague to determine the extent of the victims' and offenders' relationship.

Date rape

According to *BOR/JAG* records this type of sexual assault did not appear in Germany.

Acquaintance rape

Only two rapes in Germany were of this type. They involved offenders who had a working relationship with the victim(s). In one instance, the soldier raped a woman who had been doing his laundry. In France there were no rapes of this type; in England, acquaintance rape happened 8 times.

Partial stranger rapes

Thirty-two (19%) involved victims who had been seen by their assailant, or had been in contact with each other, prior to the crime. Forty percent of the rapes in France involved partial strangers. In England 13 percent of the rapes were of this type.

Stranger rapes

Seventy percent (N = 131) of the rapes in Germany involved rapists and victims who had never met before. Once contact had been made, the offenders and victims were not separated until the crime was completed. This type of rape represented a 14 percent increase over the same type of rape pattern in France, and a 23 percent increase over what happened in England.

Unknown

The type of relationship in 12 percent of the rape cases (N = 22) is unknown.

Other patterns

Typical pattern

The major rape pattern in Germany became so obvious that the JAG described it in more than one of their reviews. It stated, "The undisputed facts show that this case falls into the typical pattern of German rape cases."[66] Two soldiers entered a home at night in a somewhat isolated section of a town. The incident that prompted this response occurred in

Auerbach. One of the two assailants was armed with a pistol when they proceeded to the second floor where three women were sleeping. One woman was the stepmother of the other two – they were sisters. The soldier armed with a pistol took one of the women, this time the stepmother, downstairs and locked the outside door. They raped the three women and left.

Sodomy

Another trend that was discussed by *HBO/JAG* involved the fact that the rapes in Germany were often more brutal and humiliating than in the United Kingdom and France. German women were beaten, hit with rifles, fists, knocked unconscious, raped in front of the husbands, children, mothers, grandparents, friends, lodgers, and various other witnesses. In addition to the rapes, according to the official records, the German victims were increasingly forced to submit to anal and oral assaults. *HBO/JAG* concluded that "this trend reached a crescendo during the German Phase."[67]

On April 7, 1945, Waltraud S., 24 and married, was living with her child and three other women in Bremke, Germany. Between 8:30 p.m. and 8:45 p.m., she heard the glass in her door broken as it was kicked in by four American soldiers. They searched the house, found a bottle of alcohol and some eggs that one of the women was forced to fry. The soldiers left at 10:30 p.m.

After midnight, two soldiers reentered the house. One of them had been with the four soldiers who had departed earlier. The other soldier was Private First Class Jack C. Kelley, white, Battery B, of the 207th Field Artillery Battalion. He pulled Waltraud into the bedroom and placed his pistol against her child's breast when it began to cry. Waltraud managed to get the child into the kitchen. By this time, the other soldier had gathered the other women there, too.

Kelley forced Waltraud into the bedroom again, compelled her to undress, and raped her for about an hour. He also placed "his head between her legs for 'quite a while.'"[68] According to the records, "he was very brutal."[69] His blond companion then raped her.

The same night Kelly and three soldiers also raped Waltraud's neighbor, Fraulein Elfriede E., 21. She was living with her farmer parents and had retired fully dressed because of the nearby artillery fire – it probably came from Kelley's organization. She was awakened at about 10:20 p.m. by knocking on her door and several loud voices. Kelley slapped her several times on the face and forced her to accompany him as he searched the house. In her room, he forced Fraulein Elfriede to lay on her bed, removed his pants and made her "remove all her clothes."[70] All of the soldiers raped her.

Fraulein Elfriede's sister-in-law, Agnes N., lived next door with Annie M., a 30-year-old housewife with two children. She, too, was in bed fully dressed because of the shelling. About 1:00 a.m., she heard a noise in the back of the house and the sound of a window broken. Kelley entered the house, locked the door, took one of her children out of her bed and placed it in a nearby bed. He motioned for her to undress. When she refused to remove all of her clothes, Kelley hit her on the head and face with his pistol. After raping her twice, he forced her to kneel "and put his penis into her rectum."[71] She was then forced to "take his penis in her mouth and on her refusal pushed her head down, held her tight and had his penis in her mouth three times, each time causing her to throw up."[72] She finally escaped naked into another room. Kelley, 22, left the house at about 2 a.m. He was convicted of rape and sodomy, and sentenced to confinement at hard labor for life.

The afternoon attack on Louise W. in Hockenheim, Germany, is an exemplary example of an "appallingly brutal attack" by two white infantrymen, Private First Class Willie E. Lucero and Homer E. Miller.[73] The victim had ridden her bicycle to visit her mother. As she neared her, Louise W. was stopped by Lucero and Miller, and ordered to a nearby railroad station. Her mother rushed to her aid, and Lucero punched her in the face. While she scrambled away to get help, Lucero forced her daughter into a backroom of the station. She pleaded with him to no avail – he raped her. When he had finished he noticed, "he was entirely bloody." Blood was on the inside and outside of his trousers, shirt and person. "He made her lick the blood off his penis and then made her take it in her mouth."[74]

Major Roland E. Nieman, Medical Corps, examined Lucero and gave him two intelligence tests. The first test indicated that Lucero had a mental age of a little more than 8 years, with an IQ of 58. The second test suggested he had a mental age of ten years and an IQ of 73 – any score between 68 and 80 was considered borderline. Lucero could distinguish between right and wrong, according to Nieman. He was convicted and sentenced to hard labor for life.

Marauding

By late March, 1945, another pattern of rape was evident – small groups of marauding soldiers would tell other soldiers where to find women they had already raped. Illustrative is the case of three black soldiers who raped four women at night in Sprendlingen, Hesse, Germany. The soldiers were from the 642nd Quartermaster Truck Company – it had pulled into Sprendlingen at about 4 p.m., bivouacked in a field, and posted guards. Some of the company "went into the woods to look for snipers and souvenirs."[75]

About 7:45 p.m., Katherine W. and her 18-year-old daughter, Charlotte, were at home when three uninvited soldiers entered their house. They used candlelight to examine the women and tried to force them upstairs. They escaped and ran across the street and hid in their neighbor's cellar. The soldiers followed them but failed to find their hiding place.

Their neighbors feared the soldiers, and they would not allow Katherine and Charlotte to remain with them. The mother and daughter went to another neighbor who permitted them to hide in a small room next to their kitchen. The black soldiers entered this house, perhaps three times, and searched it without finding the women. Shortly after midnight, three black soldiers discovered them – two of the soldiers had been with the three soldiers who had entered the women's home the first time at about 7:45 p.m.

The soldiers separated the mother and daughter, who kept calling "Mama, Mama."[76] They were forced upstairs and each was placed on a bed in the same room. Nelums raped Katherine first, then her daughter, but not before Jackson with the help of Garrett, had raped Charlotte. Different soldiers raped the daughter repeatedly. "[T]he personnel in the room was shifting constantly during the period from 11:30 p.m. and 1:30 a.m. and that in all, six colored soldiers attacked her."[77] Later the same night, some of the same soldiers who had raped Katherine and Charlotte, entered two additional homes and raped more women. The number of rapists was fluid with one or two soldiers joining or leaving the group as it marauded from house to house.

Procurement

Most of the marauding/buddy rapes victims were assaulted in the same place they had been found. If they were moved from one place to another it was most often within the same building. Usually it was the soldiers who moved from place to place. Abducted victims were raped and thrown aside, or raped and transported back to where they had been before being raped. Perhaps the only case of explicit procurement that went to trial happened in early April, 1945. It involved two white soldiers who ended up getting charged with rapes that they did not commit.

Private First Class Alfred F. Willet and Pvt. William Carreon, Battery A, 227th Field Artillery Battalion, were both charged, first, with felonious house breaking, and the rape of Vera K., a slave laborer who had been brought to Germany in 1942.[78] On the night of April 8–9, the soldiers broke into the home of an elderly farmer, Wilhelm L. who lived with his son, two Hollanders,[79] a Pole, and Vera K. Eleven Italians slept in an adjoining barn.

The soldiers gathered all of the people into the barn, exclaiming that they were the "American control."[80] They asked their names and told them they could all go to bed. Willet and Carreon accompanied Vera to her room, covered her with a blanket, ordered her to go to sleep, and departed. "About five minutes later both accused returned to Vera's room."[81] Despite her struggles, Carreon removed her pants, nightie, and brassiere. At first he did not have intercourse because of her resistance, but he did "succeed in injecting his penis into her mouth."[82]

After Carreon finished, he held Vera's hands down, and Willet raped her while she screamed with pain – it was her first intercourse. When Willet finished, the soldiers helped dress her, and all three of them went downstairs. She was blindfolded and "escorted … to a house ten or twenty minutes distance by walking."[83] Four different and unknown men assaulted her there – three of them had sexual intercourse. Carreon sat by her feet until the four men had finished, then he "picked up Vera and … took her to another house where he lay on her the rest of the night."[84] At daybreak, he had intercourse with her again, gave her clothes and told her to go away. Carreon and Willet were charged with raping Vera. They were also charged and convicted of the rapes by the three unknown men "on the theory that they occurred, as a result of the procurement by both accused and with the active participation of Carreon who sat at her feet, as a continued threat during each intercourse."[85]

Remorse

A few of trial transcripts and reviews contained information indicating that some rapists were remorseful. Unfortunately, it is impossible to determine the extent or sincerity of this experience. The scarcity of evidence about it in the military records is not a fair measure of its nonexistence, especially among those soldiers who were drunk or under the influence of alcohol at the time of their crimes. None of the records indicated that any of the offenders were asked *ex post facto* how they felt about their crimes.

Private First Class William J. Blakely, white, Company H, 405th Infantry, however, did feel repentant and self-condemning. About 12:30 a.m., April 9, 1945, he entered a dwelling on Moor Strasse, Borgholzhausen, Westfalen, Germany. He pointed his pistol at the head of Wilhelm M. and said in German, "Daughter, sleep." At first Ruth M.'s father refused to take Blakely to her, but after Blakely released the safety on his pistol, he complied and took him to his living quarters where his wife and daughter were in bed.[86]

Pistol in hand, Blakely said to Ruth: "[S]leep (have sexual intercourse) or father and mother kaput."[87] When she did not undress quickly, he repeated the statement, and pushed the 17-year-old girl down on the bed. Every time she resisted his advances, he threatened her with the weapon and said, "Father and mother kaput." He raped her in front of her mother and father.

The record states that "After the intercourse, the accused 'appeared to feel repentant.'"[88] He gave his pistol to Ruth M. and told her she should shoot him. Blakely also told Ruth M.'s mother that he would marry the girl.[89] After 15 to 20 minutes he fell asleep and was taken by the victim's parents to the bed where he had raped her.

It is easy to doubt Blakeley's sincerity. He did nothing more than say he was sorry. He did nothing to affirm or re-affirm his statements. Perhaps he would have done something more if he had not fallen asleep, or had not been awaken by an American officer. The buddy rape involving Pvt. William D. Johnson, Jr., had a different, and arguably, an unambiguous expression of remorsefulness. He and his buddy raped two German women on the same night that Ruth M. was attacked. (Twelve German women according to official military records were raped by US soldiers on April 9, 1945.)

At about 11 p.m., April 9, Johnson and a dark-haired buddy entered a church in Merkers, Germany. It contained about thirty evacuated people from the surrounding and immediate area who were seeking shelter from the chaos caused by the Allied drive to the Elbe River. The armed soldiers asked for wine and were told none was available. At this point they lit a candle and went from bed to bed "inquiring for a red-headed girl and appraising the occupants with such remarks as 'Too young,' and 'Good, nice.'"[90]

When they reached Mrs. Frieda E, who begged to be left alone, the soldiers struck and pulled at her. After she ran away and got caught, they cut off her hair and raped her.[91] Their next victim was Gertrude S., a mother with a young child whom one of the soldiers grabbed by the neck. They tried to kiss Gertrude, but she resisted and escaped as far as the church tower. They dragged her down its steps and forced her onto a bed. The dark-haired buddy kicked, and with Johnson's assistance – he kept her mouth shut – raped her and eventually had an emission.[92]

The next day arrangements were made for the two married victims to attend an identification parade. Shortly before the parade Johnson's dark-haired buddy committed suicide with a piston. The following note was found beside his body. It was in his handwriting and signed by him:

To Whom It May Concern

Saying you're sorry doesn't mean anything but I am. I've gotten away with a lot but this time I went to [*sic*] far.

I raped the woman. I don't know what made me lose control (this was actually my first intercourse), but when drunk you do things you'd never do otherwise. I am mainly concerned about the Army's losing a man when needed, but I cannot stand the disgrace of a trial.

My only request is that my mother be informed that I was killed in action. Our family has a long record of military service to the country, and the shock of the truth may be very serious to her.

Thank you and may God speed you on to Victory and home.[93]

Private Johnson was convicted and sentenced to be confined to hard labor for life.

Who raped?

Service units

The decline of service units involved in the German rapes was the most noticeable change in the patterns of sexual assaults in the ETO.

They represented approximately one-third of the offenders' units compared to the UK and France where most of the rapists came from service units – some of the black rapists in Germany came from truck and construction units.

Frau Kaethe N., 22, married with two children, was walking in the direction of her parents-in-law at about 11:15 p.m. At an intersection on March 7, 1945, "she encountered three blacks, two mulatto and one very dark."[94]

Tech. Fifth Grade John F. Autrey, 3912th Quartermaster Truck Co., the darker one, asked her for her passport. She did not have one, and she kept on walking. Thirty minutes later he was alone and driving a truck when he overcame her. He got out of the truck, pointed his rifle at her and said, "Fuck, fuck,"at the same time he made a sign with his fingers.[95] Her detailed description of what happened merits repeating in full:

> He led me to the truck and then he clasped a hand over my mouth and fired a shot. He was standing behind me. He pushed me into the truck with one hand and held me with the other and then closed the door. He threw me on the seat. He jumped on top of me. He pulled my legs over to the side and threw himself on top of me. He pushed my skirt to the side and he pushed my bloomers over to one side and he forced his mouth on top of my mouth. I had one hand behind me and the other holding underneath the steering wheel. He opened his trousers and removed his sexual organ. With force he jumped on top of me and let everything run into me. Then he got up. I attempted to kick him with my foot. He got up and buttoned-up his trousers. He opened the door and grabbed hold of my right hand and pulled me out. I fell and he remained standing, and then he got in the truck and drove away.[96]

Autrey was found guilty and sentenced to hard labor for life. On the same day – March 7, 1945 – American soldiers sexually assaulted six other women in Germany.

Black rapists in Germany also came from units with responsibilities other than servicing supply needs. Tech. Fifth Grade Elmer L. Spohn and Private Marton L. Whelchel were in Company C, 602nd Tank Destroyer Battalion. One week after Autrey's rape, these soldiers raped Hildagard T. at Immerath, Germany. Between 11:00 p.m. and midnight on March 14, 1945, they went into the home of Matthias T. where he was living with his two daughters, Hildagard,16 and Helga, 13, a son, 9 years old, and his brother-in-law, Joseph S.[97] After being told there was no room for them to sleep, Whelchel whacked Matthias on the chest with a gun, and the two soldiers went upstairs to a bedroom with two beds. They had been drinking – Spohn was drunk – each had a bottle.

Hildagard was awakened and very frightened. Whelchel wanted her to sit on his lap, but she did not understand him. Her uncle, however, spoke English and explained what he wanted. Reluctantly, she complied and Whelchel hit her on the head with his gun, took off her pants and made all her "folk" get on one bed. He pushed her to the other bed and raped her. She fought and his penis came out twice and each time she forced her to put it back in. He stayed on her about an hour, her folks all the time on the other bed, captives.

Spohn meanwhile had vomited and gone to sleep. Whelchel awakened him, and he too raped Hildagard. Next, Whelchel dragged Helga from the bed she and the others had been on, forced her onto the bed with Hildaggard and Spohn, and attempted to rape her. All the while Spohn was on top of her, she cried out "Mother, Mother, I'll die."[98] An Army medical officer examined the girls and found that Hildagard had a torn hymen, a blood clot and purplish discoloration near the entrance. "On the younger girl he found nothing."[99]

At the soldier's trial, First Lieutenant Robert E. Graham of the accused's company, testified on cross-examination that Whelchel had never been court-martialed before. He also stated that he had known Whelchel for two and one-half years, and that "he was one of the best tank destroyer drivers in the ETO."[100] He elaborated further by stating that Whelchel took good care of his vehicle and that on several occasions when their company and been in tight places, Whelchel "always stuck by all of us every time."[101] Neither had Spohn been court-martialed. Before going to the German's home, they had played poker until about 10:30 p.m.

Each soldier was convicted and sentenced to confinement and hard labor for life. Five other German women were raped on the same day as Hildegard.

Black rapists also came from the integrated infantry. In late April 1945, Frau Ida C. was at a house in Schwabach, Germany, when two soldiers, one black the other white, knocked on the door. Private Harry L. Luckey, Company K, 394th Infantry, and a white soldier from the 394th Infantry, entered the house and was led by an old man to a room where six women were seated. A baby was lying on a couch.[102] Luckey searched a chest of drawers, showed some interest in the baby's cradle, searched two bedrooms and returned to the drawing room. He pointed his rifle around the room and showed the occupants that it was loaded. The white soldier put the safety on. Luckey asked two girls some questions, but they did not understand him. Thinking he wanted to know their ages, they replied "ten."[103] He next turned his attention to Frau C. and asked her some questions. She did not answer. From her he turned to one of the young girls – all of the women started to scream.

Luckey changed his mind and selected Frau C., who immediately threw herself on her 18-month-old baby. He pulled her away from her child, slapped her, pointed his gun at her, and directed her into one of the sleeping rooms. He put his rifle against the door, locked it, turned off the light, threw her on the bed, and despite her resistance, raped her.

The white soldier interrupted Luckey by knocking on the door. Angry, he got up and opened the door. The white soldier, thinking that Frau C. was the old man's daughter, tried to get him to call her out of the room. She indicated that she wanted to leave the room, but Luckey shut the door, turned to her, again threw her on the bed and penetrated her once more. Meanwhile, the white soldier knocked on the door again and interrupted Luckey for the second time. This time the two soldiers talked, and Luckey sat down on a bathtub.

Almost immediately thereafter the military police arrived because one of the other women had notified them of the soldiers' behavior. At his trial, Luckey protested the charges against him. He claimed that he had gone to the house looking for cognac. His rifle, he said, was carried in his hands because at 6' 1' he could not get through doorways with it slung over his shoulder. According to his testimony, Frau C. had taken him by the hand into the sleeping room, sat on the bed, and asked for chocolate. He gave it to her, unfastened his trouser, and she guided him into her private parts. The court found him guilty and sentenced him to confinement at hard labor for life.

The *BOR/JAG* records do not reveal any other rapes in Germany on April 29, 1945. Five women were raped the next day, three of them in Hanover.

Buddy rapes

According to the *BOR/JAG* records, 68 (36%) of 187 rapes in Germany involved more than one American assailant. This group of 68 had 159 rapists. Contained in the 159 were 90 (57%) blacks, 66 (42%) whites, and 3 (1%) unknown. The 159 "buddy rapists" represent 56 percent of the 284 American convicted of rape in Germany. This percentage is 3 percent less than found in France, and 9 percent greater than for the United Kingdom. (See Table 5.2.)

This and related information permits N (number) and percentage comparisons of buddy rape incidents by race per country. The results provide some of the most interesting findings of this study. (See Table 5.3.)

This table reveals three distinct patterns. One, the frequency of buddy rape incidents increased from 8 in the United Kingdom, to 42 in France, 68 in Germany, for a total of 118. This pattern is consistent with the fact that as the war became progressively more and more destructive, more and more women became vulnerable to predators. This observation is suggestive rather

Table 5.2 Number (N) and percentage (%) of buddy rapists by country*

	N	%
United Kingdom	17/36	47
France	69/116	59
Germany	159/284	56
Total	234/436	54

*The denominator represents the total number of convicted rapists per country, *BOR/JAG*.

Table 5.3   Buddy rape incidents by race per country*

	United Kingdom	France	Germany
Black	7 (88%)	35 (83%)	36 (53%)
White	1 (12%)	7 (17%)	30 (44%)
Unknown	–	–	2 (3%)
Totals	8 (100%)	42 (100%)	68 (100%) = 118
	8 (7%)	42 (36%)	68(58%) = 118

* Arguably the numbers in this table are far too small to use percentages. They are therefore more suggestive than mathematically sound. The readers are invited to make their own conclusions.

than definitive, because the number of potential rapists also increased per country – there were fewer soldiers in the UK than in the France or Germany.

Second, the number of reported buddy rape incidents involving black American soldiers increased from 7 in the United Kingdom to 35 in France and then 36 in Germany. The number of buddy rapes incidents increased for white solders from a low of 1 in the United Kingdom to 7 in France and 30 in Germany.

Explaining these changes is most challenging. Such efforts are best left to reasonable speculation. Perhaps the number (and the relative and questionable high percentage) of black buddy rape incidents in the United Kingdom happened largely because of the volatile mix of racial stereotyping endemic to America's segregated military and its system of justice, the lack of color barriers, and the lack of adequate sexual opportunities for virile young men away from home. It would certainly be difficult to sustain an argument that the brutalization of war was causal in the United Kingdom where no on-ground fighting occurred.

France had more buddy rapes than the United Kingdom. This can be reasonably explained by the fact that the social contexts in France were more conducive to assaulting vulnerable women. The three most important factors involved, 1) the American image of France and its women as more sexually liberated, especially with blacks, than in either the United States or the United Kingdom; 2) an increase in female vulnerability because of the absence of protective family members and the physical destruction of homes; and 3) a decrease in the military supervision of service units compared to the United Kingdom. The impact of brutalization and insensitivity resulting from frontline fighting and its aftermath no doubt played an indeterminable role for black and white soldiers in France and later in Germany.

There is an abundance of reasonable explanations for the changes in the patterns of buddy rape incidents found in Germany. The traditional answer suggesting that enemy women get raped because they are extremely vulnerable to the victors has great merit. This point was recognized, rightly or wrongly, in numerous military court decisions and reviews. Armed American soldiers entered German homes almost at will, despite military orders to the contrary. They did so primarily at night; frequently they were drunk, and they did not have military brothels as sexual outlets. As attractive as this simple answer is, it is inadequate because it does not address why the gap between black and white incidents of buddy rape closed so radically in Germany compared to the United Kingdom and France.

One possible explanation lies in the fact that as the US troops made progress across France and into Germany and beyond, the racial differences that had separated them in the United States and United Kingdom had begun to shrink. The organization and employment of the black and white soldiers started to more closely resemble each other. At the height of Allied fighting at the Ardennes, the US units, like the Germans, too, had problems with replacements because the manpower well in the United States was showing signs of going dry.[104] The Third Army under the American General Patton, for example, was "particularly short of infantry replacements until well along in the January campaign."[105] To address this problem Eisenhower directed "both a comb-out of rear echelon units and a program whereby Negro service troops might volunteer for the infantry."[106]

By March, 1945, the picture began to change. At this time fifty-three platoons – two or more squads and a headquarters – of black soldiers who had volunteered, "often taking reductions in grade in the process, to leave their service units, went to the front." "In the 12th Army Group the platoons were attached to a number of veteran divisions, usually one to a regiment, to serve under a white lieutenant and platoon sergeant as a fifth platoon in a rifle company."[107] This practice eventually had an impact on the Army's policy of employing blacks only in segregated units, as did the use of blacks in many other fighting units including anti-aircraft artillery, cavalry, field artillery, infantry, and tank units.[108] While the efficiency and morale of black soldiers witnessed noticeable improvements, the most obvious counter argument is that they were still in a segregated army.

Black "buddy rapes" involved more than half of all of the rape incidents that involved two or more offenders, compared to white soldiers. Buddy assailants of unknown race represented few buddy rape incidents. (See Table 5.4.)

Buddy rapes most frequently involved two soldiers and one victim. Black and white soldiers were in twenty two-to-one rape incidents each. An example is found in the case of Privates David McArthur and William "Willie" J. Lee, both of the 3119th Quartermaster Service Company. Their crime occurred in the afternoon of April 6, 1945, at Leider, Germany. Both soldiers had been drinking when they entered the home of Agatha B. Mrs. B.[109] was in the kitchen when McArthur "threw" her on the table, unbuttoned his trousers, and tried to rape her. She successfully defended herself this time, but McArthur forced her to the floor and penetrated her. Her brother-in-law, Johann H. who was repairing the roof of her house, heard Mrs. B.'s screaming and came down to help her.

Table 5.4 Number (N) and percentage (%) of buddy rape incidents by race

	N	Percentage
Black	36	53
White	30	44
Unknown	2	6
Total		100

Mr. H. saw McArthur at one of the doors of the house and was about to enter when an unnamed third soldier used his weapon to force him back up on the roof.[110] Fortunately, he was able to get down from the roof another way and report the episode to the local American commander. The soldiers were taken into custody after they had left the home of the H.s, who lived about 500 feet from the B.s residence.

McArthur and Lee had visited the H. home the same day. Hilda H. heard a knock on her door, and from her window, she could see one of them standing there "with the gun in front of him."[111] She opened the door, and "they just stormed [in] like wild"[112] into the living room where her daughter, Helga H. was located. Lee forced her onto the couch, pulled her up, and pushed her down toward the floor. From his pocket he pulled out a dagger-like knife, cut her under drawers and opened his pants. Several times he mentioned, "kill" to Helga H., but he left the room after McArthur departed. According to the records, "Immediately after the episode, Helga H. had scratches on her face, and one of her cheeks was swollen."[113]

The soldiers were tried, convicted, and sentenced. McArthur received a life sentence of hard labor; Lee got 20 years. On the same day they raped Agatha B., another woman was raped in Leider by an American soldier, Pvt. Billy Reed, 22, from the same unit as McArthur and Lee, the 3119th Quartermaster Service Company. It is possible that he was a companion of McArthur and Lee. If so, it makes more sense to consider the two incidents as involving three rapists instead of two. The victim in the Reed case testified that her assailant was the first "colored soldier" she had seen.[114] The main issue for the court was whether Reed was the alleged rapist. The victim, Frau Ella M., was confused about Reed's identification by the English-to-German translations of the prosecution and defense questions. The court, presumably all white, decided he was her assailant and noted that "It is often difficult to formulate in precise words the reason for one's recognition."[115] He was convicted and sentenced to hard labor for life.

In addition to the pattern of two soldiers assaulting one victim, there were six incidents of two black soldiers raping two victims. Further, there were seven incidents of two white soldiers raping two victims. In the following

Table 5.5 Number (N) of black and white rapists per N of victims

		V1	V2	V3	V4
Black	2 ×	15	6	–	1 = 44
	3 ×	3	5	3	= 33
	4 ×	2	–	–	= 8
	5 ×	1	–	–	= 5
White	2 ×	17	7	–	= 48
	3 ×	4	2	–	= 18
Unknown	3 ×	1	–	–	= 3
Total					= 159

Note: Blacks = 90; Whites = 66; Unknown = 3; V1 = one victim; V2 = two victims; V3 = three victims; V4 = four victims.

case, two soldiers committed various crimes, while one of them raped two women, one at night, the other the next morning. (See Table 5.5.).

On April 15, 1945 at about 7 p.m., two white soldiers, Private Leo F. Manko, 36, and Private First Class Andrew J. Wortheam, 23, each armed with M-1 carbines, entered the house of Herr Richard K., a discharged German soldier. They were searching for German pistols and SS troopers, and found neither. In the attic they found "a quantity of schnapps spirits and removed it to the kitchen," and departed.[116] About an hour and a half later they reappeared in what appeared to be a state of drunkenness. During this visit they asked about the girls and children who lived in the house. They soon departed only to return again in about 15 minutes. During the last visit they found the door locked and pounded on it with their fists. When Herr K. opened the door, Manko, – the "tall one" – seized him by the throat and accused him of watering down the schnapps.

Manko forced his rifle against Herr K.'s chest and dragged him outdoors and beat him in the face with his fists. Several shots were fired – he ran off into the woods and did not return until the next afternoon.[117]

Wortheam – the blond one – meanwhile had grabbed Herr K.'s wife, Agnes, by the throat and carried her into the kitchen and laid her on the couch. He put his M-1 on the floor, pressed his mouth to hers to prevent her from screaming, pulled down her pants, and despite her struggles, raped her.

About 7 a.m the next morning they returned to the house, armed, and because the door was locked, entered through a door connected to the barn. They asked for Herr K. (he was still in the woods) and Stefan S., a Polish farm worker. After searching the house again, Wortheam called for Agnes. When she entered the room he threw her on the bed, choked her, and despite her muffled protests of "I have a husband. I don't do it," screams and resistance, he raped her again.[118]

Later in the morning, Manko ordered Frau Hedwig F., the sister-in-law of Frau K., upstairs. She understood that she was to carry a key to Wortheam who was upstairs searching for schnapps. Wortheam pointed his gun at her as she came up the stairs, forced her to the floor, and over her protestations that she was married and the mother of a young daughter, raped her.

Following the morning rapes, the victims cooked breakfast for the soldiers and asked whether they wanted coffee.[119] Manko fell asleep on a doorstep after eating and remembered nothing, he said, of the previous evening except that he found no SS troopers. Prior to the rapes he had been withdrawn from infantry line duty to join other men in his organization to search for SS troopers. He did remember getting drunk with some Polish refugees and singing with them, however. Wortheam's account of the evening was essentially the same as Manko's. Both admitted that they had drunk excessively on the evening in question. Neither soldier denied their offenses; both were convicted. Manko got hard labor for six years, and Wortheam was sentenced to hard labor for life.[120]

According to Table 5.5, the size of the groups involved in buddy rapes varied by race. The group size for blacks ranged from two to five members. White soldiers raped groups with two or three membersp

Modus operandi: time and place

As in France, the rapes in Germany occurred around the clock. Most of the rapes (56%) took place between 6 p.m. and 6 a.m. (See Graph 5.2.)

It was between these hours that Corporal Lester Berger and Private Donald W. Bamford (probably white), Battery "C," 359th Field Artillery, raped 19-year-old Anneliesa T. Their assault occurred on the night of March 6–7, 1945, right after the US Army Operation Grenada had made a breakthrough at Uerdingen on the Rhine River.[121] On the night of the crime, approximately twelve German civilians were in the "air raid cellar" of Peter T.'s house. At about 11:15 p.m., the two soldiers knocked on the house's door and were let in by two women who led them down in the cellar. They asked for schnapps and liquor and were refused, but nevertheless, seated themselves. At first they conversed in a friendly and jovial manner among themselves. From time to time they drank from their flasks – they had them on their arrival.[122]

Berger fancied Anneliesa T., a daughter of Peter T., and after a while, he told her he was in love with her and that he wanted her to sleep with him. She answered that she slept in the shelter with the others. At this juncture according to the records, the soldiers began to show some antagonism – it increased as the evening progressed. At one point they called the people in the shelter "German swine," and at one point they wanted to shoot at the light and bed stands.

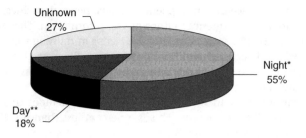

Graph 5.2   Times of rape – Germany
*Night: 6:00 p.m.–5:59 a.m; **Day: 6:00 a.m.–5:59 p.m.

Near 1 a.m. Berger ordered one of the women in the shelter, Frau Irma P. to leave. As she ran out of the shelter up to her living quarters on the second floor, she saw Berger "angrily take hold of Anneliesa's arm."[123] By this time Berger was very angry with Anneliesa, and he indicated that he was going upstairs to sleep. Bamford attempted to persuade her to join Berger, but she again refused. She was not persuaded by his argument that in France "German officers had done it much worse."[124] Peter, her father, agreed to accompany her upstairs – at least, he thought, this would get Berger out of the cellar, and he would be able to keep his daughter out of harm's way.

He was tricked. Just as Berger was out of the door with Anneliesa, Bamford went through the door and closed it. The door locked. Anneliesa testified that she followed Berger up the stairs to the ground floor where the room he wanted to enter was locked. She tried to run away, but Berger chased her upstairs. Using his carbine to threaten her, Berger forced her into a bedroom, ordered her to undress, and tore her bra in the process. Naked and shivering from the cold, she got into the bed to keep warm. Berger removed his clothes, got into bed, and raped her five or six times. Bamford was called into the room, but he was not as aggressive as Berger. He withdrew when she protested.[125]

Ten days later each soldier was tried and found guilty. They were sentenced to hard labor for life. On the April 6–7, 1945, eight other women – four of them at Altfeld – were raped by American soldiers.

Alcohol, weapons, and rape

Historian Paul Fussell, Harvard graduate, former Army lieutenant with the 103rd Infantry Division in France, and keen observer of life in the American military during world wars I and II, has written entertainingly about "drinking far too much, copulating too little."[126] He argues that the soldier, especially the conscript, "suffers so deeply from contempt and damage to his selfhood, from absurdity and boredom and chickenshit, that some anodyne is necessary."[127] In Vietnam, he says, it was drugs, in World War II it was drunkenness.

He found his evidence in songs, poems, adverts, news magazines, soldiers' letters and journals, and America's Office of War Information. The latter took it on itself to lay to "rest suspicions that the troops in training were drinking too much."[128] As insightful and amusing as Fussell is on this topic, he mentions nothing about drinking and rape, or other patterns of soldiers' criminal behavior and its connection to alcohol.

Alcohol was involved in at least 31 percent of the rapes in Germany according to the *BOR/JAG* records. This is 5 percent less than was found for the rapes in France. (See Graph 5.3.)

The percentage of rapists who claimed to be intoxicated when they committed their assaults was the same in France and Germany – 6%. Likewise, 58 percent of the cases had no information on whether the rapists were drinking or drunk.

It was typical for rapists to commit other offenses, including breaking and entering in search of alcoholic drink. The crimes of Private Charles E. Heishman,[129] Jr. and his companion, James Janes, are illustrative.

During the evening of March 19, 1945, Heishman and other members of his organization were billeted in Kottenfurst, Germany. They had been in a drinking party. About 11:30 p.m., he left and told the guard, "We are going scavenging."[130] Around 2:30 a.m., they entered the house of Bernhardt B. where he lived with his daughter and nine evacuees, including Mrs. J. and her two daughters, Helena and Agnes, Mrs. Maria W., her four-year-old son, her two brothers, and Mr. and Mrs. N. Access was gained through a window Heishman had broken with an iron bar.

After searching the provisions room, they entered Bernhardt's bedroom, held him at pistol point, and searched through everything. They found a bottle of liquor "and after forcing Bernhardt to try it, they both had some."[131]

The soldiers next entered the room occupied by Mrs. J and her two daughters. They cried and begged to be left alone. After they had searched the room, and fearing the women's screams might arouse help, the two soldiers went downstairs and waited. When no one came, they entered the bedroom used by the rest of the occupants of the house. Here Heishman beat two of the men with his hand, feet, and pistol. Then he turned to Maria W., and

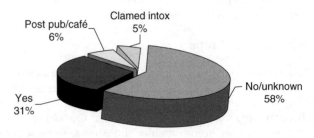

Graph 5.3   Alcohol and rape – Germany

after forcing her to undress while he held his knife against her chest, took her into the kitchen where she was raped. His pistol lay beside her head while he was on top of her.

Heishman then returned to the upstairs bedroom and ordered Helena downstairs where he tore off her nightgown and raped her on the floor – his pistol lay beside her head. "She was then made to go outside with accused where he pushed her head down on his penis."[132] He fired a shot in the hall as the two returned to the upstairs bedroom. There he forced Agnes to go to the kitchen, undress, and while holding her arms over her head, twice had sexual intercourse with her. She was then forced to kneel in front of him as he sat on sofa. He pushed his penis into her mouth – she pulled her head back when he came to an "ejection."[133] Between 6:30 a.m. and 7 a.m., the two soldiers left the house and headed back to where they were billeted carrying two bottles of liquor, and Bernhardt's gold watch.

The use of guns to perpetrate the rapes in Germany varied only a few percentage points higher (71%) than in France (68%). This is not surprising – both settings were battlefields where the soldiers were required to be armed. The use of fists to subdue and frighten their victims declined in Germany to just 1 percent, compared to 7 percent in France. Knives were also used less in Germany (2%) than in France (8%). In the United Kingdom, knives were reported to be used in 41 percent of the rapes.

The increase in the presence of guns in the rapes in France and Germany is consistent with the context within which the soldiers were located. The presence of knives at the rapes in the United Kingdom suggests two factors. Rather than carrying guns, black soldiers in the United Kingdom often relied on knives. This was consistent with black cultural heritage born in the segregated United States where blacks were often prohibited from owning or carrying guns. Military requirements on this topic changed in France and Germany. This does not mean that blacks stopped carrying personal knives for protection. It means that blacks were not only armed with guns but also armed with knives. (See Graph 5.4.)

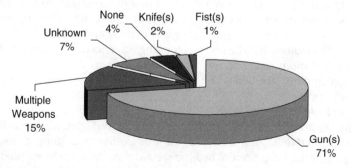

Graph 5.4 Weapons and rape – Germany

Explanation

Why is the official count of the rapes in Germany higher than in either the United Kingdom or France? The easiest and most accurate answer lies in the fact that more rapes happened in Germany. The vast devastation caused by the war, especially during 1944–1945, gave little protection to a number of populations including the aged, children, and women. Equally important is fact the victims were the *enemy's* women. In the minds of some of the rapists the German women had it coming because they were guilty by association. While some of the sexual assaults were undoubtedly influenced by what some of the soldiers had witnessed at the hands of the metaphoric "bad Germans," in other instances the causes were ambiguous. The case of Second Lieutenant Robert D. Thompson is illustrative.

Hatred of Germans?

Lost from their battalion on the night of April 30, 1945, Thompson selected for himself and two enlisted men – each white – a home in Allach, Germany, as an emergency billet for one night. They occupied the lower floor and ordered the regular occupants, Erna F., a 34-year-old widow, her nephew, and sister-in-law, to sleep upstairs. After eating and drinking, Thompson found a photograph of Erna in the nude, which he showed to the enlisted men.[134]

At about 1:30 a.m. Thompson took his .45 caliber pistol and a flashlight and entered the upstairs bedroom. According to the *BOR/JAG* review of his trial, he "insisted that Erna accompany him below, where in the presence of both enlisted men, he confronted her with the photograph."[135] He then ordered her to undress in front of the men – she was shivering and weeping. In his defense, he said that on the afternoon of the day that he billeted in Erna's house, he had been to the Dachau concentration camp. There he had seen "the horrors that those Germans perpetrated on both men and women."[136] Disrobing in front of three American men was, he said, a minor humiliation compared to what had happened at Dachau. At one point, Thompson referred to his behavior as "perhaps a whimsical action."[137]

The trial transcript contains a more thorough discussion of the complicated scenario of what occurred. Thompson spoke no German, and he relayed his instructions to Erna through one of the enlisted men who spoke German. One soldier left the room before she was naked; the second enlisted man left the room after she was nude. After she was disrobed, Thompson undressed, got into the bed with Erna, and fondled her. It is unclear whether he raped her.

She did not cooperate with Thompson, and her crying could be heard upstairs. Frustrated, he slapped her, got out of bed, got his pocketknife, opened it, and got back into bed. At this point, Erna stopped resisting Thompson. After he got out of bed the second time, he told the enlisted men that "she is hot now," and if they wanted to they could get in bed with Erna.[138]

The trial testimony indicated that Thompson may have been the victim of disgruntled enlisted men. He was a demanding officer who had received his battlefield commission in February, only two and half months earlier. On the night of the incident with Erna, one of the enlisted men allegedly said, "I'm not taking orders from you any more," or words to that effect. Thompson's defense council asked one of the enlisted men if he said to "Lt. Thompson that if he got shot in the back it would not be the first Lieutenant it happened to and you could be just the one who could do it?"[139] Another defense question asked if one of the enlisted men "hated the Lieutenant's guts."

The trial transcript indicates that on previous occasions when Thompson had stayed in a German house, his men were ordered to stay someplace else. Thompson's intimacy with Erna F., however, had been witnessed by two enlisted men who did not like their commander. In response to Lieutenant Colonel John C.F. Tillson, III's question, "What was the matter?," Staff Sergeant John F. Gerteisen replied,

> Just no cooperation sir. Any suggestion that was made was knocked in the head as fast as it was made. Not by myself alone or any of the drivers or any of those. There have been objections made by other officers how we could have gotten our work done and gotten a little rest once in awhile. That is the only trouble we have had, sir. If we could have arranged our work so we could have gotten a little rest it would have been all right.[140]

The trial did not explicitly explore whether Thompson hated Germans. His defense counsel could do little to dispute the facts – he had ordered a German woman to undress. Her credibility was nonetheless seriously damaged when the court learned that her deceased husband belonged to the Panzer Division Vansberg, an SS Division:[141] He had been killed on July 10, 1944, near Cannes, France. Her motivations were also questioned when the court learned that while she had told her neighbors what had happened, she did not report the incident to civil or military authorities. In fact, in court she said she did not intend to report the incident.

Thompson's undisputed claim that the incident was reported by one of the two enlisted men and embellished through the willing cooperation of the wife of a dead Nazi soldier helped him. He was found not guilty of rape but guilty of violating the 95th Article of War. In the presence of enlisted men he had not acted like an officer. He caused Erna "a female person, to remove her clothing."[142] The *BOR/JAG* reasoned, "Regardless of accused's resentment of German atrocities, the conduct shown exhibits individual standards of decency and decorum falling below the limit of tolerance authoritatively prescribed for officers and gentlemen."[143] He was dismissed from service.

The rape of German women by black soldiers who said they hated Germans was arguably more plausible than when white men made the same claim because these assaults contained the volatile mix of the racial ideology that permeated German society. These sexual assaults also suggest the possibility that in general black rapes of white women was a form of race-based revenge. The case involving Privates William A. Stevenson and William N. Stuart is illustrative. It contains specific language about their attitudes toward Germans, in general, and their victims. (On another level, their crimes are especially interesting because they were from the same fighting outfit, the 777th Field Artillery Battalion, that had the first rape that went to trial in Germany on February 7, 1945. This suggests that some units may have an unusually high number of rapists – this topic will be examined in future research).

Stevenson's and Stuart's crimes involved entering homes, thefts, and rapes. Between the afternoon and early evening of March 7, 1945, they entered three German homes near Altfeld. In the first home, they raped two of the three daughters who were living with their parents. Each victim was in her 20s; one was a virgin. At the second home, they raped no one because it contained no females, but they stole several items.

They entered the third home at about 3 p.m. and stayed until approximately 7:30 p.m. during which time they raped two women, twice. Their modus operandi involved each taking turns. While one held the other members of the households at gunpoint, the other selected his victim and took her into another part of the house where they were raped. In each incident the victims' loved ones and others who were living in the same dwelling overheard the assaults. They were helpless to come to their assistance because the soldiers were armed.[144] Two days later the soldiers resumed their activities and raped two more women, one time each.

Stuart was described, as "he appears to be a man of some intelligence and of a type who feels superior."[145] Stevenson was described as having an "inferior intelligence" with an IQ of 71, and he had spent one year on a Georgia chain gang before joining the Army. He "was doubtlessly influenced in his actions to a considerable degree by Stuart."[146] The record indicates that the soldiers had planned their attacks. According to Stuart's testimony, he had for sometime wanted to rape German women. However, it is not clear why he and Stevenson acted the way they did. Perhaps the explanation is no more complicated than what Stuart offered. He said that the crimes were the result of having seen what the Germans had done to England and France. He stated that once he was in Germany he found that the Germans were subservient, and this angered him. He also claimed that the Germans he met had "claimed they were not Nazis [and that] made him angry," too.[147]

Their attitude toward Germans is suggested by Stuart's words: "We wanted to hurt them in the first place," and "We started to kill them."[148] He was also influenced by his racist belief – according to the record – that "All girls are afraid of colored people."[149] The record does not indicate that the military authorities investigated whether the soldiers' crimes were instigated primarily by race-based anger or revenge. The presence of racial ideology on the part of these soldiers, especially for Stuart, is indisputable, but this does not explain why these two villains chose to rape the *younger* or *youngest* women in the homes they entered. Information on this aspect of their crimes is not in the records.

Caution is required lest we take the *BOR/JAG* account without critical scrutiny. Much of the content of the BOR's reaction in this case is inconsistent with the bulk of the legalese found in nearly all of their other summaries and opinions for rapes committed in the United Kingdom, France, and Germany. For this reasons this case is useful for gaining insight into the BOR's attitude toward Stevenson and Stuart, and German women. At the beginning of the BOR's opinion it states,

> It is not necessary to set forth the evidence of the obscene, animalistic conduct of accused which support the findings, in as much as it is corroborated by the admissions and testimony of each of them. The facts and circumstances shown by the record of trial disclose a cold-blooded, deliberately planned course of violent action by the accused having for its purpose the wholesale ravishment of German women. The Board of Review affirmatively declares that the orgy initiated by and participated in by the accused is probably the most fiendish, barbaric and brutal sexual episode, involving American soldiers, which has come before the Board on appellate review.[150]

We learn more about what might have been behind the above statement of outrage by contextualizing the BOR at this point in the European war. First, Stevenson and Stuart were black soldiers and the victims were white. At no place in the BOR's opinions on white buddy rapes is there anything close to the same level of indignation. Perhaps their comments were racially motivated. Second, the time of the crimes was in early March, 1945. At this time, the peak of the "rape season" was just beginning, and the BOR had no reason to know that a flood of similar cases would soon cross its desks. For example, there were no trials for rapes that had happened in January, 1945, according to official figures. Only four rapes in February, 1945, went to trial. By the end of March, 1945, the official figures indicate that 78 rapes had occurred during this month alone. This figure almost doubled to 140 rapes in April, 1945.

Perhaps more important than the precipitous rise in the number of rape trials it was asked to review, the BOR's outrage with Stevenson and Stuart may have stemmed from what they saw as a radical change in the composition of the rapes. All of the buddy rape incidents in Germany that went to trial *before* Stevenson and Stuart, involved *white* soldiers. Not one buddy rape had yet, according to official records, been committed by blacks.

The white buddy rapes up to this point involved 14 assailants and 9 victims. Until Stevenson and Stuart, there also had been an equal number – five each – of one-to-one rapes in Germany by black and white soldiers. In only one of these incidents was there more than one victim, and they were raped by a white first lieutenant.

This incident occurred just two days before Stevenson and Stuart started their crime spree. It involved 33-year-old First Lieutenant Joe E. Randie, 33rd Armored Regiment, who prior to his commission as second lieutenant in Fort Knox, Kentucky, April 24, 1943, had been in the National Guard between June 1930 and January 1932.[151] His pistol-pointing two rapes happened on the same day, March 5, 1945, at Rheinkassel, Germany. At his trial, officers of his command "testified to his bravery in battle, his superior performance of dangerous missions, and the award to him, for bravery and heroism, of the Silver Star (oak leaf cluster recommended) and of the Bronze Star."[152]

In other words, when in June, 1945, the BOR reviewed Stevenson and Stuart's convictions, their crimes appeared to be more outrageous than the other cases that it had thus far scrutinized from Germany. The BOR's outrage was therefore possibly a function of its limited experiential knowledge about buddy rapes, as well as an expression of racial prejudice. The rapes by Stevenson and Stuart were everything the BOR said about them, but this does not negate the possibility that the BOR was much less provoked when German women were gang raped by whites than blacks.

Third, Stevenson and Stuart's were members of a black fighting unit that had already had at least one rape in February, 1945. Perhaps the BOR's strongest sentiment was that it thought that these black soldiers were an example of troops that were incapable of handling their roles responsibly. This is, of course, difficult to gauge. However, the BOR did state that "In each instance we have the situation of [black] individuals with lethal weapons not prepared for the responsibility of being conquerors or capable of exercising the restraint that goes with power."[153] Language expressing this sentiment was not found in the buddy rapes committed by white soldiers. Stevenson had been in the 777th Field Artillery Battalion only one month before he raped – prior to this job he had been with the Quartermasters, loading 4.5 cannons.[154]

A fourth problematic that sheds some clarity on the BOR's outrage with Stevenson and Stuart involves the victims' lack of resistance. None of the women raped offered physical resistance, yet they were expected to do so according to law and custom. The accuseds' defense asked, for example, "Why didn't you resist with all of your powers?" One of the victim's replied, "Because I was afraid."[155] Each of them testified that they feared they or their loved ones would have been killed unless they complied with the soldiers' demands.

Whether true or not, this nonetheless raises the question of why Stevenson and Stuart were not charged with violation of the military's nonfraternization policy. The fact that they were charged with rape gives credence to the idea that racial prejudice influenced the BOR in this case.

Brutalization and rape?

The idea that rapes follow the brutalizations that soldiers experience in war may help explain why the number of rapes in Germany was higher than in the United Kingdom and France. This is an excellent question to explore because the movement of the American troops in many ways had some of the features of scientific experiments. It contains, for instance, variation in the form of three distinct times, as well as three distinct social/cultural contexts. Criminal behavior, therefore, should vary accordingly. The United Kingdom was not only the most protective setting for women but also arguably the least brutalizing environment for American soldiers compared to France and Germany. Germany, on the other hand, was the most brutalizing context for the American troops in Europe.

Common sense suggests that the rapists in the "peaceful" United Kingdom would have had the longest time lapse between their induction and the date of their crime(s). The logic here is based on the idea that soldiers who raped in the United Kingdom had not yet been exposed to the extreme brutalities of war. A reasonable alternative is required to the "brutalization in war" explanation for the UK rapes. It might be found in the length of time between induction and the date of the crime.

This argument is suggested by the often-noted observation that the military itself is a brutalizing and dehumanizing institution, especially for civilians who have enjoyed the relative freedoms of a democracy. Even without the impact of war, membership in the US military required numerous demanding adjustments to the loss of civilian life. The cumulative impact of the dehumanizing rigors and degradations of the military may have served as a substitute form of brutalization by war.

Rapists in Germany, on the other hand, would be expected to have had the least time lapse between induction and the date of rape. Simply put, the longer soldiers were in the war, as opposed to just being in the military, the greater the chances were that they could be brutalized, and perhaps raped. In other words, exposure to brutalization under conditions of war might very well be associated with rape within a relative short amount of time.

At first glance, the findings on the "brutalization and rape" theme are unambiguous. The time lapses between induction and the time of rape generally narrowed between 1939 and 1944. Two rapists who had entered the army in 1938 did not commit their crimes until the passage of five years and two months. One of these soldiers raped in 1943, and the other in 1944. Both rapes were committed in England.

Likewise, seven rapists who entered the Army in 1939 did not rape until 1945. All of these rapes occurred in Germany. The time lapse for these

Table 5.6 Time lapse between induction and rape

Year of induction	Year and months to rape*	% of rapes in Germany
1938	5.2	0
1939	5.6	100
1940	4.6	67
1941	3.7	61
1942	2.4	56
1943	1.8	69
1944	0.11	87

*Average time lapse = 3 years, 5 months.

assaults was five years and six months. Seventeen rapists entered the service in 1940. They did not rape until the passage of four years and six months. Seventy-six percent (13) of these rapes happened in Germany. The other rapes by this group of soldiers happened in England (1) and France (4). (See Table 5.6.)

Fifty-one rapists were inducted in 1941. Thirty-one (61%) of their rapes occurred in Germany. The remainder of their assaults happened in England (3) and France (17). The time lapse for these offenders was 3 years and 7 months. In 1942, the time lapse for 144 inductees who raped was 2 years and 4 months. Fifty-six percent of this category of rapists committed their crimes in Germany; 30 percent of their rapes were in France, the rest in England.

Of the 160 rapists who were inducted in 1943, 110 (69%) raped in Germany within 1 year and 8 months. Thirty-one soldiers who were inducted in 1944 committed rapes within 11 months; 87 percent of their rapes occurred in Germany. In summary, between 1938 and 1944, the time lapse between induction and rape decreased. However, the percentage of rapes in Germany during this time was bimodal. This suggests that the time spent in the army was less likely to be associated with rape than was the location of the crimes.

The victims

This chapter opened with the rape of the youngest victim in the records, 3 year-old Ingrid C. (It stretches one's imagination to think that she was "just a German.") About half of the victims' ages were not recorded, rendering a definitive conclusion on this topic impossible. Based on the information gleaned from the *BOR/JAG*, teenagers were raped more than any other age category – the youngest 13, the oldest 19. They comprised 40 percent of the known ages. Women in their 20s represented 29 percent of the known victims. Females in their 30s comprised 14 percent of the identified victims. Nine percent of the victims were in their 40s. Only 2 percent of the victims were in their 50s – the same percentage of victims were in their 60s.

Hildergard R., 13, was walking home with her father Karl R. at about 9:15 p.m. They were returning from the village of Konron, headed in the direction of Schrozeberg, Germany. An American soldier approached them as they neared Schrozenberg. He drew his pistol, loaded it in front of them, and in a rough voice told him to "go back."[156] He obeyed and proceeded to his home, leaving his weeping child behind. Her father did not see Hildergard again until about 11:30 p.m. when her mother, Marie R., returned to their home with her. She had found her daughter near a railroad intersection between Konbron and Schrozberg – Hildergard was crying, trembling, her hair and clothes were dirty and bloody. Her underpants were missing. She told her mother that she had been hit and raped.

On the next day, September 22, 1944, a German physician examined Hildergard. He concluded that she was an underdeveloped girl of 13 "whose sex organs were bloody and whose hymen showed evidence of violation."[157] At the trial, Hildergard testified that the soldier had taken her into a turnip field and ordered her to lie down. At first she refused, but the soldier told her to "shut up" or he would shoot her. He threw her on the ground and overpowered her.

The accused, Private First Class Joe F. Selvera, was, according to Captain Bohme, a member of Bohme's organization, was of good character, "and that he had been the kind of man he would like to have in his company."[158] Another member of his organization, Company B, 36th Armored Infantry Regiment, came to Selvera's defense and testified that from his personal observation Hildergard would "voluntarily indulge in sexual intercourse with soldiers for a bar of chocolate, and that he knew she had voluntarily engaged in sexual intercourse."[159]

Selvera was found guilty by two-thirds of the members of the court and confined to hard labor for life. The JAG's Board of Review ruled that the defense offered for Selvera tended only to establish his prior good character, and the prior (alleged) bad character of Hildergard.

There was no question at the trial of Private First Class Aelred V.J. Platta about what Elizabeth J. would do or not do for a chocolate bar. On or about March 1, 1945, shortly before midnight, she, a 74-year-old widow, was at home with her dead brother's wife, grieving because her brother had just died. He was lying dead on a bed in the living room. Elizabeth had gone outdoors to check on a fire she had previously doused with water (there were fires in her neighborhood), when two soldiers, one of them Platta, approached her, carrying guns. Platta forced her into the living room, and seeing the dead man, touched him "in order to find out if he actually was dead."[160]

He undressed partially and "quickly took her clothes off with force and raped her at once."[161] Meanwhile, a fellow soldier named Whitaker, who had just previously been on guard duty with Platta, noticed his absence and began searching for him. He saw a weak stream of light coming out of a house about 75 yards away. In it he found Platta with two elderly women, one kneeling beside a bed; the other on her back with her dress drawn up and exposing her thighs and buttocks.

Whitaker entered the house and called, "Platta, come out of this house immediately." Platta answered, "Ted, take off." He went to get assistance and in about 20 minutes, he returned with the sergeant of the guard. This time Whitaker called, "Platta, come out of this house immediately." Platta replied while reaching with a bare arm, "Ted, give me your light."[162] Whitaker refused, and he and the sergeant went for more help. In about five minutes they returned with Lieutenant Rose. By this time Platta was walking away from the house.

The victim was unable to identify Platta, but the court found him guilty nonetheless and sentenced him to hard labor for life. The record shows that he was considered an excellent soldier who had on several occasions gone "forward with the lieutenant as 'forward observer party' and 'performed his job perfectly.'"[163]

Age was not a deterrent to rape. Based on data from approximately half of the cases that the army prosecuted, American rapists preferred their victims to be teenagers. A word of caution, a reminder, is needed here. The age distribution may be nothing more than an artifact of the US Army's legal system. It is quite plausible that the predominate image of innocent rape victims were teenagers resulted from nothing more than the fact that those cases were prosecuted more assiduously than cases where the victims were older.

Information on the marital status of the 243 rape victims indicates that 25 percent were single (60), 26 percent married (64), and 4 percent widowed (9). There was no information on the marital status of 45 percent (110) of the rape victims.

Image and objectification

The question of innocence for women beyond the teen years did not discourage military court authorities from impeaching their integrity and painting them guilty by association. Nor did it prevent rapists from objectifying their victims as "chicks,"[164] "good for pricking,"[165] "a lay,"[166] "lying bitch,"[167] or saying that their brutal victimization had transformed them from being "no longer a wife but a woman."[168]

The cleanup operation by the US Army was still in progress in Fulda, Germany, on April 1, 1944 – in late March, it had been part of the American Army's sweep to the Elbe River.[169] At about 8:30 p.m. two days later, just as Miss Anna H. was locking the front door, two drunken American soldiers, Private First Class Thomas G. King and Private Denzil A. Thomas, entered uninvited. Miss H. lived there with her sister-in-law, Mrs. Anna H., Mrs. Bertha B., an American citizen, and another family unnamed in the *BOR/JAG* summary. The two H.s had been eating dinner in the kitchen with two Italian boys[170] when the armed soldier went into the kitchen. Thomas fired his rifle into the ceiling and ordered the Italians to leave.

Mrs. Bertha B. heard the shot and came downstairs from her second floor room to investigate. She told the soldiers that she was an American and showed them her papers. Afterwards Thomas escorted her back upstairs and told her to stay there. During the night, she said she "heard the girls scream for help, and also heard slamming of doors. She said she did not think of opening the window and calling for help."[171]

Both soldiers spent the night in the house, and each of them had sexual intercourse with Miss and Mrs. H. At one point, Mrs. H. was forced to lie on the kitchen floor with Thomas's rifle under her back while he was on top of her. Miss H. claimed that she had "never had intimate relations with men before [and] [h]e did that in all different positions, going for quite a while."[172] Neither of the women apparently screamed, in contrast to what Mrs. R. stated.

The soldiers left after coffee the next morning, and when Mrs. R. came downstairs, she found Mrs. and Miss H. upset and crying. They sorted out what to do and agreed that a complaint should be made at the American commandant's office. At first there was fear and confusion about what to do because the soldiers told Mrs. H. they "could shoot any damn German they found."[173] After doing her housework, Mrs. H. made the report and with the aid of a military police sergeant, she pointed out both soldiers on the street – they were in the vicinity of the battalion command post.

The sole evidence of the soldiers' guilt consisted of the testimony of German witnesses. This gave the defense the opportunity to question their integrity and character, and he wasted no time in doing so. When Mrs. R., the American, was on the witness stand the defense attorney quickly asked her if she was a member of the Nazi party. She replied that she wasn't. Next, he asked why she had left the United States. She answered that her mother was ill in Germany, and because she was not married, she agreed with her sister and brother that she "should be the one to come back and take care of my mother."[174]

The prosecution took exception to this line of questioning and objected to it as being improper and having no bearing to the case. The court's legal authority, the law member, agreed. The defense, in turn, interpreted this decision as a denial of the right to cross-examine Mrs. R. He passionately argued that according to General Bradley's Special Orders, the Germans had been taught that the "national goal of domination must be obtained regardless of the depths of treachery, murder and destruction."[175] They were not to be trusted, and anyone associated with Germans were suspected. He argued further that the interest and background of Mrs. R. was relevant to whether the court could rely on her statements. The law member disagreed.

The defense persisted and upon "recross examination," asked, "Are these Miss Anna H. and Mrs. Anna H. members of the Nazi party?" "Are their husbands or relatives serving or have they served in the German armed forces?"[176] Again, the prosecution objected and the count's law member agreed with him. This did not prevent the defense from asking many similar insinuating questions. He asked Mrs. Bertha R. to explain the circumstances of her being in Germany, to indicate the year she left the United States, and whether she was in sympathy with the Nazi cause. The prosecution objected, and the law member again agreed with him.

The defense pressed on. His theory of defense was well illustrated by his questioning of the medical witness who was called to examine the women. He wanted to know if the American woman was upset with what had happened to the German women. If she was upset, it would suggest that perhaps she had greater sympathy for the Germans than for the American soldiers accused of rape.

It was not a good time for an American to be pro-German. The war was nearly over. General Eisenhower had already decided it was not necessary to fight on to take Berlin.[177] Germany was nearly prostrate – yet still fighting – and the victorious Allies were in no mood to tolerate Germany's sympathizers.

The content of the defense questions are illuminating. He asked the medical witness, "Just what did she say, this American woman?" Upon the prosecution's objection and the law member's "objection sustained," the defense continued his impeachment of Mrs. R. He stated, "If the court please, it is our contention that these soldiers had a party with these two women and that this whole case was instigated by this busybody woman and we think we are entitled to show her as such and that is our defense and if we are not going to be permitted [*sic*]."[178]

The defense's cross-examination of Miss Anna H. stayed the course. After asking her age (29), and if her encounter with the soldiers was her first sexual intercourse with any man, to which she replied, "Yes," she was asked, "Did you ever go to a Nazi youth camp?"[179] This query generated another prosecution objection, and it, too, was sustained. Undeterred, the defense continued the efforts to vilify Miss Anna H. by saying,

> I think it is very material. It is a well known fact that Der Fuehrer encouraged or awarded medals to these German women to have children whether they were married or otherwise, for Der Fuehrer and if it can be proven that this woman is giving false testimony about this particular thing it is going to affect all the rest of her testimony.[180]

The sustained objections by the prosecution undoubtedly helped the court members – they found the soldiers guilty, and they were sentenced to hard labor for life. The JAG's Board of Review disagreed with this decision. It concluded that the law member's decisions had curtailed the defense's "right to legitimate cross-examination, abused his discretion and committed serious prejudicial error." If permitted to cross-examine Miss Anna H. the way that the defense had intended, the court would have learned that her brother – Mrs. Anna H.'s husband – was in the German army at the time of the trial. Whether this or similar damning information would have altered the court's vote is unknown. The Board of Review was of the opinion that the record of trial was legally insufficient to support, finding the soldiers guilty of rape. The soldiers were white.

Less than a month before the H.s were accosted, the Ninth Army was pushing toward the Rhine River near Krefeld, when on Sunday, March 11, 1945, five soldiers from Company C, 184th Engineers Combat Battalion, raped two sisters, Frau Gertrude P. (24 years) and Frau Maria T. (18 years). The sisters were at the home of their mother, Frau Margarete B. when three of the soldiers, two of whom where Pfcs. – Charles W. O'Neil and George B. Tweedy – "sort of invited themselves in."[181] They stayed five minutes and left. After evening chow, one of the soldiers, Private Rufus N. Casey, asked Charles W. O'Neil, if he wanted to join him and Private First Class William E. Ewing. Casey said he knew where there were two "good looking chicks and some cognac." Casey drove a 2 1/2 ton 6-by-6 truck named "Dorothy," and all of them arrived back at Frau B.'s home at about 7:30 pm. They were all armed with M-1 rifles except for O'Neil – he carried a .45 caliber automatic pistol. Casey also carried a foot-long wooden-handled whip with leather thongs also about a foot long.

There was no confusion about who was to do what. They herded Frau B., her two daughters, a boy about 12, and a recently released male French prisoner of war into a room. They drank some cognac the Frenchman had produced and then sorted the daughters into bedrooms. Frau Gertrude P. was raped by three of the soldiers while the other two raped her sister. After a while, some of the soldiers changed places with each other. One of the daughters at first refused Casey's invitation to "zig zig," and clung crying onto her mother. He struck her with his whip.[182]

They soon departed and returned to their unit in the truck. All five soldiers admitted they had sexual intercourse but denied that it was rape. They were found guilty and sentenced to be hanged – according to one source – they were black.

The alleged transforming power of turning a "mere wife" into a "real woman" by oral, anal, and vaginal intercourse represents an especially brutal form of objectification of a German mother of two by American soldiers. These assaults involved three white soldiers, two of whom were Privates Roy E. Andrews and Charlie M. Hathcock, from the 271st Ordnance Maintenance Company. Late at night of March 30, 1945, they awoke the household of Karl H. by "banging on the door."[183] His house was home for his wife and their two children, his mother, and his sister and her two children. The soldiers demanded wine and twice forced Karl H. to the cellar for it.

Around midnight, the third soldier became drunk and urinated in the hallway. One of the two remaining soldiers took him outside, returned, and laid his weapon on the kitchen table. By this time the soldiers "began to appear wild and we thought something was going to happen."[184] The larger of the soldiers looked wilder every time one of the women screamed. At one point, the grandmother was called into the kitchen to hopefully protect the children.

Shortly after midnight, Andrews took Paula into her brother's bedroom and began to assault her. The rest of the family had to go upstairs. Andrews stood in front of her with his rifle and forced her to completely undress – once he struck her with his rifle. She begged him to stop because she was menstruating and she appealed to his sense of decency, after all, he had previously shown her pictures of his wife and children.

At this point, Hathcock was brought into the room, and the soldiers talked and smoked cigarettes. Hathcock "forced her to put a rubber on his penis"[185] and he raped her vaginally and orally. She fainted. After he got up, Andrews went into the bedroom, undressed, and shook her awake, and raped her vaginally, anally, and orally. When he threatened to cut her finger off with his knife, she removed her ring and gave it to him. Each time she tried to cry out he put his hand over her mouth, or on her throat, and acted as though he was going to stab. He kept saying, "You are no longer a wife but a woman."[186]

Witnesses at the trial said her screams were heard "every second or so" until 6 a.m. the next morning.[187] She said she had never heard of oral or anal intercourse. Two non-commissioned officers testified that Hathcock was one of the "finest" and best men in the organization. Both soldiers were said to be very efficient workers with excellent records. Andrews was 31 years old, married, and the father of three children; Hathcock was unmarried.[188] The soldiers were convicted and confined at hard labor for life. According to one source, the two were white.

On the night of Paula H.'s assault, three black soldiers from Battery B, 578th Field Artillery Battalion, raped two sisters in the yard of their mother and father's house at Limbach, Germany. At first, one of soldier held the parents at bay with his pistol while his buddies assaulted the sisters outdoors, then he took his turn. "We all agreed on it, and said we would try it."[189] They were convicted and sentenced to hard labor for life.

Another soldier, Private First Class Thomas B. Janes, white, Company C, 33rd Armored Engineer Battalion, referred to his rape victim, Maria E., as a "lay" and his behavior as "being in the saddle."[190] The court recommended that he be shot with musketry, but the Board of Review reduced his sentence to hard labor for life.

Resistance versus consent

Physical resistance to sexual assault(s) was used as crucial legal evidence to determine if rape had occurred in the United Kingdom and France. The logic supporting this idea quickly became a contentious issue in Germany where victims of sexual assaults often said they did not consent. The problem for the military court was that there was no physical evidence that they had put up a fight. Again and again the records show that German women gave two reasons for submitting without physical resistance. First, German women said that they expected to be raped – their government had told its citizens that the Allied forces, including the Americans, would rape their women.

Second, German rape victims said they did not fight their attackers because they were armed, and according to what they said their government had told them, they expected to be killed if they resisted. The words of Frau Anne S. in early March, 1945, are informative: "I was too frightened to do any more because I was afraid he might kill me. We were always told if we resisted we would be killed."[191]

A third and fourth factor complicated the matter further. At one level, the American authorities knew that the above two reasons were tenable. The German government had informed its citizens by radio and other means to expect rapes and that the Allied soldiers were indeed raping. What complicated matters was the fact that the rapists were armed, often drunk, and without German language skills. Under these circumstances, the failure of German women to forcefully resist the soldier's physical advances was enough for some of the soldiers to mistakenly think – or at least to claim once caught – that sexual intercourse was consensual. These situations were akin to the ancient and discredited masculine notion that "no" means "yes". From the victims' perspective, it was rape.

There was mounting evidence that rape was increasingly becoming a major issue. While there were no rapes that went to trial in January, by the end of March more than 70 rapes were slated for trial. When coupled with the Army's move deeper and deeper into enemy territory this data means that American soldiers were facing greater and greater opportunities and risks as conquerors as they came into contact with German citizens.[192] This produced a difficult dilemma. Should the soldiers be allowed to have some contact with the vanquished – in some ways it would make their life easier and more pleasant – or no contact?

Harkening back to a nonfraternization policy that was established in 1918 when American "soldiers briefly occupied German towns along the Rhine were ordered to avoid contact with the local population," the soldiers were again ordered "Don't Fraternize."[193] The result was a controversial policy "that in the words of *Yank* [military newspaper] produced 'the loudest and most engaging international discussion of sex since Adam discovered that Eve had not been placed in the Garden purely for decorative purposes.'"[194] As it became evident that the Army's fears of German uprisings and reprisals were not going to develop, soldiers were given greater freedom to have limited contact with the Germans. Soon "Copulation without Conversation Is Not Fraternization" became a motto, if not an informal policy.[195]

It is within this context that resistance and consent took on a different meaning and urgency to the military authorities. Soon in Germany what would likely have been rape in the United Kingdom and France often became unlawful "sexual intercourse with an unmarried women."[196]

On or about March 4, 1945, two soldiers armed with rifles slung on their shoulders entered uninvited into the house of Fraulein Margarete K. She was an unmarried 19-year-old virgin who lived in Aldekerk, Germany, with her parents, brother, and a woman lodger. Private Lewis Ward touched her on the shoulder, motioned her upstairs, and she complied. He looked in the upstairs rooms until he found one with a bed, put his rifle in the corner and indicated that she was to sit on the bed. Ward's companion, Private Jessie Sharer had also ascended the stairs. After the soldiers spoke briefly with each other, Sharer stepped out of the room and remained outside of the door with his rifle. Ward proceeded to undress Fraulein Margarete even though she "was very much afraid. It was only the second day after the occupation by the Americans and before that there had been no soldiers in our house."[197]

Ward undressed and joined her in the bed for several minutes. The intercourse "hurt very much," she cried and "shook her head in the negative."[198] When he had finished, he called Sharer and motioned for her to remain on the bed. Sharer put his rifle down and had sexual intercourse with her. After he was finished, Fraulein Margarete dressed and started down the stairs only to be stopped by Ward who motioned for her to re-enter the room. He "used" her again. This time he placed his rifle on a table next to the bed. Afterwards, he put his pants back on and spoke to Sharer, who had come into the room, and Sharer "used" her again.

Ward, meanwhile, left the room and soon returned with Fraulein Margarete's mother. The record indicates that all four stood around "and drank Ward's wine."[199] He kissed Fraulein Margarete twice in the presence of her mother before taking her downstairs and to a neighbor's house. There he motioned for her to go upstairs where he again found a room with a bed,[200] removed her slacks, undressed, and "used" her again. This time he placed his rifle next to the door. After giving her more wine, he removed her ring from the third finger of her left hand and replaced it with a simple gold ring, "saying 'You-me-Frau [*sic*].'" They soon left the second house and walked to a vehicle where there were other American soldiers. One of them asked Ward and Sharer what they had been doing in the German's house. Soon he motioned for her to go home. Between 5:30 p.m. and 6 p.m., an American lieutenant asked the family what had happened and they informed him.

The record indicates the blood found on the sheets and mattress cover was from her ruptured hymen – an American medical officer established that she "had been a virgin before the first act in question." The soldiers did not act drunk even though evidence was introduced that Sharer was drunk earlier in the afternoon of the rapes. Neither soldier hit her or pointed his gun directly at her. "When they touched her, it was neither affectionately nor rough."[201] Each soldier had been instructed on the subject of nonfraternization with Germans.

Ward stated that he had no trouble entering her vagina and that he thought she was not a virgin. He gave her the ring because he "believed from her actions that she desired it because of 'his love making.'"[202] The court disagreed. Each soldier was found guilty of rape and sentenced to confinement at hard labor for life. The reviewing authority, however, disagreed. It found them guilty of attempting to fraternize with German citizens.

The legal problem for Fraulein Margarete was that by her own testimony, "she offered no [physical] resistance whatever to either accused."[203] According to the reviewing authority, she never complained of the assaults "to her family until the accuseds' departure and never made any complaint herself to American authorities."[204] Based on a previous ETO rape court-martial involving a soldier named Flackman, the authorities reasoned further that her weeping and mild "protestation by shaking her head in the negative could have reasonably charged Ward with notice of, 'the reluctance of the consent which her docility seemed to demonstrate.'"[205]

Her delay in complaining was also a negative. The reviewing authorities concluded it was "incompatible with the sense of outrage which might reasonably be expected from such a crime."[206] Again quoting from the Flackman case, they reasoned, "Such half-hearted protests as she testified to, expressed only at the eleventh hour, after she was taking and had taken off her clothes, are of a type which might be expected from almost any consenting female in the situation shown."[207] The fact that the soldiers were armed and thus quite capable of instilling fear in Frau Margarete and her family was brushed aside because the soldiers were required to be armed.

The reviewing authorities' decision that the evidence was insufficient for a finding of rape did not absolve the two soldiers. Instead, they found them guilty of violating Article of War 96 – having sexual intercourse with an *unmarried* woman. (Emphasis in the original.)[208] The Board of Review reasoned that in view of the fact that the two combat soldiers were in the midst of "a campaign in a newly occupied enemy city, of engaging in promiscuous sexual intercourse with an enemy citizen only 19 years old while unlawfully in her home, with her mother nearby, constituted … conduct to the prejudice of good order and military discipline."[209] Ward and Sharer were dismissed from the Army and sentenced to one year of hard labor.[210]

Additional evidence and insight into the Army's reluctance to charge its soldiers in Germany with rape is also found in the language it used to describe some of their sexual assaults. After early March, 1945, terms like "bestial" and "animal" were rarely used. Private Frank P. Prairiechief's March

14, 1945 brutal vaginal and anal attack on Frau Anna K., 60, for example, was referred to as "he pursued his desires."[211] A few days later shortly after midnight in Leidstadt, two soldiers, Technician 5th Grade Ray F. Daniels and Private James A. Caudill, entered the home of Frau F., an elderly German. After she got away, they raped Frau Johnana K. The record states that Caudill fell asleep "[f]ollowing satisfaction of his sexual desires."[212] Ward and Sharer, as we have seen, "used" Fraulein Margarete. Many others were guilty of "wrongly ... putting fear in her [to] induce ... sexual intercourse."[213]

Conclusion

Overall, the data on the rapes in Germany is consistent with the findings for the United Kingdom and France. The rapes committed by American soldiers varied primarily by the types of social environments they found themselves in. The social conditions of Germany were far more conducive to rape than either the United Kingdom or France.

Several related questions about brutalization and rape remain unexplored and will be addressed in further research. For example, were the rapists in any significant ways different from murders and murder/rapists? Did they have more prior convictions for military misconduct? Were they from the same or similar military units and racial backgrounds? Were rapists punished more, or less, than other capital offenders in the US Army during World War II? Before addressing those questions, we turn to the patterns of prosecution and punishment for the rapists.

6
Punishment and Context: Wartime Justice

"The law is a funny thing." Private Wesley Edmonds[1]

Introduction

Most of the information about punishment(s) in the previous chapters was presented after discussions of individual cases. This pattern of presentation changed in Chapter 4. It contained information not only about individual offenders, but also about the distribution of punishment for rape by the race of the soldiers. In this chapter, we focus and elaborate on the patterns of punishment for life sentences, death sentences, and executions in the United Kingdom, France, and Germany. It is important to explore whether the patterns of punishment were consistent with racist ideology and the importance of changes in social settings as discussed in Chapter 1.

We will also examine a behind-the-scenes battle between the leadership of the JAG's Branch Office, ETO, the Commanding General, Dwight Eisenhower, and the Secretary of War, over the issues of sentencing disparity and clemency. At the heart of this confrontation were embarrassing public relations issues for the government and military. These matters pitted *fairness* against the *power* of commanders to determine the length and severity of sentences. Intertwined amongst this debate were important arguments about the quality of military justice that would not be resolved until several years after the end of World War II. This issue has not disappeared. Recent commentators are convinced that a few, if any, improvements have been made in the quality of military justice in the United States.[2] We begin with life sentences.

Life sentences

Before the war, President Roosevelt gave approval for black soldiers "not to exceed 10 percent of the crew" in the Navy, Marine Corps, and Coast Guard, a percentage that reflected the proportion of blacks in the civilian population.[3]

Table 6.1 Disproportionate life sentences in the United Kingdom, France, and Germany (in percentages)

Race	United Kingdom	France	Germany
Black	52	78	49
White	40	19	42
Unknown	8	3	8
American Indian	–	–	1
	100	100	100

The same rule was applied to the Army. This decision was based on the approximate distribution of 10 percent blacks and 90 percent whites within the US population.

The patterns of punishments were consistent with what would be expected in a segregated society's military, but they were not proportional to the racial distribution of the population. In each of the settings – United Kingdom, France, and Germany – black soldiers received life sentences for rape greater than in proportion to their membership in the US Army and in the US population. White soldiers received life sentences less than in proportion to their membership in the US Army and US population. This information is presented in Table 6.1.

A second trend involved changes in the size of the disproportionate black representation, and the corresponding underrepresentation of white soldiers in each of the settings. It is important to note that when compared to the proportion of blacks receiving life sentences in the United Kingdom (52%), blacks in France saw a dramatic increase from 25 percent to 78 percent, and then a decrease of almost 30 percentage points in Germany (49%).

Correspondingly, the proportion of whites receiving life sentences in the United Kingdom was underrepresented at 40 percent, and then decreased to less than half of this figure at 19 percent in France. In Germany, whites were given 42 percent of the total life sentences. This number was only 2 percentage points greater than what was found in the United Kingdom for white soldiers.

These figures are consistent with what would be expected under conditions of racism and with the changes in the conditions of war discussed in Chapters 2, 4, and 5.

Death sentences

The patterns of disproportionate life sentencing for blacks and whites were replicated with the death sentences – even more so – except for Germany. This information is presented in Table 6.2.

Table 6.2 Disproportionate death sentences in the United Kingdom, France, and Germany (in percentages)

Race	UK	France	Germany
Black	91	92	46
White	9	8	33
Unknown	–	–	20
American Indian			1
	100	100	100

The percentage distributions for death sentences by race were found to be more disproportionate than for the life sentences, except in Germany. The death sentences for the black and white soldiers in the United Kingdom were almost exactly the opposite of what would be expected based on the proportion of each in the population of the United States.

A dramatic difference was found in the percentages of death sentences given for the rapes in Germany. In the United Kingdom and France, blacks had received more than 90 percent of the death sentences – they represented only 10 percent of the Army. In Germany, they received 46 percent of the death sentences, which represents an approximate decrease of 44 percent compared to the percentage of death penalty sentences they had been given in the United Kingdom and France. Yet, the figure of 46 percent was still 36 percent greater than their membership in the military and in the US population

The percentage of white soldiers receiving the death penalty for rape in the United Kingdom and France was 9 percent and 8 percent respectively. These figures represented a disproportionate underrepresentation of more than 80 percent. In Germany, the death penalty sentence for white offenders increased to 33 percent, an approximate increase over the same sentence in the United Kingdom and France of 23 percent.

The paramount question, at least in terms of math, is not proportionality compared to US population or within the military, but whether sentence disparity existed when blacks and whites were *tried*. In other words, did blacks get the death sentences more often than whites when both were tried for the same offense? This question is addressed in Table 6.3.

There is no doubt that sentence disparity existed for soldiers tried for rape in the United Kingdom and France. The picture is less clear for Germany. When black soldiers were tried for rape in the United Kingdom and France, they received the death penalty 43 percent and 44 percent of the time, respectively. White soldiers, by comparison received the death penalty only 9 percent of the time in the United Kingdom. This percentage doubled to 18 percent in France.

Table 6.3 Disparity and percent of death sentences in the United Kingdom, France, and Germany

Race	UK	France	Germany
Black	43	44	23
White	9	18	20
Unknown	–	–	43
American Indian	–		33

The large percentage of Unknowns who received the death penalty in Germany made it hazardous, if not impossible, to have clear conclusions on sentencing disparity according to race. However, it is important to note with caution that black soldiers appear to have received death sentences for rape in Germany more often than white soldiers.

Sentences received following convictions were not always the sentences that the soldiers actually served. Sentences could be reduced. In the following section, we will examine the patterns of reduced sentences. It was expected that the reductions follow race – the sentences for white offenders were expected to be reduced disproportionately more often than for black offenders.

Reduced life sentences

The data on the proportionality of the reduction of life sentences is presented in Table 6.4.

The percentages presented in Table 6.4 are based on the total number of sentences that were reduced and not on the number of sentences given. For example, in the United Kingdom, 8 sentences were reduced, 3 for blacks (37.5%), 3 for whites (37.5%), and 2 for Unknowns (25%). These findings however are somewhat ambiguous because of the small numbers involved – they should be used with caution.

In the United Kingdom, the reductions for black and white soldiers were the same at 38 percent each. This figure is higher than would be expected based on the proportion of blacks in the military. In other words, black soldiers received 38 percent of all of the life sentences that were reduced for rapes committed in the United Kingdom.

The reduction of the life sentences in France is, at first glance, curious, when it is compared to the pattern of reduced sentences in the United Kingdom. The picture of reduced sentences in France is consistent with what would be expected in an army segregated by race. It is also consistent with the argument that context matters. No blacks had their life sentences reduced for rape in France – 100 percent of the reductions went to whites. However, this figure should be interpreted very carefully because what it

Table 6.4 Disproportionate reductions of life sentences in the United Kingdom, France, and Germany (in percent)

Race	United Kingdom	France	Germany
Black	38	0	10
White	38	100	48
Unknown	25	0	42
American Indian	–	–	0
	101*	100	100

* Due to rounding up 37.5% to 38%

means, in fact, is that only one white soldier had his life sentence reduced in France. In other words, 78 percent of the life sentences in France went to blacks, and *none* of them received a reduced sentence.

By comparison, white soldiers received 19 percent of the life sentences in France, and only one of them received a reduced sentence (see Table 6.1). The overall absence of reductions in life sentences in France is, however, stretched mathematically, consistent with racist ideology – one white soldier got his life sentence reduced. More important was the fact that France was the battlefront where military discipline could ill afford a reputation for reducing sentences. Alternatively, the scarcity of reductions for life sentences may have been indicative of (1) a lack of uniformity and fairness in sentencing among commanders and (2) commanders' lack of interest in getting offenders returned to active service. These ideas will be explored later in this chapter.

Life sentence reductions in Germany had an even greater percentage (42%) for the Unknown than in the United Kingdom (25%). This made it highly problematic to reach any meaningful or insightful conclusion about a pattern of reductions for life sentences. Without considering the potential impact of the racial composition of the Unknowns, it appears that blacks received only 10 percent of the total reductions for life sentences compared to whites – they received 48 percent of the reductions.

The percentage of life sentence reductions per race in the United Kingdom, France, and Germany revealed clearer findings about sentence disparity. This information is presented in Table 6.5.

The reader is reminded that in this table the numbers are not based on overall proportionality. Rather, they are based on the question of whether as a group convicted blacks had their sentences reduced more or less than convicted white soldiers had their's. In other words, the figures presented in Table 6.5 address an *intra* race question – each group represents 100 percent.

Of the ten black soldiers who were sentenced to death in the United Kingdom, only three of them had their sentences reduced. By comparison,

Table 6.5   Disparity in the reduction of life sentences in the
United Kingdom, France, and Germany (in percent)

Race	UK	France	Germany
Black	36	4	7
White	88	100	33
Unknown	–	–	43
American Indian	–	–	–

88 percent of the white soldiers convicted of rape and sentenced to death in
the United Kingdom had their sentences reduced. This pattern was also
found in Germany. But again, the percentage (43%) of unknown who had
their sentences reduced makes it difficult to be very conclusive. It does
appear nevertheless, that the disparity in sentence reductions by race held.

Reduced death sentences

The pattern of disparity in death sentences for convicted black and white
rapists in the United Kingdom and France was reversed for reduced death
sentences. This information is presented in Table 6.6.

Black rapists were given 100 percent of the reductions of death sentences in
the United Kingdom. This does not mean that no blacks were executed for
rapes in the United Kingdom. Rather, it means that blacks received 100
percent of the total number of reductions for death that were given by the
military. Whites, on the other hand, received no death sentence reductions
for rapes.

These two patterns were also found for death sentences given in France.
Blacks received 81 percent of the reductions for death sentences there – whites
were granted the remainder of the reductions at 19 percent. It appears that the
presence and influence of racist ideology on the reduction of sentences for
rape stopped, or at least waned, when it came to reconsidering death
sentences in the United Kingdom and France.

An alternative explanation suggests that the stereotyped "fanciful image"
of French women acted as a counterweight to racial prejudices, especially
when it came to a question of whether to execute a black soldier. In other
words, were the lives of black American soldiers to be ended for having raped
French women who already had a tainted reputation for sexual looseness
with blacks following World War I, and who may have recently collaborated
with the German occupiers?

It is clear that at the level of reducing death sentences for rape, the military
was more lenient with black rapists in the United Kingdom and in France,
than it was with white assailants. As will be discussed shortly, the patterns of
racial disparity found thus far persisted unabated at the death gallows.

Table 6.6 Disparity in the reduction of death sentences in the United Kingdom, France, and Germany (in percent)

Race	United Kingdom	France	Germany
Black	100	81	100
White	0	19	100
Unknown	–	–	100
American Indian	–	–	100
	100	100	100

Interpreting the patterns of death sentence reductions in Germany is somewhat less problematic. All death sentences for rape in Germany were reduced – there were no executions for rape in Germany.

Executions

Racial disparity was present at the gallows. This information is presented in Table 6.7.

In the United Kingdom, 56 percent of the soldiers executed for rape were blacks, compared to only 28 percent of whites. One Latino, or Spanish American, named Aniceto Martinez, 22 years old, single, and from Jeaniez, New Mexico, was executed for rape in the United Kingdom. He was put into a separate category because his trial transcript was incomplete in two respects. It did not indicate his unit other than "Headquarters Detachment." This information was inadequate for determining if he was assigned to a black or white unit. Neither did his records specifically state whether he was classified as black or white. However, the record did indicate that at one time he was a member of the 202nd M.P. Co. – a unit that was activated at Camp Blanding, Florida, May 15, 1942 – where he "trained new men and did general camp duty."[4] This strongly suggests he was in a white unit. Later he was transferred to the 769th M.P. Company "in the U.K. for almost 2 years doing M.P. work of [a] police nature and convoy work without difficulty."[5] He was identified as an illiterate, quiet, calm, and "unperturbed Spanish American who g[ave] his story clearly and coherently.[6] His crime, however offensive and repugnant, was not violent. It was committed while drunk – he said he thought he was in a brothel. If he was classified as white, the percentage of white soldiers executed would increase to 44 percent, a figure that is 45 percent below proportional representation.

It is interesting that although we have seen that black and white soldiers who raped in Germany were sentenced to death, *none* were executed there. But, at the same time, the US Army was still executing its own, or paying someone else to do it. On June 15, 1945, more than a month after the German surrender, Englishmen Thomas W. Pierrepoint and Albert Pierrepoint hanged Martinez at Shepton Mallet Prison.

Table 6.7   Executions by race and country for rape (in percent)

Race	UK	France	Germany
Black	56	86	0
White	28	14	0
Latino*	16	0	0
	100	100	0

*1 Spanish American

The significant factors that explains why Martinez was executed and his counterparts in Germany lived can be found in the characteristics of the respective victims. Clearly, his crime was not distinguished by extreme brutality or violence as was sometimes present in France and Germany. Martinez's victim was a 75-year-old white Englishwoman. The German victims were, perhaps, "just Germans." Other explanations deserve consideration.

Why no executions for rape in Germany?

Rejection of racial ideology

Explanations for this development in what had been a regime of harsh responses to rape in the United Kingdom and France are intriguing. One possibility involves the notion that the military had come to realize that there were no real or significant differences between black and white soldiers and/or rapists. Perhaps the military wished to set an example that gave witness to the ugliness of its racist ideology, especially in view of how the Nazi's had practiced it in Germany. Perhaps it was therefore thought that there was little or any value to hang more blacks than whites, Or, for that matter, to hang any soldiers at all.

Joining Europe

This possibility would have been consistent with the execution policies of other countries of Europe. Many of them, if not all, had more lenient sentences for rape than the US military. England, for instance, had abolished the death penalty for rape in the late nineteenth century. Perhaps, in apparent strong contrast with the current US government's hostile opposition to the new International Criminal Court, as well as its conflict with France and Germany over Iraq, at war's end, the US military had second thoughts about its harsh rape penalties.[7] Evidence supporting this interpretation is found in the Branch Office history. It's authors state, "[B]ut critics also point to the more lenient sentences imposable for rape by the civil law in the other countries of Europe."[8]

Morale problem

It is also possible that the US military did not want to risk discouraging its soldiers in Germany or lowering their morale by telling them through various publications, including the newspaper *Stars and Stripes*, morning reports and orders read aloud at formations, that it had executed loyal and long-fighting fellow troopers for raping the enemy's women.

News about the execution of American soldiers abroad seldom appeared in domestic newspapers. One misleading exception appeared during the 1944 Christmas holiday season. On December 28, an associated press report from Paris was published on the front page of the *New York Times*. It stated that since D-Day – June 6 – not a single "American soldier in France had been executed for cowardice."[9] What the news story did not tell was that General Eisenhower had already approved scores of executions including his recent approval for the execution of Private Eddie D. Slovik for the crime of desertion. As American death penalty expert Watt Espy insightfully explained in 1992, "At that time we were making war heroes in the newspapers, executing American soldiers was not good press."[10]

Hatred of Germans

This is an especially intriguing possibility, wrought as it is with ample doses of wartime and postwar propaganda that portrayed the Germans as Godless heathen and quite suitable targets for contempt, revenge, and neglect. The argument has been made that the commanding general, Eisenhower, hated Germans so much that he was part of a policy that actively prevented available food to be distributed to German prisoners of war, thus causing the death of hundreds of thousands of unarmed soldiers and civilians. It has been claimed that upwards of a million people died because of various food and health-related neglects that Eisenhower had a hand in.

Journalist James Bacque's *Other Loses: The Shocking Truth Behind the Mass Deaths of Disarmed German Soldiers and Civilians Under General Eisenhower's Command* was called the "most controversial and hotly debated book of 1991."[11] Before it was published in the United States, it was a best seller in Canada, France, the United Kingdom, and Germany, and the subject of a BBC documentary. Within the United States it was the subject of an "unprecedented three-and-a-half page front-page attack ... in the New York Times Book Review, fully three months before the publishing date of the book."[12]

After its initial 1989 publication, it was the subject of a 1990 international conference that was sponsored by the Eisenhower Center at the University of New Orleans. At that time, Stephen Ambrose, one of the most successful historians to popularize World War II for millions of Americans – directed the Center. Two years later he co-edited a volume of the conference's papers that claimed to assess Bacque's troubling assertion.[13] The papers selected for publication countered Bacque's claim by asserting that he (1) misinterpreted documents that accounted for the disposition of the German POWs; (2) neglected important evidence that contradicted his thesis; (3) failed to take account of the acute disruption of Europe's economy and distribution networks; (4) ignored the competing needs of millions of refugees, displaced persons, and hungry civilians; as well as (5) the deployment of Allied resources to the Pacific Theater of Operations where the war continued.[14]

Curiously, none of the contributors addressed whether Eisenhower had the power, influence, motivation, and resources necessary to effectuate Bacque's thesis. The failure to execute any US soldiers for raping German women would be consistent with Eisenhower's alleged hatred of Germans. It must be pointed out in fairness to Eisenhower that at war's end many influential and powerful Americans, including President Roosevelt, went on record stating that they wanted to see the Germany military and its citizens punished. President Roosevelt, in fact, said he wanted to castrate them.[15]

Spoils of war

It is also possible that the failure to execute American soldiers for raping German women was an expression of any number of the explanations for wartime rape discussed in Chapter 2. As we know from the *HBO/JAG's* official account of its birth and work, ETO soldiers were executed in the United Kingdom and France for raping either allied nationals or females who had been under German occupation.[16] But the German rape victims differed from these two groups – they were the enemy's women. Perhaps when the hard choice of executing American soldiers for raping them came, the collective command structure of the US Army gave a nod and a wink.

Prosecutions too difficult

The acknowledged difficulties of finding witnesses and perpetrators after battles may have contributed to the failure of the military to execute American soldiers who raped German women. Perhaps the Army therefore found it unreasonable or embarrassingly difficult to justify executing only the soldiers who were convicted, knowing well that many other soldiers got away with rape. This problem was discussed in the JAG's history in chapter XXX – Sex Offenses. It said, "Inability sufficiently to identify the attackers, especially during the disordered break-through periods, was, of course, a principal reason for the failure to try many of the alleged offenders."[17]

A related problem was what to do with the large number of soldiers – more than 10,000 – who were convicted of crimes that could result in incarceration.[18] Some commanders wanted the soldiers to be sent to federal prisons in the United States, while others wanted them to be sent to the military's Disciplinary Training Centers, a position supported by some of the JAG. The problem was too many *American* prisoners.

Other more important issues

Perhaps, as Ambrose and his colleagues argued in their spirited defense of the accusation that Eisenhower was party to letting German POWs die for lack of food and sanitary living conditions, the military had many other, more pressing issues to worry about than its rapists. The world war certainly was not over, notably in the Pacific Theater. The conditions in Germany were nearly chaotic and catastrophically disorganized. Perhaps executing American soldiers under these conditions was a last, lingering dirty detail, too insignificant to matter in the larger scheme of things.

Symbolic expression of strength

According to one view of the nature of law, legal institutions serve primarily as a codification – or official reaffirmations – of definitions of social reality developed within a given social context.[19] The purpose of punishment or of legal redress generally, is construed as the reparation of social reality. Punishment, therefore, is a process by which definitions, usually official ones or at least popular views of the social world, are reaffirmed. It is not applied willy-nilly. Rather, historically it has been applied according to principles of justice that require that some people be held responsible and punished for offenses while others are not.

Consistent with this perspective is the fact that when societies have a particularly strong sense of solidarity and moral strength, crimes are forgiven. Various forms of absolution repair the harm done. Some of the features of the execution of Christ are particularly good examples of this logic.

Perhaps the lack of executions for rapes in Germany is inconsistent only at first glance. Germany, unlike the United Kingdom and France, was not an entity that the military had to appease or impress with messages about any subject, especially its own attitudes toward its misbehaving soldiers. The Army had had many opportunities in Germany to have public hangings, replete with plenty of innocent victims and interested spectators, but it did not do so. Put simply, the rape of German women was not worth taking the life of one American soldier. To do so would not repair any sense of harm that had been done to, or by, any US Army personnel, or by juxtaposition, the United States. Perhaps Ted Kadin was right – they were "just Germans." There was little if any symbolic value to executing Americans for raping Germans. The symbolic value of executing US soldiers for rapes in Germany was so low that they were in the end, ignored.

Brigit Beck's analysis of rapes committed by the German Wehrmacht is consistent with the idea that one of the purposes of punishment is the reparation of social reality or social order. German soldiers who raped in France were punished harshly because they "severely damaged the reputation of the Wehrmacht and the trust of the French population in it."[20]

Military justice in disarray?

The possible explanations for the failure to execute Americans for raping Germans has thus far focused primarily on factors external to the Branch Office of the JAG. In this section, we examine the JAG Branch Office for clues to this wartime justice anomaly. As will be shown, it operated under numerous handicaps. Some of these problems were matters of time, personnel shortages, over work, command influence, and philosophical differences about fairness, punishment, and clemency. We begin with its history.

Branch Office JAG history

The Branch Office of the JAG for the United States Army and the Board of Review in the British Isles was created as a result of a directive from President Franklin D. Roosevelt to the Secretary of the War on April 14, 1942. It was first established on May 22, 1942, in Cheltenham, Gloucestershire, England. Two years later, October 16, 1944, the Office moved to Paris, where it was housed in a modern office building at 127 Avenue des Champs Elysese. Nine months later on July 8, 1945, the Office moved from Paris to the "Parc de Montretout, St. Cloud, France, about five miles distant from its former location and on the left bank of the Seine River."[21]

Nothing for the Branch Office seems to have been very easy. "The move from England to France, as well as from Paris to St. Cloud, created tremendous problems."[22] First, the Cheltenham Office was only given six days to prepare to move its entire personnel, records, and equipment to France. With no additional manpower or outside help available, the "burden of packing, planning and moving fell upon the Executive Division and the enlisted personnel."[23] Second, it took a convoy of trucks of an unspecified number to transport the packed materials to Southampton where they were loaded onto a Liberty ship for what turned out to be a four-day trip across the Channel in bad weather. According to the records, "The entire journey was made without mishap, although there were many discomforts."[24]

The order to move to St. Cloud came suddenly, but this time there was help available from the Transportation Corps and "several 10-ton trailer trucks."[25] This move was made in one day.

Supplies and personnel

The matter of supplies was always "a question of constant application and follow-up."[26] In England the need for typewriters and other machines "became acute," in part because "[p]aper supplies were ordered from Washington, as well as from local sources."[27]

This situation did not change once the office was in Paris. With its growing staff, the "clerical and administrative sections of the office were never fully supplied, lacking typewriters being the most serious problem."[28] The Office Branch's non-legal and legally trained personnel also made the work problematic. Their "capability, previous training, and numerical sufficiency" varied.

The law clerks were often transferred to the Office Branch from the infantry, artillery, and the military police. Several of them had law review experience. Overall, "Their services were invaluable and they [were] entitled to high commendation."[29]

Workload

The workload was extraordinarily demanding, "with a volume of work never before experienced by any other Branch Office of the JAG. To handle "a base monthly volume of 500 cases (or any substantial part of that amount)" the basic staff consisted of 6 people, only 1 of whom was a typist.[30]

It is informative to remember that the economic and social conditions in the United Kingdom, and especially in France and Germany, were rife with opportunities to illegally sell US government properties in a thriving black market. One consequence for the Branch Office was a tremendous increase in its criminal work. The railway pillaging cases are illustrative.[31]

In early September, 1944, the 716th Railway Operating Battalion was assigned the mission of "operating and maintaining the military railroad, initially from Chartres forward, ultimately from Droux through Versailles to Paris."[32] The trains carried US government property intended for the Army, including uniforms, clothing, rations, cigarettes, and "all types of supplies to be distributed to post exchanges for sale to soldiers."[33]

Wholesale theft soon became evident. During part of September, October, and November, 1944, "there was a critical shortage of cigarettes in the European Theater of Operations."[34] Every five or ten days badly pilfered trains arrived in Paris. On at least a dozen occasions, officers testified that cigarettes, rations, shoes, and goods intended for post exchanges had been stolen from the train – lock, stock, and barrel.

Incognito agents from the Criminal Investigation Division investigated the thefts and "mass arrests of more than 400 enlisted and commissioned personnel" occurred at the end of November.[35] The subsequent impact of these arrests on the Branch Office is best read from the original source. It said,

> The drafting, processing and trial of these cases was handicapped by a number of adverse circumstances: (1) the cases were received at a critical period in the precipitous tenfold expansion of the Staff Judge Advocate Section, forced by the large influx of serious cases, in which it became by far the largest operating military justice section in the theater or without much doubt, in our entire Army. (2) this expansion was at in volume of work alone (e.g., some 500 General Court-Martial cases received in January) with no corresponding increase in staff, the total staff of Judge Advocates consisting at that time of 10 company grade officers (mostly Lieutenants) in addition to the Staff Judge Advocate and Executive Office.

(3) additional staff and operative personnel of more than 100 officers were supplied from junior convalescent officers assembled from the hospitals into a detachment of patients-at-large. These officers were wholly untrained for the duty required of them and needed a maximum of supervision. ... These problems were aggravated by critical shortages of such essentials as court reporters and typewriters and by the necessity of moving twice in the course of a month in midwinter, finally occupying three different unheated buildings in widely separate parts of the city.[36]

The first trial for the thieves began in January, 1945. The second and last trial ended on March 28, 1945. In between the trials, Brigadier General Pleas B. Roger wrote a terse one and one-half page letter to those soldiers who had confessed. In part, the letter stated, "You have, however, the good fortune to have a commander [Eisenhower] with a profound sense of justice and keen interest in every individual soldier in the theater."[37] After writing that the commander was well acquainted with their merits as well as their crimes, he wrote, "He has therefore authorized and directed that you, or such of you as have demonstrated [by confession] this basis for redemption, be given the opportunity to serve under suspended sentences in a special combat company."[38]

Rogers sardonically added: "[H]owever, let me make it clear that it must be a fighting unit, with a spirit of loyalty and determination to faithful service which will not only repudiate, but fully redeem the unhappy past of its members. There must be no black sheep in your midst."[39] There is no indication how many, if any, of these "volunteers" survived the war. "Altogether 190 enlisted men and 8 officers were tried."[40] From its first case in the United Kingdom until its last in Germany, the Office Branch reviewed more than 17,000 cases.

Boards of review

The Office Branch's work grew at a fast pace on the continent. In the United Kingdom, it needed only one Board of Review (BOR). By July 11, 1944, in just over one month after D-Day, BOR No. 2 was created. Additional Boards were established on (No. 3) March 12, 1945, (No. 4) June 9, 1945, and (No. 5) June 25, 1945. "Unlike the Boards of Review sitting in Washington which considered its cases against the familiar American scene, the European Theater cases had to be analyzed as apart of field operations which often violently varied from each other."[41] The cases from the United Kingdom and Iceland involved, for example, "troops in the garrison islands," compared to those "in the disorganized battle-grounds of the liberated and conquered portions of western Europe."[42]

In addition to the material shortages, personnel problems, and the increasingly demanding workload, the Office Branch's responsibilities were expanded to include the cases that came from the Army of Occupation in

Germany and Austria, and the Mediterranean Theater of Operations (MTO). These developments came after the German surrender but were nonetheless additional work for the Office Branch.[43]

The problematic nature of the Branch Office's working conditions was less an impingement to the quality and integrity of its final dispositions of the Germany rape cases – or any other disposition it made – than other less tangible factors. The most important of these elements were questions about the legitimacy of the US military and the use of its courts as a means of discipline. It is against this background that a series of hotly debated issues involving justice, clemency, and excessive sentences are illuminated.

The US military: a question of legitimacy

The literature on the US military as an institution is plentiful. In Britain, the military was viewed as an honorable "secondary" career, an alternative for the second son in the family, or preparation for the eldest's larger work in life. Because of its long continental association with oppressive government, early America did not share this respect for the military, a point frequently made by military historians,[44] including biographers of some of its most famous generals.[45]

During the US colonial period, for example, professional soldiers were hated, especially the mercenary Hessians hired by the British. Americans chose to fight its revolutionary war with the militia volunteers. Later this position was reinforced by the US government's formative *Federalist Papers*. They made it clear that while a strong central government was needed to combat the chaos of an initial confederated government, a well-armed militia would be America's fighting force, not a professional standing army.[46] One indication of the low regard for the military can be gleaned from the fact that after the American Revolutionary War, it took an Act of Congress to approve pay for its soldiers and investors. Furthermore, the US government created a Department of War, and not separate departments for each of the military services.[47]

These developments help explain why the early US government saw the military as an occasional force to be dormant until times of conflict, a view shared by its citizens who treated the military as a necessary evil needed to repulse foreign invasion, to fulfill their "manifest destiny" in the conquest of its Western frontier, and finally, to become a world power broker. Throughout its history, US armed forces have been manned by volunteers. Conscription or mass drafting of personnel was saved for a few rare occasions, including World War II. And only slowly and begrudgingly did the US government come to permit the military to train officers for careers.[48] Despite the fact that some of its military heroes, including George Washington, Andrew Jackson, US Grant, Theodore Roosevelt and Dwight D. Eisenhower would occupy the White House, the military has never been fully accepted by the US citizenry.[49]

Only after World War II did the US create a standing army and a Department of Defense.[50] Even then, the US continued zealously to guard the right of civilian rule. The unpopular President Harry S. Truman (1945–1952), for example, fired an extremely popular World War II general, Douglas MacArthur, when he labeled Truman "a temporary occupant of the White House." Americans gave MacArthur a hero's farewell but ultimately backed Truman for his actions. Today after almost 70 years of a standing army the US military is still not very popular. The US military services spend millions yearly in advertising not only to recruit new members but also to bolster their institutional legitimacy.

Military justice: part of the problem

The problem of legitimacy for the military stems in large measure from its questionable record of internal justice. The issue is conflict over the purpose of military justice: civilian rulers see military justice as extensions of civilian justice, while career militarists view the courts as a means of discipline.

Several exposes of military justice and legal commentaries illustrate this point.[51] The first cause celebre occurred under suspicious circumstances in 1883 with the court martial of James Chestnut Whittaker, a former slave. After being commissioned to West Point, Whittaker received threatening notes, hazing by cadets, and he was beaten severely and tied to his bed. His white commander concluded that he was "faking it." Whittaker's demand for justice and his request for a court of inquiry drew national newspaper coverage. The army – quick to defend itself from critics about the brutal life of a black cadet in West Point – ultimately court-martialed Whittaker rather than face the stark reality of changing two of its most cherished institutions: West Point and the military justice system.[52] Whittaker's experience and the questions it raised about the purposes of military justice was not an isolated or forgotten incident. More than 100 years after Whittaker's trial President Clinton posthumously granted Whittaker's commission in 1995.

Whittaker's experience was not an isolated incident in the history of US military justice. In World War I, black soldiers were treated very harshly. In 1917 alone, at Fort Bliss, Texas, more than 60 black soldiers were court-martialed for mutiny when they did not attend a drill formation in a racially charged Southern environment. All were promptly found guilty, dishonorably discharged, and given 10–20 years in Leavenworth prison for their protest. The incident went largely unreported in the South but was used by Northern politicians to discredit the Army as racist. During World War I, a total of 35 soldiers, all black, were executed.[53]

More horrific than the Fort Bliss incident were the riots in Houston, Texas, and also of 1917. Amid a constant war between the black 24th Infantry and the local white police, two non-commissioned officers were arrested for "disorderly conduct," and rumored to be dead. This sparked the soldiers to arms, and an ugly scene followed. Several hours later, 15 whites were dead. A "state of war" was declared and 63 soldiers, all black, were court-martialed. Forty-eight were convicted and sentenced to lengthy prison terms, 14 more were sentenced to death, and five were acquitted. The executions occurred the morning after the trial and *before* the records reached Washington for command review. A similar incident occurred in 1918 at Camp Dodge, Iowa, where three black soldiers were hanged for "assaulting and outraging" a 17-year-old white girl.[54]

The military, stinging from public criticism of these and other incidents, soon faced an enraged Congress and a gravely concerned public. "The War Department responded by ordering that no death sentence could be carried out 'until the record of trial had been reviewed in [JAGO] and the reviewing authority ha[d] been informed ... that such review [had] been made and that there [wa]s no legal objection to carrying the sentence into execution.'"[55] This decision, with revisions and expansions soon became known as General Order Number Seven. It created Boards of Review (BOR or BR) to examine all serious sentences after verdict and prior to sentence disposition. They were empowered to review the process and content of general courts-martial and to ensured that military justice was indeed just. The BORs were, unfortunately, powerless to stop the role of command influence in capital cases for World War II.

There was considerable tension among the War Department, the Army, and the JAG over the importance of reviewing capital cases, sentences, clemency, and executions. If one thing united them, it was concern about how the public would react to their collective record on punishments given to soldiers.

Justice, clemency, and excessive sentences

The problem of how to handle improper sentences soon came to the attention of the head of the JAG's World War II Branch Office in the ETO. In two separate letters from Eisenhower, Brigadier General E.C. McNeil, a lawyer, was "directed to report to your [McNeil's] headquarters, among other things, improper sentences ... of a general prisoner to be returned to the United States which should be reduced here before his return."[56] The first letter was dated August 6, 1943. The second one was dated February 4, 1944 – a year of national elections. Both letters were received by McNeil while the Branch Offices were still in the United Kingdom.

McNeil replied to the first letter December 23, 1943. In it he questioned the policy for clemency, which in the US Army addressed among other things the reductions of sentences. McNeil used the case of Private Woodrow Burns to begin what turned out to be a lengthy and, at times, acrimonious debate about fairness in sentencing. Burns had been tried and convicted for "petit larceny (3 specifications) and desertion involving an absence of 30 days."[57] He was sentenced to dishonorable discharge, total forfeitures, and confinement for 30 years in the US Penitentiary, Lewisburg, Pennsylvania.

For sake of comparison, McNeil's letter contained enclosures of several similar cases. In the cases of Nolan, Mosser, and McCutcheon, he noted that they had committed many crimes "and maintained themselves during long absences by a deliberate life of crime."[58] "However," he said, "it should be noted that the first two received sentences of 20 years," while "Burns received 30 [years] and [had] no record of crime while absent."[59] (No mention was made of McCutcheon's sentence). McNeil's letter also pointed out that two other soldiers, Specensky and Takach, had committed offenses comparable to Burns'. They had received sentences of five and four years, respectively, to be served at the Army's Disciplinary Training Center at Shepton Mallet, England.

McNeil wanted to know why one soldier, Burns, should get a dishonorable discharge and 30 years in a penitentiary in the United States, while soldiers who had committed similar offenses were not given dishonorable discharges. McNeil ended his letter by stating that he wished to comply with the instructions he had received from Eisenhower regarding uniformity of sentences. He was motivated by concerns about public relations issues for the Army back in the United States after the war. He said, "[S]o that this theater may not be subject to criticisms for returning prisoners to the United States with indefensible sentences which require immediate clemency by the War Department."[60] This was a legitimate and sensitive issue of concern for the military, and in this regard, McNeil was prescient. Finally, McNeil suggested that a method should be developed to reduce excessive sentences to a uniform figure, and he offered his cooperation.

Eisenhower replied to McNeil in January, 1945, with a letter written by Colonel T. Hughes. It stated that when McNeil (Branch Office) reviewed the cases of general prisoners to be returned to the United States and found what he deemed "unjustifiable or indefensible' sentences, he should *recommend* a change." (Emphasis added) The suggested sentence change was to be sent to Eisenhower. "[T]he Theater Commander, the Commanding General, ... would then take the final action in the matter."[61] In other words, there were to be no new methods for reviewing excessive sentences. The procedures that were already in place would work just fine, according to Eisenhower. He did not want the JAG Branch Office to override sentences that he or his commanders had approved, even if they were excessive and inconsistent.

In early February, 1945, Eisenhower's inflexibility on this topic was reaffirmed in a letter sent to McNeil. The letter from "By Command of General Eisenhower" stated that Private Burns' sentence had been reduced from 20 years to10 years hard labor. The same letter reiterated that "it is desired that you report such sentences, with your recommendations to the Commanding General ... for his consideration."[62]

McNeil refused to back away from the issues. His December 23, 1943 letter which had expressed his concerns about Private Woodrow Burns's 30-year sentence, was only one page long, and it contained only three tightly written paragraphs – none of them numbered. It had been written under the innocuous label, "SUBJECT: Policy re clemency in certain cases."[63] However, his February 16, 1945 letter to the Commanding General was altogether different.

Instead of constructing his letter under a soft, unblameworthy title, McNeil immediately gives notice that he had reached an accusatory conclusion. For his "SUBJECT," he writes, "Excessive sentences *adjudged* by general courts-martial."[64] The past tense of "adjudged" is the key word. It is not a query; it is similar to a declarative statement. It also contained an opinion that was coming from the highest-ranking officer in Branch Office of the JAG. McNeil's opinion was unmistakably clear – he thought that Eisenhower's commanders were guilty of approving excessive sentences. McNeil's evidence was presented in a three-page, single spaced letter that contained seven numbered paragraphs and a single sentence that was numbered "8," plus a chart.

The letter stressed the power and influence that context exerted on the proper punishments for felonies that had been committed when the Army had been in the United Kingdom. "There," he noted, "[was] little difficulty with respect to the punishment of felonies where there are customs and standards fixed by civil law as well as by military authorities."[65] The situation for the Branch Office and the Army had changed once there were troops on the continent. In McNeil's words, "On arrival on the Continent and entry into combat there was born, naturally, a great increase in trials for desertion, misbehavior in battle and disobedience of orders relating to combat."[66] He went on to say at the end of the first paragraph: "The sentences are not only very severe [here] but there is a great lack of uniformity in different jurisdictions. I am unable to carry out the above directives without such some advice as to the theater policies in these matters."[67]

McNeil's concerns stemmed from an empirical base that indicated that the wide range of sentences for convictions for which there were "no standards of application." As evidence, his letter contained a chart that summarized the sentences that had been given in January, 1945. It clearly indicated a lack of uniformity. Some soldiers had been sentenced to 15 years, others to confinement ranging from 20 years (93 soldiers), to life (76 soldiers).

He informed Eisenhower that he had recently studied "available general court-martial orders promulgated by the War Department" at home in Washington, DC.[68] By comparing the ETO sentences with those imposed by the JAG home office in Washington, McNeil's paragraph 5 reinforced the argument that the ETO sentences were severe and excessive. McNeil reported, for instance, that in 1943, there were 11 death sentences imposed for desertion (some were associated with escape, drunkenness, and theft), all of which were commuted. In eight of these cases, the dishonorable discharge had also been suspended. In 1944, McNeil reported that the War Department had also considered three desertion cases and that it had commuted the sentences to 10, 10, and 1 years respectively.

Finally, "for consideration as indicative of opinion at home," McNeil informed Eisenhower that the War Department had recently reconsidered a well-publicized case of disobedience of orders.[69] Death was the first sentence given in this case, and it was reduced to life. The life sentence was reduced to 20 years, and the War Department reduced this sentence to just 5 years. Ever mindful to public sentiment, McNeil wrote in the last four lines of the seventh paragraph of his letter: "While it is our duty primarily to consider the effect on the Army here, we must also try to visualize the reaction which will be caused at home, and whether it will result in criticism of this Theater."[70]

The *HBO/JAG* is curiously silent on whether McNeil's concerns about criticism for severe sentences for desertion were informed by what he knew had happened at St. Marie Aux Mines, France, on January 31, 1945. On that date, with Eisenhower's approval, the Army shot to death Private Eddie D. Slovik, 25, white, Company G. 109th Infantry, for desertion. It was the first such punishment for this offense in more than 80 years.[71] According to Slovik's trial records, McNeil registered no objections to the sentence – he agreed with Board of Review No. 1's decision that "the record of trial is legally sufficient to support the sentence."[72]

The facts of the case were straightforward. Slovik's unit had been heavily involved with front line fighting, and he refused to join in it – he did not want to kill. He deserted his group near Elbeuf, France, about August 25, 1944 and stayed with the Canadian Provost Corps for six weeks, until they returned him to military authorities near Brussels on about October 4, 1944. Four days later, he deserted again and turned himself in on October 9, 1944.

Slovik admitted in writing that he had deserted the US Army, and he also wrote that if he was caught and turned lose, he would "RUN AWAY AGAIN IF I HAVE TO GO OUT THEIR (Sic).[73] He hoped that he would be tried, found guilty, and sent to prison. His hopes were well founded. Thousands of deserters had done the same thing, and none had been executed. According to one source, by the end of the ETO, at least 40,000 soldiers had been found guilty of desertion, and none were executed but Slovik.[74]

McNeil's endorsement of BOR No. 1's findings was in sharp contradiction to his previously expressed concerns about the unfair sentences for desertion. He was well aware that life or death sentences for desertion had been routinely changed to a broad range of years in prison. Two clues give some illumination to his thinking. First, he agreed that Slovik's plan was deliberate. McNeil correctly stated that [I]t had been Slovik's intention to "secure trial and incarceration in a safe place but the imposition of a less severe sentence would only have accomplished the accused's purpose of securing his incarceration and consequent protection from the dangers which so many of our armed forces are required to face daily."[75] This was solid legal reasoning. The second clue is less convincing and smacks of hypocrisy. McNeil said, "His unfavorable civilian record indicates that he is not a worthy subject of clemency."[76]

Here McNeil referred to Slovik's early youth when he had been arrested and incarcerated for a series of crimes that the FBI's report to the army portrayed as more serious than they actually were. Slovik, for instance, was arrested once for driving a stolen car. The FBI concluded nonetheless that "[T]hey indicate a persistent refusal to conform to the rules of society in civilian life, an imperviousness to penal correction and total lack of appreciation of clemency; these qualities the accused brought with him into the military."[77] In fact, Lieutenant Colonel Henry J. Sommer, the JAG Judge for the 28th Infantry Division that Slovik's unit was in, said without independent verification or standard reference: "The accused is a habitual criminal."[78] Sommer recommended death.

Sommer and McNeil's reasoning failed to emphasize that Slovik's criminal past *did not* involve capital crimes. Nor did they recognize that the Army had thousands of known criminals in its ranks. Neither did they argue that executing Slovik would have been inconsistent with all of the sentences that thus far had been given to deserters. No consideration was given to the fact that the Army had previously found Slovik unfit for service and had accordingly classified him as 4-F; only later, under the pressure of needing more soldiers, was he drafted into the Army. As Slovik wrote on December 9, 1944, to General Eisenhower, "[T]he army didn't want anything to do with me at the time."[79] The use of "persistent refusal" and "total lack" were blatantly inconsistent with Slovik's minor criminal record.

Context killed Slovik. By the time his case got to Eisenhower, the military jails were full of deserters, and he was short of men. As we have seen in Chapter 5, black soldiers had been approved to help relieve this problem by leaving their service units and joining the infantry, often following required reductions in rank and pay. Slovik was an easy soldier to execute. Already once labeled as undesirable by the Army before he got drafted, he had few if any capital qualities. His marriage and happy home life meant nothing to the Army when it needed an execution to deter desertions. There is no indication, however, that Slovik's execution produced the desired results.

Slovik's understanding of the importance of context is unquestionable. As he stood with his execution party, an MP told him, "'Try to take it easy, Eddie. Try to make it easy on yourself – and on us.'"[80] Slovik replied, "Don't worry about me. I'm okay. They're not shooting me for deserting the US Army – thousands of guys have done that. They're shooting me for the bread I stole when I was twelve years old."[81] Eleven bullets pierced his body – only one was judged a "probably fatal wound."[82]

McNeil's campaign for wartime justice continued, nevertheless. On April 7, 1945, he wrote about his concerns to the Theater Provost Marshall. By this late date in the war, he had seen no improvements with uniform sentencing. His message was clear: "Sentencing policies are not uniform between different commands, between different courts within the same command, or even between different cases tried by the same court."[83] McNeil also complained that too little attention had been paid in the ETO to the importance of Disciplinary Training Centers and the rehabilitation that they could accomplish. He was of the opinion that clemency – reduction of sentences – should be encouraged so that the maximum number of convicted "men could be restored to useful service."[84]

Shortly afterward on April 20, 1945, Brigadier General R.B. Lovett, US Army Adjutant General, wrote to McNeil on behalf of Eisenhower. He stated categorically that the conditions in "theater on August 6, 1943 and currently" made it impracticable to define in advance what fair sentences would be.[85] The circumstances of each case and the requirements of fluid "military objectives and for the security of forces under command" prevented taking "more definitive" decisions about miscarriages of justice.[86] More emphatically, Lovett made it clear that "the administration of justice ... serve[s] command responsibilities."[87] "It is not expected that the Commanding General ... for sake of uniformity will undertake to equalize the sentences."[88] Uniformity and fairness for Eisenhower were simply unimportant.

Meanwhile, the war in Europe was winding down. Lovett's April 20, 1945 letter to McNeil was written only two weeks before Germany surrendered, and Eisenhower was still not persuaded by McNeil's arguments. His position was again reiterated and strongly supported by a three-paged, single-spaced letter dated April 23, 1945. This time it was written by Colonel Daniel L. O'Donnell, Chief of the Military Justice Division. It was labeled "*Memorandum* for General McNeil," and its contents gave additional weight to Lovett's interpretations of matters related to excessive sentences and place of confinement.[89] In essence, everything that McNeil had been fighting for was rejected. O'Donnell's last line said it all. "It may be inferred from the indorsement that a sentence is not to be deemed 'improper' ... merely because it is out of line with the theater average or some other uniform scale of maximum punishments." The Chief of Military Justice Division was loath to have any sentence questioned.

Matters began to quickly change once Germany surrendered and American soldiers began to return to the United States. On May 15, 1945, Under Secretary of War, Robert P. Patterson, wrote Eisenhower a direct and clear letter about clemency and uniformity of sentences. He had just established a board to examine sentences that had been given in the United States. It began thus, "As you know, my office in the War Department is charged with the duty of clemency and uniformity of sentences with respect to military prisoners sentenced by general courts-martial."[90]

Patterson firmly supported reducing excessive sentences, and he was of the opinion that a soldier's service record was often given too little consideration at sentencing. He said, "It is my belief that courts and reviewing authorities on initial action do not always give proper consideration to a man's long and arduous combat service, often valiant service recognized by award decorations, and to conditions of physical and mental exhaustion and other circumstances shown in the particular case."[91] The Under Secretary of War did not mention to Eisenhower the tragic and illustrative case of Private First Class Blake W. Mariano, Company C, 19th First Tank Battalion.

Mariano was a 29-year-old full-blooded Navajo from a reservation not far from Gallup, NM. He had completed the third grade at 13, having repeated it twice. He was from a broken family – his father had abandoned him and his mother. Mariano was divorced, the father of one child, a girl, and the sole supporter of his mother, grandmother, and other relatives. Mariano had fought the enemy in Africa, Italy, France, and Germany – he had been overseas for 34 months and in the Army for 4 years. A girlfriend waited for him in England.

On April 15, 1945, the town of Lauf was captured by the "victorious American army."[92] During the night of the same day, the soldiers entered the town. Private First Class Mariano parked his tank near Meier's store and began a night of drinking in a cellar with "some Polish and Russian people."[93] Later in the night, he and another American soldier, Private First Class George P. Muhlehaupt, and a Pole entered the cellar of the Castle of Lauf. Assembled there in very poor lighting were 15 German residents and 2 children. At gunpoint, Mariano forced Fraulein Elfriede W., 21, an office girl, to leave the shelter and to accompany him to the castle courtyard where she said he raped her. She testified that after Mariano was finished with her, his American companion, "the tall soldier, also raped me."[94]

Muhlehaupt could speak a little German. According to Fraulein Elfriede W.'s testimony he said he was 28 and that his father was German. She asked him why he and Mariano raped her. He replied, "[T]hat the Germans had done the same in France."[95] Upon noticing that she was wearing an engagement ring, he asked about her fiancé and whether he was an officer or a sergeant. She replied that he was an ordinary soldier (in the German Army). Sometime after the rape he followed her home, and they spent some time together.

She saw him a few times before he departed the next day at 10 a.m.[96] Investigating Officer First Lieutenant James E. Stodgel reported that Private First Class Muhlenhaupt told him that he had asked Fraulein Elfiede if she was "mad for what had happened and she replied she was not."[97] Muhlenhapt also said that at this time he asked her to kiss him "good bye," and that she compiled.

The impact of the rape on her engagement and later life was nonetheless devastating, according to Mme. Heidenreich.[98] At the time of the crime Fraulein Huber was sixteen-years-old. She and her entire family had been in the castle cellar briefly before Mariano and Muhlenhaupt entered it. Sensing that the cellar could be turned into a deadly trap, her family except for her father – Wilhelm Huber – who stayed behind because it was "warden of the cellar," ran and hid in the root cellar of a nearby neighbor. It was only a few feet past her and her parent's home at 10 Siebenkase Streetwhich. After the family emerged from hiding the next morning, their home's second – story view provided a close and clear view of the parked tank and the castle from which the two American rapists emerged and drove away.

Sixty years later, Mme. Heidereich, the owner of an electrical appliance store directly across the street from the castle, explained that her father and several others had reported that they had seen some of the crimes committed by Mariano. According to her recollection, her father overheard Fraulein Elfriede tell her own father of her rape by Mariano and Muhlenhaupt. Upon returning from the war, Fraulein Elfriede's fiancé found the rape too painful to accept and broke their engagement. Apparently, she never recovered, and she spent several years living a reclusive unmarried life with her father. She never married. Following his death, she retreated further from social life, lived a hermit-like life, drank heavily, and died a few years later.

Mariano returned to the shelter in approximately twenty minutes and with gestures told Frau Martha G. – possibly a Swedish citizen – to undress. All the time his "tommy gun" was held at ready.[99] She did not want to undress, however, and offered her wedding ring to Mariano, as well as her Swedish passport. Mariano showed no interest in these items and threw them aside.

Some of the men in the shelter encouraged Mrs. Martha G., 41, to "undress and for her to sacrifice herself by removing her clothes."[100] She was wearing slacks. She took off her coat and her blouse and folded her slacks down below her knees. The upper part of her body down to her corset [were] exposed and also her legs were exposed from her corset to her knees."[101] During this time she pleaded with Mariano to stop the ordeal. She was embarrassed to be undressing in front of others. Fraulein Elfriede W.'s father, however, told her to go ahead, "that they would not look."[102]

When she started to remove her girdle, it was evident that she was menstruating. Apparently, for no other reason, Mariano shot her (she suffered greatly and did not die until the next day) and reloaded. According to his trial records, he turned his attention to Frau Babette K., a 54-year-old storekeeper. She did not resist, and she left the shelter and went into a room where Mariano had sexual intercourse with her. At this point, all the people remaining in the shelter escaped through a window that served as an emergency exit, except for the wounded woman and the paralyzed daughter of Frau Babette K. The next day Mrs. Martha G.'s husband arrived with his discharge papers from the German Army, only to learn that his wife had been murdered by an American. "He is the one who reported the incident to the proper authorities."[103]

Before Mrs. Martha G. was shot, and also before Frau Babette K. was forced outdoors by Mariano, Fraulein Elfriede W. returned to the cellar and spoke quietly to her father. According to Frau Elizabeth M. – Mrs. Martha G.'s sister-in-law who was also in the cellar – she did not hear what Fraulein Elfriede W.'s father said, but she did hear his daughter's reply. It was "All both [sic], in the court castle."[104] At this point, Frau Elizabeth M. said that the father remarked that "they could not go on with this."[105] "[H]e gave razor blades to some of the people for them to commit suicide."[106]

Investigations before his trial on May 25 and 26, 1945, found that Mariano was considered a good soldier who remained calm under combat conditions and that he had killed many Germans.[107] His only weakness was that when drinking "he seems to go wild" and "g[o]t off his nut ... playing around with the women and chasing after them ... to get into their pants."[108] When drunk Mariano sometimes acted childish "doing foolish things, like riding a cow."[109] One witness said he was an Indian who could not hold his liquor.

He was found guilty of murder, attempted rape, and rape, and the court recommended death. At the first level of review following the court's decision on May 28, 1945, Captain George A. Fisher, Acting Staff Judge Advocate, Headquarters, 45th Infantry Division, agreed, even though Mariano had the "mentality of 11 years (high-grade moron)" and had "shown a satisfactory ability to adjust" to the Army.[110] Fisher explained his position in some of the most stinging language found in any of the capital in the cases in the European Theater. He said,

> There is but one answer to the offenses of which the accused has been convicted. To say it mildly, the offenses were heinous. They showed utter degradation and depravity second to none. The accused disgraced his country, his country's Army, and his own noble race. The fact that the crimes were committed against the persons of enemy civilians does not diminish them in my judgment, but rather, if anything, aggravates them. I make this assertion not because of the fact that the victims were Germans, but because of fact that the accused, by his conduct, did that which would serve to confirm in the minds of those who witnessed it and heard about it, that everything Hitler and his henchmen had said concerning how Americans would act as true and correct. Certainly acts like that of the accused were such as would inspire additional resistance. The court imposed the death penalty. I am of the opinion that such imposition was fully warranted and I do not think that the death sentence should be mitigated. Unless the provision for the death penalty is but an empty gesture, he deserves to die.[111]

Fisher not only wanted Mariano to die, he wanted him hanged. "As a matter of custom and practice, hanging ... has been generally been reserved for murder, rape, and the like offenses, and is considered a more shameful punishment than shooting."[112] Clearly, Fisher wanted Mariano to suffer. He elaborated thus: "Such line of thought grows out of the physical matters attendant to a hanging. I am of the opinion that accused's acts fully merit the most ignominious punished that can be imposed."[113]

On the next day the convening authorities agreed with Fisher. However, sometime between May 29 and 31 July, 1945, Major Francis J. Gafford, Assistant Staff Judge Advocate, located at the Headquarters of the United States Forces, offered his opinion on Mariano's fate; he disagreed.[114] Gafford argued that there had been contradictory evidence on the rape of one of Mariano's victims. A German civilian doctor, Welder Seybold, of Lauf had found that Fraulein Elfriede W. had not been penetrated. "He found the hymen [of Fraulein Elfriede W] not damaged."[115] Seybold testified that "in his opinion she had never had sexual intercourse."[116]

Gafford was also concerned about the violation of some of Mariano's rights. The prosecution had, for example, announced in its voire dire that it was going to ask for the death penalty. "Such a statement is not customary before court-martial. There was also some question about whether the prosecution had violated the rules of cross-examination when it had Mariano on the witness stand. Captain Joseph D. Anderson, defense counsel, had strenuously objected to some of the prosecutor's questions on the grounds that they violated Mariano's rights against having to give compulsory self-incriminating evidence."[117]

He had other concerns, though minor, which did not affect any substantial right of Mariano that, nonetheless, indicated that he had given the trial records minute and detailed attention, perhaps even greater scrutiny than had Fisher. Gafford pointed out that Fisher had not acknowledged or discussed the fact that there was no receipt for Mariano's copy of "the record of trial proper," and that there were various typographical errors that Fisher should have corrected.[118]

The most glaring technical transgression that Fisher had made was that he had not caught the fact that the *wrong person* had been identified at trial as the officer who had investigated the charges against Mariano. "The trial Judge Advocate erroneously announced to the court that the charges were investigated by First Lieutenant James E. Stodgel. Although this officer made a preliminary investigation, the officer who made the formal investigation under Article of War 70 was First Lieutenant William S Hathaway."[119]

Gafford, almost certainly knew of the May 15, 1945 letter that Under Secretary of War Patterson had sent to Eisenhower that had made it clear that he thought the soldier's service records should be considered at sentencing. Accordingly Gafford wrote, "Great consideration should be accorded him for his combat service with a battle-line unit and his long, active and continuous engagement with the enemy."[120] In the final analysis, it was Mariano's record that Gafford relied upon to recommend that the original sentence be confirmed, but commuted to dishonorable discharge, forfeiture of all pay and allowances, and confinement at hard labor for life.

Back home: public criticism of military justice

Gafford's decision did not end the debate about Mariano's fate. Brigadier General ED. W. Betts, also a staff judge advocate, appended his opinion of the evidence on the last page of Patterson's review and conclusions. On July 31, 1945, he wrote only one sentence on the matter: "Having read the record of trail, I concur, except I recommend confirmation of the sentenced as approved."[121]

As with Gafford, there is every reason to think that Betts knew about Under Secretary Patterson's attitude about considering soldier's service records. Not only was Betts' decision taken a full six weeks after Patterson's May 15, 1945 letter to Eisenhower, it was four weeks after the day Patterson had written a second letter to Eisenhower about the issue that McNeil had been prescient about – public criticism of military justice. On May 31, 1945, Patterson wrote to Eisenhower: "There has been widespread comment in the press here over the case of Private McGee, who received a court-martial sentence in your Theater of two years confinement and dishonorable discharge for striking nine German prisoners of war."[122] The *New York Times* coverage of this case is illustrative.

It reported that "A hot protest by Representative McCormack, House Majority Leader, started a War Department review tonight of a two-year sentence imposed on Private. Joseph McGee of Worcester, Mass."[123] McCormack demanded and got the Office of the Judge Advocate General to give a prompt review of the case. McGee had been tried and convicted at Le Mans, France, after he "'socked' the German prisoners when they refused to work."[124] McCormack asked for the exoneration of this soldier and his immediate restoration to duty.[125] After all, "[t]he evidence against this man came from – practically if not wholly – German people and certainly one cannot remove their testimony from the realm of prejudice." McGee had been returned to the United States and on May 26, was confined at Fort Benjamin Harrison, Indiana.

Patterson's letter to Eisenhower was written only 5 days later, on May 31, 1945. In it he stated, "[T]he sentence given to McGee was severely criticized in Congress, as well as in the press and over the radio."[126] He also informed Eisenhower that he had cancelled McGee's dishonorable discharge and restored the man to duty. Patterson also expressed concern that the military justice system might now have radical changes forced upon it. In hopes of avoiding this outcome, Patterson asked Eisenhower to control the imposition of penalties for soldiers about to be returned to the United States. Patterson was manifestly concerned about bad press "where the initial sentence is deemed by the public to be out of line with the offense committed."[127]

At this point, Eisenhower expressed only light sympathy for Under Secretary Patterson's predicament. One month after Germany's surrender, he wrote to Patterson and reaffirmed that he gave the administration of military justice "constant personal care; particularly in the serious cases in which I am called upon for personal review."[128] Eisenhower admitted that the approving authorities in McGee case "did not take into calculations its possible effect upon public opinion."[129] He also admitted that he knew "nothing whatsoever about the actual merits of the [McGee] case or the character of McGee."[130] Eisenhower agreed with Patterson "that under the circumstances you were practically compelled to take the action you did."[131]

In other words, Patterson's PR problems could and would not be laid at the feet of the Commanding General. Eisenhower implied that lesser souls, including McNeil, had been at fault. In his defense, Eisenhower's letter said, "I have already given very strict orders for reviewing sentences to assure their reasonableness and upon occasion have personally intervened both to reduce sentences and to suspend them."[132]

A copy of Eisenhower's letter to Patterson was sent to McNeil. At this juncture, McNeil, predictably, responds to Eisenhower's letter to Patterson. He stated, "I am unaware of any directive by the Theater Commander with reference to reasonableness of sentences."[133] It is worth noting that Eisenhower's letter to the Under Secretary was decidedly informal. Eisenhower's greeting to Patterson made casual reference to a former position that Patterson had before he became the Under Secretary of War. It began with "Dear Judge Patterson." The letter, in fact, contained no references to any specific "strict order" he might have made regarding the matter. In a matter so serious as to cause public outcry, it is more than curious that Eisenhower, who had spent his professional life dealing with the specifics and minutia of military life, did not take the letter as an opportunity to more thoroughly cover his backside.

McNeil also took pains to point out that during the time of McGee's offense and trial, thousands of American soldiers were in German prisoner of war camps. Any inadequate punishment of McGee "might well have been reported to the American authorities, by the protecting power and have formed the basis of reprisals against American prisoners of war."[134] Furthermore, McGee's dishonorable discharge was not ordered by any authority in this theater. This happened in the United States.

In view of the press attention given to McGee and Congress's criticism of military justice, it is reasonable to conclude that Eisenhower had been put on notice to help prevent unwanted public criticism because of excessive sentences. Nonetheless, Betts, who was near Eisenhower as the Theater Judge Advocate, signed his name and dated his one-line comment on Mariano's record. On July 31, 1945, he rejected it as irrelevant. Betts left no record indicating why he supported the original death sentence. However, Marino's final fate had yet to be decided – that was up to Eisenhower.

He confirmed Mariano's death sentence on August 4, 1945. McNeil disagreed, and on September 7,1945, he replied to Eisenhower. The concern in

Washington about excessive sentences, meanwhile, had not abated. Earlier in mid-summer (July 31,1945), the War Department had written another letter on the subject of courts-martial and combat records. McNeil's September 7, 1945 letter quoted part of it to Eisenhower. "While a credible combat record does not endow the individual with any special immunity, neglect to give it due weight is equally an injustice and an impairment of public respect for the Army's administration of military justice."[135]

McNeil's position was essentially the same as Gafford's. Both attorneys emphasized Mariano's strong service record, lack of education, weak mental facilities, and drunkenness. The latter condition did not develop, McNeil emphasized, until Mariano had been drafted and he "began using liquor by buying 'beer at the PX.'" McNeil blamed all but the Army for putting Mariano in harm's way.[136] Mariano testified that he never drank alcohol until he was in the Army.

True to his word, on September 28, 1945 "the Theater Commander gave further personal consideration to this matter ... and directed that the sentence as confirmed and approved be carried into execution."[137] Captain Fisher had his wish fulfilled. Private Blake W. Mariano was hanged at the Lorie Disciplinary Training Center, Le Mans, Sarthe, France, on October 10, 1945.[138] Eisenhower, however, did not approve the execution of any soldier in Germany for rape alone.

It was easy for the Army to kill Mariano. His death, especially, and Slovik's death came at the end of a context where military justice gave theater commanders enormous life and death power in capital cases. Neither unfortunate soldier, nor nearly seven score more, had the benefit of public concern. Mariano's story has never been told. No powerful politician – or any politician, for that matter – political body, or writer with the stature of William Bradford Huie (who wrote about Slovik) ever heard his name. Public concern about military justice nonetheless soon broadened and deepened in the United States.

On December 13, 1946, the Secretary of War received a report from his Advisory Committee on Military Affairs, soon to be known as the "Vanderbilt Report" for its chairman, New Jersey-based Honorable Arthur T. Vanderbilt, arguably the nation's legal reformer during the middle decades of the twentieth century. The committee's members had been nominated by the American Bar Association; its function was to study the administration of military justice within the Army and its courts-martial system and to make recommendations to change the existing laws and regulations. Its goal was the improvement of military justice in the Army.

The committee had been authorized to have "full freedom of action in the accomplishment of its mission."[139] It took advantage of this directive and held hearings and called witnesses it deemed desirable. These included the Judge Advocate General, the Assistant Judge Advocate General, ETO, the General Board, US Forces, European Theater, the Secretary and Under

Secretary of War, the Chief of Staff of the Army, the Commander of the Army Ground Forces, and "a number of Generals, Lieutenant Generals, Major Generals, Brigadier Generals, colonels, and representatives of five Veterans organizations."[140]

The committee also relied upon a number of "voluminous statistical and result studies by the Judge Advocate General's Department," including the two-volume *History of the Branch Office* used in this study.[141] They received and examined hundreds of letters, had numerous personal interviews, and digested 321 answers to questionnaires that had been sent to officers of all grades, enlisted men, and civilians.

The committee's efforts were unprecedented in US military justice history. In addition to the above-mentioned work, it held regional public hearings in New York, Philadelphia, Baltimore, Raleigh, Atlanta, Chicago, St. Louis, Denver, San Francisco, and Seattle.[142] Before presenting its recommendations, it made it clear that its findings were "not based on the testimony of convicted men or their friends."[143] In the committee's words,

> Our information comes from general officers, staff, judge advocates and in large part from men who served as members of the courts and as counsel for the respective parties. Many of them are known by us to be young men of unquestioned character and ability, who have become or will become leaders of the legal profession in the future, the sort of men upon who a greatly expanded army must rely in time of war and who, in giving their testimony, had no grievances to air or desire to impair or destroy the existing system but were moved to offer sympathetic and constructive suggestions for its upbuilding [*sic*].

In other words, the committee interviewed and listened primarily to men from inside the army – men *they* could trust.[144] It is with little surprise, therefore, that the committee reported to the Secretary of War that "[a]lmost without exception our informants said that the Army system of justice in general and as written in the books is a good one that it is excellent in theory and designed to secure swift and sure justice; and that the innocent are almost never convicted and the guilty seldom acquitted."[145]

Against a background of acknowledging that there was such disparity and severity in the Army's version of military justice as to "bring many military courts into disrepute both among the law-breaking element and the law-abiding element,"[146] the committee made several recommendations. They are not part of the story told here, however. For an excellent, rich, and detailed discussion of these recommendations within the history of military justice, the reader should consult Jonathan Lurie's two-volume work.[147]

The postwar reforms did not end the public's concern about the fairness of military justice. It remains a subject of debate. As recently as December 2002 it was the subject of rather scathing *U.S. News & World Report* review that concluded "[m]ilitary courts are stacked to convict – but not the brass."[148] To some observers, the military's criminal justice system is not only arcane but also deeply afflicted with unequal justice. The law remains a funny thing.

Notes

Preface to the French Edition

1. Rome Statute of the International Criminal Court, July 17, 1998, Articles 7 and 8.
2. *Violences sexuelles*, in *Les femmes et la guerre*, 2/8, Geneva, Publications of the International Committee of the Red Cross, 2001.
3. Law of December 23, 1980, Article 1, quoted by Georges Vigarello, *Histoire du viol XVIᵉ–XXᵉ siècle*, Paris, Seuil, 1998, p. 255.
4. Susan Brownmiller, *Le Viol*, Paris, Stock, 1976 (English edition: *Against Our Will: Men, Women and Rape*, New York, Simon & Schuster, 1975); Marie-Odile Fargier, *Le Viol*, Paris, Grasset, 1976.
5. Georges Vigarello, *Histoire du viol, XVIᵉ–XXᵉ siècle*, Paris, Seuil, 1998, p. 255.
6. Stéphane Audoin-Rouzeau, *L'Enfant de l'ennemi*, Paris, Aubier, 1995.
7. Véronique Nahoum-Grappe, "Guerre et différence des sexes. Les viols systématiques (ex-Yougoslavie, 1991–1995)," in Cécile Dauphin, Arlette Farge, *De la violence et des femmes*, Paris, Albin Michel, 1997
8. Raphaëlle Branche, La Torture et l'armée pendant la guerre d'Algérie, Paris, Gallimard, 2001
9. Vania Chiurloot, "Donne come noi Marocchinate 1944-Bosniache 1993," *DWF Donna Woman Femme*, no. 1, 1993, pp. 42–67.
10. Helke Sander, Barbara Johr, *Befreier und Befreite. Krieg, Vergewaltigung, Kinder*, Munich, Kunstmann Verlag, 1992, quoted by Ruth Seifert, "The Second Front. The logic of sexual violence in wars," *Women's Studies International Forum*, 19, 1996; Marc Hillel, *Vie et Mœurs des GI's en Europe, 1942–1947*, Paris, Balland, 1981.
11. Quoted by Susan Brownmiller, *Le Viol*, Paris, Stock, 1976 (English edition: *Against Our Will.: Men, Women and Rape*, New York, Simon & Schuster, 1975), p. 92.
12. David Andrew Schmidt, Ianfu. *The Comfort Women of the Japanese Imperial Army of the Pacific War, Broken Silence*, Lampeter, Edwin Mellen Press, 2000; Iris Chang, *The Rape of Nanking. The Forgotten Holocaust of World War II*, New York, Penguin, 1997 and Masahiro Yamamoto, *Nanking. Anatomy of an Atrocity*, New York, Praeger, 2000.
13. Norman Naimark, *The Russians in Germany*, Cambridge, Belknap, 1995.
14. Quoted by Omer Bartov, *L'Armée d'Hitler. La Wehrmacht, les nazis et la guerre*, Paris, Hachette Littératures, 1999, p. 105.
15. Joanna Bourke, *The Second World War. A People's History*, Oxford, Oxford University Press, 2001, p. 96.
16. Joanna Bourke, *An Intimate History of Killing*, London, Granta Books, 1999, p. 354.

Preface

1. Sean Loughlin. March 12, 2003. "House cafeterias change names for 'french fries' and 'french toast.'" www.cnn.com
2. Personal email message from rbeck5@nyc.rr.com August 7, 2004.
3. Richard Drayton. May 10, 2005. "An ethical blank cheque." *Guardian*.
4. Owen Bowcott. November 1, 2005. "Top brass feared worst as GIs and good-time girls enjoyed blackout." *The Guardian*.

5. Ben Fenton. April 25, 2006. "Wartime GIs went on rampage of rape and murder." www.telegraph.co.uk
6. *New York Times*. 1993. "When black soldiers were hanged: a war's footnote." February 7: Y-14, col. 1–5.
7. Michael D. Haydock. 1998. "Personality: born and raised in Germany, Herman J.F. Bottcher gave his life in battle for his adopted country." *World War II*. March, pp. 8–14.
8. Almost fifty years had passed before I learned that Dad's hat was called a *"cunt cap."* See Fussell. 1989. *Wartime: Understanding and Behavior in the Second World War*. Oxford: Oxford University Press, p. 92.
9. See Marc Riedel. 1965. "The poor and capital punishment: some notes on a social attitude." *The Prison Journal*. Vol. XLV, no. 1 (Spring–Summer), pp. 24–28.
10. Ibid.

1   Introduction

1. *United States vs. Private Wesley Edmonds* ETO. GCM 90. 1942. Trial transcript. October 19–20, p. 54.
2. Ibid., p. 64. Also see the US Army's Branch Office of the Judge Adjutant General's *Board of Review, United States vs. Wesley Edmonds*. Vol. 1 (1942): 87–89. Hereafter BOR/JAG.
3. Trial transcript. October 19–20, 1942. p. 11.
4. Ibid., p. 81.
5. Ibid.
6. Ibid., p. 64.
7. Ibid., p. 41.
8. Trial transcript. *Testimony of Vernon O. Kash, 1st. Lt.* October 10, 1942.
9. *United States vs. Wesley Edmonds*. ETO. CM 90 p. 74.
10. Ibid., p. 24.
11. Ibid., p. 40 and 42. According to a medical doctor consulted by the author (March 1, 2002), "normal" most likely for Drs. Burrows and Kash meant "voluntary," although this is not certain. One implication is that if the intercourse was voluntary, the size of the male organ would not likely cause lacerations.
12. Ibid., p. 40.
13. Ibid., p. 43.
14. Ibid., p. 54.
15. Ibid.
16. Ibid., p. 55. Later, he complained that after his clothes were examined by the authorities the second piece of chocolate was missing.
17. Ibid.
18. Ibid., p. 56.
19. Ibid., p. 60.
20. See the trial transcript *U.S. vs. Wesley Edmonds*. ETO 90. Handwritten note dated November 30, 1942 to Franklin Ritter, J.A.G. D, Chairman for the Board of Review.
21. See the trial transcript *U.S. vs. Wesley Edmonds*. p. 90–91.
22. See the trial transcript *U.S. vs. Wesley Edmonds*. *ETO* 90, and BOR/JAG *U.S. vs. Wesley Edmonds*. Vol. 1 (1942): 90–91.
23. See the trial transcript *U.S. vs. Wesley Edmonds*. ETO 90, and BOR/JAG *U.S. vs. Wesley Edmonds*. Vol. 1 (1942): 87–89.

24. Letter contained in the trial transcript file.
25. Ibid.
26. Nicolson Harold. 1941. "Marginal Comment." pp. 190–192 in Fiona Glass and Philip Marsden-Smedly (eds.) 1989. *Articles of War: The Spectator Book of World War II*. London: Grafton Books.
27. For a useful discussion of what has been called the "occupation of Britain," see Reynolds, David. 1995. *Rich Relations: The American Occupation of Britain, 1942–1945*. New York: Random House.
28. Gardiner Juliet. 1992. *"OVER HERE": The GIs In Wartime Britain*. London: Collins & Brown.
29. John Hope Franklin. 1956. "History of Racial Segregation in the United States." *Annals of the American Academy of Political and Social Sciences*. Vol. 304 (March): p. 8.
30. Derrick Bell. 1992. *Race, Racism and American Law*. Boston: Little, Brown and Co. p. 110.
31. Ibid., p. 111.
32. A. Russell Buchanna. 1977. *Black Americans in World War II*. Santa Barbara, CA: Clio Books, p. 78; Morris J. MacGregor, Jr. 1985. *Integration of the Armed Forces 1940–1965*. Washington, DC: U.S. Government Printing Office, p. 7.
33. Ibid., p. 37.
34. Samuel A. Stouffer, Edward A. Suchman, Leland C. De Vinney, Shirley A. Star and Robin M Williams, Jr. 1949. *The American Soldier: Adjustment During Army Life*. Vol. 1. Princeton, NJ: Princeton University Press, p. 495.
35. Ulysses Lee. 1966. *The Employment of Negro Troops*. Washington, DC: U.S. Government Printing Office, p. 300.
36. Ibid.
37. Ibid., p. 324.
38. Ibid.
39. Ibid., p. 331.
40. See Lee's chapter XI. It is essential reading for understanding the problems which affected the morale of black soldiers.
41. Bernard C. Nalty and Morris J. MacGregor. 1981. *Blacks in the Military: Essential Documents*. Wilmington, DE: Scholarly Resources Inc., pp. 239–240.
42. Harvey M. Applebaum. 1964. "Miscegenation statutes: a constitutional and social problem." *Georgetown Law Journal*. 53: 49–91.
43. Eugene Genovese. 1976. *Roll, Jordon, Roll: The World the Slaves Made*. New York: Vintage, p. 414.
44. David M. Friedman. 2001. *A Mind of its Own: A Cultural History of the Penis*. New York: Free Press, pp. 103–147. This book is an indispensable source of information on the cultural history of the penis, especially its material on the ancient debate about the size of the black penis and the fear and awe it continues to instill.
45. Ibid., p. 119.
46. Ibid. p. 125.
47. Richard A. Wright. [1940] 1989. *Native Son*. New York: Harper Collins.
48. J. Robert Lilly and Richard A. Ball. 1982. "A critical analysis of the changing concept of criminal responsibility." *Criminology: An Interdisciplinary Journal*. 20 (2) August: pp. 169–184.
49. Calvin C. Hernton. 1965. *Sex and Racism in America*. New York: Grove Press, p. 115.
50. Steward E. Tolnay and E.M. Beck. 1992. *A Festival of Violence: An Analysis of Southern Lynchings, 1882–1930*. Urbana and Chicago: University of Illinois Press, p. 50.

51. Kentucky Revised Statutes 402.020.
52. See *A Manual for Courts-Martial U.S. Army – 1928* (Corrected to April 20, 1943). 1943. Washington, DC: Government Printing Office, pp. 33–35.
53. *History Branch Office of the Judge Advocate General with the United States Forces European Theater.* July 18, 1942 – November 1, 1945. Branch Office of the Judge Advocate General with the US Forces, European Theater, St. Cloud, France.
54. Leon Radzinowicz. 1957. *Sexual Offences: A Report of the Cambridge Department of Criminal Science.* London: Macmillan, p. xv. The problem of inaccurate crime rates is discussed in detail in the next chapter.
55. Norman Longmate.1975.*The G.I.'s: The Americans in Britain, 1942–1945.* New York: Charles Scribner's Sons, especially,. pp. 124–135; Juliet Gardnier. 1992. *"OVER HERE": The GIs in Wartime Britain.* London: Collins & Brown. John Costello. 1985. *Love, Sex and War,* London.
56. Tom Brokaw. 1998. *The Greatest Generation.* New York: Random House. p. xxx.
57. A few authors have convincingly demystified the war. See for instance, Michael C.C. Adams. 1994. *The Best War Ever: American and World War II.* Baltimore, MD: Johns Hopkins University Press; Paul Fussell. 1990. *Wartime: Understanding and Behavior in World War II.* Oxford: Oxford University Press.
58. See Edward Smithies. 1982. *Crime in Wartime: A Social History of Crime in World War II.* London: George Allen & Unwin. He does not discuss rapes committed by US soldiers, but he does devote attention to their involvement in prostitution, robberies, racial conflicts amongst themselves, and drunkenness.
59. *A Manual for Courts-Martial U.S. Army – 1928* (Corrected to April 20, 1943). 1943. Washington, DC: US Government Printing Office, p. 165.
60. "Ravages of time." 2000. *New York Times,* June 4, p. 4.
61. BOR/JAG United States vs. Private James W. Shields. CM ETO 1883.Vol. 5: 353.
62. J. Le Beau. 1987. "The journey to rape: geographic distances and the rapist's method of approaching the victim." *Journal of Police Sciences and Administration,* 15(2): 129–136.

2 Wartime Rape

1. Perry R. Duis. 1996. "No time for privacy: World War II and Chicago's families," pp. 17–45 in Lewis A. Erenberg and Susan E. Hirsch (eds.) *The War in American Culture: Society and Consensus During World War II.* Chicago: University of Chicago Press.
2. Lawrence Freedman (ed.) 1994. *War.* Oxford: Oxford University Press. p. 3.
3. See Stephen E. Ambrose 1992. *Band of Brothers.* NY: Simon & Schuster; *D-Day* NY: Simon & Schuster; *Citizen Soldiers* (1997) Simon & Schuster and *The Good Fight* (2001). NY: Simon and Schuster. Some of Ambrose's World War II books came under close scrutiny in early 2002 when he was accused of plagiarism. See *New York Times.* 2002. "2 Accuse Stephen Ambrose, Popular Historian, of Plagiarism." January 5: A-8; *New York Times.* 2002. "Author admits he lifted lines from '95 book." January 6: A-22; *New York Times.* "As historian's fame grows, so do questions on methods." January 11: A-1. *New York Times.* 2002. "Many on campuses disdain historian's practice." January 15: A-14.
4. Edgar L. Jones. 1946. "One war is enough." *The Atlantic Monthly.* 177 (2): 49.
5. Ed Putter. 2002. "Mr. Smith's complaint." *The Times Literary Supplement.* December 28: 22–23.
6. Meron T. (1998). *War Crimes Law Comes of Age.* Oxford: Oxford University, p. 206.

7. Yamashita v. U.S. 327 *U.S. Reports* 1, 1946. General Yamashita's execution was very controversial and was approved by a 6–0–2 decision by the Supreme Court of the United States, on February 4, 1946, at a time when national sentiment against Japan was intensely negative. Mr. Justice Ruthledge, dissenting, stated that Yamashita's trial was unprecedented in our history because the United States had never tried and convicted an enemy general for *failing to take action* (emphasis added).

8. Fora more in-depth discussion of war crime law coming to age see Meron, T. (1998). *War Crimes Law Comes of Age.* Oxford: Oxford University Press.

9. Thomas D. Q. and R. E. Ralph (1994). Rape in War: Challenging the Tradition of Impunity. SAIS Review. Baltimore: The Johns Hopkins University Press, pp. 82–89.

10. Convention Relative to the Protection of Civilian Persons in Time of War, August 12, 1949, 6 UST 3516, 75, UNTS 287 (Geneva Convention No. IV, Article 27.

11. Seealso Control Council Law No. 10, *Control Council for Germany*, Official Gazetter, Jan. 31, 1946. Reprinted in *Naval War College, Documents on Prisoners of War (International Law Studies – 1979 – Vol. 60.* Cited in Thomas and Ralph, 1994.

12. Meron(1998), p. 207.

13. Thomasand Ralph (1994).

14. Marlise Simons. 1996. "For First Time, Court Defines Rape as War Crime." *New York Times* 28 June: A 7. In 2001 the United Nations' war crimes tribunal convicted three Serbian soldiers of raping and torturing Muslim women and girls in 1992 and 1993. Two of the soldiers were also convicted of enslaving their victims up to eight months while abusing them sexually and forcing them to do domestic work. Some of their captives were rented or sold to other soldiers. Some of the victims were as young as 12 yrs. See Marlise Marlise Simons. 2001. "3 Serbs Convicted in Wartime Rapes." *New York Times.* February 23: A-1, A-7.

15. Liz Philipose. 1996. "The Laws of War and Women's Human Rights." *Hypatia* 11: 46.

16. Claudia Card. 1997. "Addendum to 'Rape as a Weapon of War.'" *Hypatia* 12: 216.

17. A 1994 United Nations report documented that the rape and death camps in Bosnia-Herzegovia were also sites of forced castrations through such crude means as forcing other internees to bit off a prisoner's testicles (see Card 1997). As one form of male-on-male martial sexual assault, it is important for future research that victims of this form of brutality did not report that they had been victims of sex crime or even of sexual assault. Rather, they reported that they were victims of torture. One observer commented that the men attached a great stigma to the idea of being the victim of a sex crime (Card 1997).

18. [Wines– omit] Michael Wines. 2000. "Chechens Tell of Torture in Russian Camp." *New York Times.* 18 February: A-12.

19. Susan Brownmiller. 1975. *Against Our Will: Men, Women and Rape.* New York: Ballentine. p. 15. (Emphasis in the original.)

20. Peter Landesman. 2002. "A Woman's Work." *The New York Times Magazine.* 15 September: pp. 82–89; 116; 125; 130; 132; 134.

21. Nikki Tait. 2002. "Albright to testify in former Bosnian Serb leader's case." *The Financial Time.* 17 December: p. 8.

22. Morrow Lance. 1996. "Rape." pp. 378–379 in *Reader's Companion to Military History.* Ed. By Robert Cowley and Geoffrey Parker. Boston: Houghton Mifflin.

23. Morrow 1996: 378.

24. Seifert Ruth. 1994. "War and Rape: A Preliminary Analysis." pp. 54–72 in *Mass Rape: The War Against Women in Bosnia-Herzegovina.* Edited by A. Stiglmayer. Lincoln: University of Nebraska Press.

25. J. Robert Lilly and Pam Marshall. 2000. "Rape – Wartime." *The Encyclopedia of Criminology and Deviant Behavior*. Vol. 3. Philadelphia: Taylor & Francis, Inc. pp. 310–322.
26. Morrow 1996: 379.
27. According to Ma Kinnon (1994) the victims filmed were reported to be Muslims and Croatians, and their assailants were Serbian soldiers. The television broadcasts were aired on the evening news in Banja Luka, a Serbian-occupied city in western Bosnia-Herzegovia.
28. Iris Chang. 1997: x. *The Rape of Nanking: The Forgotten Holocaust of World War II*. New York: Penguin. Exactly what happened and why at Nanking remains controversial. See Masahiro Yamamoto (2000) *Nanking: Anatomy of an Atrocity* (New York: Praeger) for an excellent review of the incident and the debates that surround it.
29. Ibid. Kirby quoted in Chang 1997: x.
30. Ibid. Chang 1997: 6.
31. Ibid. Chang 1997: 7.
32. Ibid. Morrow 1996: 378.
33. Ibid. Seifert 1994: 59.
34. Carol J. Williams. 1999. "Serbs make weapon of rape: Kosovo victims 'have no future.'" *Cincinnati Enquirer*. 29 May: A 2.
35. Cornelius Ryan. 1966. *The Last Battle*. New York: Simon & Schuster.
36. See Atina Grossman. 1997. "A Question of Silence: the Rape of German Women by Occupation Soldiers." pp. 33–52 in Robert G. Moeller (Ed.), *West Germany under Construction: Politics, Society in the Adenauer Era*. University of Michigan Press: Ann Arbor, MI., and Elizabeth Heineman.1996. "The Hour of the Woman: Memories of Germany's 'Crisis years' and West Germany National Identity." *American Historical Review*. April: 354–395; Anthony Beevor. 2002. *The Fall of Berlin 1945*. New York: Viking; Maria Hohn. 2002. *GIs and Frauleins: The German-American Encounter in 1950s West Germany*. Chapel Hill, NC: University of North Carolina Press. p. 9.
37. Ibid. Fn. 29. Beevor. 2002. *The Fall of Berlin 1945*. p. 32.
38. Ibid. Beevor. pp. 28–29; Anthony Beevor. 2002. "They raped every German female from eight to 80." *The Guardian*. Inside Story. 1 May: 6–7.
39. Ibid. Beevor. 2002. "They raped every German Female from eight to 80;" Kate Connolly. 2002. "German war rape victims find a voice." *The Observer*. 13 June: 18, col.1–6; Cal McCrystal. 2002. "Red Army on the Rampage." *The Independent on Sunday*. 28 April: Arts Etc. 15, col. 1–5; Anthony Beevor. 2002. "They raped every German female from eight to 80." *The Guardian*. Inside Story. pp. 6–7.
40. Ibid. Naimark 1995: 89.
41. Kate Connolly. 2002. "German war rape victims find a voice." *The Observer*. 23 June: 18, col. 4.
42. Madeline Morris. 1996. "By Force of Arms: Rape, War and Military Culture." *Duke Law Journal*. Vol. 45, No. 4: 651–781.
43. *History Branch Office of the Judge Advocate General with the United States Forces European Theater*. 18 July 1942 – 1 November 1945. Branch Office of the Judge Advocate General with the United States Forces European Theater. St. Cloud, France. 1 November 1945. p. 13.
44. Jews in the World War: A Study in Jewish Patriotism and Heroism. Nd. New York: Jewish War Veterans of the United States; Deborah Dash Moore. 1994. When Jews Were GIs: How World War II Changed a Generation and Remade American Jewry. Ann Arbor, MI: University of Michigan.
45. Bernd Wegner. 1995. "SS." In I.C.B. Dear and M. R. D. Foot (eds). *The Oxford Companion to World War II*. Oxford: Oxford University Press. p. 1004.

46. Peter Neumann. 1958. *The Black March*. New York: Bantam. p. 83.
47. Joseph Nathan and Nicholas Alex. 1971–72. "The Uniform: A Sociological Perspective." *American Journal of Sociology*. Vol. 77, No. 4: 719–730. See also Paul Fussell. 2002. *Uniforms: Why We Are What We Wear*. Boston: Houghton Mifflin. pp. 10–18; 38–47.
48. EB. Sledge. 1991. *With the Old Breed at Peleliu and Okinawa*. New York: Oxford University Press. p. 134.
49. John Gregory Dunne. 2001. "The Hardest Way." *The New York Review of Books*. 20 December: 50.
50. Bernard C. Nalty.1986. Strength for the Fight: A History of Black Americans in the Military. New York: Free Press. p. 204.
51. Ibid. Natly. 1986. p. 204.
52. Ibid. Natly. 1986. p. 204.
53. *New York Times*. 1996. "His Medals Questioned, Top Admiral Kills Himself." 17 May: A-1; C-19
54. Ibid. *New York Times*. 1996. 17 May: A-1; C-19.
55. Ibid. p. A1. Questions about his medals were but one of several stressful aspects of Adm. Boorda's Navy responsibilities. Some of his troubles included scandals involving cheating at the Naval Academy and sexual assaults at a convention of naval aviators.
56. *New York Times*. 1996. "Admiral, in Suicide Note, Apologized to 'My Sailors.'" 18 May: A1–A9.
57. *New York Times* 1996. "Commit Suicide Over a Medal? An Ex-General Gives His View." 20 May: A-8.
58. Lance Morrow. 1993. "Unspeakable Behavior." *Time*. 22 February: 48–50.
59. Ibid. Chang, 1997.
60. Cliffton D. Bryant. 1979. Khaki-Collar Crime: Deviant Behavior in the Military Context. New York: Free Press. p. 223.
61. Peter Karstens. 1978. *Law, Soldiers and Combat*. Westport, Conn.: Greenwood. Quoted in Bryant, 1979, p. 224.
62. Ibid. Chang. 1997. Other authors have elaborated on this theme and offered their different interpretations. See Masahiro Yamamoto. 2000. *Nanking: Anatomy of an Atrocity*. Westport, Ct.: Prager.
63. Ibid. Chang, 1997: 53.
64. Peter Schrijvers. 1998. The Crash of Ruin: American Combat Soldiers in Europe during World War II. New York: New York University Press.
65. Gustavo Gonzales. 1997. "Chile-Human Rights: Government Rejects Trial of Pinochet in Spain." Inter Press Service. May 29.
66. Susan Jackson. 1995. "In Chile, Pinochet Stands in the Path of Reconciliation." *San Francisco Chronicle*. 19 September: A-8; Timerman, Jacob. 1997. *Death in the South*. Translated by Robert Cox. New York: Knopf; Calvin Sims. 1997. "Era Ending for Chile as Pinochet Plans Exit." *New York Times*. 28 September: A-17.
67. Bunster-Bunalto Ximena. 1993. "Surviving Beyond Fear: Women and Torture in Latin America." In Alison M. Jaggar and Paula S. Rothenberg (Eds.). *Feminist Frameworks: Alternative Theoretical Accounts of the Relations between Women and Men*. New York: McGraw-Hill, Inc, pp. 252–261.
68. See Alain Boureau. 1998. *The Lord's First Night: the Myth of the Droit De Cuissage*. Chicago: University of Chicago Press; Juiette Benzoni. 1983. *Dans le lit Des Rois: Nuits de Noces*. Paris: Plon Litvack; E. P. Frances. 1984. *Le Drit du Seigneur in European and American Literature: From the Seventeenth through the Twentieth*

Century. Birmingham, Ala.: Summa Publications, and Louis Veuillot.1813–1883. *Le Droit du Signeur au Moyen Age*. Paris: L. Vivies.

69. See War Department – Annual Reports, 1919, Vol. I. Washington: Government Printing Office. p. 674. Also see Hearings Before a Special Committee on Charges of Alleged Executions without Trial in France. Sixty-Seventh Congress. Washington: Government Printing Office. 1923. p. IV.

70. *New York Times*. 1917. "American Soldier Hanged." December 4: p. 6:4.

71. General George S. Patton, Jr. 1947. *War As I Knew It*. New York: Houghton Mifflin. p. 23.

72. Thisstatement was given to me by a history professor, who said it came to him from Forrest C. Pogue, the World War II historian best known for his four-volume biography of General George C. Marshall and for *The Supreme Command*. Because the statement cannot be verified, the historian requested that I not identify him. I respect his decision, though I would not be surprised if Patton indeed made the comment.

73. Norman Naimark. 1995. *The Russians in Germany: A History of the Soviet Zone Occupation*, 1945–1959. Cambridge, Mass.: Harvard University Press. p. 70.

74. Ibid. Nairmark. 1995. pp. 71. James Wakefield Burke's 1952 *the Big Rape* – a documentary novel – provided a graphic and sensitive account of the Russian soldiers' "initiatives" in and around Berlin, spring 1945, fifty years before Beevor.

75. Peter Schrijvers. 1998. *The Crash of Ruin: American Combat Soldiers in Europe during World War II*. Washington Square, NY: New York University Press. p. 183.

76. Writingin 1997, World War II veteran and author, Samuel Hynes, states that the memoirs of World War II "tend to ignore the sex lives of soldiers." See Samuel Hynes.1997. *The Soldiers' Tale*.New York: Penguin.

77. Harold P. Leinbaugh and John D. Campbell. 1985. New York: William Morrow and Company, Inc. p. 235.

78. Yuki Tanaka. 1998. *Hidden Horrors: Japanese War Crimes in World War II*. Boulder, CO: Westview Press. p. 103

79. John W. Dower. 1999. *Embracing Defeat: Japan in the Wake of World War II*. New York: Norton. p. 579. Fn. 16.

80. Ibid. Dower. p. 126.

81. Brownmiller 1975: 99.

82. Brownmiller 1975: 99.

83. Gary D. Solis 2000, "Military Justice, Civilian Clemency: The Sentence of Marine Corps War Crimes in South Vietnam." *10 Transnational Law & Contemporary Problems* 59.

84. *Chicago Sun-Times*. 1992. "Imperfect Soldiers Fight Imperfect War." August 1: Editorial. p. 21.

85. Ibid.

86. Ibid.

87. *Wisconsin State Journal*. 1992. "New 'War' for Pentagon." August 3: 5 A.

88. Ibid.

89. *New York Times*. 2000. "U.S. Sergeant in Kosovo Is Accused Of Killing Girl." January 17: A-3: 1.

90. Ibid.

91. *New York Times*. 2000. "G.I.'s in Kosovo Face a Barrage of Complaints." 29 January: A-6:1.

92. *New York Times*. 2000. "Details Emerge in Kosovo Girl's Slaying." February 19: A-1.

93. Ibid.

94. *New York Times*. 2000. "U.S. Sergeant Gets Life in Murder of Kosovo Girl." August 2: A-3: 1.
95. Ibid.
96. Wisconsin State Journal.1992. Ibid.
97. *New York Times*.1996. "Sexual Harassment in Military Dips, but Remains Problem, Survey Finds." March 7: C-19.
98. Ibid.
99. *New York Times*. 1997. "Army Trial Raises Questions of Sex, Power and Discipline." April 12: A1, 8.
100. *New York Times*. 1997. "Sergeant Convicted of 18 Counts of Raping Female Subordinates." April 30: A1-A12; *New York Times*.1997. "Drill Sergeant Convicted of Sex with Trainees." May 30: A-12.
101. *New York Times*. 1997. "Sergeant Convicted of 18 Counts Of Raping Female Subordinates." April 30: A1-A12.
102. Ibid.
103. *New York Times*. 1997. "Sergeant Is Given 25 Years For 18 Rapes at Aberdeen." May 7: A-19.
104. New York Times. 2003. "Military Policy on Sex Abuse Under Scrutiny: Air Force Accusations Raise New Questions." 2 March: A-1;A-24.
105. Ibid. New York Times, p. A-24.
106. Stephen E. Ambrose. 1997. Citizen Soldiers: The U.S. Army from the Normandy Beaches to the Bulge to the Surrender of Germany. New York: Simon & Schuster. p. 450.
107. Ibid. Ambrose. 1997, p. 450.
108. Myron C. Cramer 1945. The Opinions of the Judge Advocate General Branch Office, European Theater of Operations. Forward. Vol. 1.
109. Seethe trial transcript U.S. vs. Wesley Edmonds., ETO 90, and BOR/JAG U.S. vs. Wesley Edmonds. Vol. 1 (1942): 90–91.
110. *History Branch Office of the Judge Advocate general with the United States Forces European Theater*. 18 July 1942–1 November 1945. Branch Office of the Judge Advocate General with the United States Forces European Theater. St. Cloud, France, 1 November 1945. pp. 3–4. Hereafter HBO/JAG.
111. Ibid. HBO/JAG. p. 7.
112. Ibid. HBO/JAG. p. 8.
113. Ibid. HBO/JAG. p. 9.
114. Ibid. HBO/JAG. p. 9.
115. Barry Hindless. 1973. *The Use of Official Statistics in Sociology*. London: Macmillian.
116. Thereis a well-developed body of literature on the problems of official statistics that was used to inform this discussion. See Marvin E. Wolfgang. 1963. "Uniform Crime Reports: A Critical Appraisal." *University of Pennsylvania.* 111 (April): 709–736; David Sudnow. 1965. "Normal Crimes: Sociological Features of the Penal Code in a Public Defender Office." *Social Problems.* 12 (Winter): 255–76; Albert D. Biderman and Albert J. Reiss. 1967. "On Exploring the Dark figure of Crime." *Annals of the American Academy of Political and Social Sciences.* 374 (November): 1–15; Leslie T. Wilkins. 1965. "New Thinking in Criminal Justice Statistics." *Journal of Criminal Law, Criminology, and Police Science.* 56 (September): 277–84.
117. Hindless 1973; Cressey, Donald B. 1966. "Crime." pp. 136–92 in *Contemporary Social Problems*. 2nd. Edition. Robert K. Merton and Robert K. Nisbet. New York: Harcourt, Brace & World, Inc., and T.B. Sarbinand John I. Kitsuse. Eds.1994. *Constructing the Social*. Thousand Oaks, CA: Sage Publications.

118. Someof the most interesting and informative discussions of the problems with official reports can be found in research that has demonstrated the influence of private conceptions, or typifications, used by rule enforcers.

119. Thereare several easily available discussions of the problems associated with reporting rape. See Duncan Chappell, Robley Geis and Gilbert Geis. 1977. *Forcible Rape: The Crime, the Victim, and the Offender*. New York: Columbia University Press; Susan Estrich. 1987. *Real Rape: How the Legal System Victimizes Women Who Say No*. Cambridge: Harvard University Press; Linda S. Williams.1984."The Classic Rape: When Do Victims Report?" *Social Problems* 31(4):459–467; Susan Brownmiller. 1975. *Against Our Will: Men, Women and Rape*. New York: Fawcett Columbine; L.A. Greenfeld. 1997. *Sex Offenses and Offenders: An Analysis of Data on Rape and Sexual Assault*. (NCJ-163392). Washington, DC: Department of Justice, Office of Justice Programs; R. L. Binder. 1981. "Why women don't report sexual assault." *Journal of Clinical Psychiatry*, (42): 437–438.

120. See Marc P. Riedel. 1998. "Counting Stranger Homicides: A Case Study of Statistical Prestidigitation." *Homicide Studies*. 2: 209–219; Marc Riedel and Tammy A. Rinehart. 1996. "Murder Clearances and Missing Data." *Journal of Crime and Justice*. 19: 83–102.

121. Julien C. Hyner et al. nd. *Military Justice Administration in the Theater of Operations*. Reports to the General Board, United States Forces, Europe, no. 84.

122. Ibid. Hyer et al. p. 16.

123. Ibid. Hyer et al. p. 16. Fn. 79.

124. Ibid. Hyer et al. p. 16, fn. 79.

125. Ibid. HBO/JAG. p. 249.

126. See Phillippe Burrin. 1993. *France Under the Germans: Collaboration and Compromise*. New York: Free Press. p. 206.

127. John Steinbeck.1959/1990. *Once There Was a War*. London: Mandarin, p. 4.

128. Peter Schrijvers. 1998. *The Crash of Ruin: American Combat Soldiers in Europe during World War II*. New York: New York University Press. p. 180.

129. Ibid. p. 181.

130. Elderidge Clever. 1968. *Soul on Ice*. New York: Dell Publishing. pp. 160–161.

131. Ibid. p. 14.

132. "Thereason I haven't" U.S. Sex Survey – W and "VD Problems of Negro Enlisted Men in MTOISA." Report 122 M2, 25 September 1945." Cited in John Costello. 1985.*Viture under Fire: How World War II Changed Our Social and Sexual Attitudes*. Boston: Little, Brown and Co. p. 97.

133. Samuela. Stouffer, Edward A. Suchman, Leland C. De Vinney, Shirley A. Star and Robin M. Williams. 1949. *The American Soldier: Adjusting During Army Life*. Princeton, NJ: Princeton University Press. pp. 546–547.

134. Julien C. Hyner et al. Nd. *Military Offender in Theater of Operations*. Reports of the General Board, United States Forces, European Theater, no. 84. p. 8.

135. Ibid. Hyer, et al. Nd. No. 84, p. 12.

136. For accuracy sake, rapes occurred in Wales and Ireland. For simplicity sake, I use the United Kingdom because there was no difference in the military authority governing the soldiers while US soldiers were in the British Isles.

3   England: White Women

1. Angus Calder. 1991. *The Myth of the Blitz*. London: Pimlico.

2. Michael C.C. Adams. 2002. *Echoes of War: A Thousand Years of Military History in Popular Culture*. Lexington, KY: The University of Kentucky Press.

3. UPI/Bettmann International News Photo.
4. Ray John. 1996. *The Night Blitz: 1940–1941*. London: Cassell & Co. p. 12.
5. Quotedin Angus Calder. 1969. *The People's War: Britain 1939–1945*. New York: Pantheon, p. 85.
6. C.L. Sulzberger. 1966. *The American Heritage Picture History of World War II*. New York: American Heritage Publishing Co, p. 114.
7. Quotedin Angus Calder. 1969. *The People's War: Britain 1939–1945*. New York: Pantheon, p. 214.
8. Sulzberger 1966, p. 114.
9. Calder, p. 17.
10. Ibid.
11. Priestley J.B., *Out of the People*, quoted in Calder, p. 163.
12. David Reynolds. 1995. *Rich Relations: The American Occupation of Britain, 1942–*New York: Random House.
13. A.P. Herbert. 1919 [1981]. *The Secret Battle*. New York: Atheneum. Winston Churchill described this book as one that "should be read in each generation, so that men and women may rest under no illusion about what war means." See Introduction (p. v), of the 1981 edition.
14. *The Atlantic Monthly*. 1946. April. Vol. 177, no. 4, p. 135. An editor's note accompanying the poem states that "This poem has been printed on postcards and mailed to thousands of Americans. Written by England's famed author and Member of Parliament, P. Herbert, it first appeared in the London *Sunday Graphic* and then in *This Week*. It deserves to travel."
15. George Orwell. January 3, 1943. Letter to the Editors, *Partisan Review*. p. 277 in *My Country Right or Left 1940 – 1943*. Edited by Sonia Orwell and Ian Angus. 1968. New York: Harcourt Brace Javanovich, Inc.
16. Ibid. p. 279.
17. George Orwell. 1943. "As I please." in SoniaOrwell and Ian Angus (eds.) 1968. *As I Please, 1943–1945*. New York: Harcourt Brace Javanovich, Inc., p. 54.
18. Christopher Hitchens. 2002. *Orwell's Victory*. London: Allen Lane, chapter 4.
19. David Reynolds. 1995. *Rich Relations: The American Occupation of Britain, 1942–1945*. New York: Random House. p. 216.
20. See Roi Ottley. 1951. *No Green Pastures*. New York: Charles Schribner's Sons, pp. 34–48, 49–68.
21. Thomas E. Hachey. 1974. "Jim Crow with a British accent: attitudes of London Government officials toward American Negro soldiers in England during World War II." *Journal of Negro History*, 59 (1) January: 65.
22. This aspect of Anglo-American relations during World War II has been discussed so thoroughly in a number of places that it need not be reviewed in depth here. See ibid. Reynolds. 1995, chapter 14, chapter 18; Graham Smith. 1987. *When Jim Crow met John Bull: Black American Soldiers in World War II Britain*. London: I.B. Tauris; Christopher Thorne. 1988. *Border Crossing: Studies in International History*. Oxford: Basil Blackwell. chapter 12; Norman Longmate. 1975. *The G.I.'s: The Americans in Britain, 1942–1945*. New York; Charles Schribner's Sons, chapter 11, pp. 23–25; Thomas E. Hachey. "Jim Crow with a British accent: attitudes of London Government officials toward American Negro soldiers in England during World War II." *Journal of Negro History*, pp. 65–77.
23. Ibid. See Thorne. 1988, p. 260.
24. Ibid. Thorne, p. 266.
25. Ibid. Reynolds.1995. *Rich Relations*, p. 218.

26. Ibid.
27. Ibid. Reynolds. 1995. *Rich Relations*, p. 232.
28. Hermann Manheim. 1965. *Comparative Criminology*. Boston, MA: Houghton Mifflin Company, p. 591.
29. Angus Calder.1969. *The People's War: Britain 1939–1945*. New York: Pantheon. p. 35.
30. Ibid., p. 38.
31. Ibid., p. 48.
32. Ibid., p. 50.
33. Ibid.,
34. Ibid., p. 267.
35. Ibid.
36. "Coupons and nylons: the underside of VE Day." Radio 4. May 8, 1995. Matt Thompson, Producer. Interview by Dick Hobbs. Also see: F. Fraser. 1994. *Mad Frank*. London: Little, Brown & Co.
37. T. Lambrianou. 1992. *Inside the Firm*. London: Pan, p. 20. See also C. Kray and J. Sykes. 1997. *Me and My Brothers*. London: Everest; R. Kray. 1991. *Born Fighter*. London: Arrow; R. Kray and R. Kray. 1989. *Our Story*. London: Pan; J. Pearson. 1973. *The Profession of Violence*. London: Granda; W. Probyn. 1977. *Angle Face. The Making of a Criminal*. London: Allen and Unwin; C. Richardson. 1992. *My Manor*. London: Pan; B. Webb. 1993. *Running with the Krays*. Edinburgh: Mainstream.
38. Hermann Mannheim. 1965. *Comparative Criminology*. Boston, MA: Houghton Mifflin Company, p. 596. See also Manheim's 1971 (1955) 2nd and enlarged the edition of *Group Problems in Crime and Punishment*. Montclair, NJ: Patterson Smith, chapter 3 – "Three contributions to the history of crime in the Second World War and after."
39. Angus Calder, p. 337.
40. Ibid. pp. 225–226.
41. Edward Smithies. 1982. *Crime in Wartime: A Social History of Crime in World War II*. London: George Allen & Unwin, p. 2.
42. Ibid., chapter 2 – "Theft at work," pp. 25–39. Caution is advised when interpreting these numbers. They are based on crimes *known* to the police.
43. Ibid., chapter 3 – "Theft: mainly professional," pp. 40–57.
44. Ibid., p. 40.
45. Ibid., p. 51.
46. Ibid., chapter 7 – Betting, gaming and drink, pp. 106–129.
47. Ibid., p. 121.
48. Ibid., pp. 119–120. Emphasis in the original.
49. Ibid., p. 120.
50. Ibid., pp. 120–121.
51. Ibid., p. 121.
52. Ibid., pp. 137–138. See also John Costello. 1985. *Love Sex and War: Changing Values, 1939–1945*. London: Collins for an excellent discussion and documentation on World War II as a turning point in relations between the sexes in the United States and Britain.
53. Smithies. 1982, p. 138.
54. Norman Longmate. 1975. *The G.I's: The Americans in Britain, 1942–1945*. New York: Charles Scribner's Sons, p. 271.
55. Smithies. 1982, p. 142.
56. Philip Ziegler. 1995. *London at War: 1939–1945*. New York: Alfred A. Knopf, p. 53.

57. Costello. 1985, p. 126.

58. Smithies. 1982, pp. 139–141.

59. Graham Smith. 1987. *When Jim Crow met John Bull: Black American Soldiers in World War II Britain*. London: I.B. Tauris, pp. 183–184.

60. Karl Gustav Hulten was executed on his 23rd birthday, March 8, 1945 at Pentonville prison. At his hanging he wore civilian clothes following a request by the US authorities that he should not be executed in his Army uniform. He left behind a wife and child in Boston, Massachusetts. See *Stars and Stripes*. 1945. "U.S. soldier dies as civilian for slaying of London Cabby." March 9. Paris edition. Vol. 1, no. 225; Steve Jones. 2000. *When the Lights Went Down: Crime in Wartime*. Nottingham: Wicked Publications, pp. 61–65. This crime was the subject of the journalist and war correspondent, R. Alwyn Raymonds's 1945 booklet, *The Cleft Chin Murder*. London: Claud Morris Books, Ltd., and M. Gaynor's 1990 *Chicago Joe and the Show Girl* (London: Hodder and Stoughton), and was also portrayed in a major movie by the same name.

61. George Orwell. January15, 1944. "London letter to *Partisan Review*" in Sonia Orwell and Ian Angus. (eds.) 1968. *As IPlease, 1943–1945*. New York: Harcourt Brace Javanovich, Inc, p. 77.

62. Ibid.

63. *History Branch Office of the Judge Advocate General with the United States Forces European Theater*. July 18, 1942–November 1, 1945. Issued by the Branch Office of the Judge Advocate General. St. Cloud, France. Vol. 1, p. 13. Hereafter *HBO/JAG*.

64. Historian David Reynolds mentions the 121 rapes and the convictions of black soldiers, but he does not discuss the 101 "English girls." See David Reynolds. 1995. *Rich Relations: The American Occupation of Britain, 1942–1945*. New York: Random House, p. 232.

65. Ibid. *HBO/JAG*, p. 13. See the note under Chart 17.

66. Ordinary rape involved females 16 years and older. However, because the definition of rape used by the US Army was "the unlawful carnal knowledge of a woman by force and without her consent," (*Manual of Courts Martial*. 1928, para. 148b, p. 165), age was not an essential part of the offense. Sometimes age was mentioned, sometimes it was not.

67. I hasten to reemphasize that these data are based on the trials that occurred, not the number of rapes that took place. The later number is unknown.

68. BOR/JAG United States v. Private Kenneth M. Waite. Vol. 2, pp. 379–389.

69. Ibid., p. 380.

70. Ibid.

71. Ibid.

72. Ibid.

73. Ibid.

74. Ibid., pp. 380–381.

75. Ibid., p. 381.

76. BOR/JAG United States v. Private Thomas (NMI) Bell. Vol. 3, pp. 373–382.

77. Ibid., p. 374.

78. Ibid.

79. Ibid.

80. Ibid.

81. Ibid.

82. Ibid., pp. 374–375.

83. Ibid., p. 375.

84. Ibid.
85. Ibid.
86. Ibid.
87. Ibid.
88. Ibid., p. 377.
89. Ibid., p. 373.
90. BOR/JAG United States v. Private Madison Thomas. Vol.10, pp. 249–253.
91. Ibid., p. 250.
92. Ibid.
93. Ibid.
94. *United States vs. Private Madison Thomas*. Trial Transcript. Exhibit "C." Dated October 12, 1944.
95. BOR/JAG *United States v. Private William (NMI) Cooper*. Vol. 2., pp. 317–323.
96. Ibid., p. 318.
97. Ibid., p. 319.
98. Ibid.
99. Ibid.
100. Ibid.
101. Ibid.
102. Ibid.
103. Ibid.
104. Ibid., p. 322.
105. BOR/JAG *United States v. Private Aniceto Martinez*. Vol. 22, pp. 71–76.
106. Ibid., p. 72.
107. Ibid.
108. Ibid.
109. Ibid., pp. 72–73.
110. Ibid., p. 71.
111. BOR/JAG *United States v. Private Clarence (NMI) English*. Vol. 4. CM ETO 1366. 1944, pp. 247–251.
112. BOR/JAG *United States v. Private Melvin C. Tallent*. Vol. 7. CM ETO 2550. 1944, pp. 141–145.
113. BOR/JAG *United States v. Lee A. Davis*. Vol. 3. CM ETO 969. 1943, pp. 201–227.
114. BOR/JAG *United States v. Private Jack H. Morgan*. Vol. 31. CM ETO 16978. 1945, pp. 317–325.
115. BOR/JAG *United States v. Corporal Ernest Lee Clark*. Vol. 14. CM ETO 5156. 1944, pp. 199–207, and *United States v. Private Augustine M. Guerra*. Vol. 14. CM ETO 5157. 1944. pp. 209–220.
116. *United States v. Private William Harrison, Jr*. CM ETO 5747. 1944. (A summary of this case does not appear in the 34 volumes of BOR records. This reference is to the complete trial transcript.)
117. BOR/JAG *United States v. Second Lieutenant Arthur C. Blevins, Jr*. Vol. 7. CM ETO 2472. 1944, pp. 41–54.
118. Ibid., p. 42.
119. Ibid., p. 43.
120. C. Ryan. 1966. *The Last Battle*. London: Touchstone.
121. Ibid., p. 487.
122. I. Chang. 1997. *The Rape of Nanking: The Forgotten Holocaust of World War II*, New York, Penguin.
123. Peter Schrijvers. 1998. *The Crash of Ruin: American Combat Soldiers in Europe during World War II*. New York: New York University Press, pp. 177–190.

124. IPeter Schrijvers. 1998. *The Crash of Ruin: American Combat Soldiers in Europe during World War II*. New York: New York University Press, p. 183.
125. Hyer Julien C., Col. JAGD, nd. *Military Offenders in Theater of Operations*. U.S. Army Military History Institute. Carlisle Barracks, PA
126. I hesitate to say "fighting men," because this might imply that non-infantrymen were not engaged in war. This would be an error.
127. The second rape trial involved Private Charles A. Shaffer, white, from the 846th Engineer Aviation Battalion, a service unit. See *Board of Review*. [Hereafter BOR/JAG]. *United States v. Private Charles A. Shaffer*. Vol. 1, pp. 339–344.
128. BOR/JAG Vol. 2. *U.S. v. Private Isiah (NMI) Porter*, p. 190.
129. Ibid.
130. Ibid.
131. Ibid.
132. Ibid.
133. Ibid.
134. Ibid., p. 196.
135. Ibid., p. 197.
136. BOR/JAG *United States v. First Lieutenant Hugh I. Malley*. Vol. 14., pp. 117–118.
137. Ibid., p. 118.
138. Ibid.
139. Ibid., p. 112.
140. Ibid., p. 113.
141. Ibid., p. 114.
142. Ibid.
143. Ibid.
144. Ibid.
145. Ibid.
146. Ibid. p. 119.
147. Ibid.
148. Ibid., p. 120.
149. Ibid., p. 122.
150. Ibid., p. 112.
151. See Reynolds. *Rich Relations*, pp. 298–299 for an excellent review of the real life of flyboys, including what some women identified as "an air of sexual aggression, particularly after a mission."
152. *A Manual for Courts-Martial – U.S. Army*. 1928. (Revised 1943). Washington: US Government Printing Office, pp. 224–225.
153. BOR/JAG *United States v. Captain John F. Kenney*. Vol. 1, pp 13–28.
154. Ibid., p. 22.
155. Ibid., p. 23.
156. Ibid.
157. Ibid., p. 28.
158. Ibid., p. 27.
159. The terms "buddy," "Army buddy," or the "buddy system" have been referred to as members of a new society or clique that often developed in basic training camps as new soldiers start to become familiar and comfortable with their new social world. See Lee Kennett. 1997. *G.I.: The American Soldier in World War II* (Norman: University of Oklahoma Press.).
160. Ibid. Edwards and Ramsey. See fn. 125.
161. BOR/JAG *United States v. Corporal Robert L. Pearson and Private Cubia Jones*. Vol. 18, pp. 51–57.

162. Ibid., p. 52.
163. Ibid.
164. Ibid., p. 53.
165. Ibid.
166. Marcus Felson. 2002. *Crime and Everyday Life.* Thousand Oaks, CA: Sage Publications, pp. 32–33.
167. See the Introduction. *United States v. Wesley Edmonds.* Vol. 1, pp. 81–89.
168. BOR/JAG *United States v. Private Henry (NMI) Lakas.* Vol. 2, pp. 221–228.
169. Ibid., p. 222.
170. BOA/JAG *United States v. Privates James (NMI) Ramsey and Bennie L. Edwards.* Vol. 4, pp. 109–119.
171. Ibid., p. 110.
172. Ibid.
173. Ibid., p. 111.
174. Ibid.
175. BOA/JAG *United States v. Privates Alfonso Josie Lewis and Freddie Moses Sexton.* Vol. 16, pp. 7–14.
176. Ibid., p. 8.
177. Ibid.
178. Ibid., p. 9.
179. Ibid.
180. Ibid.
181. Ibid., p. 10.
182. BOG/JAG *United States v. Private Donald Hicks.* Vol. 5, pp. 367–380.
183. Ibid., p. 368.
184. Ibid.
185. Ibid.
186. Ibid., pp. 368–369.
187. Ibid., p. 369.
188. Ibid.
189. BOR/JAG *United States v. Private First Class Conway Green.* Vol. 9, pp. 361–373.
190. Ibid., pp. 362–363.
191. Ibid., p. 363.
192. Ibid.
193. Ibid.
194. Ibid.
195. Ibid., p. 365.
196. Ibid., p. 361.
197. BOR/JAB *United States v. Private Leonard K. Steele.* Vol. 10, pp. 223–231.
198. Ibid., p. 224.
199. Ibid. p. 225.
200. Ibid.
201. BOR/JAG. *United States v. Private First Class Conway Green.* Vol. 9, pp. 361– 373.
202. Ibid., p. 366.
203. Ibid., p. 367.
204. Ibid.
205. Ibid.
206. Ibid.
207. Ibid.
208. Ibid.
209. John Braithwaite. 2007. "Rape, shame and pride."

210. John Hagan.
211. Phone interview with Annie Kalotschke, a daughter of Patsy's sister. December 7, 1995.
212. See Lieutenant Colonel John W. Rees's, Senior Claims Officer, July 15, 1943 letter to the Branch Office, Judge Advocate General, contained in the Record of Trial for *United States v. Private Wesley Edmonds*. ETO CM 90.
213. Ibid., first paragraph.
214. Ibid., third paragraph.
215. BOR/JAG *United States v. Private First Class Fred L. Lofton*. Vol. 27, p. 289. The other rapist was not identified. Two of Queenie's female companions, ages 12 and 10, also identified Lofton.
216. Ibid., p. 291.
217. Ibid.
218. Ibid., p. 290.
219. This information is not contained in the BOR/JAG record. It was found in the trial transcript.
220. Ibid., fn. 56. Porter, p. 195.
221. Ibid., fn. 125. Ramsey and Edwards.
222. BOR/JAG *United States v. Privates Archie S. Bowman and Joseph Glover, Jr.* Vol. 9, CM ETO 3253. 1944, pp. 135–144.
223. Ibid., fn. 66, p. 112.
224. Ibid., fn. 130, p. 9.

4   France: Liberation, Occupation, and Criminality

1. A few authors have convincingly demystified the war. See for instance, Michael C.C. 1994. Adams, *The Best War Ever: America and World War II* (Baltimore, MD: Johns Hopkins University Press. 1994); Paul Fussell, *Wartime: Understanding and Behavior in World War II* (Oxford: Oxford University Press).
2. For the best account on the behavior of American troops in the ETO, see Marc Hillel. 1981. *Vie et Moeurs des G.I.'s en Europe, 1942–1947* (Paris). Unfortunately, this book is not available in translation.
3. Hermann Mannheim. 1965.*Comparative Criminology*. Boston, MA: Houghton Mifflin, p. 595; *Group Problems in Crime and Punishment*. 1955. London: Routhledge and Kegan Paul, pp. 85–114.
4. Trial transcript. *United States vs. PFC. John David Cooper*. CM ETO 5362. October 25–26, 1944. See "Report of proceedings at the execution of general prisoner John D. Cooper." January 12, 1945.
5. Ibid., p. 5.
6. Ibid.
7. Hermann Mannheim. 1965, p. 594.
8. Ibid., p. 595.
9. Philippe Burrin. 1993. *France Under The Germans: Collaboration and Compromise*. New York: The New Press.
10. Marc Block. 1968. *Strange Defeat: A Statement of Evidence Written in 1940*. New York: W.W. Norton.
11. See H.R. Kedward. 1978. *Resistance in Vichy France*. Oxford: Oxford University; H.R. Kedward. 1985. *Occupied France: Collaboration and Resistance. 1940–1944*. Oxford and New York: Blackwell; R.O. Paxton. 1972. *Vichy France: Old Guard and New Order*. New York: Columbia University Press; John. F. Sweets. 1986. *Choices in*

Vichy France: The French Under Nazi Occupation. Oxford: Oxford University Press; Ian Ousby. 1997. *Occupation: The Ordeal of France 1940–1945.* New York: St. Martin's Press.

12. This is done primarily for non-French readers.
13. Ibid. Berrin, p. 2.
14. Adam Nossiter. 1998. "Wartime nightmare is still alive in French town." *New York Times* June 18: A-12; Philip Beck. 1979. *Oradour: Village of the Dead.* London: Leo Cooper; Ibid., fn. 11; Ousby, pp. 287–288. See also William L. Shirer. 1960. *The Rise and Fall of the Third Reich.* New York: Simon and Schuster, pp. 993–994.
15. Nossiter. 1998, A-12.
16. Ibid.
17. Ibid.
18. William L. Shirer. 1960. *The Rise and Fall of the Third Reich: A History of Nazi Germany.* New York: Simon and Schuster, p. 957.
19. Unless otherwise noted the information used here comes from Roderick Kedward. 1995. "France." I.C.B. Dear and M.R.D. Foot (eds.) *The Oxford Companion to World War II.* Oxford: Oxford University Press, pp. 391–408.
20. Ibid., p. 392.
21. Ibid.
22. Ibid., p. 393.
23. Ibid., p. 392. See Table 1, "German requisitions, percentage of French output."
24. Ibid., p. 393.
25. Ibid.
26. Ibid., fn. 11; Ousby. 1997, p. 118.
27. Ibid., fn. 11; Ousby, pp. 119–120.
28. Ibid., fn. 11; Ousby, p. 123.
29. Ibid., fn. 11; Ousby, p. 124.
30. Ibid., fn. 11; Ousby, pp. 124–125.
31. Ibid., fn. 11; Ousby, pp. 120–122.
32. Ibid., fn. 11; Ousby, p. 120.
33. Ibid.
34. Ibid., Fn. 11; Ousby, p. 121.
35. Ibid.
36. [Note:This reference was submitted to Payot but did not appear in the book] Bruno Aubusson de Cavarlay, Marie-Sylvie Mure and Marie-Lys Pottier. *La justice penale en France: Resultants statistiques (1934–1954).* Cahier No. 23. Avril 1993. Also see Jean-Claude Brunschvicg. 1951. "Etude statistique des effets de la criminalite en Fance." In LES EFFETS DE LA GUERRE SUR LA CRIMINALITE. *Commission International Penale et Penitentair.* Stempfli & Cie. Berne, pp. 55–84.
37. Dick Hobbs.1988. *Doing the Business.* Oxford: Oxford University Press.
38. Ibid., Berrin, p. 278.
39. Ibid.
40. Ibid.; Ousby, p. 135.
41. Sebastian Faulks. 1999. *Charlotte Gray.* London: Vintage.
42. M.R.D. Foot. 1995. "Witherington, Pearl." In I.C.B. Dear and M.R.D. Foot (eds.) 1995. *The Oxford Companion to World War II.* Oxford: Oxford University Press, p. 1275. See also M.R.D. Foot. 1977. *Resistance: An Analysis of European Resistance to nazism 1940–1945.* London: Oxford University Press.
43. Ibid., p. 1275.

44. I am grateful to Mike Nellis, University of Birmingham, for offering me this possible interpretation of English sentiment, circa World War II.

45. Martin Blumenson. 1961. *Breakout and Pursuit*. Washington, DC: Office of the Chief Military History, pp. 9–10.

46. Ibid.

47. Ibid.

48. Adam Roberts. 1995. In I.C.B. Dear and M.R.D. Foot. 1995. "Resistance." *The Oxford Companion to World War II*. Oxford: oxford University Press, p. 946.

49. Ordinary rapes involve females 16 years of age or older. Sometimes in France, however, the US military made no distinction between victims under or over 16 years.

50. One refugee came from Poland, the others were French citizens who had fled their homes.

51. HBO/JAG, p. 13.

52. Leon Radzinowicz. 1957. *Sexual Offences: A Report of the Cambridge Department of Criminal Science*. London: Macmillan, Preface, p. xv.

53. According to one source, of the 2,000,000 Americans passing through Great Britain during and right after World War II, 100,000 married British women. See Elfrieda Berthiaume Shukert and Barbara Smith Scibetta. 1989. *War Brides of World War II* (New York: Penguin.), p. 7.

54. BOJAG *U.S. v. Private Clarence Whitfield, CM ETO 3142*. 1944. Vol. 8, pp. 351–361.

55. Clarence Whitfield. Trial Transcript. C.M. ETO. 3142. 1944. I have found no instance in which the kin of an executed soldier received insurance payment.

56. Ibid. See "Proceedings: execution of Private Clarence (NMI) Whitfield."

57. BOR/JAG *United States v. Pvts. Melvin Welch and John H. Dollar.*. CM ETO 10851. 1945. Vol. 23, pp. 187–191.

58. BOR/JAG *US v. Privates James B. Sanders, Florine Wilson and Roy W. Anderson*. CM ETO 3740. 1944. Vol. 10, p. 255.

59. BO/JAG. Vol. 10, p. 258.

60. BO/JAG Vol. 10, p. 259.

61. BO/JAG Vol. 12, p. 55.

62. BOR/JAG *United States v. Privates Horace G. Adams and Hugh L. Harris*. CM ETO 7869. 1944. Vol. 18, p. 298.

63. For details and accuracy I acquired copies of a few original trial transcripts.

64. BOR/JAG. *United States v. Sergeant Obbie L. Myles*. CM ETO 8542. 1945. Vol. 19, pp. 305–309.

65. Vol. 19, p. 307.

66. BOR/JAG *United States v. Technician Fifth Grade Kenneth W. Nelson*. CM ETO 11590. 1944. Vol. 24, p. 231.

67. Ibid.; Teton and Farrell. Trial Transcript. See "Review by Staff Judge Advocate."

68. *US vs. Pvt. Roy Anderson*. CM ETO 3740. 1944. Vol. 10, p. 260.

69. William D. Pennyfeather. 1944. Trial Transcript. See also *BOR/JAG. U.S. vs. Pvt. William D. Pennyfeather*. CM ETO 4017. 1944. Vol. 11, p. 245.

70. BOR/JAG *United States v. Privates George W. Ferguson and Henry D. Rorie*. Vol. 11, p. 133.

71. T. McGann. Trial Transcript.

72. *BOR/JAG*. Vol. 13, p. 111.

73. See Tyler Stovall. 1996. *Paris Noir: African Americans in the City of Lights*. (New York: Houghton Mifflin Co.), especially, chapters 1–5.

74. Marcus Felson. 2002. *Crime and Everyday Life*. Thousand Oaks, CA: Sage Publications.

75. Arthur E. Barbeau and Flotette Henri. 1974. The *Unknown Soldiers: Black American Troops in World War I*. Philadelphia, PA: Temple University Press. p. 143.

76. Ibid. p. 144. See also Tyler Stovall. 1996. *Paris Noir: African Americans in the City of Light*. Boston, MA: Houghton Mifflin Co, pp. 1–24.

77. Ibid., p. 177. Quoted in Barbeau and Henri.

78. K. Craig Gibson. 2001. "Sex and soldiering in France and Flanders: the British expeditionary forces along the Western Front, 1914–1919." *The International History Review*. XXXIII (3) September: 546.

79. Ibid., p. 546.

80. Omar N. Bradley. 1951. *A Soldier's Story*. New York: Henry Holt and Company.

81. Personal file. Dated April 18, 2002.

82. Other animals assaulted include a fowl, a cow, and an attempted assault on a ewe. See *HBO/JAG. Chapter XXII Sex Offenses*, pp. 254–255.

83. Ibid., Stovall, p. 17.

84. Ibid., Stovall, p. 18.

85. Tyler Stovall. 1998. "The color line behind the lines: racial violence in France during the Great War." *American Historical Review*. June, pp. 737–769.

86. Ibid., p. 739.

87. For excellent overviews of France in World War I see: Jean-Baptiste Duroselle. 1972. *La France et les Franccais, 1914–1920*. Paris; Jean-Jacques Becker. 1997. *Comment les francais sont entres dans la guerre*. Paris; and H. Pearl Adam. 1919. *Paris Sees it Through*. London.

88. Expressions of hostility and disgust about France's submission to Germany in 1940 are still heard in casual conversations in the United States. At the annual meeting of the American Society of Criminology, I heard a prominent American criminologist in a casual conversation say, "I hate the fucking French ... the way they rolled over for the Germans is cowardly. What do ya expect from a bunch of men who ride around on bicycles with a beret on their head!"

89. Lee Kennett. 1997. *G.I.: The American Soldier in World War II*. Norman: University of Oklahoma Press, p. 206.

90. "The wrong ambassadors." 1945. *Time*. November 19, 1945, p. 21.

91. Ibid.

92. Ibid.

93. Ibid.

94. BO/JAG. *U.S v Private Tommie Davison*, CM ETO 8163. 1944. Vol. 19, pp. 39–45.

95. BO/JAG *United States v. Private Frank Williams*. CM ETO 5869. 1944. Vol. 16, pp. 27–31.

96. BO/JAG *United States v. Private Luther W. Carter*. CM ETO 6207. 1944. Vol. 16, pp. 197–202.

97. Blumenson. 1996, pp. 3–50.

98. Dwight D. Eisenhower.1948. *Crusade in Europe*. Garden City, NY: Doubleday & Co., p. 277.

99. Blumenson. 1996, p. 10.

100. BOR/JAG *United States v. Privates James R. Parrott, Grant U. Smith and William C. Downes*. CM ETO 6193. 1944. Vol. 16, p. 169.

101. Ibid. pp. 160–161.

102. Ibid., p. 161.

103. Eisenhower. 1948, chapter 15, pp. 266–287.

104. Trial Transcript. *United States vs. Pvt. Theron W. McGann*. CM ETO 4309.

105. Eisenhower. 1948, p. 279.

106. Ibid.

107. See Blumenson. 1961, chapters XXX–XXXII for an excellent review of the Battle for Brest.
108. BOR/JAG *US v. Private Forrest E. Washington.* CM ETO 10103. 1945. Vol. 22, p. 92.
109. Ibid.
110. Ibid., p. 93.
111. Blumenson. 1961, p. 666.
112. Ibid., p. 702.
113. Ibid., p. 688.
114. BOR/JAG *US v. Corporal Wilford Tenton and Private Arthur J. Farrell.* CM ETO 4775. 1944. Vol. 13, pp. 281–288, and Trial Transcript.
115. Trial Transcript. See section titled "Review of the Staff Judge Advocate."
116. Ibid., subsection "6. Data as to accused."
117. Trial Transcript.
118. Ibid.
119. Ibid.
120. Comments of former World War II Military Police Corporal made to Lilly in 1999.
121. BOR/JAG. Vol. 10, pp. 391–407.
122. The trial record is unclear about whether her father came back to assist her.
123. *United States vs. Private Wesley Edmonds.* ETO. GCM 90, 1942, Trail Transcript.
124. Trial Transcript. *United States vs. PFC John David Cooper.* CM ETO 5362.
125. Interview on May, 2006 with the current owner of the house, a 35-year-old German man.
126. Christine Doublet, Program 33, shared this information with me just prior to the interview with Mirielle W., May 2005.
127. Trial Transcript. *United States vs. Robert L. Skinner.* ETO CM 5363.
128. Trial Transcript. *United States vs. Yancy Waiters.* ETO CM 5584.
129. Additional US soldiers were executed in France for crimes, especially murder committed against fellow soldiers. Five more US soldiers were executed for murder/rape crimes involving French victims. An additional two soldiers were executed in France for murder/rape, but their crimes were committed in Germany, and the victims were Polish.
130. Fabrice Virgili. 2002. *Shorn Women: Gender and Punishment in Liberation France.* Oxford: Berg.
131. US military justice has a long history of questionable harsh and swift decisions. See Robert Sherrill's *Military Justice is to Justice as Military Music is to Music.* (New York: Harper & Row.1969).

5 Germany – Operation Plunder

1. Technically the war was over by the time of this crime. I have included it in an effort to (1) demonstrate that the abuse of females in Germany did not end on May 8, 1945, and (2) because it was included in the BOR's records of crimes committed during the war by US soldiers in Germany. According to this source, 27 women were raped in Germany between May 10 and September 23, 1945.
2. BOR/JAG *United States v. Private Gilbert F. Newburn.* CM ETO 18381. 1945. Vol. 33, p. 2.
3. Ibid., p. 353.
4. Ibid., p. 354.
5. Richard Bessel (ed.) 1987. *Life in the Third Reich.* Oxford: Oxford University Press. p, xi.

6. Charles B. MacDonald. 1973. *The Last Offensive*. Washington, DC: US Government Printing Office, chapter VIII.

7. Charles Messenger. 1995. "Aachen." In. I.C.B. Dear and M.R.D. Foot. (eds.) 1995. *The Oxford Companion to World War II*. Oxford: Oxford University Press, p. 1. (Anne Frank's parents were married in Aachen in 1925. She lived there with her grandmother in 1933).

8. BOR/JAG *United States v. Private First Class Wardell W. Willson*. CM ETO 8837. 1945. Vol. 20, pp. 67–70.

9. See Cornelius Ryan. 1966. *The Last Battle*. New York: Touchstone; Antony Beevor. 2002. *The Fall of Berlin 1945*. New York: Viking; David Schoenbaum. 1966. *Hitler's Social Revolution*. New York: Doubleday; Atina Grossman. 1997. "A question of silence: the rape of German women by occupation soldiers." In Robert G. Moeller (ed.) 1997. *West Germany under Construction: politics, society, and culture in the Adenauer era*. Ann Arbor, MI: The University of Michigan Press, p. 33–54.

10. See the novel by James Burke. 1951. *The Big Rape*. New York: Farrar Straus & Young.

11. MacDonald. 1973, p. 475.

12. Ibid., p. 481.

13. Jurgen Forster, Charles Messenger, and Wolfgang Petter. 1995."Germany." in I.C.B. Dear and M.R.D. Foot (eds.) *The Oxford Companion to World War II*. Oxford: Oxford University Press, p. 456.

14. Ibid.

15. There already exists an enormous and growing legacy of work on the Third Reich. See William I. Shirer. 1960. *The Rise and Fall of the Third Reich: A History of Nazi Germany*. New York: Simon and Schuster; Christopher R. Browning. 1992. *Ordinary Men: Reserve Police Battalion 101 and the Final Solution in Poland*. New York; Omer Bartov. 1992. *Hitler's Army: Soldiers, Nazis, and War in the Third Reich*. Oxford: Oxford University Press; Omer Bartov. 1996; *Murder in Our Midst: The Holocaust, Industrial Killing and Representation*. Oxford: Oxford University Press; Antony Beevor. 2002. *The Fall of Berlin 1945*. New York: Viking; Anthony Read and David Fishner. 1992. *The Fall of Berlin*. New York: W.W. Norton; James Lucas. 2002. *The Last Days of the Reich: The Collapse of Nazi Germany, May 1945*. London: Cassell.

16. MacDonald. 1973, p. 331.

17. Author's notes, 1993. Unfortunately, I have not found the trial transcript to confirm Kadin's recollections. He died in 1997 after a long and successful business career in New York City. I met Ted Kadin after the *New York Times* reporter, Francis X. Clines, wrote an article about the research a colleague and I were doing on the execution of black soldiers by the US Army, ETO. Ted said he had had second thoughts about his choice of words, but he had no doubts about the outcome of the trial. See Francis X. Clines. 1993. "When black soldiers were hanged: a war's footnote." *The New York Times*. February 7: A-14.

18. Forster et al., p. 457.

19. R. Bessel. 1987. *Life in the Third Reich*. Oxford: Oxford University, p. 97. Quoted in Ibid. Forster et al., p. 457.

20. Michael Geyer. 1987. "The Nazi state reconsidered." In Richard Bessel. 1987. *Life in the Third Reich*. Oxford: Oxford University Press, pp. 57–58.

21. Forster et al., p. 459.

22. Ibid.

23. Michael Geyer. 1987, picture caption.

24. William L. Shirer. 1960. *The Rise and Fall of the Third Reich: A History of Nazi Germany*. New York: Simon and Schuster, p. 941.

25. See Steven Erlanger. 2002. "Vienna skewered as a Nazi-era pillager of its Jews." *New York Times*. March 7: A-3; Celestine Bohlen. 2002. "Judge revives case of Nazi-looted art." *New York Times*. April 27: B-9; Ralph Bumenthal 2001. "Twice stolen, twice found: a case of art on the Lam. *New York Times*. July 19: E-1.
26. Shirer. 1960, p. 944.
27. Ibid.
28. Forster et al., p. 459.
29. Ibid., p. 461. See Table 7.
30. Edith Hahn Beer with Susan Dworkin. 1999. *The Nazi Officer's Wife: How One Jewish Woman Survived the Holocaust*. New York: Weisbach and Morrow, p. 3.
31. Forster et al., p. 457.
32. Shirer. 1960, p. 946.
33. Forster et al., p. 460.
34. Ibid.
35. Shirer. 1960, p. 947. Taken from a memorandum that Shirer cited regarding Germany occupied Russia.
36. Forster et al., p. 457.
37. Ibid.
38. Shirer. 1960. Quoted on page 951.
39. Gerhard Wilke. 1987. "Village life in Nazi Germany." In Richard Bessel. 1987. *Life in the Third Reich*. Oxford: Oxford University Press, pp. 20–21.
40. Ibid., p. 23.
41. Shirer. 1960. p. 951.
42. Ibid., p. 949.
43. Ibid., p. 948.
44. Ibid., p. 949.
45. Bessel, Richard (ed.). 1987. *Life in the Third Reich*. Oxford: Oxford University Press, p. xv.
46. Ibid. Forster et al., p. 460.
47. Ibid.
48. Ibid.
49. Ibid.
50. Ibid., p. 464.
51. Ibid., p. 465.
52. Ibid.
53. Shirer, 1960, p. 950.
54. *New York Times*. 1944. "Freakish cold spell strikes Germany." November 23: p. 6. col. 5.
55. Forster et al., p. 465.
56. Ibid. p. 465.
57. Henry Steele Commager (ed.). 1945. *The Pocket History of the Second World War*. New York: Pocket Book, p. 317.
58. Ibid.
59. Shirer. 1960, p. 995.
60. Ibid., fn. 54. *New York Times*. 1944. November 23.
61. Ibid., Shirer. 1960, p. 1006.
62. Ibid., p. 1007.
63. MacDonald. 1973, p. 15.
64. Ibid., p. 330.
65. Mathematical or statistical purist might object to including rapes committed after the war officially ended on May 8, 1945. However, only 12 rapes were committed between June and September 1945.

66. BOR/JAG *United States v. Private First Class Rito Mendez and Private Joseph R. Rego*. CM ETO 12604. 1945. Vol. 25, pp. 269–274; *United States v. Private (formerly Technician Fifth Grade) Michael A. McDonald*. CM ETO 12662. 1945. Vol. 25, pp. 331–333.
67. HBO/JAG, chapter XXII, p. 255.
68. BOR/JAG *United States v. Private First Class Jack C. Kelley*. CM ETO 13425. 1945. Vol. 26, pp. 359–363.
69. Ibid., p. 361.
70. Ibid.
71. Ibid., p. 362.
72. Ibid.
73. BOR/JAG *United States v. Privates First Class Willie M. Lucero and Homer E. Miller*. CM ETO 18165. 1945. Vol. 33, pp. 213–219.
74. Ibid. Vol. 33, p. 215.
75. BOR/JAG *United States v. Technician Fifth Grade Jeremiah C. Nelums, Technician Fifth Grade Henry Garrett, Jr. and Private First Class Ernest Jackson*. CM ETO 13568. 1945. Vol. 27, pp. 35–44.
76. Ibid. Vol. 27, p. 37.
77. Ibid. Vol. 27, p. 38.
78. BOR/JAG *United States v. Private First Class Alfred F. Willet and Private William Carreon*. CM ETO 16640. 1945. Vol. 31, pp. 119–126.
79. The term "Hollanders" appears in the record. It refers to two Dutch people.
80. BOR/JAG *United States v. Private First Class Alfred F. Willet and Private William Carreon*. CM ETO 16640. 1945. Vol. 31, p. 122.
81. Ibid.
82. Ibid.
83. Ibid.
84. BOR/JAG Ibid. Vol. 32, p. 122.
85. BOR/JAG *United States v. Private First Class Alfred F. Willet and Private William Carreon*. CM ETO 16640. 1945. Vol. 31, p. 124.
86. BOR/JAG *United States v. Private First Class William J. Blakely*. CM ETO 17442. 1945. Vol. 32, pp. 125–131.
87. Ibid. p. 127.
88. Ibid.
89. The *BOR/JAG* states that after 15 to 20 minutes Blakely fell asleep and was taken to the bed where he had raped. The family stayed in the kitchen until 5:30 a.m. when, against her parents' advice, Ruth M. reported the incident. An officer came and got Blakely out of bed. He was arrested, charged, and put in stockade to await trial. He escaped from the stockade on May 15, 1945, and turned himself in on May 27, 1945. Blakely was convicted and sentenced to be shot, but this punishment was reduced to hard labor for life.
90. BOR/JAG *United States v. Private William D. Johnson, Jr*. Vol. 29. CM ETO 15250. 1945. pp. 43–48.
91. See Fabrice Virgili. 2002. *Shorn Women: Gender and Punishment in Liberation France*. (English edition). New York: Berg, for an excellent and unprecedented discussion of the practice of punishing French women for real and alleged collaboration with German occupiers and German sympathizers.
92. *BOR/JAG United States v. Private William D. Johnson, Jr*. Vol. 29. CM ETO 15250. 1945. p. 44.
93. *History Branch Office of the Judge Advocate General with the United States Forces – European Theater*. 18 July 1942 – 1 November, 1945. Branch Office of the Judge Advocate General with the United States Forces European Theater. St. Cloud, France. p. 248.

94. *BOR/JAG United States v. Technician Fifth Grade John F. Autrey.* CM ETO 10696. 1945, Vol. 23, pp. 23–27.

95. *BOR/JAG United States v. Technician Fifth Grade John F. Autrey.* CM ETO 10696. 1945, Vol. 23, p. 24.

96. Ibid.

97. *BOR/JAG* Technician Fifth Grade Elmer L. Spohn and Private Marton L. Whelchel. CM ETO. 12873. 1945. Vol. 26, pp. 39–45.

98. Ibid., p. 41.

99. Ibid.

100. Ibid.

101. Ibid.

102. BOR/JAG *United States v. Private Harry L. Luckey.* CM ETO 14448. 1945. Vol. 27, pp. 395–399. See David P. Colley. 2002. *Blood for Dignity: The Story of the First Integrated Combat Unit of the U.S. Army.* New York: St. Martin's Press.

103. Ibid., p. 396.

104. MacDonald. 1973/1984,. p. 54.

105. Ibid.

106. Ibid.

107. Ibid., pp. 334–335.

108. Ibid., p. 335.

109. I have used the names as they appeared in the records. In some instances "Frau" was used, at other times "Mrs." was recorded.

110. BOR/JAG *United States v. Private First Class David McArthur and Willie J. Lee.* CM ETO 15604. 1945. Vol. 28, pp. 99–103.

111. Ibid., p. 101.

112. Ibid., p. 101.

113. Ibid., p. 101.

114. Ibid. BOR/JAG. *United States v. Private First Class Billy Reed.* CM ETO 14338. 1945. Vol. 27, pp. 327–331.

115. Ibid. *BOR/JAG.* Reed, p. 331.

116. BOR/JAG *United States v. Private Leo F. Manko and Private First Class Andrew J. Wortheam.* CM ETO 11970. 1945. Vol. 24, pp. 397–402.

117. BOR/JAG. *Manko and Wortheam.* Vol. 24, p. 399.

118. Ibid., p. 400.

119. Ibid.

120. Ibid., p. 401.

121. MacDonald. 1973/1984, pp. 174–178.

122. BOR/JAG *United States v. Corporal Lester Berger and Private Donald W. Bamford.* CM ETO 9083. 1945. Vol. 20, pp. 107–117.

123. *BOR/JAG.* Berger and Bamford, p. 110.

124. Ibid.

125. *BOR/JAG* Ibid., p. 111.

126. Paul Fussell.1989. *Wartime: Understanding and Behavior in the Second World War.* Oxford: Oxford University Press. See chapter 8.

127. Ibid., p. 96.

128. Ibid., p. 103.

129. BOR/JAG *United States v. Private Charles E. Heishman.* CM ETO 14066. 1945. Vol. 27, pp. 191–196.

130. Ibid., p. 193.

131. Ibid.

132. Ibid., p. 194.

133. Ibid.

134. Trial transcript. *United States v. Second Lieutenant Robert D. Thompson, Service Company, 232nd Infantry. CM ETO 16888*. 1945. See also BOR/JAG, Vol. 31, pp. 235–236.
135. *BOR/JAG United States v. Second Lieutenant Robert D. Thompson*. ETO 16888. Vol. 31, p. 236.
136. Ibid.
137. Ibid.
138. Trial transcript. p. 18.
139. Ibid., p. 14.
140. Ibid., p. 19.
141. Ibid., p. 34.
142. *BOR/JAG* Ibid. Vol. 31. p. 235.
143. Ibid., p. 236.
144. BOR/JAG *United States v. Privates William A. Stevenson and William N. Stuart*. CM ETO 10671. 1945. Vol. 23, pp. 221–225; also, see trial transcript of the same name, CM ETO 10671.
145. Trial transcript, *United States v. Privates William A. Stevenson and William N. Stuart*. CM ETO 10671. 1945, p. 1
146. Ibid.
147. Ibid.
148. Ibid., p. 5.
149. Ibid.
150. BOR/JAG *United States v. Privates William A. Stevenson and William N. Stuart*. Vol. 23, Vol. 221–225. See also trial transcript by the same name, CM ETO 10871. 1945.
151. BOR/JAG *United States v. First Lieutenant Joe H. Randie*. CM ETO 15251. 1945. Vol. 29, pp. 49–52.
152. Ibid., p. 51.
153. Trial transcript, *United States v. First Lieutenant Joe H. Randi*. CM ETO 15251. p. 1.
154. Trial transcript. Statement of Private William A. Stevenson taken by Lt. Colonel John P. Oliver, p. 1.
155. Ibid., pp. 19–20.
156. BOR/JAG *United States v. Private First Class Joe F. Selvera*. CM ETO 17918. 1945. Vol. 33, pp. 143–146.
157. Ibid., p. 144.
158. Ibid., p. 145.
159. Ibid.
160. *BOR/JAG United States v. Private First Class Aelred V. J. Platta*. CM ETO 14206. 1945. Vol. 27, p. 277.
161. Ibid., p. 280.
162. Ibid., p. 281
163. Ibid.
164. BOR/JAG *United States v. PFC Charles w. O'Neil and George B. Tweedy and Privates William E. Ewing, Rufus N. Casey and Mack Shelvin*. EM ETO 13178. Vol. 26, pp. 183–191.
165. BOR/JAG *United States v. Private Wayne H. Hitchcock*. CM ETO 14174. 1945. Vol. 27, pp. 253–264.
166. BOR/JAG *United States v. Private First Class Thomas B. Jane*. CM ETO 14382. 1945. Vol. 27, pp. 373–379.
167. BOR/JAG *United States v. Private Alfred L. Prinely*. CM ETO 16971. 1945, Vol. 31. pp. 303–309.
168. BOR/JAG *United States v. Privates Roy E. Andrews and Charlie M. Hathcock*. CM ETO 14032. 1945. Vol. 27, pp. 155–161.

169. MacDonald. 1973/1984, pp. 373–379.
170. BOR/JAG *United States v. Private First Class Thomas G. King and Private Denzil A. Thomas*. CM ETO 13125. 1945. Vol. 26, pp. 133–148.
171. Ibid., Vol. 26, p. 135.
172. BOR/JAG *United States v. Private First Class Thomas G. King and Private Denzil A. Thomas*. CM ETO 13125. 1945. Vol. 26, p. 136.
173. Ibid., p. 137
174. Ibid., p. 138.
175. Ibid., p. 139.
176. Ibid., p. 140.
177. MacDonald. 1973/1984, pp. 339–343.
178. *BOR/JAG* Ibid. Vol. 26. p. 141.
179. Ibid., p. 142.
180. Ibid.
181. BOR/JAG *United States v. PFC Charles W. O'Neil, George B. Tweedy, and Privates William E. Ewing, Rufus N. Casey and Mack Shelvin*. CM ETO 13178. 1945. Vol. 26, pp. 183–191.
182. Ibid. p. 188.
183. BOR/JAG *United States vs. Privates Roy E. Andrews and Charlie M. Hathcock*. CM ETO 14032. 1945. Vol. 27, p. 155–161.
184. Ibid., p. 157.
185. Ibid.
186. Ibid., p. 158.
187. Ibid., p. 157.
188. Ibid., p. 159.
189. BOR/JAG *United States vs. Privates Lucious C.N. Johnson, Thomas Henderson and Ira J. Smith*. CM ETO 18047. 1945. Vol. 33, pp. 163–166.
190. BOR/JAG *Janes* Vol. 27, pp. 373–379.
191. BOR/JAG United States v. Technician Fifth Grade Thomas J. Smalls. Vol. 23. CM ETO 10700. 1945, p. 32.
192. See MacDonald, p. 330; Lee Kennett. 1987. *The American Soldier in World War II*. Norman: Oklahoma University Press, pp. 211–227.
193. Ibid., p. 212.
194. Ibid.
195. Peter Schrijvers. 1998. *The Crash of Ruin: American Combat Soldiers in Europe during World War II*. New York: New York University Press, p. 183.
196. BOR/JAG *United States v. Privates Lewis R. Ward and Jessie W. Sharer*. CM ETO 10446. 1845. Vol. 22, pp. 297– 306.
197. Ibid., p. 299.
198. Ibid.
199. Ibid., p. 300.
200. Ibid.
201. Ibid.
202. Ibid., p. 301.
203. Ibid., p. 302.
204. Ibid.
205. Ibid.
206. Ibid., p. 303.
207. Ibid.
208. Ibid.
209. Ibid.

210. Ibid., p. 305.
211. BOR/JAG *United States v. Private Frank P. Prairiechief.*CM ETO 9611. 1945. Vol. 21, p. 134.
212. BOR/JAG *United States v. Technician Fifth Grade Ray F. Daniels and Private James A. Caudill.* CM ETO 10141. 1945. Vol. 22, pp. 99–103.
213. BOR/JAG *United States v. Staff Sergeant Richard Allen.* Vol. 27. CM ETO 13767. 2:1945.103.

6   Punishment and Context: Wartime Justice

1. Trial transcript. *United States v. Private Wesley Edmonds.* CM 90 ETO. See "Statement by 1st. Lt. Agustus A. Marchetti," p. 4.
2. Edward T. Pound. 2002. "Unequal justice." *U.S. News & World Report.* December 16: pp. 18–30.
3. B.C. Nalty and M.J. MacGregor. 1981. *Blacks in the Military: Essential Documents.* Wilmington, DE: Scholarly Resources, p. 133.
4. *United States v. Private Aniceto Martinez.* Trial Transcript. See "Psychiatric examination of Martinez, Aniceto, (NMI), ASN 38168482, 16 Jan. 1945," p. 1. CM ETO 10079.
5. Ibid.
6. Ibid.
7. See Serge Schmemann. 2002. "U.S. peacekeepers given year's immunity from New Court." *New York Times.* July 13: A3; Marlise Simons. 2002. "Without fanfare or cases, International Court sets up." *New York Times.* June 16: A-4; Serge Schememann. 2002. "U.S. links peacekeeping to immunity from New Court." *New York Times.* June 19: A-3.
8. Ibid. *History Branch Office of the Judge Advocate General with the United States Forces – European Theater.* July 18, 1942 – November 1, 1945. Branch Office of the Judge Advocate General with the United States Forces European Theater. St. Cloud, France. p. 248.
9. *New York Times.* 1944. "No coward's death mars U.S. in France." December 28: p. 1.
10. Phone interview with the author, August 17, 1992. Also see Ronald Smothers. 1987. "Historian's death penalty obsession." *New York Times.* October 21.
11. James Bacque. 1991. *Other Loses: The Shocking Truth behind the Mass Deaths of Disarmed German Soldiers and Civilians under General Eisenhower's Command.* New York: Prima Publishing. Dust jacket.
12. Ibid.
13. Gunter Bischof and Stephen E. Ambrose. 1991. *Eisenhower and the German POWs: Facts against Falsehood.* Baton Rouge, LA: Louisiana State University Press.
14. Ibid.
15. "The perilous fight: America's war in color." *PBS* Television. Four-part documentary, February 19. WCET. It is unclear whether Roosevelt was speaking literally or metaphorically.
16. *History Branch Office of the Judge Advocate General with the United States Forces – European Theater.* See Appendix 83. pp. 557–617.
17. Ibid., p. 249.
18. Ibid., p. 4.
19. Richard A. Ball. 1979. "Restricted reprobation and the reparation of social reality." In P.J. Brantingham and J.M. Kress (eds.) *Structure, Law and Power: Essays in the Sociology of Law.* Beverly Hills, CA: Sage, pp. 135–149.

20. Birgit Beck. 2002. "Rape: the military trials of sexual crimes committed by soldiers in the Wehrmacht, 1939–1944." In Karen Hagemann and Stefanie Schuller-Springorum. Editors. 2002. *Home/Front: The Military, War and Gender in Twentieth-Century Germany*. Oxford: Berg, pp. 255–273.

21. Ibid. *History Branch Office of the Judge Advocate General with the United States Forces – European Theater*. July 18, 1942 – November 1, 1945. Branch Office of the Judge Advocate General with the United States Forces European Theater. St. Cloud, France. p. 31.

22. Ibid., p. 33.

23. Birgit Beck. 2002. "Rape: the military trials of sexual crimes committed by soldiers in the Wehrmacht, 1939–1944." In Karen Hagemann and Stefanie Schuller-Springorum. Editors. 2002. *Home/Front: The Military, War and Gender in Twentieth-Century Germany*. Oxford: Berg, p. 33.

24. Ibid.

25. Ibid.

26. Ibid., p. 32.

27. Ibid., p. 33.

28. Ibid.

29. Ibid., p. 51.

30. Ibid., p. 43.

31. *HBO/JAG*. Appendix 58, pp. 478–499.

32. Ibid., p. 496.

33. Ibid.

34. Ibid.

35. Ibid., p. 478.

36. Ibid., p. 479.

37. Ibid., p. 485.

38. Ibid., p. 486.

39. Ibid., p. 485.

40. Ibid., p. 496.

41. Ibid., p. 46.

42. Ibid.

43. Ibid. See also Appendixes pages 375–380; 383.

44. Stephen E. Ambrose and J. A. Barber (eds.). 1972. *The Military and American Society: Essays and Readings*. New York: Free Press; Morris Janowitz. 1974. *The Military Establishment*. Beverly Hills: Sage; Charles C. Moskos. 1970. *The American Enlisted Man*. New York: Russell Sage Foundation; Robert Sherril. 1970. *Military Justice is to Justice as Military Music is to Music*. New York: Harper & Row; Russel Weigely. 1967. *History of the United States Army*. New York: Macmillan; B. Williams. 1989. "Should military personnel be court martialed for offenses that are not service connected?" *Oklahoma Law Review*, 42: 116–31.

45. See Omar N. Bradley.1951. *A Soldier's Story*. New York: Henry Holt and Company; Dwight D. Eisenhower. 1948. *Crusade in Europe*. Garden City, New York: Doubleday; U. S. Grant. 1982. *Personal Memoirs of U.S. Grant*. New York: De Capo; Douglas McArthur. 1964. *Reminiscences*. New York: McGraw-Hill.

46. Russell F. Weigley. 1967. *History of the United States Army*. New York: Macmillian. The *Federalist Papers* were a series of political pamphlets written by Alexander Hamilton, John Jay, and James Madison. They were used to persuade votes in individual state ratification campaigns of the usefulness of the US Constitution. Given the brevity of the US Constitution – approximately 3,000 words – scholars cite these papers to demonstrate the "framer intent" of the documents.

47. J. Bishop. 1974. *Justice Under Fire*. New York: Charterhouse.
48. Stephen E. Ambrose.1966. *Duty, Honor, Country: A History of West Point*. Baltimore, MD: The John Hopkins Press.
49. See Eisenhower, 1948; Grant, 1982.
50. See Janowitz, 1974.
51. See C. Chomsky. 1990. "The United States-Dakota war trials: a study of ilitary injustice." *Stanford Law Review*. 43: 13–98; J. Sykes and J. Putkowski. 1989. *Shot at Dawn*. Warncliffe: Barnsley.
52. J.F. Marszalek. 1972. *Court Martial: A Black Man in America*. New York: Scribner's.
53. See J. Bishop. 1974. *Justice Under Fire*. New York: Charterhouse; N.E. Felder. 1987. "A long way since Houston: the treatment of blacks in the military justice system." *Army Lawyer*. October: 8–11.
54. *New York Times*. 1918. "Whole army division sees Negroes hanged." July 6: pp. 4, 5.
55. Jonathan Lurie. 1992. *Arming Military Justice: The Origins of the United States Court of Military Appeals, 1775–1950*. Vol. 1. Princeton, NJ: Princeton University Press.
56. Ibid. *History Branch Office of the Judge Advocate General with the United States Forces – European Theater*. July 18, 1942 – November 1, 1945. Branch Office of the Judge Advocate General with the United States Forces European Theater. St. Cloud, France. p. 512.
57. Ibid., p. 462.
58. Ibid.
59. Ibid. McNeil's letter contains an error. He mistakenly wrote "days" instead of "years."
60. Ibid.
61. Ibid., p. 463.
62. Ibid., p. 464.
63. Ibid., p. 462.
64. Ibid., p. 512. Emphasis added.
65. Ibid.
66. Ibid.
67. Ibid.
68. Ibid., p. 513.
69. Ibid.
70. Ibid., p. 514.
71. Ibid. *HBO/JAG*. Appendix 83, pp. 584–585. Slovik's death was an anomaly of such proportions that it later became the subject of a best-selling book and movie. William Bradford Huie. 1954. *The Execution of Private Slovik*. New York: Duell, Sloan and Pearce. "The execution of Private Slovik." 1974. NBC tv documentary, was reviewed as "very good television, a successful competitor" to "The Autobiography of Jane Pittman," "Catholics," and "The Glass Menagerie." See *The Washington Post*. 1974. "Execution of Private Slovik." March 19: B-1, B-17.
72. Trial Transcript. *United States v. Private Eddie D. Slovik*. CM ETO 5555, p. 1.
73. Ibid., p. 5.
74. *Washington Star-News*. 1974. "40,000 deserted, 1 executed." March 31: A-3. Also see ibid. Huie. 1954, p. 11.
75. Slovik, p. 1.
76. Ibid.
77. Ibid. See Review by Staff Judge Advocate, pp. 1–4, signed by Major Frederick J. Bertolet, JAG.
78. Slovik. See p. 6 of "Review of the Staff Judge Advocate."

79. Ibid. See handwritten letter to General Eisenhower, December 9, 1944.
80. Huie. 1954, p. 21.
81. Ibid.
82. Ibid. Trial Transcript. See "Report of execution by shooting," p. 3. Signed by Lieutenant Colonel Henry J. Sommer, Division Judge Advocate and Recorder.
83. *HBO/JAG*. Appendix 63, p. 508.
84. Ibid.
85. *HBO/JAG*. Appendix 65, p. 515.
86. Ibid.
87. Ibid. *HBO/JAG*. Appendix 65, p. 516.
88. *HBO/JAG*. Appendix. 65, p. 517.
89. Ibid. *HBO/JAG*. Appendix 66, pp. 519–521. It is entirely possible that many other letters were exchanged that I do know about. I relied on the letters that are contained in the *HBO/JAG*'s extensive Appendixes.
90. Ibid. *HBO/JAG*. Appendix 68. pp. 525–526.
91. Ibid., p. 525.
92. Trial Transcript. *United States v. Private First Class Blake W. Mariano.* CM ETO 15902. 1945.
93. Ibid., p. 13.
94. Ibid. See Exhibit A., p. 3.
95. Ibid., p. 4.
96. Ibid., p. 5.
97. Ibid. See "Investigation of alleged murder and alleged rapes." May 3, 1945, p. 3.
98. Interview, May 15, 2005. Lauf, Germany.
99. Trial Transcript. There was disagreement about whether the weapon Mariano carried. It might have been a rifle.
100. Ibid. See Exhibit D, p. 2
101. Ibid., p. 3.
102. Ibid.
103. Ibid., p. 4.
104. Ibid., p. 1.
105. Ibid.
106. Ibid.
107. Ibid. Trial Transcript, p. 12.
108. Ibid., p. 4.
109. Ibid. See "Proceedings of a board of officers which convened at Munich, Germany." May 10, 1945,. p. 6.
110. Ibid. "Staff Judge Advocate review," p. 14.
111. Ibid. Fisher, p. 15.
112. Ibid., p. 16.
113. Ibid.
114. Ibid. Gafford, pp. 1–6.
115. Ibid. Fisher p. 6.
116. Ibid. Gafford, p. 3.
117. Ibid. Trial Transcript, p. 47.
118. Ibid. Trial Transcript. "Staff Judge Advocate review." Gafford, pp. 4–5.
119. Ibid., p. 5.
120. Ibid.
121. Ibid., p. 6.
122. *HBO/JAG*. Appendix 69, p. 1.

123. *New York Times*. 1945. "Jailing of soldier who beat Nazis hit." May 26: p. 4, col. 8.
124. Ibid.
125. Ibid.
126. *HBO/JAG*. Appendix 69, p. 1
127. Ibid, p. 2.
128. Ibid., Appendix 70, p. 1.
129. Ibid.
130. Ibid.
131. Ibid.
132. Ibid.
133. Ibid.
134. Ibid.
135. Ibid. Trial Transcript. McNeil's September 7, 1945 letter "TO: Commanding General, United States Forces, European Theater (Main), APO 757, U.S. Army," p. 1.
136. Ibid.
137. Ibid., p. 2.
138. *HBO/JAG*. Appendix 83, p. 584.
139. Advisory Committee Report. 1946. p. 1.
140. Ibid., p. 2.
141. Ibid.
142. Ibid.
143. Ibid.
144. Former Justice Owen J. Roberts considered complaints from convicted men, or their friends. He examined court-martial sentences for severity "after the war and in many instances reduced them." See ibid, p. 2–3.
145. Ibid., p. 3.
146. Ibid., p. 3–4.
147. Jonathan Lurie. 1992. *Arming Military Justice: The Origins of the United States Court of Military Appeals, 1775–1950*. Vol. 1. Princeton, NJ: Princeton University Press; 1998; *Pursuing Military Justice: The History of the United States Court of Military Appeals for the Armed Forces, 1950–1980*, Vol. 2. Princeton, NJ: Princeton University Press.
148. Edward T. Pound. 2002. "Unequal justice." *U.S. News & World Report*. December 16: 18–30.

References

Books and articles

Adam, H. Pearl. 1919. *Paris See It Through*. London.

Adams, Michael C.C. 1994. *The Best War Ever: America and World War II*. Baltimore, MD: Johns Hopkins University Press.

Adams, Michael C.C. 2002. *Echoes of War: A Thousand Years of Military History in Popular Culture*. Lexington, KY: University of Kentucky Press.

Ambrose, Stephen E. 1966. *Duty, Honor, Country: A History of West Point*. Baltimore, MD: The John Hopkins Press.

Ambrose, Stephen E. 1992. *Band of Brothers*. New York: Simon & Schuster.

Ambrose, Stephen E. 1994. *D-Day: June 6, 1944: The Climatic Battle of World War II*. New York: Simon & Schuster.

Ambrose, Stephen E. 1997. *Citizen Soldiers: The U.S. Army from the Normandy Beaches to the Bulge to the Surrender of Germany, June 7, 1944–May 7, 1945*. New York: Simon & Schuster.

Ambrose, Stephen E. 2001. *The Good Fight*. New York: Simon & Schuster.

Ambrose, Stephen E. and J.A. Barber (eds.) 1972. *The Military and American Society: Essays and Readings*. New York: Free Press.

Bacque, James. 1991. *Other Loses: The Shocking Truth Behind the Mass Deaths of Disarmed German Soldiers and Civilians Under General Eisenhower's Command*. New York: Prima Publishing.

Ball, Richard A. 1979. "Restricted reprobation and the reparation of social reality." In P.J. Brantingham and J.M. Kress (eds.). *Structure, Law and Power: Essays in the Sociology of Law*. Beverly Hills, CA: Sage.

Barbeau, Arthur E. and Flotette Henri. 1974. *The Unknown Soldiers: Black American Troops in World War I*. Philadelphia, PA: Temple University Press.

Bartov, Omer. 1992. *Hitler's Army: Soldiers, Nazis, and War in the Third Reich*. Oxford: Oxford University Press.

Bartov, Omer. 1996. *Murder in our Midst: The Holocaust, Industrial Killing and Representation*. Oxford: Oxford University Press.

Beck, Philip. 1979. *Oradour: Village of the Dead*. London: Leo Cooper.

Becker, Jean-Jacques. 1997. *Comment les francais sont entres dans la guerre*. Paris: Presses De Science Po.

Beer, Edith with Susan Dworkin. 1999. *The Nazi Officer's Wife: How One Jewish Woman Survived the Holocaust*. New York: Weisbach and Morrow.

Beevor, Anthony. 2002. *The Fall of Berlin, 1945*. New York: Viking.

Benzoni, Juiette. 1983. *Dans le lit Des Rois: Nuits de Noces*. Paris: Plon Litvack.

Bessel, Richard (ed.). 1987. *Life in the Third Reich*. Oxford: Oxford University Press.

Biderman, Albert D. and Albert J. Reiss. 1967. "On Exploring the Dark Figure of Crime." *Annals of the American Academy of Political and Social Science*. 374 (November): 1–15.

Binder, R.L. 1981. "Why women don't report sexual assault." *Journal of Clinical Psychiatry*. 42(11): 437–438.

Bischof, Gunter and Stephen E. Ambrose. 1991. *Eisenhower and the German POWs: Facts Against Falsehood*. Baton Rouge, LA: Louisiana State University Press.

Bishop, J. 1974. *Justice under Fire*. New York: Charterhouse.

Bloch, Marc. 1968. *Strange Defeat: A Statement of Evidence Written in 1940*. New York: W.W. Norton.

Blumenson, Martin. 1961. *Breakout and Pursuit*. Washington, DC: Office of the Chief of Military History.

Boureau, Alain. 1998. *The Lord's First Night: the Myth of the Droit De Cuissage*. Chicago: University of Chicago Press.

Bradley, Omar N. 1951. *A Soldier's Story*. New York: Henry Holt and Company.

Brokaw, Tom. 1998. *The Greatest Generation*. New York: Random House.

Browning, Christopher R. 1992. *Ordinary Men: Reserve Police Battalion 101 and the Final Solution in Poland*. New York: Harper Collins.

Brownmiller, Susan. 1975. *Against Our Will: Women and Rape*. New York: Ballentine.

Bryant, Cliffton D. 1979. *Khaki-Collar Crime: Deviant Behavior in the Military Context*. New York: Free Press.

Buchanna, A. Russell. 1977. *Blacks Americans in World War II*. Santa Barbara, CA: Clio Books.

Burke, James Wakefield. 1951. *The Big Rape: A Documentary Novel*. New York: Farrar, Straus & Young.

Burrin, Phillippe. 1993. *France Under the Germans: Collaboration and Compromise*. New York: Free Press.

Calder, Angus. 1969. *The People's War: Britain 1939–1945*. New York: Pantheon.

Calder, Angus. 1991. *The Myth of the Blitz*. London: Pimlico.

Card, Claudia. 1997. "Addendum to 'Rape as a Weapon of War.'" *Hypatia*. 12: 216.

Chang, Iris. 1997. *The Rape of Nanking: The Forgotten Holocaust of World War II*. New York: Penguin.

Chappell, Duncan, Robley Geis, and Gilbert Geis. 1997. *Forcible Rape: The Crime, the Victim and the Offender*. New York: Columbia University Press.

Chomsky, C. 1990. "The United States-Dakota War Trials: A Study of Military Injustice." *Sanford Law Review*. 43: 13–98.

Clever, Elderidge. 1968. *Soul on Ice*. New York: Dell Publishing.

Colley, David. 2003. *Blood for Dignity: The Story of the First Integrated Combat Unit in the U.S. Army*. New York: St. Martin's Press.

Commager, Henry Steele (ed.). 1945. *The Pocket Histosry of the Second World War*. New York: Pocket Book.

Costello, John. 1958. *Love, Sex and War*. London: Collins.

Cressey, Donald B. 1966. "Crime." In Robert K. Merton and Robert K. Nisbet. (Eds.) *Contemporary Social Problems*. Second edition. New York: Harcourt, Brace & World, Inc., pp. 136–192.

Dower, John W. 1999. *Embracing Defeat: Japan in the Wake of World War II*. New York: Norton.

Duis, Perry R. 1966. "No Time for Privacy: World War II and Chicago's Families." In Lewis A. Erenberg and Susan E. Hirsch. (Eds.) *The War in American Culture: Society and Consensus During World War II*. Chicago: University of Chicago Press, pp. 17–45.

Duroselle, Jean-Baptiste. 1972. *La France et les Franccais, 1914–1920*. Paris: Editions Richelieu.

Eisenhower, Dwight D. 1948. *Crusade in Europe*. Garden City, NY: Doubleday & Co.

Estrich, Susan. 1987. *Real Rape: How the Legal System Victimizes Women Who Say No*. Cambridge, MA: Harvard University Press.

Ehrenburg, Ilya and Vasily Grossman. 2002. *The Complete Black Book of Russian Jewry*. Trans. by David Patterson. New Brunswick, NJ: Transaction.

Faulks, Sebastian. 1999. *Charlotte Gray*. London: Vintage.

Felder, N.E. 1987. "A Long Way Since Houston: The treatment of Blacks in the Military Justice System." *Army Lawyer*. Vol. 87 (October): 8–11.

Felson, Marcus. 2002. *Crime and Everyday Life*. Thousand Oaks, CA: Sage.

Foot, M.R.D. 1995. "Witherington, Pearl." In I.C.B. Dear and M.R.D. Foot. (Eds.) *The Oxford Companion to World War II*. Oxford: Oxford University Press, p. 1275.

Foot, M.R.D. 1977. *Resistance: An Analysis of European Resistance to Nazism 1040–1945*. London: Oxford University Press.

Forster, Jurgen, Charles Messenger and Wolfgang Petter. 1995. "Germany." in I.C.B. Dear and M.R.D. Foot. (Eds.) *The Oxford Companion to World War II*. Oxford: Oxford University Press, pp. 455–480.

Frances, E.P. 1984. *le Drit du Seigneur in European and American Literature: From the Seventeenth through the Twentieth Century*. Birmingham, AL: Summa Publications.

Franklin, John Hope. 1956. "History of Racial Segregation in the United States. *Annals of The American Academy of Political and Social Sciences*. Vol. 304 (March): 1–9.

Fraser, Frank. 1994. *Mad Frank*. London: Little, Brown and Co.

Freedman, Lawrence. (Ed.) 1994. *War*. Oxford: Oxford University Press.

Friedman, David M. 2001. *A Mind of its Own: A Cultural History of the Penis*. New York: Free Press.

Fussell, Paul. 1980. *Wartime: Understanding and Behavior in the Second World War*. Oxford: Oxford University Press.

Fussell, Paul. 2002. *Uniforms: Why We are What We Wear*. Boston: Houghton Mifflin.

Gardiner, Juliet. 1992. *"OVER HERE": The GIs In Wartime Britain*. London: Collins & Brown.

Gaynor, M. 1990. *Chicago Joe and the Show Girl*. London: Hodder and Stoughton.

Genovese, Eugene. 1976. *Roll, Jordon, Roll: The World the Slaves Made*. New York: Vintage.

Geyer, Michael. 1987. "The Nazi State Reconsidered." In Richard Bessel. (Ed.) *Life in the Third Reich*. Oxford: Oxford University Press, pp. 57–67.

Gibson, K. Craig. 2001. "Sex and Soldering in France and Flanders: The British Expeditionary Forces along the Western Front, 1914–1919." *The International History Review*. XXXIII (3) September: 505–756.

Grant, U.S. 1982.*Personal Memoirs of U.S. Grant*. New York: De Capo.

Greenfeld, L.A. 1997. *Sex Offenses and Offenders: An Analysis of Data on Rape and Sexual Assault*. (NCJ-163392). Washington, DC: Department of Justice, Office of Justice Programs.

Grossmann, Atina. 1997. "A Question of Silence: The Rape of German Women by Occupation Soldiers." In Robert G. Moeller. (Ed.) *West Germany under Construction: Politics, Society, and Culture in the Adenauer Era*. Ann Arbor, MI: University of Michigan Press, pp. 33–52.

Hachey, Thomas E. 1974. "Jim Crow with a British Accent: Attitudes of London Government Official Toward American Negro Soldiers in England During World War II." *Journal of Negro History*. 59 (1) January: 65.

Heineman, Elizabeth. 1996. "The Hour of the Woman: Memories of Germany's 'Crisis Years,' and West Germany National Idenity." *American Historical Review*. 101 (2) April: 354–395.

Herbert, A.P. 1919 [1981]. *The Secret Battle*. New York: Atheneum.

Hernton, Calvin. C. 1965. *Sex and Racism in America*. New York: Grove Press.

Hillel, Marc. 1981. *Vie et Moeurs des G.I.'s en Europe, 1942–1947*. Paris.

Hindless, Barry. 1973. *The Use of Official Statistics in Sociology*. London: Macmillian.

Hitchens, Christopher. 2002. *Orwell's Victory*. London: Allen Lane.

Hobbs, Dick. 1988. *Doing the Business*. Oxford: Oxford University Press.

Hohn, Maria. 2002. *Gis and Frauleins: The German-American Encounter in 1950s West Germany*. Chapel Hill, NC: University of North Carolina Press.

Huie, William Bradford. 1954. *The Execution of Private Slovik*. New York: Duell, Sloan and Pearce.

Hynes, Samuel. 1997. *The Soldiers' Tale*. New York: Penguin.

Janowitz, Morris. 1974. *The Military Establishment*. Beverly Hills, CA: Sage.

Jones, Steve. 2000. *When the Lights Went Down: Crime in Wartime*. Nottingham: Wicked Publications.

Karstens, Peter. 1978. *Laws, Soldiers and Combat*. Westport, CT: Greenwood.

Kedward, H.R. 1978. *Resistance in Vichy France*. Oxford: Oxford University.

Kedward, H.R. 1985. *Occupied France: Collaboration and Resistance. 1940–1944*. Oxford and New York: Blackwell.

Kedward, H.R. 1995. "France." in I.C.B. Dear and M.R.D. Foot. (Eds.) *The Oxford Companion to World War II*. Oxford: Oxford University Press, pp. 391–408.

Kennett, Lee. 1977. *G.I.: The American Soldier in World War II*. Norman: University of Oklahoma.

Kray, C. and J. Sykes. 1997. *Me and My Brothers*. London: Everest.

Kray, R. and R. Kray. 1989. *Our Story*. London: Pan.

Lambrianou, T. 1992. *Inside the Firm*. London: Pan.

LeBeau, J. 1987. "The Journey to Rape: Geographic Distances and the Rapist's Method of Approaching the Victim." *Journal of Police Sciences and Administration*. 15(2): 129–136.

Lee, Ulysses. 1966. *The Employment of Negro Troops*. Washington, DC: U.S. Government Printing Office.

Leinbaugh, Harold P. and John D. Campbell. 1985. *The Men of Company K*. New York: William Morrow and Company.

Lilly, J. Robert and Pam Marshall. 2000. "Rape – Wartime." In Clifton D. Bryant. *The Encyclopedia of Criminology and Deviant Behavior*. Vol. 3. Philadelphia, PA: Taylor & Francis, Inc., pp. 310–322.

Lilly, J. Robert and Richard A. Ball. 1982. "A Critical Analysis of the Changing Concept of Criminal Responsibility." *Criminology: An Interdisciplinary Journal*. 20 (2) August: 169–184.

Longmate, Norman. 1975. *The G.I.'s: The Americans in Britain, 1942–1945*. New York: Charles Scribner's Sons.

Lucus, James. 2002. *The Last Days of the Reich, May 1945*. London: Cassell Company, Inc.

Lurie, Johnathan. 1992. *Arming Military Justice: The Origins of the United States Court of Military Appeals*. Vol. 1. Princeton, NJ: Princeton University Press.

Lurie, Johnathan. 1998. *Pursuing Military Justice: The History of the United States Court of Military Appeals for the Armed Forces, 1950–1980*. Vol. 2. Princeton, NJ: Princeton University Press.

MacDonald, Charles B. 1973. *The Last Offensive*. Washington, DC: U.S. Government Printing Office.

MacGregor, Jr., Morris J. 1985. *Integration of the Armed Forces 1940–1965*. Washington, DC: U.S. Government Printing Office.

McArthur, Douglas. 1964. *Reminiscences*. New York: McGraw-Hill.

Mannheim, Hermann 1965. *Comparative Criminology*. Boston: Houghton Mifflin Company.

Mannheim, Hermann. 1971 [1955]. *Group Problems in Crime and Punishment*. Montclair, NJ: Patterson Smith.

Messenger, Charles. 1995. "Aachen." In I.C.B. Dear and M.R.D. Foot. (Eds.) *The Oxford Companion to World War II*. Oxford: Oxford University Press, p. 1.

Moore, Deborah Dash. 1994. *When Jews Were GIs: How World War II Changed a Generation and Remade American Jewry*. Ann Arbor, MI: University of Michigan.

Morris, Madeline. 1996."By Force of Arms: Rape, War and Military Culture." *Duke Law Journal*. 45(4): 651–781.

Morrow, Lance. 1996. "Rape." In Robert Cowley and Geogrey Parker. *Reader's Companion to Military History*. Boston, MA: Houghton Mifflin, pp. 378–379.

Moskos, Charles C. 1970. *The American Enlisted Man*. New York: Russell Sage Foundation.

Naimark, Norman. 1995. *The Russians in Germany: A History of the Soviet Zone Occupation, 1945–1959*. Cambridge, MA: Harvard University Press.

Nalty, Bernard C. 1986. *Strength for the Fight: A History of Black Americans in the Military*. New York: Free Press.

Nalty, Bernard C. and Morris J. MacGregor. 1981. *Blacks in the Military: Essential Documents*. Wilmington, DE: Scholarly Resources Inc.

Nathan, Joseph and Nicholas Alex. 1971–1972. "The Uniform: A Sociological Perspective." *American Journal of Sociology*. 77 (4): 719–730.

Neumann, Peter. 1958. *The Black March*. New York: Bantam.

Nicolson, Harold. [1941] "Marginal Comment." In Fiona Glass and Philip Marsden-Smedly (Eds.) 1989. *Articles of War: The Spectator Book of World War II*. London: Grafton Books.

Orwell, George. 1943. Letter to the Editors. *Partisan Review*. In Sonia Orwell and Ian Angus. (Eds.) 1968. *My Country Right or Left 1940–1943*. New York: Harcourt Brace Javanovich, Inc., p. 277.

Orwell, George. 1943. "As I Please." In Sonia Orwell and Ian Angus. (Eds.) 1968. *As I Please, 1943–1945*. New York: Harcourt Brace Javanovich, Inc., p. 54.

Orwell, George. 1944. "London Letter to *Partisan Review*." In Sonia Orwell and Ian Angus. 1968. *As I Please, 1943–1945*. New York: Harcourt Brace Javanovich, Inc., p. 77.

Ottley, Roi. 1951. *No Green Pastures*. New York: Charles Schribner's Sons.

Ousby, Ian. 1997. *Occupation: The Ordeal of France 1940–1945*. New York: St. Martin's Press.

Patton, General George S. Patton, Jr. 1947. *War As I Knew It*. New York: Houghton Mifflin.

Paxton, R.O. 1972. *Vichy France: Old Guard and New Order*. New York: Columbia University Press.

Pearson., J. 1973. *The Profession of Violence*. London: Granda.

Philipose, Liz. 1966. "The Laws of War and Women's Human Rights." *Hypatia*. 12: 216.

Probyn. W. 1977. *Angle Face: The Making of a Criminal*. London: Allen and Unwin.

Radzinowicz, Leon. 1957. *Sexual Offences: A Report of the Cambridge Department of Criminal Science*. London: Macmillan.

Ray, John. 1996. *The Night Blitz: 1940–1941*. London: Cassell & Co.

Raymonds, R. Alwyn. 1945. *The Cleft Chin Murder*. London: Claud Morris Books, Ltd.

Read, Anthony and David Fishner 1992. *The Fall of Berlin*. New York: Norton.

Reynolds, David. 1995. *Rich Relations: The American Occupation of Britain, 1942–1945*. New York: Random House.

Richardson, C. 1992. *My Manor*. London: Pan.

Riedel, Marc P. 1998. "Counting Stranger Homicides: A Case Study of Statistical Prestidigitation." *Homicide Studies*. 2: 209–219.

Riedel, Marc and Tammy A. Rinehart. 1996. "Murder Clearances and Missing Data." *Journal of Crime and Justice*. 19: 83–102.

Roberts, Adam. 1995. "Resistance." In I.C.B. Dear and M.R.D. Foot. (Eds). *The Oxford Companion to World War II*. Oxford: Oxford University Press, p. 946.

Ryan, Cornelius. 1966. *The Last Battle*. New York: Simon & Schuster.

Sarbinand, T.B. and John I. Kitsuse. (Eds.) 1994. *Constructing the Social*. Thousand Oaks, CA: Sage Publications.

Schoenbaum, David. 1966. *Hitler's Social Revolution*. New York: Doubleday.

Schrijvers, Peter. 1998. *The Crash of Ruin: American Combat Soldiers in Europe during World War II*. New York: New York University Press.

Seifert, Ruth. 1994. "War and Rape: A Preliminary Analysis." In A. Stiglmayer. (Ed.) *Mass Rape: The War Against Women in Bosnia-Herzegovia*. Lincoln, NE: University of Nebraska Press, pp. 54–72.

Sherrill, Robert. 1969. *Military Justice is to Justice as Military Music is to Music*. New York: Harper & Row.

Shirer, William L. 1960. *The Rise and Fall of the Third Reich*. New York: Simon and Schuster.

Shukert, Elfrieda Berthiaume and Barbara Smith Scibetta. 1989. *War Brides of World War II*. New York: Penguin.

Sledge, E. B. 1991. *With the Old Breed at Peleliu and Okinawa*. New York: Oxford University Press.

Smith, Graham. 1987. *When Jim Crow met John Bull: Black American Soldiers in World War II Britain*. London: I. B. Tauris.

Smithies, Edward. 1982. *Crime in Wartime: A Social History of Crime in World War II*. London: George Allen & Unwin.

Solis, Gary D. 2000. "Military Justice, Civilian Clemency: The Sentence of Marine Corps Crimes in South Vietnam." *10 Transnational Law & Contemporary Problems*.

Steinbeck, John. 1959/1990. *Once There Was a War*. London: Mandarin.

Stouffer, Samuel A., Edward A. Suchman, Leland C. DeViney, Shirley A. Star, and Robin M. Williams, Jr., 1949. *The American Soldier: Adjusting During Army Life*. Vol. 1. Princeton, NJ: Princeton University Press.

Stovall, Tyler. 1996. *Paris Noir: African Americans in the City of Light*. Boston, MA: Houghton Mifflin Co.

Stovall, Tyler. 1998. "The Color Line behind the Lines: Racial Violence in France during the Great War." *American Historical Review*. 103 (3) June: 737–769.

Sudnow, David. 1965. "Normal Crimes: Sociological Features of the Penal Code in a Public Defender Office." *Social Problems*. 12 (Winter): 255–276.

Sulzberger, C. L. 1966. *The American Heritage Picture History of World War II*. New York: American Heritage Publishing Co.

Sweets, John F. 1986. *Choices in Vichy France: The French Under Nazi Occupation* Oxford: Oxford University Press.

Sykes, J. and J. Putkowski. 1989. *Shot at Dawn*. Warncliffe: Barnsley.

Tanaka, Yuki. 1998. *Hidden Horrors: Japanese War Crimes in World War II*. Boulder, CO: Westview Press.

Thorne, Christopher. 1988. *Border Crossing: Studies in International History*. Oxford: Basil Blackwell.

Timerman, Jacob. 1997. *Death in the South*. Translated by Robert Cox. New York: Knopf.

Tolnay, Steward and E.M. Beck. 1992. *A Festival of Violence: An Analysis of Southern Lynchings, 1882–1930*. Urbana and Chicago: University of Illinois Press.

Veuillot, Louis. 1813–1883. *Le Droit du signeur au Moyen Age*. Paris: L. Vivies.

Virgili, Fabrice. 2002. *Shorn Women: Gender and Punishment in Liberation France*. Oxford: Berg.

Webb, B. 1993. *Running with the Krays*. Edinburgh: Mainstream.

Wegner, Bernd. 1995. "SS." In I.C.B. Dear and M.R.D. Foot. (Eds.) *The Oxford Companion to World War II*. Oxford University Press, p. 1004.

Weigely, Russell. 1967. *History of the United States Army*. New York: Macmillan.

Wilke, Gerhard. 1987. "Village Life in Nazi Germany." In Richard Bessel. (Ed.) *Life in the Third Reich*. Oxford: Oxford University Press, pp. 17–24.

Wilkins, Leslie T. 1965. "New Thinking in Criminal Justice Statistics." *Journal of Criminal Law, Criminology, and Police Science.* 56 (September): 277–284.

Wolfgang, Marvin E. 1963. "Uniform crime reports: a critical appraisal." *University of Pennsylvania Law Review.* 111 (April): 709–736.

Williams, B. 1989. "Should military personnel be court martialed for offenses that are not connected." *Oklahoma Law Review,* 42: 116–131.

Williams, Linda S. 1984. "The classic rape: when do victims report?" *Social Problems.* 331 (4): 459–467.

Ximena, Bunster-Bunalto. 1993. "Surviving beyond fear: women and torture in Latin America." In Alison M. Jaggar and Paula S. Rothenberg. (Eds.) *Feminist Frameworks: Alternative Theoretical Accounts of the Relations between Women and Men.* New York: McGraw-Hill, Inc., pp. 252–261.

Yamamoto, Masahiro. 2000. *Nanking: Anatomy of an Atrocity.* New York: Praeger.

Ziegler, Philip. 1995. *London at War: 1939–1945.* New York: Alfred A. Knopf.

Laws

Kentucky Revised Statutes. 1978. 402.020.

Yamashita v. U.S. 327. *U.S. Reports* 1, 1946.

Media

Newspapers

Beevor, Anthony. 2002. "They raped every German female from eight to 80." *The Guardian: Inside Story.* 1 May: 6–7.

Bohlen, Celestine. 2002. "Judge revives case of Nazi-looted art." *New York Times.* April 27: B-9.

Bumenthal, Ralph. 2001. "Twice stolen, twice Found: A case of art on the Lam." *New York Times.* 19 July: E-1.

Clines, Francis X. *1993.* "When black soldiers were hanged: a war's footnote." *New York Times.* February 7: A-14.

Connolly, Kate. 2002. "German war rape victims find a voice." *The Observer.* June 13, p. 18.

Chicago Sun-Times. 1992. "Imperfect soldiers fight imperfect war." August 1: Editorial. p. 21.

Erlanger, Steven. 2002. "Vienna skewered as a Nazi-era pillager of its Jews." *New York Times.* March 7: A-3.

Jackson, Susan. 1995. "In Chile, Pinochet stands in the path of reconciliation." *San Francisco Chronicle.* September 19: A-8.

McCrystal, Cal. 2002. "Red Army on the rampage." *The Independent on Sunday.* April: Arts Etc. 15, col. 1–5.

New York Times. 1917. "American soldier hanged." December 4: p. 6:4.

New York Times. 1918. "Whole Army division sees Negroes hanged." July 6: p. 4, 5.

New York Times. 1944. "Freakish cold spell strikes in Germany." November 23, p. 6, col. 5.

New York Times. 1944. "No coward's death mars U.S. in France." December 28: p. 1.

New York Times. 1945. "Jailing of soldier who beat Nazis hit." May 26: p. 4, col. 8.

New York Times. 1996. "Sexual harassment in military dips, but remains problem, survey finds." March 7: C-19.

New York Times. 1996. "His medals questioned, top admiral kills himself." May 17: A-1; C-19.

New York Times. 1996. "Admiral, in suicide note, apologized to 'My Sailors.'" May: A-1; A-9.

New York Times. 1996. "Commit suicide over a medal? An ex-general gives his view." May 20: A-8.

New York Times. 1997. "Army trial raises questions of sex, power and discipline." April 12: A1, 8.

New York Times. 1997. "Sergeant convicted of 18 counts of raping female subordinates." April 30: A1–A12.

New York Times. 1997. "Sergeant is given 25 years for 18 rapes at Aberdeen." May 7: A-19.

New York Times. 1997. "Drill Sergeant convicted of sex with trainees." May 30: A-12.

New York Times. 2000. "U.S. sergeant in Kosovo is accused of killing girl." January 17: A-3:1.

New York Times. 2000. "G.I.'s in Kosovo face a barrage of complaints." January 29: A-6: 1.

New York Times. 2000. "Details emerge in Kosovo girl's slaying." February 19: A-1.

New York Times. 2000. "U.S. sergeant gets life in murder of Kosovo girl." August 2: A-3: 1.

New York Times. 2000. "Ravages of time." June 4. p. 4.

New York Times. 2002. "2 accuse Stephen Ambrose, popular historian, of plagiarism." January 5: A-8.

New York Times. 2002. "Author admits he lifted lines form '95 book." January 6: A-22.

New York Times. 2002. "As historian's fame grows, so do questions on methods." January 11: A-1.

New York Times. 2002. "Many campuses disdain historian's practice." January 15: A-14.

New York Times. 2003. "Military policy on sex abuse under scrutiny: Air Force accusations raises new questions." March 2: A-1, A-24.

Nossiter, Adam. 1998. "Wartime nightmare ss still alive in French town." *New York Times*. June 18: A-12.

Schmemann, Serge. 2002. "U.S. peacekeepers given year's immunity from new court." *New York Times*. July 13: A-3.

Schememann, Serge. 2002. "U.S. links peacekeeping to immunity from New Court." *New York Times*. June 19: A-3.

Stars and Stripes. 1945. "U.S. soldier dies as civilian for slaying of London cabby." March 9. Paris edition, vol. 1, no. 225.

Simons, Marlise. 1996. "First time, court defines rape as war crime." *New York Times*. June 28: A7.

Simons, Marlise. 2001. "3 Serbs convicted in wartime rapes." *New York Times*. February 23: A-1, A-7.

Simons, Marlise. 2002. "Without fanfare or cases, International Court sets up." *New York Times*. June 16: A-4.

Sims, Calvin. 1997. "Era ending for Chile as Pinochet plans exit." *New York Times*. September 28: A-17.

Smothers, Ronald. 1987. "Historian's death penalty obsession." *New York Times*. October 21: A-16.

Tait, Nikki. 2002. "Albright to testify in former Bosnian Serb leader's case." *The Financial Times*. December 17: p. 8.

The Washington Post. 1974. "Execution of Private Slovik." March 19: B-1; B-17.

Washington Star-News. 1974. "40,000 deserted, 1 executed." March: A-3.

Williams, Carol J. 1999. "Serbs make weapon of rape: Kosovo victims 'have no future.'" *Cincinnati Enquirer*. May 29: A-2.

Wines, Michael. 2002. "Chechens tell of torture in Russian camp." *New York Times*. February 18: A-12.

Wisconsin State Journal. 1992. "New 'War' for Pentagon." August 3: 5-A.

Press services

Gonzales, Gustavo. 1997. "Chile-Human Rights: Government rejects trial of Pinochet in Spain. Inter Press Service. May 29.

Radio and television documentaries

"Coupons a nd Nylons: The Underside of VE Day." May 8. Radio 4 [England]. Matt Thompson, Producer.

"The Perilous Fight: America's War in Color." PBS Television. Four-part documentary. February 19, 2003. WCET TV.

Magazines:

Editor's Note. 1946. *The Atlantic Monthly*. April. 177(4): 135.

Jones, Edgar L. 1946. "One war is enough." *The Atlantic Monthly*. 177 (49).

Landesman, Peter. 2002. "A woman's work." *The New York Times Magazine*. September 15: pp. 82–89, 116, 125, 130, 132, 134.

Morrow, Lance. 1993. "Unspeakable behavior." *Time*. February 22: 48–50.

Putter, Ed. 2002. "Mr. Smith's complaint." *The Times Literary Supplement*. December 28: 22–23.

Pound, Edward T. 2002. "Unequal justice." *U.S. News & World Report*. December 16: pp. 18–30

"The wrong ambassadors." 1945. *Time*. November 19: p. 21.

Movies

"Chicago Joe and the Show Girl."

"The Execution of Private Slovik." 1974. NBC TV documentary.

Pamphlets

Jews in the world war: a study of Jewish patriotism and heroism. Nd. New York: Jewish War Veterans of the United States.

Military resources

A Manual for Courts-Martial U.S. Army – 1928 (Corrected to April 20, 1943). Washington, DC: U.S. Government Printing Office.

Hyner, Julien C., Colonel, JAGD, nd. *Military Justice Administration in the Theater of Operations*. [ETO]. Report to the General Board, United States Forces, Europe. No. 83.

Hyner et al, Julien C. nd. *Military Offender in Theater of Operations*. Report of the General Board, United States Forces, European Theater. No. 84.

"The reason I haven't." U.S. Sex Survey-W and "VD Problems of Negro Enlisted Men in MTOISA." Report 122 M2, 25 September 1945." Cited in John Cosello. 1985. *Virtue Under Fire: How World War II Changed Our Social Attitudes*. Boston: Little, Brown, and Co.

The Opinions of Judge Advocate General Branch Office, European Theater of Operations: Myron C. Cramer. 1945. Foreword. Vol. 1.

Officers

United States vs. Captain John F. Kenney. Vol. 1. 1942, pp. 13–28.

United States vs. First Lieutenant Hugh I. Malley. Vol. 14. ETO. 5052. 1944, pp. 111–126.

United States vs. First Lieutenant Joe H. Randie. Vol. 29. CM ETO 15251.1945, pp. 49–52.

United States vs. Second Lieutenant Arthur C. Blevins, Jr. Vol. 7. ETO.2472. 1944, pp. 41–54.

United States vs. Second Lieutenant Robert D. Thompson. Vol. 31. CM ETO 16888. 1945, pp. 235–238.

Non-commissioned officers

United States vs. Corporal Ernest Lee Clark. Vol. 14. ETO 5156. 1944, pp. 199–207.

United States vs. Corporal Lester Berger and Private Donald W. Bamford. Vol. 20. CM ETO 9083. 1945, pp. 107–117.

United States vs. Corporal Robert L. Person and Private Cubia Jones. Vol. 18. Vol. 7252. 1944, pp. 51–57.

United States vs Sergeant Obbie L. Mylies. Vol. 19. CM ETO 8542. 1945, pp. 305–309.

United States vs. Staff Sergeant Richard Allen. Vol. 27. CM ETO 13767. 1945, pp. 103–105.

United States vs. Technician Fifth Grade Elmer L. Spohn and Private Marton L. Whelchel. Vol. 26. CM ETO 12873. 1945, pp. 39–45.

United States vs. Technician Fifth Grade Jeremiah c. Nelums, Technician Fifth Grade Henry Garrett, Jr., and Private First Class Ernest Jackson. Vol. 27. CM ETO 13568. 1945, pp. 35–44.

United States vs. Technician Fifth Grade John F. Autrey. Vol. 23. CM ETO 10699. 1945, pp. 23–27.

United States vs. Technician Fifth Grade Kenneth W. Wilson. Vol. 24. CM ETO 11590. 1944, p. 231.

United States vs. Technician Fifth Grade Ray F. Daniels and Private James A. Caudill. Vol. 22. CM ETO 10141. 1945, pp. 99–104.

United States vs. Technician Fifth Grade Thomas J. Smalls. Vol. 23. CM ETO. 10700. 1945, pp. 29–48.

Privates first class

United States vs. Private First Class Aelred V.J. Plataa. Vol. 27. CM ETO 14206. 1945, pp. 280–284.

United States vs. Private First Class Alfred F. Willet and Private William Correon. Vol. 31. CM ETO 16640. 1945, pp. 119–126.

United States vs. Private First Class Billy Reed. Vol. 27. CM ETO 14338. 1945, pp. 327–331.

United States vs. Private First Class Charles W. O'Neil, George B.Tweedy, and Privates William E. Ewing, Rufus N. Casey and Mack Shelvin. Vol. 26 CM ETO 13178. 1945, pp. 183–191.

United States vs. Private First Class Conway Green. Vol. 9. ETO 3469. 1944, pp. 361–371.

United States vs. Private First Class David McArthur and Willie J. Lee. Vol. 28. CM ETO 14604. 1945, pp. 99–103.

United States vs. Private First Class Fed L. Lofton. Vol. 27. ETO 14210. 1945, pp. 289–291.

United States vs. Private First Class Jack C. Kelley. Vol. 26. CM ETO 13425. 1945, pp. 359–363.

United States vs. Private First Class Joe F. Selvera. Vol. 33. CM ETO 17918. 1945, pp. 143–146.

United States vs. Private First Class Rito Mendez and Private Joseph R. Rego. Vol. 25. CM ETO 12604. 1945, pp. 269– 274.

United States vs. Private First Class Thomas B. Jane. Vol. 27. CM ETO 14382. 1945, pp. 373–379.

United States vs. Private First Class Thomas G. King and Private Denzil A. Thomas. Vol. 26 CM ETO 13125. 1945, pp. 133–148.

United States vs. Private First Class Wardell W. Wislon. Vol. 20. CM ETO 8837. 1945, pp. 67–70.

United States vs. Private First Class William J. Blakely. Vol. 32. CM ETO 17442. 1945, pp. 125–131.

United States vs. Privates First Class Willie M. Lucero and Homer E. Miller. Vol. 33. CM ETO 18165. 1945, pp. 213–219.

Privates

United States vs. Privates Alfonso Josie Lewis and Freddie Moses Sexton. Vol. 16. ETO 5805. 1944, pp. 7–127.

United States vs. Private Alfred L. Prinely. Vol. 31. CM ETO 16971.1945, pp. 303–309.

United States vs. Private Aniceto Martinez. Vol. 22. ETO 10079. 1945, pp. 71–76.

United States vs. Privates Archie S. Bowman and Joseph Glover, Jr. Vol. 9. ETO 3253. 1945, pp. 135–144.

United States vs. Private Augustine M. Guerra. Vol. 14. ETO 5157. 1944, pp. 209–220.

United States vs. Private Charles A. Shaffer. Vol. 1. ETO.397. 1943, pp. 339–344.

United States vs. Private Charles E. Heishman. Vol. 27. CM ETO 14066. 1945, pp. 191–196.

United States vs. Private Clarence (NMI) English. Vol. 4. ETO. 1366. 1945, pp. 247–251.

United States vs. Private Clarence Whitfield. Vol. 8. CM ETO 3141. 1944, pp. 351–361.

United States v. Private Donald Hicks. Vol. 5. ETO 1899. 1944, pp. 367–380.

United States vs. Private Frank P. Prairiechief. Vol. 21. CM ETO 9611. 1945, pp. 129–134.

United States v. Private Forrest E. Washington. Vol. 22. CM ETO 10103. 1945, pp. 92–95.

United States vs. Private Frank Williams. Vol. 16. CM ETO 5869. 1944, pp. 27–31.

United States vs. Private Gilbert F. Newburn. Vol. 33. CM ETO 18381. 1945, pp. 352–354.

United States vs. Private Harry L. Luckey. Vol. 27. CM ETO 14448. 1945, pp. 395–399.

United States vs. Horace G. Adams and Hugh L. Harris. Vol. 18. CM ETO 7869. 1944, p. 298.

United States. vs. Private Isiah (NMI) Porter. Vol. 2. ETO 611. 1943. pp. 189–197.

United States vs. Private Jack H. Morgan. Vol. 31. ETO. 16978. 1945, pp. 317–325.

United States vs. Private James (NMI) Ramsey and Bennie L. Edwards. Vol. 4. ETO 1202. 1943, pp. 109–119.

United States vs. Privates James B. Sanders, Florine Wilson and Roy W. Anderson. Vol. 10. CM ETO 3740. 1944.

United States vs. Private James W. Shields. Vol. 5. ETO. 1883. 1944, pp. 353–357.

United States vs. Privates James R. Parrot, Grant U. Smith, and William C. Downes. Vol. 16. CM ETO 6193. 1944, pp. 160–169.

United States vs. Private Kenneth M. Waite. Vol. 2. ETO. 832. 1943, pp. 379–389.

United States vs. Private Lee A. Davis. Vol. 3. ETO. 969. 1943, pp. 210–227.

United States vs. Private Leo F. Manko and Private First Class Andrew J. Wortheam. Vol. 24. CM ETO 11970. 1945, pp. 397–402.

United States vs. Privates Lewis R. Ward and Jessie W. Sharer. Vol. 22. CM ETO 10446. 1945, pp. 297–306.

United States vs. Privates Lucious C.N. Johnson, Thomas Henderson and Ira J. Smith. Vol. 33. CM ETO 18047. 1945, pp. 163–166.

United States vs Private Luther W. Carter. Vol. 16. CM ETO 6207. 1944, pp. 197–202.

United States vs. Private Madison Thomas. Vol. 10. ET0 3726. 1944, pp. 249–253.

United States vs Privates Melvin Welch and John H. Dollar. Vol. 23. CM ETO 10851. 1944, pp. 187–191.

United States vs. Private Melvin C. Tallent. Vol. 7. ETO. 2550, pp. 141–145.

United States vs. Private Michael A. McDonald. Vol. 25. M ETO 12662. 1945, pp. 331–333.

United States vs. Private Leonard K. Steele. Vol. 10. ETO. 3718. 1944, p. 260.

United States vs. Private Roy Anderson. Vol. 10. CM ETO 3740. 1944, pp. 223–231.

United States vs. Private Roy E. Andrews and Charles M. Hathcock. Vol. 27. CM ETO 14032. 1945, pp. 155–161.

United States vs. Private Thomas (NMI) Bell. Vol. 3.ETO. 1069. 1943, pp. 373–382.

United States vs Private Tommie Davison. Vol. 19. CM ETO 8163. 1944, pp. 39–45.

United States vs. Private William (NMI) Cooper, Jr. Vol. 2. ETO 774. 1943, pp. 317–324.

United States vs. Privates William A. Stevenson and William N. Stuart. Vol. 23. CM ETO 10671. 1945, pp 221–225.

United States vs. Private William Harrison, Jr. CM ETO 5747. 1944.

United States vs. Private Wesley Edmonds. Vol. 1. 1942, pp. 87–89.

United States vs. Private William D. Johnson, Jr. Vol. 29. CM ETO 15250. 1945, pp. 43–48.

Hearings Before a Special Committee on Charges of Alleged Executions without Trial in France. 1923, Sixty-Seventh Congress. Washington: Government

Printing Office

History Branch Office of the Judge Advocate General with the United States Forces – European Theater. July 18, 1942 – November 1, 1945. Branch Office of the Judge Advocate General with the United States Forces European Theater. St. Cloud, Fr.

*War Department – Annual Reports, 1919, Vol. 1.*Washington: Government Printing Office.

National Archives

Trials Transcripts

Non-commissioned officers

United States vs. Corporal Wilford Tenton and Private Arthur J. Farrell.CM ETO. 4775. 1944.

Private First Class

United States vs. Private First Class Blake W. Mariano. CM ETO 15902/ 1945.

United States vs. PFC John Cooper. CM ETO 5362. 1944.

Privates

United States vs. Private Eddie D. Slovik. CM ETO 5555. 1945.

United States vs. Private Madison Thomas. ETO 3726. 1944.

United States vs. Wesley Edmonds. ETO. GCM. 90. 1942.

Faulks, Sebastian. 1999. *Charlotte Gray*. London: Vintage.

Name Index

Subject Index